D1316426

Jolie Gabor

Jolie Gabor

as told to
CINDY ADAMS

MASON/CHARTER

NEW YORK 1975

Library of Congress Cataloging in Publication Data

Gabor, Jolie.
    Jolie Gabor, as told to Cindy Adams.

    1. Gabor, Jolie. I. Adams, Cindy (Heller)
PN2287.G323A34   791.43'028'0924 [B]   75-19176
ISBN 0-88405-125-0

To my Edmund, who brought real happiness into my life.

INTRODUCTION

For my age I am a miracle. I am attractive. I am talented. I play the piano. I am the life of a party. I have always friends. I have a younger husband who adores me. I have three beautiful daughters and we all love one another and they don't need anything from me and I don't need anything from them and that's probably why we still all love one another.

So, I am in a very lucky position because I am a happy woman. There is a Hungarian proverb which says that you can only know happiness after you have gone through much suffering. I have lived long enough and through enough heartache to know this is true. As I look back on the sacrifices I made, I feel I *deserve* happiness.

I walk with the sunshine. I go always under the sun. I cannot stay with unhappiness. When I am unhappy I want to die and I quickly wrench myself out of it. I have no patience with tragedy or unpleasantness. It only stays with me for a few minutes. It is ugly, and I won't allow ugliness in my life. Always I live with a smile. For this reason, I look the way I look for my age. I see 60-year-old women who are old compared to me. They complain about their husbands or their lack of husbands. They complain about their lives. They complain about their children.

I tell such a woman, "Look here, darling, if you are unhappy with your husband find a lover." To another who is miserable because she cannot find a rich husband I tell, "Marry a poor one and support him and be glad anyone will even bother with an old lady like you." When they tell to me they are lonely and nobody invites them, I say to them, "So you invite." For every invitation I get I give two back.

As for children, every mother can be unhappy. Mothers are very sensitive. My girls are not saints just because they are successes. In their relationship with me they are not different from anyone else's children. I am grateful that they adore me even though maybe they don't adore me every single moment so much now as they did when they were children.

We have many times arguments, and when they phone and someone can answer for me, I say loudly so they can hear on the other end, "Tell them I have no time," or I take it myself and I say, "Sorry, darling, I am very busy," and I hang the receiver. They are sensitive and they do not like to have words with me. Therefore, before they say something that upsets me, they think it over. They are a little afraid to argue with me, but not so afraid that they don't still do it. Always I tell them when they displease me and always Zsa Zsa says, "But, *Nuci* . . ." (*nuci* and *nucika* are their Hungarian nicknames for me). "*Nuci*, we are grown up. We are not children. We know what to do."

All the girls call me *Nuci*. Only lately does Magda call me "Mother," and sometimes it is not good. I was on Fifth Avenue looking very young in an antelope pants suit from Paris with suede boots and lush furs and Magda, who was then very fat, shouted at me, "Mother. . . . Mother. . . ." I was so ashamed because she looked so fat. I said, "Now, look here, Magduska, you must lose weight because when you are thirty pounds too heavy and you call me 'mother,' you put on me another ten years!"

My girls are all very egotistical. Spoiled. They think everything is coming to them and that everybody must bow down. They don't want that I am so demanding. When we have words we suffer like lovers. Still, sometimes we hang up on one another in anger. This hurts a mother. If she is the one who hangs up, then she is hurt. It is easy for a mother to be hurt. It is her one and only big weapon.

A recent Sunday, as I was gathering my thoughts for this book, Edmund, my beautiful husband, was in the kitchen of our winter house in Palm Springs making us lunch. He was cutting up a piece of *kolbász* for me—that's the long, skinny, smelly Hungarian salami without which none of us can exist—particularly when we have a green pepper to go with it—and the phone rang.

"Oh, hello, Zsa Zsika, just a minute," said Edmund. It was from London and, naturally, Zsa Zsa only talks to me.

"*Nucika*, darling," began Zsa Zsa, "I am doing a big performance on British TV and must know what to wear. Please choose for me between my pink with the feathers at the throat or the white beaded sheath with the high neck."

"Which white beaded sheath?" I asked. "You have so many gowns I cannot remember."

"*Nucika*, you know all my dresses. It's the new Oscar de la Renta I showed you when you came to the Waldorf to have lunch with me the afternoon we went shopping in New York."

"Oh, yes."

"Well, which is more beautiful? What is your opinion? Quick, *Nuci.* . . ."

"I am in the middle of having lunch and you call from London, and I don't know what kind of performance you are doing, so I can't imagine what is best to wear and you say quick. I can't give so quick advice. I must think."

"This is an important show and we all know that when we don't ask *Nuci's* advice we don't have luck."

"And when it doesn't turn out good then you can say, '*Nuci*, this was *your* advice,' which takes the whole responsibility off you and puts it on me."

"No, no, you know I believe you. When they called me to do *Forty Carats* in London you said when I am working late at night in the theatre I will have no time to see people and make new friends. Who is going to want to come out at one or two o'clock in the morning to be with me, I didn't take the show. So, you see, I do take your advice, and I want it again now."

"Wear the pink. The white is not flattering for you. It makes you a little bit fat. I never liked the white."

"In that case, I will give it away. Okay, I will wear the pink, but if the show doesn't turn out well and I regret it, then it will be all your fault."

"All right," I sighed, then just to give her some news I said, "Eva was on Merv Griffin last night."

"Don't speak of Eva and what she is doing on my phone call. I pay for this call and I want only to speak about me."

Often they call me three times a day when they have some problem about a man or a business decision but, always, to talk about themselves. When the world is going good they don't call much. In good times the calls are on Saturday or Sunday or in the evening because the rates are cheaper. If my phone rings on a Tuesday morning when our average call could be $20, I know it is some terrible problem.

Zsa Zsa told me the story of the famous singer Richard Tauber, who earned $20,000 for one week in Carnegie Hall but died broke. He was a telephone maniac. When he was in New York he called Vienna, when he was in Vienna he phoned South America, when he was in Budapest he called Los Angeles. When once I complained that Zsa Zsa was going to hang up so soon, she said, "When Tauber died he had a phone bill of about $8,000, and this is probably why he died because he had such a huge phone bill. Do you want us to die without money like Richard Tauber?"

And I said, "You are right. Thank you. And now that you mention all this, I am grateful you don't reverse the charges!"

That particular Sunday lunch was again interrupted by Eva from Washington. "How did you like me on Merv Griffin?" she asked.

I did not tell her that I had almost forgotten she was to be on and luckily only remembered to tune in the last few minutes. "You are more beautiful than you appeared on Merv Griffin last night. I was really not delighted with how you looked."

Minutes later Magda called from a few blocks away to tell me Eva was unhappy with what I had said to her.

"But I have to be sincere, Magduska. Nobody else will tell the truth. She asked me so I told. Everybody else would tell her she was delightful. I am honest. Who else will be honest? I tell the truth. They call me after every TV appearance to find out how they were. You know they always want to know how I liked the dress or how I liked what they said. If they would not ask me I would not tell."

When, eventually, we sat down to eat our *kolbász* and green pepper, Edmund said, "*Angyalka,* I cannot believe Eva, Zsa Zsa and Magda are your children." *Angyalka* means "little angel," and that's what he calls me.

"Why, Edmuska?"

"Because they are so selfish and you are not. You don't think about yourself only."

This is true. I think of myself first before anyone else, but this is only natural. It's just that I don't think of myself first if it means to harm somebody. I could not ever harm anyone, but aside from that I do admit that I come first. I want to be the first most elegant, first most beautiful, first most lovely—but this is normal I think. Whoever says this is not so with them lies.

My personality is not the same as Eva's or Zsa Zsa's. It is not even the same as Magda's. I am quite different. We are like another family. They are the same as their father. They are precise. They are exact. They are orderly. I am bohemian. They are smart about money. I am a spender. They have tempers. I am easygoing.

The girls love only themselves. The best in the world above all else they love themselves. Zsa Zsa and Eva are the same. They look the same, sound the same, and act the same. They are often mistaken for one another and both hate it. Even I mix them up. One was born February sixth and the other February eleventh. I never remember which is which and always I send the present to the wrong daughter. They get furious.

Sometimes the girls are jealous of one another. Eva may steal Zsa Zsa's hairstyle or something and Zsa Zsa gets so angry. They are each a little cruel to the other, but we are all very devoted. When any of us is in trouble we are a team; we close ranks.

But first they believe that number one, they come; after that, everybody else comes. They do not take after me who enjoys to do everything for everybody. They take after their father.

Inside, I am full of music. The piano is relaxation for me. When I get depressed and I say, "Oh, what is the use of anything?" I go to the piano. I play Gypsy love songs and this lifts me and I am cheered. If I feel love going through my veins, it is life to me. Then the whole dark feeling is over.

Now, I tell you something about Hungarians. They don't like to tell each other something good. With Hungarian women I am not always on such good terms. That is because we are very competitive. However, I know in my heart they adore me, and that is good enough for me.

Like I have a Hungarian neighbor near my summer home in Ridgefield, Connecticut. She had the house for thirty years. Only after I moved in did she make some little alterations like fashioning a dining area out of the kitchen and making a larger swimming pool than mine. One afternoon she came over to my doll-like house, glanced around and saw all my pictures of Zsa Zsa, Eva, Magda, myself with Mamie Eisenhower and all my celebrity friends—glamor, glamor, glamor—on top of my white piano. The type who criticizes everything with her hands on her hips and her nose in the air she sniffed, "Well, all I can say is that I keep *my* photographs in an album. I don't put them out."

For once in my life I had a quick come-back. I pirouetted right around and said to her, "It's a good thing you have an album then since you don't have a piano. And, anyhow, whose pictures would you put out? Your aunts with the *babushkas* from Hungary?" So many times you can wake up late at night and think of this great line you should have said about five hours earlier, but to have been sharp right then was exciting for me.

At a canasta party recently, even though there were some Hungarians whom I knew didn't like me at this card party, still I went because I hate to miss anything. So everybody was sitting around this apartment but nothing much was happening. There was no *joie de vivre*, no happy ambience in the room. Just tables and ladies with little mouths with little boring talk. Then I swept in wearing a big hat and with a gift for everybody from my shop, and it was the signal for everything to blossom. One close friend said to another, "I told you that when Jolie Gabor comes in the sun comes in. Until she arrives, we are like stones doing nothing then she lets herself in the door and everybody is talking and the whole air is alive."

There is not usually much jealousy of me, and if there is they don't show it, but at this party there were two or three Hungarian women who I could feel did not like me. So I went up to them, spoke a few friendly words and conquered them. I said to the one with the big nose who didn't like me the most, "Oh, how pretty you are today. You lost weight I think, no?" The ladies who were her friends were immediately melting. Even the one with the nose beamed, "Oh, Jolie, you are the one and only."

I must have life. I have to keep going. When I get up in the morning and my calendar is empty I get nervous. Whatever, wherever, a luncheon, card party, shopping, exchanging, anything. Without this activity I would die.

Now that I am not so anymore young—but only in years—I wake up and go quickly to the mirror in fear that at this age I have not skin left on my face anymore. I look in the magnifying mirror and I see that I not only have skin left on me but it is better and better each year, and then I sigh with relief and I relax a little. In the morning I occasionally get these feelings of depression and I sigh to myself, "Oh, what is there left for me now?" Then I run quickly out and do something.

About ten years ago at a big party in a townhouse on Fifth Avenue, a theatrical producer with a flower in his buttonhole came over and introduced himself. So I introduced myself. "I am the mother of three famous daughters, Magda, Zsa Zsa, and Eva."

"Why do you find it necessary to bring them up immediately in the conversation?" he asked.

This question I hadn't thought about before. "My daughters are my claim to fame and I think the reason I bring them up," I explained to this man, "is because consciously or unconsciously I feel they are my only *raison d'être*, my only reason for showing off and pretending that I am a somebody."

"But you are a valuable person on your own," he told me. "You are more than your three daughters put together."

"You are maybe a little angry at them?" I asked. "Because why else would you say this to me?"

"This has nothing to do with what I'm saying," he replied. "It's simply that you mustn't be self-conscious and think you have to mention them within the first two minutes. People enjoy speaking to you for what you are by yourself. Don't knock your brains out. You don't need their help."

I never forgot this. Since then I don't always bring them up so much in my conversations. At least not in the first two minutes. Now I wait five minutes.

People used to ask me, "Are you related to Zsa Zsa Gabor?" Now they ask, "Are you Jolie Gabor?" Then they say, "Oh, you are so famous. My wife adores you. My sister loves you. They always speak about you." Even if it is not 100 per cent the truth, I don't mind.

The other day my taxi driver pulled over to the side, took out a camera, took a picture of me and, best of all, he wouldn't take money. I was very flattered but I was late to a luncheon and he took so much time that I thought maybe it would have been better to take a bus. For some reason I am always recognized in taxis. Even if they don't see my face, they hear my voice and they ask, "Are you a Gabor? You sound like a Gabor." I am so proud that even though I am in a hurry, I can't resist saying "Yes" no matter how much time it takes. I stop off to say, "Yes, Eva Gabor is my daughter. Zsa Zsa Gabor is my daughter." Then they ask, "How are they? What are they doing now—

where is Magda?" It's a nuisance. Of course it's my fault. I don't have to say, "Yes, I am a Gabor." But how can I not? I am so proud.

Zsa Zsa Gabor is the most famous name in the world. In 1959 Edmund and I were driving through Europe. We were in a little village in Germany and had lost our way. There was nobody around to help except a few children playing off to the side of the road. In his halting German Edmund inquired, "Could you help us?" No reply. Then he pointed to me and said, "Here is Zsa Zsa Gabor's mother." They became excited, and they ran over to the car and repeated, "Zsa Zsa Gabor's *Mutter*. Zsa Zsa Gabor's *Mutter*," and they helped us find our way. I couldn't believe it. So, how can I not be proud?

My children are proud of me a little, too. Of course, I do think they would like it better if I were a plain, gray haired, elderly woman. This is normal. When some people tell so stupidly that I am the most pretty of all the Gabors, I hate it. This is only because the person saying it envies them. I am very attractive when I am alone, but when I am with them I am nowhere like them. Thank God I know it.

When Eva has been with me in New York and she goes home to Beverly Hills, Zsa Zsa immediately calls with, *"Nuci,* I hear you are even more beautiful than you were. Evika tells me she went to the theatre with you, and more people looked at you than at her." This is overexaggeration but it is anyhow good to hear it from your own children.

They never said outright that they don't think it is proper for a mother to have such blonde hair or low-cut dresses or false eyelashes. They might think it but never have they said it. Once I sort of sensed it. It was several years ago when I discovered false eyelashes, which I think is the best makeup invention that ever happened. Even when you have not lipstick or face makeup, the whole face is brighter with eyelashes. This is the greatest.

Today's young people were born knowing how to apply this. From Woolworth's even 16-year-old girls are making up like stars. For me, though, this was something strange and new. I asked Eva to help me the first time. "Show me how to put these on," I said.

"Don't bother, *Nucika,"* she said, "because it won't look well on you. This is not for you."

"Why? Because you are not too anxious for me to look so glamorous?"

"Oh, no," she said.

"Why do you then try to talk me out of it?"

"You have nice eyelashes," she told me. "You don't need it. Besides, you won't be able to put them on by yourself."

When I finally learned to put them on and they made such a difference Eva asked, "Who put your eyelashes on for you?"

"Never mind," I said. "I will wear them even though I know it doesn't suit me."

Once I was offended because of my eyelashes. I had given an all-girl celebrity luncheon with such of my friends as Constance Woodworth, Anita Loos, Jacqueline Susann, Joan Fontaine, Virginia Graham, and Ann Miller. Another of my friends who was invited was Vera Swift. Her little daughter who was maybe seven or so at the time came to pick her up. The little girl kept staring at me closely and following me around and abruptly she asked, "Are you a grandmother?"

I told, "Yes."

"In that case," she squeaked, "you don't have to wear false eyelashes."

Oh, this hurt me so. For months after that whenever I put on my lashes, I kept thinking of her. And from a child, yet . . . it was awful. I hated her.

I ask only that when I die I have on my eyelashes. A few Monday mornings ago I didn't feel well. I thought maybe this is it. I thought I was about to die immediately and I have only minutes to live. I ran to my *toilette*. I had no strength to stick on those damn lashes, so I dabbed blue on my lids and smeared on a little rouge. I did not have any fear or panic. I thought only that I must make myself a little pretty because I had just come out of the bathtub and did not want to die looking unattractive.

I want to go in my sleep and I want to be very beautiful with my hair done and my lipstick perfect so when they put me out everybody will exclaim, "Oh, how beautiful she is." I want not to die when nobody knows or cares. I want everybody to come and say, "Good-bye, Jolie," and make a fuss over me.

Maybe I am sounding egotistical but I want people to cry over me when I go, and I want them to drink champagne and I really want to have another party. My final party. I want them all to say, "Oh, that wonderful Jolie. She was such fun. She was such a beauty." I have told this to my husband so and I am sure I can trust him to do this for me.

Also I want to rest in a mausoleum where we can all be together. Twenty-five years ago, I did some preliminary work. I had correspondence with a man in Hollywood, and Magda and I went to see what he had. He showed us, "Now here is Jean Harlow, here is Valentino, and over there is more room for you."

"It's a beautiful area but it costs $50,000 so what do you think?" I asked Magda.

Magda thought she has only to pay a portion because we would all chip in, but Zsa Zsa said she wants to be cremated and Eva also. When Magda found she had to pay this alone with just me, she wanted something cheaper. So I found a place in New Rochelle, figuring eventually all the girls would also come there, but when Magda found she had to pay all the money right away even before her death she wasn't anymore interested.

When we were considering New Rochelle, Magda was upset with me about something and she shouted, *"Nuci,* I am so angry with you that I don't want to lie with you. No, I don't buy a plot together with you!" I must ask her now that a quarter of a century has gone by if she has changed her mind.

I don't want to die but I don't want to stay either. I don't want to be ninety and be less beautiful at the end because always you get just a bit weaker. Formerly when I had a free half hour I would put on my coat and run around shopping. Now I don't do it so quickly. Now, instead of rushing out to do some stupid thing I take sometimes a nap for ten minutes. I darken the room and put on a stupid movie and in one minute with the low, steady drone of the terrible TV movie I am asleep. For me ten minutes is like I slept a whole hour. The other day, though, this was not enough to refresh me. I was still tired. I thought to myself, "So who wants to be ninety?"

But, anyhow, if I were born again I would want this same life again. When a woman has never had affairs and is always married to one man whom she doesn't love so very much, then, when she grows older, she becomes bitter. I cannot be bitter. I don't envy anybody. I have enjoyed a great life. I have had many men in my life plus two enormous love affairs (which no matter what else they took out of me gave me great pleasure) plus three husbands. I am not supported by my children. I have made it all myself. I have my health. I have kept my looks.

I know soon I will be alone for a very long time, therefore I try to go out every single day even for a little bit. I feel compelled to wander through the shops and be where things are happening otherwise you suddenly realize every day you are getting older and if you stay home in a quiet apartment you sense only death.

There are a few benefits when you get older. For one, you no longer experience extremes of love and pain. This dies out a little. I have had little flirts. I have had bitter love affairs, and when they were going good I was in ecstasy—but these were only moments and hours—and when they were bitter they were very bitter. Anyhow, when I think back and I read about all the sex today, I can know that I had it. I have a good feeling. I don't feel frustrated. I am a woman who is really happy.

I was born with romance in my blood, a Gypsy spirit in my soul. When I am loved and I love in return, nothing else matters. Sometimes I cried and sometimes I loved, but I loved life fully, beautifully, excitingly. I had much sex around me and I had much love around me. Not always so seriously did I love, but at least I loved. Yes, I have had a beautiful experience on this earth, and I think not even big stars or famous courtesans can boast that they had such a colorful one.

And so, now, in the winter of my life I am writing a book. The theme is "It's never too late." My life should be an inspiration to all women who shudder at the passing years, who fail to realize that love can come to a woman in her middle years. At forty when I felt who will want an old lady, everything began for me. It began once again many years later. I have learned that there

are no wrinkles on the heart. In 1953 I was driving to Southampton with my
secretary, Bimba Beck. I was all wound up telling her about my life and my
lovers. According to Bimba, only once in the two-and-a-half-hour drive did I
take a breath, and then I stopped the car in the middle of the highway and
said to her, "Now, tell me about you!"

And she answered, "Oh, you are much more fascinating. Besides, you
don't really care to hear about me, do you?"

And I said, "No, not really." With that I started the car and my life story
up again.

At Southampton, Bimba said to me, "You should write down everything
you told me today and put it in a book." Next morning I bought a tape
recorder, but then a man came into my life or a card game or a party and that
was that.

In 1958 a Hollywood writer whom I met in a bar sued me for a million
dollars because she claimed I told her I wanted to do my life story. True. I
told everybody I wanted to do my life story—but not with *her!* In 1959 I again
prepared to do it but Zsa Zsa also wanted to do her autobiography so she and
her coauthor, Gerold Frank, took me to lunch at "21."

"We will build you up so much in our book and you will come out so
important that eventually the book you will write must be a best seller," Zsa
Zsa said.

"Please don't do your book at the same time as ours. Please wait another
year," Gerold Frank said.

"Okay, I am still young enough not to have to do it so fast, so you do
it and I will wait," I said.

They not only didn't print much about me, but they only put one tiny
snapshot of me in the whole book.

Before that Eva did her story. Someone opened her refrigerator and
found only orchids and salami in it so that's what they named the book. Not
a very good title. Not a very good book. She didn't even put me in the book.
"I was afraid to write about you," she said, "for fear you would sue me, so
instead I wrote about Papa." So no wonder it was not a terrific success. How
could it be good without me in it?

Years ago Anita Loos wanted to write my biography. She explained to me,
"A biography is only good when you can put your finger on a person."

"Can you put yours on me?" I asked.

"Well," she declared positively, "the average woman at your age and with
your looks and your success has got to have become a vicious bitch."

"And I am that?" I asked her in horror.

"No," she sighed. "You are not. That's the trouble. You are still very
much the innocent child."

I've tried ten times before to write this book. Always I had interest, but now I almost have less interest than before. Peter Hurkos, the clairvoyant, said I should have written this ten years ago. Perhaps he is right. Anyway, it's never too late.

So why am I now writing it? A little of several reasons. First, people have been always telling me to write it. Ever since I am alive people have been telling me. I drove to Zsa Zsa's house in Beverly Hills from Palm Springs one day with Mr. and Mrs. Dumont and Princess Tumanoff. I said, "I have ten parties coming up this week, so I will save my voice. I will not open my mouth the whole drive in." I got in the car and didn't stop until we pulled up in Zsa Zsa's driveway, and the others insisted they never, but never, in or out of the theatre, laughed so much or were so entertained. When they said good-bye, they said, "You should write a book."

Secondly, I have come to the stage where it is the last five minutes for me and if I am ever to do it then I must do it now. Thirdly, my Edmund agrees to my doing it. Since I no longer work in my shop and he worries that sometimes I get depressed, he thinks this book is good for me. It is therapy. It will keep me busy.

Fourthly, I love Cindy Adams, who understands me and loves me back a little I think.

Fifthly, and I don't 100 per cent admit that this is true, but I mention it out of honesty, I think a little bit I want to show my girls that I can do it, too. And, maybe a little bit that I can do it better than they did.

Somehow I fear it will be a Hungarian tragedy sooner or later when this comes out. I am convinced that this memoir will be the end of me and that it will ruin my life. I am certain that the girls will be unhappy no matter what I say about them. I am positive Edmund will throw me out when he reads about my lovers. So, knowing all this I know I should take care what I say, but knowing me I know I will not.

BOOK ONE

Jancsi Tilleman

I was the third child of Francesca and Josef Tilleman. I was also the third girl. First came Janette, then Dora, and by the time I came around my parents were so eager to have a son they named me Jancsi, which translated comes out Little John or Johnny.

I was skinny with mousy brown hair, which no matter how my beloved mother wanted to curl still hung straight and stringy. It was square cut with bangs. My face wasn't just plain pale—it was green. And my left eye would not focus properly. Today they call it a "lazy eye." The specialists assured my divine mother I would grow out of this eventually (she would always ask them, *"When?"*), but she was ashamed of me because by now she had her fourth daughter, Rosalie, and with one exception all her girls were pretty. Particularly Rosalie. Rozsika was an angel with blonde hair that looked like a cloud, blue eyes, pink skin, and dimples. Even her baby fat was exquisite.

When I was growing up, Budapest was a dream city. Tourists would clap their hands and exclaim, "Oh, what a joy to live in such a city." Now it is not the same. Now it is gray, but then it was gay. The women were chic, the cafés were noisy, and the air was heavy with perfume, excitement, and *joie de vivre.* The Hungarian author Ladislas Farago called it "the frivolous capital of a lighthearted country."

One sunny afternoon we four girls were out promenading with Mama on the Váczi Utca. It was *the* place to promenade. On one side the men, on the other the fashionable ladies. A family friend twirling a pink parasol came up and smiled, "Congratulations, Mrs. Tilleman, on having such an attractive bouquet of children."

"Thank you," acknowledged Mama politely, then, pushing me in the background, she sighed, "With this one I was not overly successful."

My mother, Francesca Reinherz, was born in Vienna. Her parents had a chain of jewelry shops and some little property. They weren't a rich family —just a good family—but they wanted their beautiful Francesca to marry well, and they felt confident she'd make a suitable match because everyone agreed Francie Reinherz was the neighborhood beauty.

At seventeen she fell deeply in love with a university student and her parents were not exactly delighted. A proper match, marrying someone from a high background and financial position was important, and Josef Tilleman was pleasant but penniless. His finances were in such a bad way that he had to tutor other students to pay for his education.

They knew they would never get permission to marry, so Francesca did something unbelievable in those days—she eloped. Just before dark she packed a suitcase and ran away to Budapest and she and Josef were immediately married. After six months of tutoring he saved enough to invest in a small luncheonette which they ran themselves. With her white graceful hands, Francie Reinherz Tilleman, who was raised like a queen, worked eighteen hours a day, cooking, washing dishes, and personally serving the customers.

A little while later an uncle came from Vienna and he had the idea to establish the same sort of jewelry shops that Mama's family had. Mama was smart, and with her uncle's help the Tillemans went up very quickly in the world. She established The Diamond House, where they made a fortune on a clever new idea. In those days there were no cultured pearls, only fabulously expensive natural ones. Mama didn't see why they couldn't make good imitations to look genuine, so they created strands of fake pearls but with real diamond and gem clasps.

Mama and Papa quickly became richer than Mama's own mama and papa. By the time I was born we had a nanny and a maid and a cook and everything. Being Viennese, Mama and Papa spoke *Deutsch* at home, so German was my first language. All my growing up life I had a German fraulein for a nanny. Mama wanted us so much to be so fine and elegant that she even stole one fraulein from a high-class senator.

Budapest is divided by the Duna or Danube, which, by the way, is not blue. It's brown and muddy. On the right bank is ancient Buda, on the left is modern Pest. We lived in Pest, but Fraulein took us every afternoon on outings to Gellért Hegy, a wooded area on the Buda side. Always a man just happened to come around at the time we were there. Although we were very young we knew he was her lover and we knew enough not to tell at home. Always she would say to us littler ones, "Girls, you go around in the park and look for birdies and things. Go. Go." Unfortunately, our oldest sister, Janette, knew the bench where Fraulein and her lover smooched, and she took great pleasure in smearing mud on it deliberately. Janette was a bad girl.

So sometimes was I. There was that afternoon Mama was in the park with all of us when an old woman hobbled along, saw a penny under our bench, and stooped to pick it up. Snapped Mama, "No, don't touch. This is my daughter's stolen money." I had reached into her purse when she wasn't looking. I had watched Rozsika do this often and with great success. A day earlier she had come away with twenty silver pengős without being caught. Unfortunately I became so nervous that I only got my fingers on a few kreutzers, a few pennies, and trembled so as I brought my hand back that I spilled them and they clattered on the ground. Oh, so embarrassing.

Another afternoon we were in the country, and there swam a pretty yellow duck. "Oh, won't this make Mama happy," I thought, so I stole it. It didn't make Mama too happy because by the time I dragged it home she was entertaining the small, shriveled peasant farmer who owned the duck. "Where did you get this?" she thundered when I arrived.

"From my little farm," answered the peasant.

Father was our friend but Mama was our everything. Simple love wasn't enough for how we felt about her. We adored her. We worshiped her. She always wore sables and pearls and smelled of perfume. Even when she became heavy her face remained beautiful. Mama was a rich woman and a queenly one. She lived in the greatest of luxury and elegance. I considered myself honored if I could only lace up her boots because there was nothing you could do for her. She had everything. She was a strong force, and we were all afraid of her.

Papa also adored Mama. She also loved him but not so much. I remember Mama resting her hand on the tablecloth and when she lifted her hand up Papa kissed the place where it had been. Easy and gentle Papa was just a very nice man; Mama was the everything.

She was highly intelligent and people said this was because she was a little mixed. She had some Jewish blood. Even in the business she was the central figure. In those days when nobody knew about public relations, Mama did. There was a terrible tragedy in Hungary—a coal mine collapsed and took twenty lives, and nobody could speak of anything else for weeks. Mama had the idea to give a gold watch to each of the survivors, and the story came out on the front pages that Mrs. Tilleman, the owner of The Diamond House, gave a watch to each of the eleven survivors and wasn't that a tremendous thing for her to have done! Of course, some jealous people sniped that "she makes this only for publicity not just for her good heart," but Mama was a woman who wanted to become important and to make something of herself and her family and her daughters and she did.

Mama never spent time with her children the way other mothers did. She didn't play with us or take us to school or sit and listen to our problems. She remained always a big distance from us. If any of us called to her when she came home from work, she handled it by replying, "Keep still. Don't shout. God should only help me that you will someday be out from here." I don't remember her as ever being involved with us.

Fortunately, we had one another. I went always with my unhappinesses to the children's room. We shared one big, big room like a dormitory, which we unflatteringly called a *kaszárnya* or barracks. People always came to see it. Whoever had not seen it was told about it. This was the most famous nursery in all Budapest. It had four desks and four plain cots like in an armory and what we made in those cots with the rumpled sheets and the pillow fights made Mama want to die.

Besides that there was this one special girl's room, a huge room with blue ceiling, white carpet, double-sized brass bed on a pedestal in the center, light blue silk coverlet, and exquisite untouched silk bedclothes. It was like for a bride. The only trouble was none of us could sleep in it. It was strictly for show.

Never will I forget when Mama brought home a friend to see her lavish twelve-room apartment in the five-story corner building she owned on the Kaiser Wilhelm Strasse. Mama showed her their fancy bedroom, the mirrored dining room, the salon, everything, and then Mama walked her into the special girl's room. Swinging open the doors wide, she announced, "And here . . . this is for my eldest daughter, Janette."

Janette was a rebel. She had followed behind and she said, "Mama, don't tell that in front of me because I am the eldest and never am I allowed to sleep here."

Slowly and deliberately Mama replied to the lady friend, "Janette will soon begin to sleep here because this is her room. After she gets married, it will go to Doruska and—"

"It is not true," insisted Janette. "I wanted to sleep here, but I could not. I could never sleep here. This is only made for show, for showing off."

Mother began to cry. "Janette," she said, "you must not cause me to be a liar. This is what makes a parent unhappy."

"But what you say is untrue," insisted Janette. "We can only sleep here when one of us is sick but so far none of us is ever sick so that not even me, the eldest, has ever one night slept in this gorgeous bed. We sleep only in the *kasárnya* like the army."

Mother was angry. *"Schrechlich . . . nicht Herrschaflich,"* she kept saying when the friend left. *Herrschaften* was a German word I was always to hear as I was growing up. It means "ruling classes, nobility." Mama would complain, *"Herrschaften* don't act this way. Only low-class children that would do this."

The family revolutionary, Janette, was daring and outspoken. Doruska, the lady of the group, always managed to look neat and clean. Rozsika was fun-loving. I was the most trouble of all. I had an inferiority complex. My unprettiness led to frustration, and sometimes I would make a spectacle of myself.

Except for an occasional outburst from Janette the rebel, none of us would ever fight with our refined, elegant mother. How would we dare? Because I would create grand dramas to gain her attention, there were times she was rough on me and I would cry very much and think secretly with my head buried in my pillow that Mama was an egotist. Never, however, would I open my mouth except to say, "Whatever happened was my fault and I ask your forgiveness." After that she would go to the others and be soft with them for a second, and I would wish she would have been soft with me, too, but then the moment passed. I never saw my mother in her bathrobe or with her hair undone or even in her underwear. She was always 100 per cent perfect. The only time I saw her truly soft and adoring was when her son was born. Janette was thirteen, Doruska eleven, I was nine, and Rozsika was seven when Sebastyen was born. Mama adored Sebi. Sebika. Her only son! The moment she had him, the rest of us became stepchildren.

Oh what a big fuss when Sebastyen was born. It was Mama's custom to give birth at home. We four were in our children's room and next door we could hear Mama going, "Aaaahhhh . . . Aaaahhhh. . . ." We huddled together listening to her groaning and Papa running around like mad. Nobody was paying any attention to us and it was late in the night. Just as the clock struck two, Rozsika sat upright and whispered, "I saw it. . . . I saw the stork go in."

Sebastyen was like a king. He had a wet nurse with a gigantic bosom. Because Mama didn't give him her milk, the nanny spoiled him terribly. She bathed him in cream and eggs. "Eggs are the best," she said. And when the nanny pushed him in the carriage, every few blocks she had to stop and take a glass of beer because "This is good to make milk," she claimed. This nanny had two enormous busts, but every half hour she needed beer. Mama loved Sebika so much. Always he wanted to be with her and be cuddled by her. Always he went to her. Even on Sundays when the others would go off for fun he wanted to stay with Mama but she was not the type to spend time with her children even if one of them was Sebi, so she shooed him off. "You are a boy. You don't need to spend time on your mother's lap." Still, even if she wouldn't give him attention, he adored her and preferred to play wherever she was.

Sebi was the special angel in the family. We played with him as if he were our little doll. Sebi transferred a little of his affection and adoration to Janette. He snuggled into her and when he was three he crept into bed to cuddle with Janette, who was sixteen, and we saw his little thing go up. We were all very proud of Sebika.

This was the second time I had seen something like this. When I was seven we had all gone to our summer house at Lake Balaton. Many relatives had gathered for an outdoor lunch. As they prepared spits and coal and wood and fire and set deep kettles on to bubble, I wandered off a little ways. I had to go to the bathroom. I was wearing a starched white pinafore and my little boy cousin, who was only five, watched me as I skipped into the outdoor toilet.

I was sitting there on the toilet doing what I had to do when the wooden door squeaked, a head poked in and up came my small boy cousin Miksika. The door flung wide behind him and I could see the Balaton and the green grass and nothing but open field around us. Miksika was eating an apple. Not a nice, inviting apple but a green and wormy chewed-up thing. Half the apple he'd managed to eat already. He just stood there gaping at me while I was making pipi.

Miksika was wearing a tiny bikini which was not totally covering all of him and he was sort of leaning against the door. Slowly he began to rub against the door a little and to sort of jump up and down. As he jumped I could see his thing. I couldn't see it always but I saw it sometimes. I didn't know exactly what it was I saw, but I knew I saw *something* I didn't usually see. "Jancsika," he said finally, "when you allow me to put my pimpi to your poompi . . . ," and he pointed to his pants and to me, "then I give you the other half of my apple."

I didn't quite know for sure what was this ootzie pootzie he was suggesting but I knew for sure I didn't want his rotten apple, so I guess I didn't look too enthusiastic because he said again, "When you let me put my thing next to your thing you can have my apple." I did not want his rotten apple. I wanted only to go to the toilet. However, I shall always remember this as my very first invitation—and the apple in exchange for him could really be thought of as my first offer of a business transaction!

The one pain in my childhood was that I was not pretty. To add to my other troubles, I developed pimples. Mama took me with my bad skin from one doctor to another. None of them helped and they all told me different things. One told, "I warn you, don't go to a cosmetician. Don't clean your face with lotions or cleansing creams. Stick to water." When he couldn't help me I went to a cosmetician who warned me, "Don't clean your face with water. Stick to lotions and cleansing creams." I think the best treatment was age. As I got older, it went away by itself.

In terms of sisterly closeness I was closest to Rozsika. The difficulty was that Rozsika forever teased me that she was beautiful and I not. She scraped one forefinger against the other as though saying, "Shame. Shame." She would bat her long, thick, black lashes at me, shake her heavenly crowning glory in my face and boast, "See? Blonde and curly," and then finger my brown stringy hair and go, "Uggghhh!" She also had pink skin and a dimple. I could forgive the pink skin, but the dimple I could never forgive.

I had my first love affair at seven. The object of my one-sided affection was a handsome lawyer who lived on our top floor. He was tall dark and romantic-looking and, I was told, was thirty-two years old. Every evening before supper I would stand on the landing, wishing with all my heart that my beloved would come home or go out or come down the hall stairs or go in or do something so I could catch a glimpse of him.

The first moment I saw him I was in deep trouble. I was sitting on the steps when this tall god ran up the stairs two at a time and patted me on the head like a little doggy. "Nice girlie," he patted, and this was enough to make me pledge myself to him forever. Sometimes he would say something as exciting as "Hello," and this for me was seventh heaven. I would wait for hours until he was due.

Rosalie delighted to tease me about "The Man," as she called him. One Friday it was rainy and we had just returned from school and I heard his voice outside the door. I ran to the hallway and gazed in the big antique mirror standing next to the umbrella rack. I was ugly. No doubt about it. I trembled because at that moment I would have given half my life for one little dimple. As I gazed at myself, Rozsika came up. We stood almost shoulder to shoulder;

9

I was about an inch taller. She, gave a smug, conceited smile to the mirror. "Don't you think The Man would prefer me?" she asked.

I had pulled open the drawer of the mirror stand and had in my hand a pointed rattail comb. I ran it through my hair but no matter how I worked it still hung limply like an old mop. In her baby voice Rozsika taunted me, "Jancsi, you're ugly. If The Man marries anybody, it will be me!"

Whatever possessed me I don't know, but I dug the sharp, pointed rattail right into her skull. She began screaming. She felt the thing in her head and when she went past the mirror she could see it sticking out of the top of her head like an Indian arrow, but no blood spilled out. I wanted to pull the thing out, but she ran shrieking to *Mamuska*. I ran after her. When I got close enough to grab the comb, it broke off right in her head.

I couldn't believe my sister sat screaming in the salon with the evidence of what I had done still lodged in her scalp, while I stood there stupidly clutching the other half of the broken comb. And this was the sister I was closest to, so you can imagine how close I was to the others. Oh, this was a tragedy. I threw myself on the bed. The tears came down my cheeks. Eventually I washed my face and went out to apologize but the salon was empty. Fraulein shook her finger at me. "Your Mama took Rozsika to the First Aid Station," she said.

I was waiting for them all alone in the big room when they came home an hour later. I felt awful when I saw the whole center of Rozsika's head shaved and a huge adhesive patch stuck in the center of it. I walked over to kiss her, but Fraulein with the anger of a bear roared, "Jancsi, you could have been a murderer. It is only by chance that your sister didn't die. Go to bed. You will have no supper."

I smelled the huge crock of goose fat rendering on the back of the stove and heard the sizzling sounds when the sliced onions were added to it. I thought of the cracklings seasoned with salt and pepper, which we piled onto dark bread, and I wanted to say that I was sorry. I wanted to say I also needed sympathy because didn't they know I was in love and Rozsika was telling me how unappetizing I was? Didn't they realize I had feelings too? Rozsika enjoyed being the center of attention, and the whole thing was really nothing. In three days the adhesive patch came off, and it was all over—and so was my love affair.

The next afternoon we were at Városliget, and a woman asked, "Can my children play with your children?" Fraulein answered, "Rozsika and Doruska you can take, but not this one. This one is a murderer." I was so ashamed.

I needed love very much as a child. Once I was even in love with my mathematics teacher. He was awful; short and redhaired, but he was nice to me. He rubbed the back of his hand against my cheek and it was enough for me to die for him after that. Maybe because I wanted to impress him, I learned a little more that year. I was not a good student. In fact, I was the worst.

In school they all said the Tilleman girls were elegant. Mama liked it that way. Mama dressed us identically in matching velvet suits or the same pleated skirts with golden buttons, exactly alike even to the hats and gloves. With the two older girls in front and us younger ones in back like a formation, everybody would turn when we walked into school or when we marched down the Andrassy Ut, which is the equivalent of the Champs-Élysées. Mama loved that sort of attention.

When Mama came to school, all the girls said that when they grew up they wanted to look just like that. When I was seven years old, I begged her to wear an evening dress to school. "But I can't," she said.

"But you must," I pleaded. "I want to show you off." Finally she did. She wore a jade green gown with black lace over it and a long veil and big hat. All the teachers came from their classrooms to look. They asked me, "Is your mother an actress?" And I'd reply, "Yes, she is an actress. Furthermore, I was born on stage." For years I lied and said, "My mother was actually singing on the very stage when the stork came and announced, 'Mrs. Tilleman, I have here your child.' " Oh, did they give me attention after that.

School was eight in the morning until one and then extra afternoons for French. When Sebi was eight, he went to Berlin to the military academy. Oh, how I wished I had a big brother instead of a little one and that he went to school at home so that he could bring his boyfriends home. My good friend Sari always had boys in the house because she had brothers, but I had only girls around me all my growing up life.

In my all-girls school I didn't even see a boy. We didn't have knowledge of boys or even birds or bees. Nobody taught us. We had no teaching about this at all. Mother would never stoop to instruct us in terms of sex. I knew only that you marry a man and he gets on top of you and that's that. But how or with what I didn't know. This I learned from friends, and it wasn't exactly what you'd call a full education.

It was particularly terrible because I was very sexy. Mama knew I was trouble and knew she'd better not delay in getting me married. When I was still a child, I asked her, "*Mamuska,* when can I get married?" And she said, "Not before sixteen." But the way she glared at me I had the feeling she would stretch that even lower if she had the opportunity.

I kissed Rozsika a little and we touched each other a little to sort of see what sex was, but that was my only experience and it wasn't very thrilling. We were cautioned to go not even near a broom, so we didn't, but we none of us had ever seen a male body—not Sebi nude, not my father, nobody—so I couldn't imagine what the broom meant or who has what that you stick where.

We didn't even know a boy we could rub up against or even who had a hand we could hold. Mama wouldn't let us any place where we could meet any. Fraulein took us by coach and horse to dancing school every Friday. For me it was seventh heaven. I loved the music and the piano playing and the pirouetting and everything about this sort of gay party life. In time to the music the teacher would chant, "Right foot out, left foot out," but from excitement my tongue stuck out, so she would chant, "Right foot out, left foot out, Jancsi's tongue *in.*"

When I was ten, Mama stopped dancing school because the little boy partners were then also age ten, and she considered this too much fraternization. She was afraid someone would put his pimpi to my poompi. Oh, so disappointed I was. I was good at dancing and wanted badly to show that I could be special at something.

The summer before my twelfth birthday started out to be the happiest I'd ever known. Every summer Mama and Papa took us to the villa at Lake Balaton. The Tillemans on the move resembled a traveling caravan—Janette, Dora, Rosalie, Sebastyen, Sebastyen's nurse, the cook, chambermaid, coachman, Mama, Papa, Fraulein, and me. From our apartment across the Chain Bridge and into the village overlooking the lake took a whole day. After seeing us settled, Mama and Papa would leave for their own holiday at the spa in Karlsbad, Czechoslovakia. By this time they had thirty-six jewelry shops throughout Europe, and their main shop, The Diamond House, on the ground floor of our apartment building was a showplace. It had eighteen windows. Although we were not millionaires we lived very well. Everything was beautiful for us at the lake.

Five years had passed since my first crush, and in all this time my passionate, romantic nature had been bottled up. Then I met Miklós! It was a hot day. The sun was high in the heavens. I dived underwater and bumped headlong into a boy. "Oh, excuse me," I gasped as I bobbed up, short of breath.

"That's all right," said a handsome face. He looked about thirteen and was tan and when he stood up I saw he was quite tall.

"I apologize for knocking you down," I said, wiping the water out of my eyes so I could see this god I had captured.

"My name is Miklós," he said.

"I'm Jancsi Tilleman."

"Oh, yes, you live in that small villa down the road."

I was in ecstasy talking with a real boy. We promised to meet each other down by the water the following day.

We became a steady item. Every afternoon we would swim, walk along the beach laughing and talking and trying to impress one another with our worldly knowledge. He talked of his dream to be an engineer and inventor. I spoke to him about love and life.

He was staying in a cheap hotel which had a chicken *paprikás* smell coming from its kitchen. Mikloska and his mother, who was maybe thirty-five and was always having some adventure with some man, would sit in the garden of the hotel and have lunch. This impressed me greatly. I would sit in our kitchen and think of my *bon vivant*, my man of the world, eating his lunch in a real restaurant!

I thought a little he was also impressed with me. Finally, however, he must have become unimpressed because I caught him being untrue to me. Her name was Gladys and this made my pain all the more unbearable because in Budapest nobody had such a name as Gladys. This was a foreign name and this sort of ammunition was difficult for me to fight.

After three weeks we had even discussed the probability of getting married in a few years. On the day of his betrayal I had on a blue pinafore with red dots and braids with bows on them to match and I was pretty nice. I waited at our secret meeting place ten minutes, twenty minutes, a half hour. I was frantic. Surely something drastic had happened to prevent him from keeping our rendezvous. I wanted to run down the beach looking for him. I wanted to run into the hotel to see if he was alive, but Fraulein came in sight. She had been seated quietly enjoying the music and suddenly realized I had been gone for some while. "Time to go home," she ordered. I couldn't protest for fear she'd become suspicious.

That evening I could not eat and there is almost never a time I cannot eat. Stuffed goose—with chestnuts, oranges, apricots, and bread soaked in white wine—was on the menu. For me to refuse it you must understand how serious was my condition. I pleaded a headache and went to bed early. When everybody was tucked in, I dressed and sneaked out the window. I had to find Miklós.

Hidden by a hedge which enclosed the sidewalk café, I could see the tables gaily decorated with checkered cloths and catch glimpses of fresh corn drenched in butter, newly baked rolls, and steaming rice pilaf. I was hungry, but what a time to think of food. A fiddler cried the words to that sad Gypsy song which goes, "It hurts my heart very badly that my little angel left me." *My* heart hurt very badly. Through the hedge I saw a party of laughing diners. Near the end sat my beloved and holding hands with him was this other woman. She had to be at least fifteen! Plump, rosy cheeks, blue eyes, such a beauty! The two of them in the garden of this cheap hotel with one lousy Gypsy playing, a fat waitress running around bowing and serving, and I thought I would break in two with pain. I shut my eyes as though the very act would cause my Miklós to disappear from my rival's side. Then I caught him giving Gladys one of *our* looks—a look I thought reserved only for me. Tears rolled down my cheeks as I made it home. I couldn't sleep. I vowed I would never sleep.

The following day I ran along the beach until I bumped into Miklós and That Other Woman. I called him coldly, "Miklós, I'd like to speak with you for a moment, please."

Annoyed but polite, he came over. I fought back the tears. I tried to act grown up. I had rehearsed a speech, but all I could manage was a whimpered, "Why?"

From his thirteen-year-old height, he looked at me patronizingly. "Jancsi, look, you're a sweet kid and I've enjoyed our talks, but Gladys is a woman. She's fifteen. And she's beautiful. After all, if I can be with a woman, what do I need with a little girl with braids?"

Nobly I shook his hand and whispered, "Good-bye." Silently I walked back to where my sisters were playing and ran past them into the lake. I swam as far as I could. I floated around on my back crying such tears that I thought it would cause a tidal wave. Would I never find someone who cared about me?

We could meet boys during wintertime only when we were taken to Alatkert, the ice-skating rink in the zoo. That winter I went skating with Fraulein and I met three boys. One was again named Miklós. And I learned early you cannot overcome a love affair except you have another. Until you have a fresh love the old one never dies. For me love was all. I hungered for it. I did not have enough of it. From childhood love was very important to my life, and until now it is the same.

I wore a skating cap in white silk from under which tumbled long, false curls, which I was convinced made me absolutely not to be resisted. I had three curls on one side and two on the other and three boys around me. It was exciting and romantic because I was the center of attraction. I was the sun with three moons circling around me. Oh, I was so happy—particularly when Miklós was around.

Then, on another skating day, Ilonka entered the picture. Ilonka's mother was our washwoman, and her father used to come home in daylight in a tuxedo and top hat because he worked as a waiter in a nightclub. They lived in a one-room cell with only two treasures—a red mahogany piano on a pedestal in one corner and a handpainted antique armoire. This was my first experience with poverty and I couldn't believe people existed like this. We went up to this apartment for the first time and the mother asked Fraulein if she would please take Ilonka along with us for ice-skating. Ilonka was a beauty contest winner who had won a gold watch, and I could not breathe when I was with her because she was so ravishing compared to me. We arrived to the park and I introduced Ilonka to my Miklós and I lost him immediately.

Later I said to him, "Why is it you don't love me anymore?"

"Because Ilonka is much prettier," he retorted cruelly.

"But you told me I am so witty."

"Yes, but Ilonka is so much more pretty than you."

At that moment I decided I had to become beautiful, I had to turn into the pretty creature I longed to be, I had to have men at my feet no matter what it took to get them there. Much of my desire for glamor began in those days when I knew the heartache of being homely. I spent hours daydreaming about being desirable. It gave me the hunger for self-improvement.

The years between twelve and fourteen were my turning point. On September 30, my twelfth birthday, Fraulein took Rozsika and me to the theatre. Rozsika was delighted. "It's my first play," she exclaimed happily.

I tried to camouflage my excitement. "Oh, Rozsika, you're such a child."

"And when did you go to the theatre last?" asked Rozsika.

"Never," snapped Fraulein as we climbed into the coach. "This is her first time, too."

"What's playing?" I asked.

"*Sulamit,*" replied Fraulein as the coachman started the horses up. "Why? You saw it before?"

I ignored her remark. "What's *Sulamit?*"

"It's an operetta about an Arab sheik."

We drove up to the theatre and paid our forty kreutzers or pennies per seat. Mobs of people were jostling and elbowing. "The theatre is so packed that maybe we won't get in," I trembled.

"We already have seats," announced Fraulein, "but they're in the balcony. We will have to walk up to the topmost balcony."

Our seats were so high that we two little girls had to bow our heads when we came through the halls. "I can barely see the stage," I whispered.

"Me either," Rozsie whispered back.

"Sssshhhh," hissed Fraulein as the people turned around to glare.

"You know, I think I am developing a headache," I said into Rozsie's ear.

"How come?" she whispered back. "You have never ever before in your life had a headache."

"I know but I'm getting sick from the excitement."

"Sssshhhh," repeated Fraulein.

I sat rigid throughout the performance. When the curtain rang down, I could hardly move. As we filed out, I grabbed Rozsika's arm. "Suddenly it has come to me," I said. "What better way to have men at your feet than to be an actress?"

"What men at your feet?" stupidly asked my little sister.

Aloud I said only, "I, Jancsi Tilleman, will become a star."

"What men at your feet?" repeated Rozsie.

"Even if you don't understand," I explained patronizingly, "Mama will, because it was Mama herself who always wanted to make something of herself so she will understand this feeling which I have inherited. I must become a star."

"Come, star," ordered Fraulein, pushing me down the steps. "It is time to get home and have supper."

I swore in my bed as I lay in my cot in the children's room that I would devote my life to the theatre. The next morning I confided this momentous decision to Mama and her hurried response was, "Yes, yes, but first get good marks in school."

From then on my dream never let up. The subject was never fully discussed at home because whenever I pleaded to study dramatics I was told, "Concentrate on your lessons. Learn to play the piano. Perfect your French," commanded Mama. "Grow up to be a well-rounded lady ready for marriage. That is your career."

"Never will I get over my desire to be an actress," I vowed.

"All right," sighed Mama one night, "but be one later because it is now bedtime."

At age thirteen, I changed physically. My face cleared up. One day, my teacher came to me before class and told me to move my belongings into a seat in the front row. That was where the *pretty* girls sat. Mama was so thrilled.

"You will see," promised the teacher. "This one will be the prettiest."

Within that year Rozsie became fattish and Janette began to grow a little less attractive and before you know it I had become the most beautiful of them all. Six months later the teacher whispered to Mama, "Didn't I tell you she would be the prettiest?"

My hair then was darkish blonde with red highlights. My friend Sari, who was also in high school with me, suggested, "Let's bleach our hair. All the girls who are blonde have more dates than the others."

"What would Mama say?" I was afraid.

"Whatever she says it will be too late," reasoned Sari practically. "Anyway, to be an actress you have to be maximum pretty."

I took a deep breath. "Okay. What have we to do?"

My worldly friend handed me peroxide. "That's super strength bleach," she said and went inside to bring out a huge mixing bowl. "Dunk your head in it," she said. I dunked, and she slopped my hair around in it until I was covered with the peroxide. "Now do the same for me," she ordered.

We came out bright yellow. And awful. The principal wanted to throw us out of school but my mother and Sari's hysterical mother both came to school to plead for us even though they themselves wanted to kill us.

For my fourteenth birthday I was invited to visit Janette, who was married and living in Vienna. I was so excited. I was also excited because I had developed a bosom a little bit. I had become a woman!

To do the things that other women with bosoms did, I took my first drink of beer. Janette took me to Grinzing, the outdoor café, and I sipped the warm beer slowly as I'd seen adults do with liqueurs. It was so bitter I had to spit it out on the floor. Janette rebuked me. "Ladies with blonde hair and bosoms do not spit beer out on floors!"

That night I couldn't sleep. In the next room I heard my sister and her husband *baszniing*. It went on for some while and I heard the bed creaking and the springs going up and down with a crash. It made me nervous and my heart beat doublefast because I knew what they must be doing but I didn't actually know *how* they were doing. I lay still in my narrow bed with my ear to the wall. And I made a poem. In Hungarian it comes out good, in English not so good. In English it is just that these two love each other so much and the bed comes up and down with a crash with the rhythm of their love.

The next morning I looked at them carefully to see if you could tell that they had been *baszniing* the night before. You could tell nothing. So, I told *them*. I read the poem to them and they were hysterical. While I was there, those springs went up and down with a crash many nights.

On my second Sunday Janette's husband said, "We are going to the Prater, Jancsi. It's a famous place. You must see it."

"What is it?" I asked.

"It's a playland—with a merry-go-round and ferris wheel and all sorts of rides. It is the first in all Europe. Nowhere else do they have such a place."

For this special event I dressed carefully in a short white Madeira lace dress. I wore also a black picture hat with bright red poppies surrounding jet black centers. It was a little much for playland and, accordingly, I attracted attention. I pushed way out my chest and I was like a star and everybody was looking at me.

I was such a success at the amusement park that when I returned home, I organized an outing to the little Ringelspiel playland we had in Budapest. To ensure my success as a *femme fatale* I wore the same outfit and, sure enough, a young man began following me. He even snapped a photo of me. He carried a newspaper under his arm and, once, when he caught my eye, he pointed to the newspaper.

"Jancsika," exclaimed my girl friend Sari, who was so excited she was quivering, "he is telling you he will advertise for you."

"What does it mean, 'advertise' for me?"

Sari, who was months older than I and thus much more mature, looked at me patronizingly. "A person who wishes to communicate with another person and doesn't know how puts an ad in the newspaper hoping the other person will see it and reply."

"You mean he puts in the papers my photograph?" I said breathlessly.

"If he really wants to find you he will."

Every day the whole class brought all the city's newspapers to school. A week later there it was. A bold caption, "Who is this beautiful girl?" and underneath was my snapshot.

"Look," squealed Sari, "there is an *article* about you in the newspaper."

I, who would have preferred to play it casual, ripped the pages out of Sari's hand and began eagerly devouring the words: "Who is this beautiful girl in white dress and black hat whom I admire?"

About ten of us stood in a circle in the school corridor reading the paper.

"Oh," gasped Ilona, a not-so-very-pretty girl, "Jancsi *is* the girl in the newspaper."

Another sucked her breath in and exclaimed, "Oh, Jancsi is having an *affair.*'"

"You must answer his advertisement," reasoned Sari.

"He has written he is twenty-four and he is an engineer. Isn't that too old for me?" I licked my dry lips nervously.

"Certainly not," pronounced Sari. "Ten years difference is the perfect amount between a man and wife."

I reread aloud what he said: "Whoever you are I would like to see you again."

"Oh, how romantic—but I cannot see him," I whined. "I am allowed only to school and back."

Sari said, "Write him that much as you would like to see him you cannot, but thank him anyway for his attentions."

And so came to an end the first publicized affair of Jancsi Tilleman.

By age sixteen I'd been told repeatedly that "actresses are not of the better class" and were offstage socially unacceptable. Still I continued to bring up the subject. At this point all my theatrical abilities were confined to the house. Mother would tell her friends, "Jancsika wants to be an actress," and they all laughed. Nonetheless, she was proud of me because when she had guests, I would sing some of the little things I learned from the operettas I had seen.

Besides singing I possessed another great talent. I had perfected the ability to "faint" magnificently. Fainting was big in movies in those days. My breasts heaved, my knees crumpled, and I could fall down dead quite nicely.

Once when we had a houseguest I stood in the pantry one afternoon and saw her consume four cups of tea. "Who is she?" I asked my mother.

"A relative of ours," Mama explained.

"Yes, but whose? She must be a relative of Papa's, because you have such style and this lady does not."

Mama laughed. "You must be nice. She is your Auntie Ethel and you are quite right. She is your aunt on your father's side."

"How long will she be here?" I asked.

"I don't know," frowned Mama. "She says she wants to stay a week or more." We watched Fraulein bringing her another cup of tea. "And she is an expensive houseguest with all her cups of tea."

"But tea is only water," I said.

"Yes, all right, so it is only water, but into the water she puts many sugars and many lemons and many swallows of rum, so with all this all day she is a pain in the neck."

I wanted very much to help Mama so I went into Auntie Ethel's room.

I had first to run around the apartment to make myself panting and weak and when I went into her room I heaved my breasts and crumpled my knees and fell right down at her feet in a heap. She ran into Mama's room screaming, "Jancsi is dying . . . Jancsi is dying. . . ." When Auntie Ethel's back was turned I winked at Mama and her eyes gleamed with delight. Auntie Ethel packed her bags and went immediately away after that. Mama was so grateful that she bought me a present.

I pleaded with her for permission to study acting professionally. She had a slight cold one day and Cook made her apostle's milk punch, which she always served when anyone had a cold. Made with milk, egg yolk, sugar, vanilla, a pinch of black pepper, and brandy, and served boiling hot in a tall mug, it was soothing and gentle to the spirit even if you didn't have a cold. Papa often pretended to have a cold. This day Mama was propped up with satin bolster pillows, wearing a pink satin quilted bed jacket. I came in eager to sympathize. It seemed a moment of this rare intimacy so I begged again, "Mama, you must please allow me to take acting lessons."

Weakened by her cold and anxious to silence me, Mama said, "Your Papa and I are soon to take our vacation in Karlsbad. I promise you when we return . . ."

". . . You will then give me permission to go to acting school next year," I finished for her.

"No," said Mama, "I will then discuss the subject with you more fully."

"Why can't we discuss it now?"

"I promise we will discuss it when Papa and I return."

I kissed her fingers. "Oh, thank you, *Mamuska*, thank you." I ran out bursting with happiness.

That night I eavesdropped on a family problem. It seems Doruska, my second sister, who was now married a year, was still physically untouched. There was a big meeting in the dining room and Rozsika and I had our ears to the door and our eyes to the keyhole. The husband was actually crying. Mama sat at the head of the table with her hands tightly folded. She said, "Can you imagine that my Doruska is still a virgin? She is a year virgin!"

Papa, who usually had very little to say, spoke up this one time to the husband. "You were well known to be a playboy before you married our daughter. You were well known to love women. How is it this could be the result?"

"That is the trouble," replied the husband, a heavyset strong man of twenty-four who was all crumpled up in a chair looking sad.

"What is the trouble?" demanded Mama.

"I am accustomed to dating lower-class women. Some were washwomen, peasant women. I liked them. I enjoyed their company and they were no challenge for me. But Doruska is different."

"You . . ." accused Mama, pointing a finger at him, "you are the one who is different. There is nothing different about my Doruska."

His eyes downcast, he said in a low voice, "But Doruska is for me a saint."

Mama pounded the table angrily. "A saint doesn't marry," she said hotly.

Dora, who had been sitting at the far end of the table, got to her feet. She opened her mouth to say something then closed it again. Mama looked at her. "My poor daughter," she said softly. Doruska sighed and bit her lip. Papa put his arm around Doruska's shoulder. The husband wiped his eyes.

"Why is this such a tragedy?" I whispered to Rozsika when it came her turn to look through the keyhole. "Why is *Mamuska* so upset? It is good to be a virgin, no? Always I am told not to let any man near this little *pina* of mine. Always I am told to let not even a broom slip into my *pina* let alone a man, so why is *Mamuska* complaining?"

"I don't know," shrugged Rozsika. "Can it be Doruska is pregnant?"

"How can she be pregnant, you stupid?" I hissed back. "This whole argument is because Mama complains nothing has happened down there. She says they never *baszni.*"

"I don't know then what is the whole problem," said my younger sister, still with her eyes to the keyhole. "All I know is we are told to take care of this treasure we have down there so why we must take care and Doruska not I don't know."

"Get away from there," I commanded her. "Let me look."

The husband was pacing. "The problem for me is that Doruska is so ladylike and perfect. Too much so for me. She is an exquisite creation."

"How is that a problem?" asked Mama.

"Well," he explained slowly, "she is like a perfect canvas. Could I cut into an expensive painting? Could I go with a knife and slash at the *Mona Lisa?*"

Mama stood up in a rage. "You don't have to go with a knife!"

"He has tried with me, Mama," offered Doruska quietly. "It isn't as though he hasn't tried."

"You mean," said Papa very slowly, "that he is impotent?"

She nodded.

"I try and I want to," said the husband in a voice so low I could barely make it out, "but with her I cannot."

"And with the common washwomen you can?" inquired Papa.

He nodded.

"You know," I turned to Rozsika, while there was a few minutes worth of heavy silence in the dining room, "Doruska's husband likes hard drinking and Gypsy music and he is a liker of low women. I saw him with the peasant woman who came with a big wicker basket to take the wash away. He didn't know I was there and he put her to the wall and I couldn't see exactly what he did because his back was to me but he lifted up her skirts, made some motions in front with his pants, and his hips moved in and out. What actually went on I don't know, but that much I saw."

Mama's voice came through the door. "You, a man who likes to go out late at night into the cafés and sit and talk and drink. You, a man's man. You . . . you can't do anything."

They were divorced but by then I was completely involved in my own world. I, too, had met a man. A real man, not a boy. He was an army officer and his name was Vilmos Gabor.

I went away for a week to the home of a fifteen-year-old cousin, Elizabeth, who was to be married in a big wedding. I was to be a bridesmaid. There were many pre-wedding parties and I had a pre-arranged escort for the week. He was Ferenc Christhaber, a business partner of Papa's. Mama was unhappy Ferenc was to be my escort because he was thirty. "He is much too old for you," she clucked unhappily.

"But I'm not unhappy," I said to her. "Ferenc is as handsome as a movie star."

I felt suddenly quite wicked being paired off with someone so devastatingly handsome. "Everybody says you're just like Roman Navarro," I teased Ferenc. "Can you make a deep backbend kiss like he does in the movies?"

My head pounded crazily as he smiled, "Sure." He put his arms around my waist and over I went as he kissed me full on the lips. I was dizzy with excitement. It was my first kiss and it dizzied me. His lips were soft but he smelled very male. I felt butterflies flitting around inside that little *pinuska* I was sworn never ever to even let a broom near. When Ferenc released me, my eyes fell on a stranger, sandyhaired and with a small moustache and good-looking in a dashing sort of way. Major Vilmos Gabor reacted to my gaze by bowing deeply and applauding our kiss.

While I paraded about with my sheik, it was baby sister Rosalie who was paired off with Vilmos. Vilmos was an "older man"—he was thirty-three. Ferenc was only loaned to me for a week. He wasn't for settling-down purposes —at least not with me, who was nearly a member of his family. I wasn't so sure about that Vilmos. He looked ripe for marriage. He looked ripe for *something,* that was for sure.

I took Rozsika aside. "Look," I reasoned, "how does it look for you, my baby sister, to have a romance while I have nobody?"

"But you have *Papuska's* business partner," said Rozsika, whom I could see was not going to give up easily.

"He is nothing. He is only temporary. You have a man who could be permanent. I mean, he might turn out to be a potential husband."

"Since when are you interested in anything besides becoming an actress?"

"That's true, but actresses are supposed to be seductive and alluring. How can I be that when I don't have anybody to be it with?"

"So what do you want with me?"

"I want you to give Vilmos over to me."

Rozsika did not like to give up anything that was hers. The wedding came and went and my parents went to Karlsbad and we returned to Budapest and my rented Roman Navarro went back to his jewelry shops because he had known me since I was a baby and didn't entertain any ideas that I was anything. As for Vilmos, I didn't know where he went until my sister received a postcard.

A postcard of her very own! Vilmos wrote that he had gone to Lake Balaton on business and was happy he had met her and hoped to see her soon again. Rozsie was beside herself with happiness. All she could think of to say was, "Poor Jancsi. I bet *I* will be married first."

Mama wrote us how happy she was that Rozsie seemed able to win the attentions of such a rich man as Mr. Gabor, adding, "However, Rozsie, in our family girls marry according to age. Therefore it would be best for you not to speak to Mr. Gabor should he call because first Jancsi has to find a suitor." Vilmos' card and Mama's letter changed my whole life.

I cornered Rozsie. "You must not encourage Mr. Gabor."

"But he is *mine,*" she said defiantly. "He is coming to call on me this week."

"As your older sister, I tell you that you cannot see this man. If Mama heard about this it would be terrible. I tell you what I will do for you. I will be your chaperone."

"The only thing you will do for me is steal him," she snapped.

When Vilmos came to call, our old maid Fraulein wouldn't let them alone. Neither would I. Vilmos was such a dandy that he came with two detachable stiff wing collars and halfway through the evening he changed to a fresh one. As he prepared to leave he said to Rozsie, "Would you like to take a ride with me on Sunday afternoon?"

Walking with dignity to the door I reached for the doorknob, drew myself up tall, choked down my anger and smiled sweetly, "Mr. Gabor, my parents would never allow a child of Rozsika's age to go driving with a man alone. If you wish to take her out I'll have to go along, too." Then, without a backward glance, I slammed the salon door behind me and left.

The following Sunday dashing Villie, who was out of the army now and in business, came to take both of us. In those days it was fashionable to ride or walk along Stephanie Ut. Here the young men and women outfitted in their finest leisurely strolled to see and be seen. Lovers promenaded hand in hand and families with eligible daughters paraded them by rolling along in open horse-drawn carriages. Women sat proudly, their plumed hats waving in the breeze, nodding to friends or to anybody, just to be nodding.

Rozsie and I were very impressed when we got to the curb outside our house. "Look at his coach," nudged Rozsie. "He has *two* white horses."

"I don't know why Papa is so conservative," I complained. "He will never let us have two horses at one time."

Beamed Rozsie, "Obviously my Vilmos is a sport. I hear he's a big spender. Seems he was a poor boy and now he enjoys grandiose extravagances. I intend to enjoy them, too," she said with a meaningful glance at me as we climbed into the coach. Vilmos sat between us. Moments after we started, Vilmos took my hand. I was delighted until I peered over and saw he was holding *her* hand, too.

She sat demurely. I flirted madly, batting my eyelashes, squeezing his hand, monopolizing the conversation. The glorious afternoon passed rapidly. He took us to the door, kissed each of us politely on the hand, and promised to call. As soon as he left Rozsie burst into tears. "I'm going to tell Mama on you for acting so awful."

"You're right on one count," I assured her, "that I was acting. That's all I care about. I don't care two pins about your Vilmos Gabor."

"Then why are you playing up to him?"

"Listen, if I win him over it's better for *your* sake. Then there will be no need for you to wait your turn because if Mama's assured I'm so alluring that all I have to do is crook my little finger and get a husband, she won't worry about me and you then can go on about your life."

"All right, then," agreed Rozsie, adding, "to be honest I don't particularly have a burning desire for Vilmos either. I'm just in love with the idea of being in love."

In view of this development I had a long talk with myself and decided to take Vilmos away by force if necessary. Placing a call to his office I laid on my sexiest voice. "Hello, this is Miss Tilleman. How are you?"

"Oh, hello Rozsika," said Vilmos.

"Not Rozsika—Jancsika," I corrected, forgetting to sound sexy.

"Jancsika, darling." His voice was warm and low. "I am happy to hear you."

"I would like to speak to you," I said with what I hoped was sultry mystery. "Is it possible to come to your office some afternoon?"

"Of course, my dear." A pause, then, "How about tomorrow at three?"

"That's perfect. See you then."

"Good-bye, Jancsika." Then, the voice still warm and low, "I look forward to it."

I hugged myself. I would show Vilmos Gabor a thing or two. I went straight to Mama's pink dressing room with its array of silver-framed photographs and jewel boxes and perfume bottles, and through the double doors leading to her bedroom, which was the size of most people's apartments.

I found a bright royal blue skirt, slit and tapered at the bottom but wide at the hips, like riding breeches. Pirouetting in front of the mirror I decided that this was the real me—particularly with the addition of an equally bright yellow gilet. It didn't fit me much better than the skirt, so I solved the whole problem by borrowing a wide belt, pulled so tight I could hardly breathe. From another armoire I selected a floor-length white cape with a black velvet collar. I flung one end over my left shoulder and topped it all with a gigantic white hat with huge goose feathers which swept seductively across my face.

The next afternoon, with half a bottle of Mama's perfume on me for Vilmos to have smelled me across the Austrian border, I sallied forth.

His secretary ushered me in and Vilmos rose from behind his shiny mahogany desk and came toward me on the thick red and blue Oriental carpet with both hands extended. He wore fawn gray with another stiff white wing collar, hospitally clean. Although I wanted only to conquer him so that Mama would be proud of me, suddenly he looked quite acceptable to me. "Jancsika," he said softly, "How nice to see you. Please take a seat."

He held the chair for me while I sat down swathed like a mummy because I still had the cloak wrapped around me. It was hot in his office. I realized that before I could dazzle him I had to get out of that damn long white cape with the black velvet collar which was smothering me. I couldn't slip it grandly from my shoulders because the stupid thing was wound around my neck and then went down the back of my left shoulder. It took some doing to move it out from behind and then from under my bottom. I had to lean forward and then hoist myself up out of the seat and I was terribly busy for about five minutes.

Finally, with this goddamn cape off I settled into being a temptress. Vilmos waited patiently. "I called to ask you a question, Mr. Gabor," I began finally.

"Yes," he smiled.

"Do you intend to propose to my sister?"

He said nothing for a bit and then he cleared his throat and asked, "Why should you be concerned about my intentions toward your sister?"

"I have no man," I blurted out. "And I mind very much because our family custom is to marry according to age and I am next in line."

"But you do have a man," he smiled. "You were with Mr. Christhaber at the wedding."

"Ferenc was only my date for the week. He's like an uncle to me. Anyhow," I added seductively, "Mr. Christhaber is not my type."

Vilmos leaned forward attentively across his desk. "I see," he said, nodding to me to press on with my unsubtle conversation.

I stood up then and struck what I considered a glamorous pose—one knee bent provocatively—and I tossed my head until the feather plumes were falling all over my face. "The fact is you must wait several years for Rozsika. You see, I will be an actress and I won't marry in a hurry so it will be an awfully long wait for my much younger sister."

All Vilmos said was, "Oh, yes?"

I fell silent for a moment, hoping that he might find something more to say. Finally, his face broke into a smile. "Thank you for troubling yourself to tell me you are not spoken for. This pleases me because I was thrown into courting Rozsie—but it was you I wanted all along."

"Honestly?" I lost all my composure.

"Honestly," he said, taking a few steps toward me. He stood alongside me a moment, then rubbed his hand against my cheek. "Pretty girl," he murmured, "Pretty girl."

It was a little too much like my love affair with the lawyer on the stairs. I wasn't too happy about his gesture but tried not to show it.

"Always, all along I have wanted a Tilleman girl," he said. That was not so flattering, but never mind.

"Well, then," I clapped my hands together. "It's settled."

"My heart and my eyes were turned toward you from the beginning. I want very much to marry you," he said.

"I am not certain about marriage as yet," I told him carefully, now that I had him where I wanted him.

"But I am very rich," he said looking intently into my eyes. "I am already comfortably established in an import-export business. I own fruit trees, real estate, and businesses in Sardinia and Portugal. I can make you happy. I can buy you beautiful things."

He came close—I could see he wasn't much taller than I was—and patted my cheek again. This time I was really insulted but I thought to myself, "Concentrate on the beautiful things, Jancsi."

Vilmos was serious. He sent flowers and a basket of fruit to Mama in Karlsbad. Each time Vilmos called I unsettled him. One moment I played hard to get. The next I'd gaze at him and whisper, "Ah, Vilmuska, I think I have fallen for you." He became crazy from me. On one visit, he handed me a black velvet jewel box. Inside, on the plush purple velvet, was a diamond choker studded with deep blue sapphires plus a bow of diamonds on the choker. Also, resting in their own carved-out beds were a pair of diamond earrings. Vilmos told me later that each diamond was ten carats.

When I opened it he stood back to watch my face. I didn't know what to do. Was I to take it out and try it on without Mama being home? I just held it and gaped at it.

"The girl who will marry me," he announced, "will have all this." I was impressed with his jewelry but not too impressed with his manners. He was a little parvenu, a little *nouveau riche*. I thought wouldn't it be wonderful to have all this jewelry without this man.

I had a friend named Ethel, whose wealthy father was a successful glove merchant. They lived lavishly on the Stephanie Ut. I took the jewels over to her house. I didn't take them out at once because Ethel's mother was there and this was going to be talk for girls not mothers. Eventually, though, unable to stand it, I dived into my purse and brought out the jewels.

Ethel's mother went pale. "Where did you get this?"

"From a man who wants to marry me," I boasted.

"Have you accepted him?"

"Not yet," I answered airily.

"What do you mean, 'not yet'?" the mother repeated, fingering the jewels. "I wish my Ethel had a man who would give this to her."

"Well," I said, trying on the choker, which did not go very well over my shirtwaist blouse, "I don't really want to marry this man because I want to be an actress. I can sing and I can dance."

"Yes," nodded Ethel still staring at the choker, "you can sing and you can dance—but not really *well.*"

I ignored the insult and took comfort in the size of the earrings.

A few days before Mama and Papa returned, Vilmos was visiting me in the parlor, his jewels safely back in his pocket. "Jancsika, try to understand what I am going to tell you. Regardless of any promises your parents made about your studying dramatics, I'm sure that as long as you are under their roof they will never allow you to be an actress. If you marry me, your parents will lose their legal rights over you. Besides, as a married woman you will look mature—and be twice as appealing."

I decided to tell him the truth. "I like you very much but I do not love you so very much. I really began this flirtation only to show Mama and Papa how talented I am."

Vilmos became upset. "You mean you will not marry me because you only did this for fun?"

"Oh, no. I mean I will not marry you because I do not wish to marry anyone. I want only to be an actress."

Angrily he stormed out and slammed the door. He was in such a hurry that he left behind his soiled wing collar. For four days I didn't hear from him. On the fifth day he had a plan. "Be my wife and I promise that at the end of six months if you still want to be an actress I will give you your freedom."

I couldn't believe it. "You mean that you will divorce me?"

He nodded his agreement. "This we will do for six months and when you are not hilarious happy I guarantee you can then leave me and you can keep the diamonds."

"How about the dowry money Mama and Papa will give you for me?"

"You can have that back, too. I give you the diamonds and the dowry and I take your virginity."

To get my thinking straight before Mama and Papa arrived the following day, I thought I should discuss this with Ethel, since she was an older girl. She was seventeen-and-a-half. "Can we get away from your mother?" I whispered. "This is strictly a personal matter between close girl friends."

We went into Ethel's room and closed the door. "I have decided to tell you all and ask your advice," I began.

She was struck speechless when she heard he would let me keep the jewels.

"So I will marry him and in six months get out. I really only want to lose my virginity so I can sleep with a man since it is well known that this is necessary to be an actress because actresses are fallen women."

"Yes," agreed Ethel. "It is well known that actresses are very sexy and sleep with producers."

"I want to also," I said. "Anyhow, I want desperately to have a love affair."

"Who doesn't?" sighed my older and wiser counselor.

"I know I cannot be an actress if I am a virgin. When I am divorced I can go into the theatre where they will die for me."

"How do you know they will die for you there?" asked Ethel.

"Because," I replied sharply, "I am so excellent at fainting scenes. Getting weak and gasping and crumpling to the floor delicately I do better than anyone else in the world."

Before Ethel could address herself to this logic, her mother knocked on the door and picked up the subject from the last time she had seen me. "How is the man who wants to give you such a gift of jewels?"

"And can you believe Jancsi is thinking of giving him up to go on the stage?" said the daughter.

"You don't mean it," gasped the mother.

"Yes, she does," answered Ethel.

"You are crazy," said her mother. "Do you realize, Jancsi, my husband and I have been married twenty years and even I do not own such glorious diamonds?"

"Marry him," breathed Ethel rapturously, "even if it only lasts six months or as long as it takes to get a matching bracelet."

"My advice," put in her mother, "is to marry him right away. By the way, who is he? What does he do?"

"He does things like go to Italy and arrange to buy whole crops of fruit just after they have been planted. By doing this in advance he is able to get them cheaply, but it is almost like he is a gambler because if there is bad weather then the fruits won't be harvested and he'll lose money."

Ethel's mother said only, "Marry him as quickly as you can."

Mamuska and *Papuska* were coming home in the morning. That night I couldn't sleep.

Papa agreed to a dowry of 50,000 pengös. Mama agreed to a wedding in our home. Vilmos agreed to give me a matching bracelet and a villa at Lake Balaton. And I agreed to a marriage based on Vilmos Gabor's promise to divorce me in six months.

Despite his generosity the more I knew him the more unsure I was. There were sides of this man's nature that made me less and less happy about living with him even for six months. The truth is I thought he was a little parvenu. He took me for shoes and directed the shopkeeper to "Show me only the most expensive." This I thought was a little crude. Mama and Papa would never have done anything like this. After I made my selections, Vilmos tried on a pair of boots for himself, but he didn't like the workmanship so in a rage he kicked the salesman.

I worried so much that he would not keep his promise to me and that I would be stuck with him that I wanted a contract guaranteeing the divorce. I insisted he accompany me to a lawyer on the Andrassy Ut. We drew up this strange contract and then the problem was to get witnesses. Not Mama nor anybody else in the family knew of our six-month plan, so they were no good. Ethel and her mother wouldn't sign, so he had no choice but to go in the street and ask the first passerby.

On the corner outside the lawyer's office stood four Jews with *peis*, the long sideburns that end up in curls. They all wore red caps, which meant that when somebody wanted a parcel carried, they would do it for five cents. So he brought up these porters as witnesses and for their part in our future, Vilmos tipped them enough to retire from delivering parcels for a whole week.

I had known Vilmos two months, and the wedding was to be the following Sunday afternoon with about fifty people in the living room of our apartment on the fifth floor of Rákóczi Ut, number 54. I thought I might as well be worth Papa's 50,000 pengös, so I went to have my legs shaved specially for my wedding night. This was the top cosmetician in town and only for one half hour of hot wax she charged me 500 pengös! I was so upset. "You mean," I said, "that just for this hot wax, which I could have made by myself, you are costing me 500 pengös?"

"Yes, madam," she said firmly. "And you will have to pay because I cannot put you back your leg hairs."

I had not this amount of money and could not ask Vilmos for it before we were married and could not ask Mama for it because she would have killed me. So I gave to her a gold ring that my grandmother had given me, plus a gold chain from my mother.

I loved that gold chain very much and as I looked at Vilmos Gabor that Sunday morning, I wondered if he had been worth it. But . . . too late. The music struck up, and the Jancsi Tilleman Gabor six-month plan had begun.

BOOK TWO

Jancsi Gabor

1 My first night with Vilmos was not the most thrilling thing that has ever happened to me. He had checked us into the Astoria Hotel in the city because our honeymoon was not to start until another three days.

I had told my friends that I will put a white towel on the terrace when I lose my virginity. We were staying in a front suite on the second floor of the hotel and the balcony was directly over a busy street.

When we checked into the two rooms, Vilmos was very nervous. To me this was another great dramatic episode in my life and not to be over and done in two minutes. I made a big production out of it while Vilmos was sweating and cracking his knuckles from nervousness. I put on over my nude body a thin pink veil which I had packed in among my trousseau clothes. I wrapped the end around my face just under my eyes à la Salome. Then I danced for him, weaving and swaying to the rhythm of my own voice. Vilmos went out of his mind.

He stood in the center of the room under the heavy crystal chandelier watching me. Each time he'd reach out his arm for me, I danced just out of his grasp. Finally he stammered, "Enough . . . enough. . . ."

But then I was hungry. There is almost never a time when I am not hungry. The dark wooden table in the salon was heaped high with gooseliver, which is my favorite, and pastrami and sardines, and I stuffed myself. Vilmos could not eat. I, however, could not stop. It was now two o'clock in the night and again he said, "Enough. Let's go to bed."

He disappeared inside into the bedroom and when he came out I had nothing on except little panties. Nothing else. I had a beautiful bust. He could not take his eyes off my breasts. My pink nipples just stood straight up. He cupped one hand around one breast and just as he touched me I ran out on the terrace. He nearly died. It was dark on the street and our lights were on and I was lit up like in a spotlight. Each time I danced near him he'd grab for my breast and each time I ran out onto the terrace. Then we went inside to the bed and that's when the excitement and the fun was over. Nothing happened. I know now it because he was too excited. The room was dark and I didn't see him in the nude. I only felt. So, I still could only imagine what a man had. Here I was already legally married and the only *pimpi* I had ever

31

seen wiggling in my direction was the tiny one of my little cousin who offered me half his wormy rotten apple.

I never got to hang the white towel out that night. I was so dying for sex and all that I had was a sweating husband who slid off me.

But on the second night he succeeded, and I screamed and I screamed. This wasn't romantic or beautiful. This was painful. Vilmos told me afterwards that the crack in the ceiling plaster in the hotel bedroom came from my scream.

His passion made for our first big argument. He kissed me so hard on my breasts and my arms that he made marks on them. The third day we left for the beautiful resort town of Abbazia in Italy. We were sitting there in the bar on our third honeymoon night and I was wearing a décolleté dress. Unfortunately, when I selected it I didn't know that I would have highly visible big black marks and raised red welts from him biting me and kissing me so hard. A handsome silver-haired man with a cigarette holder leaned over to me as he passed and said, "What a beautiful hot night you must have had."

Vilmos was furious. We had a big quarrel. "You are embarrassing me," he stormed.

"It's your fault that I am this way," I hollered at him.

"You should have a different dress," he shouted back. "You should have a dress that doesn't show these marks."

"How am I supposed to know that I married a deranged sex maniac not a husband and that I must buy special dresses to hide the marks he makes?"

"Only *kurvas* wear dresses like that . . . only prostitutes," he spat. "You look just like one!"

And so ended our third day of this blissful marriage.

I was maybe a month married when we went to a concert. In the foyer of the concert hall was a huge marble staircase with a gilt bannister and red plush winding steps. I posed at the top of the stairs surveying the crowd in the foyer and then slowly, very slowly, I walked down in my elegant ball gown. As I reached the bottom stair, an old family friend rushed toward me with his hand outstretched and with a big bellow he exclaimed excitedly, "Jancsika! How are you, Jancsika?" Vilmos rushed up to him and in an arch manner announced, "This is Madame Gabor. You happen to be speaking to Madame Gabor. How dare you be so friendly." Madame Gabor! I was seventeen. Madame Gabor!

The man was taken aback, but since he was already poised to kiss my hand he carried through with it. Vilmos lifted high his rolled-up program and came down hard with it across the man's face. A fist fight broke out and Vilmos had to pay a fine. Another evening at the theatre we were standing in the lobby at intermission. A young boy whom I knew from my early schooldays offered to buy me chocolates. Vilmos thundered to the startled boy, "You don't give chocolates to my wife. If she wants chocolates I will buy the whole Stummer manufactury for her." Oh, Vilmos was so wild.

Another time, a gentleman paid me a polite compliment. Vilmos slapped him. Slapping was an offense punishable in Budapest by paying a fine. Within those first months, my brand new husband paid nine fines.

He was unbelievably jealous. We were three men and three women on a skiing excursion on Sunday in the Schwabhedge. We went afterwards for a cup of hot chocolate. Vilmos told me, "You and the other two walk before us," so we did. The other two were oldish. One was nearing forty and Vilmos was very vulgar, so he figured her hair would be gray down there by then and he referred to this girl as "Gray *Pinuska.*"

Anyway, a couple of men approached us and eyed me. The man on the left said admiringly, "What a cute little bitch that one in the middle is. I wouldn't mind having her." My husband heard the word "bitch" and half a minute later they were rolling in the snow. Vilmos hit him with his skis and the man hit back. Fighting over me, creating scandal over me, making my life miserable, this he loved. He really wanted to protect me but it had to be on his terms.

One morning the German butler tiptoed into our bedroom silently to bring shoes for Herr Gabor. Accidently the butler dropped one shoe, which didn't waken me, but Vilmos shouted at him, "You idiot. How stupid of you. Do you realize you'll wake up my wife!" It was *his* shouting that woke me, of course.

I was unhappy. Six weeks after I married him I ran away from him. It was an impulsive act but not so impulsive that I didn't first gather up my jewels. I had by this time added to my collection two rings. I cleverly put on everything I had which is the only way to do and I escaped in broad daylight wearing all my jewels. I thought, "Better not to stick to the bargain and wait six months."

The truth was that I did not love him even a little at this point. I called my parents to tell them what happened. "Where are you?" cried Mama. Snuggling back into my pillows and picking at my room service tray I replied grandly, "I am checked in at the Grand Hotel in Vienna."

Mama's voice came through the phone sharply. "Do you know that Vilmos has called the police?"

"Really? What is he saying to them?"

"He's saying that his beautiful wife has been kidnapped. He has called me and your sisters and everybody is asking, 'Where is she? . . . have you heard from her? . . .' The whole of Budapest is burning."

I closed my eyes happily, reveling in the aggravation I was causing him. The next morning I called for my breakfast. As it arrived, I fainted. When I came to, I saw the chambermaid, waiter, all the employees standing around the very small bedroom I had. In my daze I heard the chambermaid whisper, "Maybe she has cholera."

In an hour the doctor came in and diagnosed my case. I was pregnant. Vilmos arrived later and with him in his pocket were more diamonds. I don't really say that I was happy to go back because of the diamonds—I was still unhappy with him personally, and I did not love him, but he was rich and life with his money was good. For the first time since my marriage I was in cheap, small, dark rooms facing the court. So, I was happy to go back. Vilmos meant servants, big lavish lunches, luxury.

Magda was born with red hair and Vilmos was blonde. There was always a joke that Magda must have came from somebody else. Later, when Vilmos' white-haired mother died and I saw her in the nude, I saw Magda came by her red hair naturally because she also had a little red down there.

I was very happy to have a child. She was red and wrinkled and ugly, but I pushed her in a carriage as though she were a beauty queen. She was maybe six months old when I dressed myself in a black velvet hat and went for a walk along Andrassy Ut. A young man with a little moustache came up to me on the street from the other direction. "Good afternoon, Mme. Gabor," he said pleasantly. "How nice to see you."

"Thank you," I said, fluffing up the pillows around my baby's head.

"Do you remember me?" he asked.

"Of course," I replied. "Who are you?"

"Darvas."

"Darvas? Darvas who?"

"Darvas who used to court your eldest sister, Janette."

"Oh, yes," I smiled, "of course I remember. But you must excuse my memory because I am so occupied here with my brand new baby." Magda at that moment was crying. She had begun to cry from the moment she was born and cried for one and a half years with stopping.

"She's crying," said Darvas, making a brilliant discovery.

"Yes," I said, rocking the carriage. "I know. Would you like to see this pride and joy of my life?"

"Oh, very much," replied Darvas, leaning over as I moved the pink coverlet down from my angel's face.

"But," he stammered, "but . . . but she's so red . . . and wrinkled . . ."

How dare you say such a thing?" I snapped. Oh, I was so hurt I nearly fainted. "She is the most beautiful baby in the world. What do *you* know of babies, Mr. Darvas!"

With that Magda added to her dried apricot look by setting up a squealing that no amount of rocking would stop, and I hastily hurried away from Mr. Darvas with this ugly, red, screaming pride and joy of mine. I took her home to feed her in hope this would stop her mouth.

In this time the bottles weren't so good. Since only the mother's milk was good, I was forced to breast-feed my children. Magda was very demanding. She wanted my milk even at ten months and she would cry if I took it away for one meal. Fortunately I had enough because I was healthy. As soon as I was married, I gained weight, and from the moment of my first sex I became pregnant. When you are pregnant, everybody stuffs you with food. I gained weight and never from that moment was I ever as thin again.

Immediately after Magda was born Vilmos said, "Now we must have a boy—I want very much to have a son."

"But I have already been married to you longer than our original six months plan."

"Yes, but if you do not give me a son I will not keep to our bargain and you know that in Hungary a woman can never get a divorce by herself."

"Please," I begged him. "I have lived up to our bargain. Let me go."

"Get again pregnant. Give me a son and I will let you go," was his answer.

I was so frustrated with Vilmos' trickery that I packed up my baby and my things and prepared to leave him. He was wearing a flowing garnet silk dressing gown with big tassels at the ends of the belt. He grabbed Magda out of my arms and walked to the front window in the salon. He opened the window and held the baby high above his head out over the open window sill. I began to scream. "My baby . . . my baby. . . . This maniac is trying to kill my baby. . . . Help . . . !" Cook ran in, the nurse ran in, Sandor, our coachman, ran in.

"Out . . . out . . . get out," shrieked Vilmos, kicking the door behind him with his foot.

I had picked up a heavy bronze statue from off the mantelpiece and held it high. I wanted to hit him over the head but then I was afraid if I did he would drop the baby so I didn't know what to do. I just stood there holding the statue and glaring at him.

"If you leave me," he said, "then I will let her drop."

"But we are five floors up. You will kill her," I cried.

"Promise me you will not leave me or I will let her drop," he threatened.

Oh, it was a big drama. Eventually I promised and he gave me back the baby but he could tell by the look in my eyes that I was not satisfied. He kept watching me and he kept backing up into the inner room with me following him closely. He still clung to the baby and it was in my mind to pull her out of his clutches then make a run for it. He backed up into the bathroom, which also had a window opening onto the court. The bathtub was filled with water because he had been preparing to take a bath when this big drama unfolded. All dressed and with my hat still on my head, I made a grab for the baby and we struggled. I lost my balance and fell into the tub.

My whole life, my whole future, my whole heartache had to stop while

I made myself dry and changed my clothes and wept and it was a big drama.

By this time I really didn't want so much to leave because it was cold outside and I was now chilled and wet. I went inside to the bedroom, I put on a silk gown with a quilted silk peignoir, and I lay down on my bed to ponder when I will someday go away from this man and how I will go and if ever I will go. In about twenty minutes I became warm and cozy. The cook knocked on the door. "Dinner is ready." In a haughty tone I replied, "Maruska, I will not eat tonight here. I will be gone from this house forever. Please prepare just for Herr Gabor."

The smell of the fine dinner that was being prepared just for him drifted through the house to the silk bolster pillows I was lying on. After all the crying and screaming and struggling, I became also a little hungry. We were having chicken goulash *à la Szeged* with chicken fat and caraway seeds and baked hot buttered noodles with poppy seeds. "This is a bad time to run away from home," I said to myself.

Vilmos came in to me, wiping the edge of his mouth with a linen napkin, and he sat on the edge of the bed. From him I could almost taste the chicken let alone smell it. "Look, my darling," he said to me softly. "When we have a son, you can take your little girl and you can leave. I must also have something of my own because I love you so much."

"So you will take the son and let me leave?" I said, smelling the chicken every time he opened his mouth.

"Exactly," he said. "At least then I can remember you when you leave me a son."

"All right," I sighed. "We will make us a little boy and then I will leave."

"Agreed," he said.

I got up, walked to the door to shut it and got back in the bed, pulled aside the bedclothes on his side so he could crawl in and said, "So, now, let us not waste time. Let us immediately go and make a son."

"Very well," he nodded, extending both his hands to lift me up, "but first I would like to finish dinner. Come."

In four years I had three babies. I had always natural childbirth, without a single injection, and it was a great thrill to feel this big big pain and to know the moment when the baby is out of you is heaven. To actually see a new life is exciting and I was always thrilled with it. I've always treasured that first instant of birth.

I wanted a boy. I prayed for a boy. It happened on a wintry evening in February. It was one o'clock in the night. I was enjoying an elegant supper at a fashionable supper club after the theatre. I was eating my favorite dessert —apricot *palacsinta* with fresh whipped cream. Suddenly, I felt pains and I knew this was it. "Ugh," I groaned. "This rotten son of mine is not due for another two weeks but he is not going to wait!" Our carriage sped me back to the bedroom.

There was no king-size bed then. I lay down on my twin bed which had a pedestal under it and a huge silk pink canopy over it and one hour later Zsa Zsa was born. The doctor had not yet arrived but we had a midwife living in.

The midwife washed the baby with warm water and wrapped her up and placed her on my breast and while she breast-fed, the midwife stood right close by to see that I didn't harm her charge, and it was all over before the doctor arrived.

It was a good thing that the midwife was there to help because this second daughter of mine sucked the milk from my breast so greedily and so quickly that she began to choke. On the second day she became blue.

The doctor came in and ordered, "Put cold water in a bowl and when the child begins to choke, sprinkle her with the water."

"Where?" I asked nervously. "On her body?"

"No," he said, cradling the baby and examining her carefully, "on her face."

"How will this make her stop choking?"

"It is not necessary for you to know how. It is only necessary for you to know enough to do it," the doctor replied shortly.

Rozsika came to pay me a visit and I cried to her, "Oh, Rozsika, maybe this sick child is the result of my fears and my disordered thoughts because I wanted a boy so much and I do not want this second girl."

"Don't be silly, Jancsika," comforted my sister. "You are not being punished. The child is just sick. She will outgrow this."

"No," I said, tortured by my black thoughts. "God is punishing me. Maybe I am harming my child. Maybe what I should do is run away. Maybe I will never have a boy. Maybe I should not ever think about having a boy. Maybe I should put an end to all this."

"You are talking crazy, Jancsika," said my sister. "You are talking out of your head. You must calm down. You must get some rest."

I was sweating. My forehead was dripping with perspiration. Rosalie took a damp cloth and wiped my face and head and chest.

I tried to calm down and think only rational thoughts while she was there. As soon as Rozsie left I said to myself, "Now, now you must do something. Now you must make your arrangements. Now is your time. Now."

The door to my bedroom opened and in came the nanny with the bowl of water. "Very well," I said imperiously. "You may deposit the bowl and then you may leave."

"But I am not supposed to go while you feed the baby. The doctor says I am to be present during the feeding."

"You are dismissed," I ordered.

"Please, Mme. Gabor," stammered the nanny nervously. "Please, take care." She brought the baby and placed her on my breast and lingered at the doorway, watching me anxiously.

"Go," I commanded.

"Don't forget the water for her choking spell," called the nanny as she reluctantly closed the door behind her.

"I will take care," I called to the closed door. "Yes, I will take care," I thought to myself bitterly. "When she will choke I will make it like it would be an accident. I will let her choke and I will pretend I am asleep."

I don't know how I could have pretended I was asleep because the whole house at this moment was like the noise of a world war. Our German shepherd dog, Lady, was barking excitedly at my door. Emmy, my maid, insisted at that moment to come in and tie a bright pink bow in my hair. Magda was, as usual, howling and crying in the nearby nursery, and Cuki, the nanny, was babbling prayers in German outside my bedroom door.

It happened that this second daughter of mine didn't choke. She just sucked greedily and after she was full, she just went a very little "Aha . . . aha. . . ." and with that I turned over the bowl of water on her and saved her. I didn't really save her life or anything because nothing dramatic happened. But, somehow, in my mind I saved myself because of the noise around me that drowned out my thoughts. I was convinced that my change of mood changed the mood of my daughter, and on this second day of her life she was saved.

That very night, Emmy, my maid, brought into my bedroom a summons. It seems that a woman was suing Mr. Gabor because she claimed he was the father of her child. I didn't believe it but it didn't matter—I was deliriously happy because I thought this could mean grounds for divorce.

When Vilmos came home he came into my bedroom where I was sitting up in bed. Pink orchids were in my hair and I was sipping a little champagne. "What is this story, Mr. Gabor?" I said archly.

"I don't understand, my angel Jancsika," he began guiltily. "It is not true. It could not be so because nobody in my whole life could I look at after you. You are my sun, you are my stars. Never could I. . . ."

"Please never mind this story," I said. "I want only the truth." Oh, I was so happy that for once I had Vilmos on the defensive. I did not care even if it was the truth. I did not love him, so I had no jealousy.

"I only helped this woman to get onto the trolley car," he explained, pulling up an antique petit point armchair. I was so emotionally involved in his explanation that I thought only at this moment that I wish he would not pull the chair by its arms because he could damage the tapestry.

Aloud I said only, "And how is it that a woman can become pregnant by being helped onto the tramway?"

"She was so fat that she needed an assist onto the tramway and since I was behind her I assisted her. She was just a poor woman and I helped her."

"Indeed," I sniffed, taking another sip of champagne and enjoying every moment.

"I think she was already pregnant," he offered, "because she was so fat. I swear to you I had nothing with her. I swear to you on my life."

Then he laughed. I also laughed a little. "She was like an elephant and I only reached under her behind and gave her a little shove," he insisted.

"How can a woman have a baby by your putting your hand on her behind and shoving her?"

This particular problem was quickly resolved the next day when he came home with a blue fox coat and a large green emerald. Operation Cheating was now very all right and definitely put to rest as far as I was concerned.

When Eva was ready to be born, I was at the Orpheum Theatre when it began, and again my family was upset at the way I was going out every night. Again it was two o'clock in the night and again the doctor was not yet arrived. There is a Hungarian slogan that "the third is the best" so we all were sure I would have a boy. When the midwife came the first word she said to me was *"Kislány."* This means "little girl." Another girl! I thought I cannot stand this. Another daughter! Never ever will I get free of this bastard husband!

Out of my womb and into my arms came this beautiful, blonde, blue-eyed girl baby sucking a finger. She made such loudly sucking sounds that the whole room was laughing. The doctor said he had delivered 2,000 babies and that this one was the most beautiful he had ever delivered. So, what could I do? She was so beautiful that I had not the heart to hate her.

I could not stop looking at her. I decided to name her Eva just because it was in fashion at the time. Magda I named Magda just because it was a very chic name. Zsa Zsa was originally Sari, which was the name of my mother's sister. Oh, I was so in love with these children. From the moment of birth each had skin that was perfect. They had not a blemish, not a pimple. Nothing. They were so beautiful, so sweet, so healthy. While I was bitterly unhappy with Vilmos, I was deliriously happy with my babies.

To tell you the truth after the birth of my third daughter I didn't even want to go away from Vilmos so much. I still did not love him even a little but I didn't want so much to go because my whole thought was to be an actress. I was so very young that I thought a woman who has children can not any longer be considered desirable. I thought I can not now be considered desirable to any other man again. I was so stupid. And because of that I tortured him. Three times a day I told Vilmos he ruined my life.

After Eva, my maternal instinct was so great that it outweighed any thoughts of leaving home. I was determined to see that my daughters never knew the frustrations I had known. I wanted for them the glamorous life I had so desperately wanted for myself. I decided that it was better for me to make something out of them than out of myself, and so I devoted myself to teaching them and making them and moulding them. Thus was my entire ambition transferred. I made them like dolls. I made big parties for them. I brought Magda on stage in a charity show when she was only ten months old. I made a masked ball for them when they were only one, three, and five.

Every morning at 9 A.M. I paid a visit to the nursery. It was so cute to see the three little beauties in their bathroom. Magda was redhaired, Zsa Zsa blonde, and Eva platinum. We always had much help around because the child of five needs a Fraulein and the baby of one year needs a nanny, and I remember standing there one morning watching Eva getting a bath while Magda was getting wiped while Zsa Zsa was sitting on the potty trying to make. She was going "Eh . . . eh . . . eh." Oh, how I wish I had a picture of it now. We didn't have cameras in the house in those days and how can you order a professional photographer to come and watch your Eva making pipi or your Zsa Zsa sitting on the potty.

I spent more time with them in their early growing up years than my mother ever did in her whole life with me. Maybe it was because I didn't want to spend time with my husband like Mama did. Anyhow, my children loved me as though I were a god. My children weren't afraid of me as I was of my Mama but they obeyed me. I can't ever remember when they disobeyed me. They couldn't speak with Papa because he was too busy and too strong with them. He gave them money but he was never close. He was shouting always and adoring only me. So they came to me with everything. I was the whole world to them. They were very sweet with me, and when I was unhappy with Vilmos they would soothe me. "Don't cry," they'd say. "Did daddy hurt you?" Always they were with me. When I spoke they ate me up with their ears and eyes.

I wanted them to do everything, know everything, experience everything. Once, I even made them have a fight. A real fight with their tiny fists. Eva was about two, Zsa Zsa four, and Magda six when they were in the apartment on a rainy afternoon. Magda said, *"Nucika,* what shall we do today?"

"Why not have a fight?" I suggested.

"With pillows?" she asked.

"No," I said. "A fight. A fist fight. A fight with hitting one another." I tell to them, "Children, you must try everything. So now you will try to fight." They began hitting each other. Eva had a bloody nose and was crying.

When Vilmos came home he stormed into the room and banged open the double doors with a loud crash demanding to know, "What is going on here? Are you crazy?" he screamed. "You are mad." I didn't answer. I was fascinated with what had happened.

"Are you crazy?" he shouted over Eva's screams.

"No," I said. "For me it was very interesting. I like when they fight. I like when they do *everything.*"

It is for that reason that I threw them into Lake Balaton one summer. I wanted them to know how to swim and the lake was calm and so I threw them into the water. There was no time for them to learn. They just simply had to swim and so they swam. My friend gasped, "How can you throw them in?"

"They will paddle like dogs," I said calmly—and they did.

I always had difficulty when Cuki, their Fraulein, had a day off. Terrible tragedies happened only on the days when I was minding my own children. Or, at least, I was supposed to be minding them.

The Budapest of those days was a center of enormous zest for living. Even after the First World War, which was so disastrous for Hungary, Hungarians still lived their lives in huge flourishes. No one approached life timidly. The Hungarian character is a blend of the wild *csárdas* and the Gypsy lament. One moment a Hungarian can explode into a temperamental fury and the next simmer down to an apologetic sweetness. At the least, we Hungarians are never boring and never bored. Like our paprika, our fiery tang turns at once to be mellow and sweet to the taste. This grandiose passion for life flavors our social world, our professional lives, our very breath.

With me I always had to be out doing, making, seeing, experiencing. On a morning when Fraulein Cuki was off in the afternoon and Mama Jancsi was to be on, I was off enjoying the *Gemütlichkeit* of my countrymen. We were off enjoying a light *tizorai*. The *tizorai* is a before-lunch snack, something to give you the strength to pull up the chair and sit down to eat. In Hungary we ate about seven times a day. Morning started with a light breakfast, followed by a heavier one at 10 o'clock (that was the *tizorai*), which was only so we would have the strength to wait for lunch. Early afternoon another bite followed by tea, dinner, and a late supper. Mind you, this did not take into account the many cups of coffee with whipped cream or glasses of wine which were consumed in between at our many coffee houses.

So, this particular day a group of us in fashionable clothes and big feather hats were lingering over our *tizorai*, and I didn't get home until late in the afternoon. Although we had central heating in our apartment on the Múzeum Körut, overlooking the museum, we also had a small stove in the center of the room. I came home to a small Hungarian tragedy. Magda had been dancing around the stove, which was red-hot. She had lost her balance and fallen in and both hands were badly burned. It was my duty to speed her off to the hospital. I was so ashamed because these things only seemed to happen when it was Cuki's day off and I was minding the children.

Mostly it was some tragedy with Zsa Zsa. When Zsa Zsa was a baby she was fat. She was also a tomboy who liked to play rough. Another time when I was playing nursemaid, my poor Zsa Zsa fell down on our shiny wooden parquet floor and split her lip. Back I went to the doctor, who told me she is truly a miracle child to live through all that happens to her.

Another time I was in the nursery and Zsa Zsa was playing with a hoop which had a small wooden handle attached to it on top. How this wooden handle ended up stuck into the roof of her mouth, imbedded deep into her palate, I don't know. Quickly I comforted her as best I could and made her not to cry but I didn't know how badly she was damaged. She was whimpering a little but I comforted her and thought that this was all there was to it.

Vilmos stopped at every crib to see how they all were that night before he went to sleep. I hadn't told him this latest crisis because I was ashamed that these things only happen when it is my turn to be the nursemaid. I tiptoed into the nursery with him and there we found Zsa Zsa crying and black blood seeping out of the corner of her mouth. When we opened her mouth, she was literally full with blood. Black blood. "Quickly," said Vilmos, scooping her up in his arms. "We will take her right away to the Payor Sanatorium."

"But it is midnight," I protested.

"Even so," he answered, already out the door. "It is not far away and as you know there is a famous professor doctor there."

I followed on his heels all the way to the clinic, which was the best known in Budapest, and we were lucky that the famous doctor was on at that hour. He took one look at her and prepared to operate immediately. Within an hour he had taken twelve stitches in the roof of her mouth.

"You were very fortunate that you went into her room and saw the black blood running from the sides of her mouth," he told us.

"And to think I had been afraid to tell my husband what had happened," I moaned.

"If not operated on so quickly," continued the doctor, "she might not have been able to speak properly the rest of her life. It could have permanently impaired her speech."

When the time came that she had to have those twelve stitches taken out, we were waiting in the doctor's waiting room, and we heard another child screaming. But screaming! "What is happening?" I asked the nurse.

"Another child the same age as yours is having her stitches taken out," she replied.

"*Nuci*, if I die then I will die, but I will die before I will scream," whispered Zsa Zsa.

When we went in and he was removing the stitches, she was blue from pain but not a sound came from her. The doctor said afterwards, "I am twenty-five years in the medical profession, and I never saw before such a child with such strength. This miracle child will grow up to be something special. Such strength can never be held down."

When Magda was born, we lived in a huge apartment once belonging to Count Nako Sándor, who had been governor of Fiume. We had many servants. My favorite servant, Rozsika, was nineteen. When she came to work for me, she said, "But Madame, I always thought that the lady of the house should be older than I am.

"I always worked for older ladies of thirty or forty years old who were the madames of the house," said Rozsika a little hesitantly.

After a particularly loud fight with Vilmos, which was on the heels of another loud fight I had had with Vilmos, I said to her, "Don't worry about my age. I will get older very quickly with this husband of mine."

Rozsika was only a servant girl and a not pretty one but I envied her. She had known passionate sex and romance in her life while I had nothing but Vilmos. Rozsika had a child but no husband. She had been employed earlier by an army captain and his wife and the wife was a little bit of a *kurva*. There was a period when several soldiers were camped in the house while her husband was away. Unfortunately, they couldn't all make love to the lady of the house at the same time, and they were young, hot, and a little impatient. One of them was in need one night and couldn't wait for his commanding officer to finish his tour of duty with the lady, so he decided to do his basic training with the servant girl. However, her bedroom door was locked. Anyhow, this hot soldier crawled through the transom. It was dark and she didn't know what was happening but all of a sudden she felt him jump on top of her. Now, you must admit that is a much more pleasant way to wake up than with an alarm clock. So he made good sex with her and, as Rozsika told, she didn't ever know who the father of her child was because it was dark and she was sleeping.

We also had a butler named Simon. Simon was very regal like a British butler. Sometimes he was so regal that I thought he looked down on Vilmos and me altogether. I loved parties and I gave lots of them. I was always having big expensive parties just so I could perform at them. I would sing or I would dance or just plain pirouette and the guests—since I was paying for everything —would applaud. This always made me feel excited. Without a real stage I made the whole world a stage.

It was my birthday night once and we were having a big party in our showplace . . . the only apartment in Budapest with three bathrooms. One of our guests was overfriendly to me that night. He had probably had a little too much of my champagne and he was smiling a little unsteadily in my direction. This was enough for the host to pick up a chair and lift it high over his head and bring it down on the overfriendly guest. Our own guest in our own house! I quickly ran to Simon, who looked down on me imperiously as though I shouldn't be caught running even if quarts of genuine blue blood were gushing all over my floors. As I rushed up to him in the pantry obviously all upset and with my face streaked with tears, Simon said merely, "Madame wishes something?"

"Herr Gabor hit one of our own guests over the head with one of our own chairs in our very own house! They are fighting in the salon. My party is ruined. Everything is a mess. It is a disaster. Do something."

"Quite so, Madame," said Simon, handing me a napkin to dry my tears.

"But you don't understand," I cried. "They were good friends. They are not now friendly. They are killing each other."

"They will be friendly again," explained Simon, not removing his white gloves nor quickening his leisurely stride toward the salon.

"No, Simon. No. You do not understand. There will be no party. My guests will all leave."

"They will not leave, Madame," replied this butler of mine with what amounted to a final regal proclamation. "No one leaves a good party. Your champagne is the best. Your caviar the most expensive. Your table is laid with the best cuisine in Budapest. No one will leave."

"I will be so embarrassed that I will not be able to lift my head. What am I to say to my guest who has been hit?"

"May I suggest, Madame, that you offer him another glass of champagne?"

"He will probably have left by now."

"He will not leave, Madame. It will be like Count Nako and the Prince of Hapsburg. They had a fight and they were friends again. This is a gentleman's fight in a drawing room, Madame, not a street fight amongst ruffians. They will be friendly again."

Simon and I approached the crowded salon, and we saw Vilmos and the man walking off into a corner arm-in-arm, and exactly as Simon predicted, not one guest left.

Then as now I loved life and I loved to go out and look and shop and meet friends, and I particularly loved this life during the day because that's when I could enjoy without Vilmos. By 11 o'clock I'd be out of the house, but I must call him every half hour or he would create tension for me. The most I could go was one hour or he would call detectives. Never, never would he allow me to go anywhere alone. He would even send Sandor, our coachman, to follow me. I used to enjoy the excitement of the Váczi Utcza, which is the equivalent of Fifth Avenue. It's like a miniature Paris, with shops, ladies in big hats, boutiques with fancy garments, and friends all along the avenue. Sandor took me to the Váczi Utcza and I said to him, "Sandor, now I walk maybe six, eight blocks."

"Oh, but you cannot walk," he declared emphatically.

"What do you mean I cannot walk? I have legs, haven't I?" I answered sharply.

Sandor took his cap off and wrung it in his hand as he looked at the ground. "Herr Gabor says I must accompany you."

"But it is early in the day. It is not late. It is not night. It is not dark. It is not raining. Why must you accompany me?" I demanded.

Sandor still avoided my eyes. "It is Herr Gabor's order. It's in case you get tired. He says that maybe you'll faint on the street."

"Faint?" I repeated. "I'll faint? I'm twenty-three years old. How do I faint? I am so strong like your horse. It is only 11 o'clock and I know I must be home by 1:30 for lunch and I will walk perhaps six, eight blocks and I guarantee you I won't faint. Now go away. I order you go away."

I began to walk. Three blocks down in front of a hat shop I saw a girl friend. The girl friend had a lover and I was so envious. She told me everything of how she got away from her husband. I was fascinated, and I was storing up ideas when I felt something hot and wet at the back of my head. I turned around and there was Sandor in the fiacre and Olga, the stupid horse, so close that she actually had her big wet lips on my neck.

Lamely, Sandor said only, "Olga loves you."

If I liked a girl friend and I walked with her on the Corso, Vilmos would say, "She's a *kurva.*" Even if she was a fine lady and I went with her, he would tell to me, "She's a *kurva.* Why do you go with her?" He didn't like me to like anybody but him.

Sometimes I could spend an afternoon playing cards with friends and then Vilmos didn't mind but they had to be the people who were his friends, not just mine. I could play tennis, too, because then he would know exactly where I was and with whom.

It wasn't that I would not like to have cheated with even the first man I would meet anywhere any time, but he gave me no opportunity. Besides, there wasn't anybody. At our summer place at Lake Balaton we were a half dozen women with no husbands. Our husbands were in Budapest during the week working and our social life was to visit one another at the different villas every night. It was boring.

During the week the Balaton was very quiet. I had a villa. My sister Rozsika had a villa. Janette had a villa. Only Dora did not because she had no children. Lelle, our little village on the Balaton, was divided. There was upper Lelle Tersolelle, and bottom Lelle Alsólele, where we lived. Ours was a residential area. No businesses. No shops. Even the nearest train was five miles away in upper Lelle Tersolelle. That was the so-called exciting area. They not only had a train depot but they even had a lone restaurant—a *csárda* with a single third-rate violinist.

I loved even the third-rate violinist because I loved life so desperately. One evening they advertised a whole Hungarian orchestra, so we made up a party and just to make it a longer evening we decided to walk. One neighbor, an elderly, very much married professor, was going. Another neighbor, a soubrette from Budapest named Biller Iran, was going. She had a lover and I was so jealous. He once wrote her a letter which she showed me and it said, "You are my prayer." Oh, I was so heartbroken that I had never had a lover —an actor yet who would write me such things.

We ladies all wore pretty dresses and flat shoes and carried a bag with our high heels in them. It was a two-mile walk. This *csárda* we were all heading to was dark and stinking from goulash, but it had tzigane music. Oh, how I love Gypsy Hungarian music.

We were still far off when I heard music. I didn't know where it came from and there was no visible activity but I definitely heard music, so I sat down on a step and put on my heels, which were high enough so that it wasn't easy to walk twenty steps in that road in them. My friends were all laughing at me. Suddenly out of the dark skipped three little Gypsies about eight years old. And they began to play the violin and my friends all teased, "Aaahh, that Jancsi, she heard the *tzigane* from miles away. . . ."

It was true. It was because I died to have life. I lived for it. The next night I had an argument with Vilmos on the phone. He was angry because he heard I had been rowing in a boat with a young man. It wasn't true but inevitably we had a fight. I was especially angry because I wished it could have been true.

There was so little to do in Lelle that when Vilmos accused me I could not stand it. "Who was this doctor with whom you were on the Balaton rowing?" he demanded to know on the phone.

"What you heard was nothing because there is no doctor and I wasn't rowing," I replied annoyed. "I don't even know a doctor up here."

"All right, then, a lawyer."

I shouted into the telephone, "I don't have anybody up here. I don't even know anybody up here to go rowing with if I wanted to! Anybody here is a married man and there is nothing . . . nothing. . . ."

I put down the telephone and returned to the party which was in my villa. I was feeling sorry for myself so I drank a little wine and as the evening progressed I found myself in a romantic mood.

I made long curls for myself. I didn't usually have curls but this one night I did and I had made myself very beautiful and I had a lacy, frilly nightgown on. When I slept with Vilmos I never wore an expensive nightgown because he would just tear it right off and climb right on top of me and buy me another nightgown when he was finished.

My villa fronted the beach which was on the lake. The back side opened onto a two-acre garden. When everybody left I was feeling lonely and frustrated and unhappy and I'd had wine. I was in my beautiful nightgown and I had perfumed myself and I was in a romantic mood and I was unhappy with my husband and the argument and his lack of understanding and romance and I decided that the first man who will come along I will tell I want love.

I went outside after all the ladies left. I don't really know why I went outside because nobody really walked here in the evening, but I stood there in the dark all alone listening to the sounds of the stillness. I thought to myself, "The first man who comes along and he is under fifty I will tell 'I want to make love!' " And a man came along. A young man. He was swinging a lantern up and down. As he came nearer I could see who it was. Here stood Jancsi Gabor planning to take revenge on her husband and the first man to come along in the darkened street to sweep me up in his arms and make passionate love to me as I had forever imagined in my dreams turned out to be the night watchman.

Awestruck at the sight of me in my golden curls and flowing nightgown, he shouted at me, shaking his stick, "Go inside! What are you doing here? Are you not ashamed? Go in!" He shook the lantern up and down in front of my face and hollered at me again, "Get into the house!"

I went back. I was crying. I thought God also doesn't want that I cheat on Vilmos—even God was on Vilmos' side.

I was an incurable romantic. After four years of marriage I had begun to read Elinor Glyn's book *The Three Weeks*, which is about a princess and a commoner and how they make love all day long, and from beginning to end it was all about making love. Reading this book was the tragedy of my life. I thought, "I will die if I don't have three such weeks." I needed romance—love and kisses and passion. Oh, how I wanted to be in bed with someone I loved. It didn't seem much for a husband to allow a wife who had given up stardom and international acclaim as a film actress for him!

Vilmos and I were always arguing. Over anything. For no reason we would have a fight. Once I threw my white gold wedding ring out of a fourth floor window and heard it drop. It was after a fight late at night on a street as busy as Fifth Avenue. I didn't even try to find it. I knew he would buy me a second one. Another time he bought a bronze gondola as a souvenir of an ardent reconciliation in Venice. For the hundredth time we had a wild quarrel and I threatened at the top of my lungs, "Vilmos, I go. I leave you."

He called my bluff, "Go!" he shouted, "Leave. Move out. Talk to your lawyer," and he heaved the brand new bronze gondola at the mirror.

He loved bronze. He bought everything bronze. I figured any minute our apartment has to sink for all the bronzes—we must have had 20,000 kilos of bronze in the damn place. One night, in fact, we were fighting about the bronzes, and I slipped out and gave the concierge ten pengös and instructed, "When you hear some noise quick come in because Mr. Gabor will be beating me, and I want a witness to that so I can get a divorce."

"But how do you know he will be beating you?" asked the astonished concierge.

"Because I will push him to do it. Now, do as I say." Well, he heard the noise and he broke in, but there was no divorce.

Another wintry autumn I had decided to take singing lessons. I was always the frustrated actress and it was on an exceptionally cold, windy Sunday in November that I had taken a hot bath and we then suddenly had to go across the bridge to the Buda side. I had on a black Persian coat which Vilmos had given to me and which I hated. Usually there was one horse for my carriage but at night with Vilmos there were always two horses, so we were going along briskly.

"Close your neck," he commanded me.

"No," I said angrily.

"The wind is strong. Close your neck," he insisted.

"No, I don't," I insisted just as strongly.

"You will catch cold," he said.

"So then I will sneeze," I said.

He unwound the silk scarf from his own neck and wrapped it around me. I was already annoyed with him so I tore the scarf off and opened the neck of the hated coat and screamed, "I prefer to die."

Vilmos reached toward me and began to button the coat which I had kept open. I pushed him away and flung the coat open wide. "Leave me alone. I don't mind to die."

"Jancsi . . ." began Vilmos sternly.

"Leave me alone, Vilmos," I spat back. "It is your command to wear this coat. I hate this coat. So, all right, I am now wearing it. Now it is your command to button it. Leave me alone." My voice rose hysterically. "I prefer to die than to do more of what you tell me. I am tired of your always telling me. I don't care if I die. Now leave me alone."

We galloped across the bridge and, of course, I caught a chill and lost my voice. A half hour in the night air in the open carriage and I couldn't speak when we arrived at the party. There was a married man, the husband of a good friend of mine, who was my admirer, but we had nothing, only looks and flirtation between us. We had never even had a kiss or a moment of hand-holding between us. It was only a look from afar.

Naturally, I wanted to show off in front of him because he was always so flabbergasted when I sang at parties. He thought my voice was so beautiful. He told me, "Your voice is like a canary's" and this night I could not even speak, let alone sing. I was so unhappy that I thought better I would lose my arm than to suffer this loss.

It was particularly bitter because I had already scheduled an appointment with an old opera singer who was now giving lessons because he could not more sing professionally. Naturally, with my cold I got hoarser and hoarser so I couldn't keep my appointment. I went to three doctors and they pronounced the bad news that for a week I could not speak. However, even after the week I could not speak. I had to write on a paper what I wanted.

When I finally went to the last specialist he informed me, "I am sorry, Madame Gabor, but for a very long time you will not be able to sing."

Not that I ever *could* sing, but this now infuriated me. "What do you mean for a very long time I will not be able?"

"Your larynx has become enlarged."

"So shrink it."

"Madame," insisted the specialist, "when your larynx has become enlarged there is nothing you can do because it has become enlarged!"

From my deep knowledge of medical science I made a profound statement. "But that is impossible," I said.

"Before you even make an attempt to sing you must first heal your throat."

"But you must do something. Prescribe something."

"I prescribe that you go to the shore and that you live there for a long period."

"I like this idea," I said, thinking that Vilmos could not take off from his business and this was at least one way of getting away from him. "Where do you prescribe that I go?"

"To Abbazia and there you must live for a period of six months."

"Excellent. I will do that," I beamed.

"Six months!" exclaimed Vilmos when I happily gave him the news in my froglike whisper that night.

Vilmos would never stand in the way of my health, however, so he compromised and did send me to Abbazia—for three days. And with his mother to watch me. And in adjoining rooms so she could look in on me at odd hours.

My mother-in-law was an awful woman. Vilmos always had her there to watch me if he was away. Magda was three years old and we were in Lelle and Magda got the measles. The local doctor did not seem to know what to do with her. "She can not eat *kolbász* or *hurka* or *szalona* anymore, for at least three weeks," pronounced the doctor solemnly.

Fraulein said to me, "That doctor must be crazy. In her whole life she has never this food."

"This country doctor I can not trust," I told Vilmos. "He is very bad. I think I must take Magda immediately home to Budapest."

"But how will you go?"

"By train."

They wanted to throw me off the train because I was transporting a child with measles and then when I arrived in Budapest, the doctor wanted to throw me out for bringing her to the office. "I have a five-year-old child myself and I don't need an epidemic," he shouted at me.

"I apologize," I said tearfully, "but if I wait until she is well before I am allowed to see you I then won't need you."

"Put a compress on her every three hours," he instructed.

"Every three hours?" I said. "I have already been placing one right after another on her and she has so much fever that the compress becomes hot in two minutes."

"Then place it on her every two minutes," was his instruction.

"But Magda is so hot I am afraid she will die," I cried.

"She will not die," he said, and pushed me outside.

I had left Zsa Zsa in Lelle and shortly I received a telegram that now Zsa Zsa was dying! My children were never just sick. They were always dying.

When I arrived my mother-in-law who had sent me the telegram announced at the gate, "You cannot come in. Your daughter has the pox."

"But I have brought medicine. I showed Magda's doctor the telegram and he gave me what was needed to bring."

"She has wounds all over her body. Her eyes are sealed from the disease. She will become blind from this," predicted this impossible woman.

"Do not dare to say such a thing to me," I shouted, "and do not try to keep me from my daughter."

"But she cannot see you."

"But she can *sense* me. My daughter can feel my presence from 200 yards away like an animal."

It was true. Her eyes could not open but she sensed that I was there and that comforted her. "*Nuci . . . Nuci . . . ,*" she whimpered. I spoon-fed her the medicine the doctor gave me, never for one instant leaving her bedside, holding all the while to her hand tightly. Within hours my little Zsa Zsa passed the crisis.

Unfortunately, my children were always dying at inconvenient moments. Burned into my memory is that bitter cold winter when I escaped with Fraulein Cuki and my three babies to the Balaton. Although Hungarian winters are long and cold, we loved them because of the winter sleigh-ride parties. Our sleigh was shiny black, upholstered in bright red broadcloth with black wolf lap robes lined in red. The ebony horses wore necklaces of silver bells which tinkled merrily as we raced them through the countryside.

After hours of outdoor fun the young people would return home for singing, dancing, and refreshments. What a glorious sight they were to behold! Their eyes would sparkle with the excitement, their cheeks would be rosy as apples. Once inside, their delight was preparing the fiery red snowballs. The softest, whitest snow was scraped up and formed into lightly packed balls and placed in paper containers. A thick syrup was made from beets and sugar and poured over the snow. Oh, it was delicious. We also made roasted nuts and drank a hot punch of boiling tea with sugar, lemon, and a dash of red wine. Little cakes were baked in pans with rounded bottoms and served with sandwiches stuffed with apricot jam and rolled into soft powdered sugar until their thick coats resembled snowballs.

So, we never found Hungarian winters weary because indoors it was always warm and full of good cheer. When I packed up this particular wintry, snowy day to leave Vilmos again, this is how I imagined it would be. There was only one difficulty. Our villa at Balaton was a summer place. There was no heat. It is difficult to be warm and full of good cheer when your children are screaming and freezing.

We had to check into a small room in a small hotel. All of us in this one small room. The children had caught cold and were vomiting. All developed whooping cough. Three nights in this hotel and Cuki whimpered, "Let's go home. There we have a beautiful nursery and it's warm and there is beautiful food. If we stay here the children will die."

"Why do these stupid children of mine have to always die whenever I am escaping from their father?" I said shivering.

"If you go back," continued warm-hearted, lovable, fat Cuki, whose lumpy nose was also dripping, "you know Herr Gabor will buy you something glamorous for a welcome-home present like he always does when you come back from running away. And remember, the last time you ran away and he negotiated with you to come back, he came to terms with you in advance for the next time you would run away."

"What did I ask for? I don't remember."

"A ruby. Herr Gabor promised you that the next time you escaped and came back he would give you a ruby."

At this point Zsa Zsa was whooping loudly like a crane and Magda was again throwing up. "I tell you the truth," I admitted to Cuki, "right now I would be happy to see Vilmos. Right now I would go back to that warm beautiful home with the servants and the food even without the ruby."

Cuki pulled out the suitcases and I began to pack.

Five months later I was off again. My friend Alice had come to the apartment to stay with me. For the party in her honor I wore for the first time a black beaded dress, which Vilmos had bought in a department store on the Champs-Élysées. When we were undressing that night he made a grandiose statement in the *nouveau riche* manner of his. "Everybody was staring at the gown tonight because it's so expensive looking, therefore I am going to order six more."

"Six more of the *same* dress?"

"In different colors. White, green, blue . . ."

"But identical dresses? How gauche. You can't possibly wear the same dress all the time. I never heard of anything so ridiculous."

"I am never ridiculous. It is you who are ridiculous!"

"Yes. You have finally said one thing in your life with which I can agree. For me to have married you was just that—ridiculous!" And from such a nothing we had a bitter fight.

"If I gave you heaven you would not be happy," he shouted at me.

"That is true," I shouted back. "I will be happy only when I find another man."

"Okay, so I don't mind if you don't love me; but if you cheat on me then I will wipe out your whole family, beginning with your Jewish mother."

"Leave my beloved mother out of this. You are not good enough even to mention my mother's name," I screamed at him.

"You are a *kurva.*"

"And you I hate!"

The next morning, while we were still glaring at one another, my friend Alice received flowers. An admirer of hers sent her a huge basket of roses, which had to weigh ten kilos. Vilmos believed it was for me from a secret admirer and he became angry, flew into a jealous rage and ended up hitting me on my thigh. The thigh turned blue. So I thought, "Aha, this is good. This is again a reason to escape."

Again I pulled out the suitcases, but this time I went to visit my mother, who was in Marienbad. Being very beautiful, she had always many men around her and I was dying for romance. Sex I didn't really need because Vilmos was very good.

Vilmos was a very sexy man. He could have with me sex in the morning, in the evening, in the afternoon. He was always interested even as an hors d'oeuvre. We would make love just before dinner. Even when we were long-time married he was very passionate and it was good. Even when I didn't like him in the daytime, I always loved him in the night. We had already been married eight years when he came home after being away in Germany for a few days' business trip. We had a long apartment opposite the museum and we looked out over the statue of the great poet and patriot Sándor Petőfi. The apartment was in one line—it was ten rooms but we had a mirror at the end of the hall so it looked like twenty rooms. He came home about 8:00 in the evening. The house was quiet. The servants were way down at the other end of the hall in their quarters.

Immediately he stepped into the vestibule he began pulling at my clothes, "Vilmos," I whispered sharply, "please . . . don't . . . let's go to the bedroom. It's only a few steps."

But he couldn't wait. Right there in the vestibule he unzipped his pants and pulled me down on the floor.

"Vilmos . . . the servants. . . ."

But he was not hearing me. He lifted up my skirts, got on top of me with the mirrors reflecting us for miles and right there in the hallway it was the best we ever had. He was good many nights but I remember this as being his very best. It was six times that one night.

So I wasn't really just interested for sex but I wanted very much romance.

The Palace Hotel in Marienbad was for me especially exciting. There many rich ladies sipped tea and came for the waters. There one sat after dinner in the big music salon. I sat there with my mother, all alone. Everybody else had somebody. "Why," I asked my mother, "doesn't some man come over to speak to ask me for a dance?"

"I think it is because you look so sophisticated and unapproachable," she explained. "You are wearing that black beaded dress from Paris with that big black velvet hat and you just seem to be perhaps too unattainable. And you have so many diamonds that a man might be frightened of you."

There was this one stunning man. Tall. Slim. I even envied him his slimness because he was smaller in the hips than I was. He had black, black hair and always a flower in his buttonhole. Oh, I thought this was so elegant. A friend of my mother's saw me staring at this man. "You would like to be presented to him?" inquired my mother's friend.

"Oh, yes," I sighed. "I adore him already. Who is he, a gigolo for some rich lady?"

"No," he shook his head, glancing at my beautiful man. "No, I don't think so. I think I heard that he is the *Eintaentzar.*"

"You mean that glorious creature is the house dancer—hired by the hotel to teach ladies how to dance and to actually dance with them himself?"

"Yes, I think so," he nodded.

I picked up my wine glass and clinked my diamond bracelets in an airy wave of the other wrist. "In that case I don't think I shall speak to him much."

But I could not take my eyes off him. Eager to take me out of my misery, my mother's friend brought my Adonis *Eintaentzer* over to me. I surveyed him carefully. His hands were lovely. His shoes were not overpolished as though he were eager to make a good impression and he appeared to be wellborn. He did not appear to be an *Eintaentzer.* He said in well-spoken German, "I have been looking at you since you arrived, Madame, but who would dare to speak to you or to approach you—you give the appearance of being a French star."

"Well, I am not," I laughed. "Please sit down."

We spent about an hour, with a little wine, a little conversation, a little flirtatious talk with the eyes, and then he took out a very flat watch with numbers on it that were foreign and excused himself to go back to his hotel. His car and chauffeur were waiting. "Will you do me the honor of joining me tomorrow for five o'clock tea at my hotel, Madame?" he asked bowing slightly.

Even without seeing the car and chauffeur I replied, "It would be my pleasure."

The next day he told me he was from Berlin, that he was a millionaire, and that he was not the hotel *Eintaenzer.* Who he was or what he was I did not know because this, somehow, he never told me. He was my mystery man but I adored him. He smelled faintly of cologne. His shirt, cuffs, and collar were gleaming white. His teeth were not completely perfect but this suited him and made him even more masculine in my eyes. He held my hand. He kissed my hand. He kissed the tip of my nose. I was in ecstasy.

The next morning my rooms were filled with flowers from him. That night he invited me to a charity ball and presented me with paid tickets for my mother and her friends.

The next few days we had a few kisses and a little flirtation but then Vilmos got in touch with me and told me that one of the children was dying. One of those little devils of mine was always dying.

My heart stopped. I had come so close to almost lying naked next to this stirring creature that I was quivering from head to toe.

I wanted him so much. I wanted to touch him. I wanted to feel him. I wanted him to kiss my whole body the way he kissed my face. I wanted him to take his time and slowly run his beautiful fingers all over me, not rip off my nightgown and climb up and off like Vilmos did. I was so near to this exalting experience that I could almost taste it—and now at the point of fulfillment, Vilmos uses the old weapon, my children.

I had to go home. He presented me with flowers and tears streamed down my cheeks. I leaned out the train window and handed him one rose. He ran alongside the train as it began to move and he cried, "I shall never forget." It lasted only four days. And yet I, too, did not forget.

Back in Budapest life in our emotional household was the usual turmoil. Vilmos would bring home things that, like himself, were weighty: bookends, busts, full-length statues, more goddamn bronzes in the shapes of snarling tigers and charging rhinoceroses, which I would try to throw out or break to make room for my flowers, beautiful exquisite paintings, crystal, five canaries, dainty gilt objects, perfume, and candy. Our apartment was enormous, with pillars and high ceilings, gigantic burgundy silk brocade upholstered chairs, heavy rosewood furniture, two immense salons, and everywhere aunts, uncles, cousins, my continual parade of guests and friends and the ceaseless procession of servants.

If servants stayed longer than two months we considered them faithful family retainers. With Vilmos' disposition and my parties and our children, the Gabor household always looked like an employment agency. When I didn't have a broke baroness as a governess I would trade a few bronzes for an old duchess, but through it all ran the rhythm of the Gabor household: temperament, passion, loud voices, *Sturm und Drang*.

Crisis followed crisis. We were like characters in a giant play. According to the book Zsa Zsa later wrote, there was "Mama, a strikingly beautiful girl with blonde hair falling to her shoulders, an exquisitely fair complexion, huge dark eyes, and a zest for living" and "Papa, powerfully built, a suspicious distrustful stubborn man whose temper was ungovernable."

Most of our sudden, violent quarrels happened at the lunch table. The Hungarian custom was a big lunch. But Vilmos always wanted a bigger lunch than anybody, with such heavy things as goose and duck and gooseliver. Once he heard we would *not* have a big lunch because I was tired of so much food. So what he did was to bring home three live geese. He let them loose in the house and they relieved themselves on my carpet and we had a big argument. After that we always had a big big lunch. Anyway, one reason for most of our violent quarrels happening at the lunch table was that everything else was going on at the lunch table. We always began with a minimum of nine people. Our table seated twelve and was usually full. There was Papa and Mama, the three kids, Fraulein Cuki, the private tutor and her daughter and the piano teacher, who almost lived in with us.

We had two pianos in the house. One was in the dining room, another in the hall. I would drink beer at lunch and be sleepy but still with my head nodding I'd sit with my musically untalented daughters while they practiced their terrible piano. You can believe me that musically my daughters are only 10 per cent as talented as I am. I can play piano even now but they can not. The piano teacher lady came to our house every day for ten years. I fed the piano teacher lady lunch every day for ten years. It cost me 15,000 pengös because I wanted so much for them to be accomplished, but what they learned wasn't worth ten cents.

I was so talented that every time a new servant joined our household he or she asked, "Are you an actress, Madame?" I only got mad at that question once. It was after I had been married a long time and a new servant asked me, "Were you an actress, Madame?" I fired her the same day.

I tried to make stars of my children from their babyhood. I wanted them not just to ice-skate but to outdo a Sonja Henie. I wanted them to play piano so magnificently that a Rubinstein would suffer by comparison—but even with all the money I spent on their piano lessons not one of them can today go ping ping.

With all the people at the table, lunch was like a ceremony, like a wedding. The biggest eaters were the tutor and her daughter. With three children in our family one of them always needed tutoring in something, so this woman was a steady member of the lunch table. Her fee was 100 pengös a month but she reduced it to 80 so that her daughter could eat. It was well known that the Gabors set a good table. Our table often included a seamstress and the fencing instructor (I was always giving my children lessons), whose fees included lunch and a talent to pretend they heard and saw nothing.

Vilmos' table and his wines were always better than anybody else's. He was that type. Everything with him was larger than life—including his fantasies, his suspicions, and his temper. I liked living on his scale. I just didn't like *him.* If not for having to take his medieval ways, I would have been happy taking his beautiful life of abundance.

For all its being like a banquet, lunchtime was often traumatic because Vilmos came home every day for lunch. I recall the rainy day we had a new girl serving at the table. Vilmos was already seated at the head dressed formally in his jacket and wing collar and tie. The children were late and he was tapping his foot impatiently. I was beginning to get nervous. I could sense this would be another day of tensions between us. He took out his watch, adjusted the antique rosewood grandfather clock in the dining room and then returned to the gleaming mahogany table, laid with a damask cloth, Limoges dinnerware and crystal goblets.

"They are late," he said, drumming his fingers on the cloth.

"Please do not begin a scene," I said. "It is raining and so they are late getting home. But do not create tension at the table. It is bad for them to see us always this way."

"If you would not run around to card parties and would raise them properly, this would not happen," he thundered at me. The tutor and her daughter exchanged looks. Lady, our dog, began yelping. I stood up embarrassed and asked Vilmos, "Would you please step into another room with me?"

"No, Madame, I will not," he replied.

So, instead of speaking to him across the length of the table, I came around and sat down in the seat next to him and pleaded in a low tone, "Please, Vilmos, do not embarrass me again in front of the piano teacher and the tutor and her daughter. I am so ashamed that this kind of talk goes on in front of them."

Vilmos raised his voice. "If you are ashamed in front of the piano teacher, then let the piano teacher eat somewhere else."

The piano teacher dropped her eyes and I did the same with my voice. It was now so low Vilmos could barely hear it. "Please . . . please," I begged him. "Do not be so loud at the table."

"I am the head of the household," he said for everybody to hear, "and if anybody at my table does not like the way I am acting, then they may leave my table."

The fencing instructor, the seamstress, the piano teacher, the tutor and her daughter all began examining their fingernails. Therefore I hated him.

"The worst thing is to be loud," I whispered to him. "Mama always used to say to me, 'Speak softly for that is a sign of good breeding.' I do not say I am always so softly spoken but please, I plead with you, do not embarrass me further in front of our guests and our children. Tell me everything . . . tell me anything . . . only not loud."

"I am not interested in your *kurva* mother."

"My mother doesn't even mind when you insult her. She says 'I will ignore it as long as he is good to you.' And you are good to me, Vilmos," I said softly, trying to be conciliatory. "And I do appreciate it. Only I beg of you do not be so loud. Mama always used the German word, '*Herrschaften.*'

She always told me I spoke too loud. It is a bad habit that I have and you also have. *Herrschaften*, the noble people with good breeding, always speak softly and . . ."

"Bring me the soup," shouted Vilmos, bringing his fist down on the table so that two of the Limoges service plates crashed to the floor and the massive Czechoslovakian crystal chandelier tinkled.

At this moment Zsa Zsa came in from school with her schoolbooks harnessed around her shoulders. "Oh I can see this will be another lovely meal," she teased. Then, grinning, she threw out the standard family joke, "Did you get the divorce yet?"

"No," I smiled, bowing graciously to all the smirks that the familiar joke provoked around the table, "not yet."

Vilmos just sat there stonily. Zsa Zsa kissed him on the cheek and took her place at the table. She was followed by Eva, whose greeting was, "Divorce? Did I hear talk about divorce as usual?" Her big black eyes took in the usual scene and, sliding in next to Zsa Zsa, she turned to her Papa and asked, "Did you and Mama come to an understanding yet?"

"No, not yet," said Zsa Zsa.

"Okay," said Eva, "Then we can eat."

"Yes, there is still money in the family because Papa has not given back the dowry money to Mama yet," teased Zsa Zsa.

Then Magda skipped in, caught the wink and the look toward Vilmos and me that Eva threw at her and went along with the joke, "Mama get the divorce yet?"

"No, not yet," answered Eva, buttering a slice of dark bread.

"Good, then we can eat," said Magda, also helping herself to bread.

Vilmos never entered into this banter. He sat there like a stick until the nervous new servant girl brought him the soup. This is a famous Hungarian soup which takes forever to prepare. *Halászlé*, like bouillabaisse, is prepared with fresh fish immediately after the catch and several varieties are used— carp, pike, whitefish, and bass. These are scaled, cleaned, washed, cut into three-inch pieces and then layered into a large kettle with onions, carrots, celery, celery leaves, salt, pepper, a good dash of the splendid, sweet Hungarian *Szeged* (paprika), which is an essential ingredient in our food. After simmering gently, with the pot carefully shaken from time to time, each slice is gently removed with a slotted spoon to prevent the fish from falling apart and placed into deep soup bowls. To this is added the hot broth. The *halászlé* is served with dark bread and sweet butter.

Vilmos sampled it, spat it out right on the table, thumped his fist so hard that the soup bowl spilled, and ranted, "It is not hot enough."

"Oh, but it is boiling hot, sir," trembled the nervous maid.

"Please, Vilmos," I cried from across the table. "Heat is coming up from the kettle that is how hot it is." Vilmos, his temper even hotter than the soup, rose and with a mighty tug of his powerful arms pulled the tablecloth off the table and soup, fish, onions, Limoges, crystal, bread, butter, wine, beer, flowers, bowls, everything spilled over and crashed to the floor with nothing left of the *halászlé* but slices of fish all over our laps and the Oriental carpet.

Vilmos stormed out. I picked up a porcelain vase and threw it after him. It missed but it didn't miss the bronze lamp in the corner, where it came to rest in a thousand pieces.

A door slammed in the background. "And stay out," I shouted after him. "I hate you. . . ."

The servant girl began crying, the piano teacher fled in fright, my dog was barking, the crystal chandelier from Czechoslovakia was quivering, Eva burst into tears, the tutor and her daughter were slopping up the fish, Magda stooped down trying to pick up the broken cups and saucers and from the floor she sighed, "Oh, Mama, you must stop laying the table with Limoges. It costs too much money."

"Mama," said Magda, "Why don't you divorce Papa?"

"I am embarrassed for you children that I am so bad to him," I admitted. "I know I am no angel. But he is so loud that I am ashamed of him and it makes me hate him."

The servants came in and I herded the children into their room while the storm passed and they relaid the table. A half hour later the cook came in to announce that luncheon would be again served. Shifting from one foot to the other and with a troubled look in her eyes she then said softly, "I am sorry to tell you, Mme. Gabor, but I would clean the floor with my nose rather than live with that man."

All four of us looked at her wide-eyed. Therese was not the sort to be disrespectful. She had witnessed such scenes before and always looked away.

I extended both hands to Therese. "What is it, Therese? Why do you say that? Has Herr Gabor done something to you?"

Tears welled up in her soft brown eyes and one tear squeezed its way down her cheek. "I never told you this story before but . . ." her lip quivered and she faltered.

"Go on, Therese," I said.

"Remember the other week when Herr Gabor was up at the Balaton on business and stayed overnight? Well, I was up there staffing the house for him as you had ordered. After I had completed my work I had coffee in the kitchen with the night watchman. Herr Gabor heard the door close when the watchman left and he came tearing out of the house shouting, "Who is this? Who is there?" He raced out and found the watchman walking rapidly out of the servants' quarters. Do you know what Herr Gabor did?"

"What?" I asked terrified.

"What?" asked Magda echoing me.

"He said to the watchman 'You are a peasant and I will teach you to become friendly with my servants' and do you know what he did?"

"What?" I asked.

"He gave the watchman two slaps across the face."

There was a law then that at night a man can take a shotgun and defend himself by shooting if he hears something, so I mumbled, "Well, I guess the watchman is lucky that he just got two slaps."

"The watchman is harmless. He is well known to us all and he only came to call on me to have a cup of coffee. He said to me the next day that he could kill Herr Gabor for this."

"So give him a message for me," I instructed her. "Tell him to kill him. This way I wouldn't have to sell my diamonds to have the money to pay someone to kill him. Tell the watchman it's a good idea to kill him. He has my permission."

Therese wiped her eyes and we hugged each other and then she handed me the mail. It contained a letter from an unknown admirer. It said, "You are so beautiful and you have such gorgeous legs and you have such a captivating smile. I have seen you twice and I am in love with you."

I was happy that I had captivated someone; but then I heard Vilmos coming back to the luncheon table and I quickly stuffed the letter inside my dress. When we sat down again to a much less lavishly decorated table, I was still in a euphoria about some strange man noticing me so I must have had a faraway look because he was immediately suspicious.

"What is the matter with you?" he demanded. The piano teacher, the seamstress, the fencing instructor, the tutor's daughter looked up quickly. Magda, Zsa Zsa, and Eva looked down quickly. My hand instinctively flew to my bosom and the paper crackled.

He pointed a long finger across the table at me. "You are hiding something."

"Nothing. I swear to you."

"You are hiding something in your dress."

"Nothing . . . I have nothing . . . I swear to you." I always lied to him for everything. Even when I had not things to lie to him about I would lie to him.

"If you are having an affair with anybody, then I will kill your mother and your sisters and I will kill the whole family; but first I will begin with your mother."

"I have never had even a sniff of an affair during our marriage. I have never even had a platonic love," I answered in front of the piano teacher, the fencing instructor, the seamstress, the tutor and the tutor's daughter, who all seemed to have lost their appetites.

"Your mother is lying to me," he said to the girls. "Your mother is crazy. She has everything and still she wants more."

The new servant girl wouldn't come anywhere near us, so Therese served what was left of the lunch. A bowl of vegetables thickened with sauce or *rántás* prepared with butter, flour, sautéed minced onions, and sweet cream and seasoned with chives and dill was placed at each end of the table. A crock of gooseliver, my favorite, was put in the center.

The glorious aroma lifted to my nostrils and I was hungry. As I reached for the bowl of vegetables, Vilmos began again.

"Your mother is never satisfied. What's more she has never satisfied *me*. I wanted a boy. All she gave me were you girls."

"It's not true. You wanted only girls because if I had a boy I would have left you. You lie."

"No," he screamed, *"You* lie. And you are lying to me right now about what you are hiding inside your neckline!"

Getting up, he raced toward me and collided with Therese, who was bearing down on my end of the table with an enormous casserole of something which quickly joined the bits of *halászlé* still clinging to the floor. I took advantage of the melee to dive under the table. I quickly began shredding the letter and eating it. I also ate the envelope, which was silly because there was nothing written on it.

I don't know what all the others above me ate for lunch. I only know all I ate that day was a letter and parts of an envelope.

I decided then that I had to get a divorce. Not even getting pregnant again could change my mind. In Budapest, abortions were a very quick thing. Into the office, boom, out of the office. I did away with six more brothers or sisters that my three girls might have had. My doctor was a big rich man who used to say, "Take off your little panties, my darling, and open the little legs and put the 500 pengős on the table."

He would do it in ten minutes and then we would go right home. By the fifth time I was such a steady customer that he should have given me a discount.

It happened we were in a coffeehouse. Coffeehouses at this time were landmarks in Budapest. The New York was informal and Bohemian and very popular. The Japan was a grand café where one transacted business, had a flirtation, impressed a friend. The Abbazia was where the fashionable people came to engage in conversation, read the world press, and dream fancy dreams. You could sit there forever. No limit was placed on time or money. It was a Thursday evening and we two were in a coffeehouse. Temperamental Vilmos had naturally had a fight with the waiter. Vilmos had insulted him with "You are a stupid nothing, go away," and then in a rage stood up and slapped him.

I was so angry that I left the café and took a suite in the Hotel Gellert.

I had my freedom and every day at three I had an appointment to come to see the children. My bills at the hotel were being paid by him and my friends came nightly and we played rummy and I was happy.

Vilmos' lawyer asked him a fee of $1,000 and he guaranteed that with this single payment from Vilmos to him I would be back home in three days. All this lawyer did was give advice to Vilmos to don't give me money, don't pay her suite, don't let her see the children. Usually when I came to see the children Vilmos would have left me a note saying, "I adore you," and there would be for me flowers and delicacies I loved on the table. This first time after Vilmos hired his lawyer a tearful Cuki wouldn't let me in. She opened the front door barely enough for me to see her face perspiring and her big bosom heaving. "You cannot come in. Herr Gabor's orders. He says you can't see the children."

"Cuki, I'll have you fired. You know Mr. Gabor always does what I want." I was in shock. Crying hysterically, I called Vilmos. He said, "When you see me then we can work things out." I went immediately to a big divorce lawyer with the contract I had made Vilmos sign before we were married, the contract which guaranteed me a divorce automatically after six months.

The divorce lawyer told me, "This paper isn't even good enough for you to wipe yourself with." I had no choice but to go back and make up. On the telephone Vilmos said, "You come and meet me in the same coffeehouse where I insulted the waiter." So, we met at four o'clock. Nobody was there at that early hour. Maybe only three people. Vilmos smelled of his customary heady cologne.

When I arrived he stood up, kissed me, ordered champagne for us both, then asked for a light from that very waiter. And then he said to the waiter gently, "Kiss the hand." In Hungarian this is the most polite and noble and gracious manner. Just "Kiss the hand . . . thank you."

The waiter had tears in his eyes. He replied only, "And thank *you* very much." The waiter said later to me, "Herr Gabor is really a very fine man. He is just a little nervous."

We'd been there about four hours and we were a little *shicker*, a little drunk, and Vilmos suggested we go to Margaret Island, that elegant little section in Budapest in the middle of a park where very chic ladies with big hats go to see and be seen. They had restaurants there and hotels and it was now evening and I was feeling good and I said, "Okay, let's go."

"I adore you," he said. "That's why I'm happy. You are only miserable because you don't love me."

At Margaret Island was sitting my lawyer, who saw me walk in on the arm of my about-to-be-divorced husband and called to me, "Are you crazy? How can I make a divorce if you are with him?" Vilmos had booked a room for us and since I was always in the mood, we went upstairs together. As I went up, my lawyer hollered to me, "My fee is 6,000 pengös!" Oh, he was so upset that we went upstairs to sleep together. Unless a man is so very bad in bed that you cannot stand him—which Vilmos was not—how can you be angry with him afterwards, right? So, naturally, we went back together again.

My personal problems were thrown aside suddenly when I fell ill. I was never sick a day in my life until the epidemic of Spanish influenza. Many died all around us. We were acquainted with one family where the mother and father both died and had left a seven-year-old girl. Everybody warned me, "Don't touch this orphan. Leave her alone. It is not smart to take her because maybe the child also has the sickness in her what with her mother and father dying." But, still, I took her into my house and, true, the child fell ill. Vilmos said, "Let's get her to the hospital" but I wanted to take care of her myself. She grew well, but I became sick.

I was taken to the Payor Sanitorium and diagnosed as suffering with both pneumonia and diphtheria. I felt disembodied, as though I were already in the other world and yet how interesting it was that I could hear everything. I couldn't speak and yet I could hear Mama, Papa and her sister around me.

Mama was saying, "We have to wait for a room. One is coming empty right now; but we must wait until they carry the people out." I felt as though an unseen hand was strangling me because I could not speak. A while later three dead people were carried out of the room. Two children and a mother. Only the father was still alive.

Then they wheeled me into this same green, antiseptic-smelling room, and I could hear some doctor's voice saying about me, "What a pity, such a beautiful young woman and there is no hope." I was in the hospital four weeks.

I couldn't retain any food. Not even liquids would stay with me. And I was hallucinating. I kept seeing big black birds circling me. Mother never left me. Mother would feed me boiling hot coffee. She'd force it down my throat. Her sister Bertha and she would take turns shaking me. They even pulled my hair. Never for two minutes would they let me go to sleep. They poured ice cold water on me, then soaked me in hot water. They pried open my mouth —they forcefed water into me and it kept running right out of me. Again they repeated the treatment. Ice water, hot water, shake her, pull her hair, feed her boiling hot coffee, move her arms, pull her legs, keep her awake, don't let her go to sleep, ice water, hot water . . .

They cried and I could hear them crying, but I couldn't speak even a sound. Not for one second, twenty-four hours a day around the clock, for four weeks did either of them leave me alone. One or the other or both of them stayed always with me. They kept my body alive.

The doctors admitted it is they who brought me back. They said that I was actually dead. It is written even now in the record book of the Payor Sanatorium in Budapest that it is a miracle that Mme. Jancsi Gabor survived.

Physically I had been resurrected. I was lifeless only emotionally. That part of my heart and soul that yearned for another life, another love, another man had been burned out in the fever. I was grateful to be alive. I was grateful to Vilmos for having paid the bills even though it was my mother who kept me alive. I threw myself into my children.

In Budapest we had a nightclub called The Arizona. You push a button and the tables went down and there were telephones on the tables and there were little dark nooks. Two Hungarians owned this establishment. She was a singer and he a musician and they had met in Arizona, which is why that was the name of this high-class place.

Such a place I wanted to see. More than that, I wanted my girls to see. I wanted them to share with me this terrific zest for life. On a Sunday afternoon when Vilmos was someplace, I dressed all three in identical outfits with identical gray nutria fur coats, and we left our ultra-refined home.

This street of our stately apartment building was a wide, tree-lined avenue of superb shops. Across was a jewel of a park with purple lilac trees and white acacia trees and our National Museum. In spring it smelled like perfume and at night it echoed with the strains of Gypsy music from the open air cafés alongside.

From this wealthy, sophisticated, superprotected side of life I shepherded my darling babies to The Arizona, which had a show in the afternoon. There was never such an exciting nightclub in the world like The Arizona and we went with a friend named Elizabeth. I prayed to God that He should save us and my husband shouldn't see us there although I was doing nothing wrong.

My little doll babies sat there in the dark and watched a rising stage come up from a pit with a girl on it. She stood there in a gown with a huge crinoline. From under her enormous crinoline skirt came music. At the point where the stage had risen to its maximum height, she lifted her crinolines high and a gasp went from the audience. I myself was so excited at viewing such wickedness that I could barely sit still. The drums rolled, the lights flickered, and from under her skirt came out her husband playing the piano.

I took the three of them, Magda nine, Zsa Zsa seven and Eva five, to the National Opera every Saturday, and to the National Theatre once a week to stick stardust and showbusiness into their veins early. I took them myself personally to the circus. I would not let their snobby governesses take them. At times we had a tall, gray haired French baroness, who quit after a few weeks for some reason I don't remember, a skinny German, and an English one. A chauffeur drove my babies to school and a governess took them home. But for the important things like their cultural life, I took them.

At the circus we sat spellbound as an Indian fakir swallowed fire while flames spurted from his mouth and he climbed a ladder of razor-sharp swords on naked feet. I punched my Zsa Zsa in her ribs, "Now," I hissed in the darkness, "When will you be able to do that!"

Her little eyes opened as wide as saucers and she gasped, "I must swallow fire???"

For me nothing was to be impossible. If anyone could do something, we Gabors could do it. My children would not be ordinary children. They would be taught every accomplishment. The Gabor children would be the most glamorous, most elegant, most beautiful, most pursued, most talented, most multifaceted of any human beings anywhere. And why not? Hadn't their mother denied herself her career for them?

I gave them ballet lessons, tennis lessons, riding lessons. It was on an icy cold day when I decided, "Come, children, we will learn ice-skating. Today we will go to the most fashionable rink in town, Stadtwaldchen in Városliget." It was very expensive because to go skating here at this artificial lake one had to be a member of the skating club, so Vilmos bought six memberships, including one for Fraulein Cuki and one for me. It cost 2,000 pengös. In keeping with the costliness I dressed myself in a forest green ensemble with a mink trim. I considered this the perfect skating costume particularly since I added a matching mink toque.

We were all outfitted with skates. I helped the children as they slipped and slid forward to the railing, to which they clung for dear life. I then put on my skates. It was not easy because you had to go down ten steps to put the stupid skates on. I tried to get a teacher, which it was impossible because they were too professional and too occupied to bother with us for just one hour. "Never mind, children," I sang out, "I will teach you myself."

My little ones did not seem to feel too great a degree of security in putting their lives in my hands particularly since I began a run and once I picked up speed I could not stop. I sped right by them totally unable to control the speed or to bring myself to a stop, and the poor frozen frightened children thought I didn't see them so they started to cry and call out piteously, *"Nuci . . . Nuci."*

They were cold and unhappy. At one end was the usual little house where the skaters warmed themselves before the potbellied stove and bought a candy at the commissary. There was a wooden gate there and if I didn't keep skating and running and if I stopped too short, I could run headlong into that wooden barrier and crash it right down. So, my third time around I fell down. I was blue with cold. My behind hurt because I fell on my left hip. My beautiful forest green suit was slushy and wet, and my toque, which had been sitting right on the top of my head, was now an eyebrow hat. However, a young man in uniform, I guessed he was at least a captain, executed a smart skating formation to swing quickly around at my side and pick me up. He gazed down at me with adoration, and once I pushed my hat off my eye, I gazed back at him with rapt attention. He was so dashing in his uniform that I didn't want him to know I am married with three daughters. "My sister's three little ones are over there by the round gate," I fluttered helplessly, "Can you teach them to skate?"

He looked over to see a platinum head, a blonde head and a redhead clinging to one another and to the guard rail with all three noses running and all six eyes crying. Waiting and shivering and frozen to the ice they were. Too appetizing they did not look so he dismissed with, "Sure. In a bit."

Meanwhile, he took my arm and we were half-skating and he was supporting me. "I can't stop for your nieces on this particular turn," he puffed, "because I am holding you up and if I stop now you'll fall down."

The girls screamed as around and around I went with my captain. On the fourth turn around I caught the rhythm of his long gliding steps, and I now had my breath under control sufficiently to glance at him more carefully. A better look at his uniform and I suddenly realized my captain was a mailman. At that point I ordered him to stop immediately.

When we arrived home we herded my children into their big bathroom. My three treasures were blue with frost. Cuki filled the bathroom with steam from the shower and showed me that Zsa Zsa had icicles hanging off her little *pinuska*. She had made pipi in her panties and it was so cold that ice formed. So, in a few minutes it was a little *Titanic* in my bathroom.

I also cooked one time in order to show them the culinary arts. The children were very young and it was Zsa Zsa's birthday which I somehow had forgotten. I had to make up in some way because she was sulking, therefore I decided to cook a meal for everybody as sort of a special feast. The big problem was that never had I done this before; but I figured if a cook can do it so can I. What cannot a Gabor do?! "You," I ordered to the cook. "You are to go into the nursery and I will prepare the feast."

"Mama," as we called the cook, was our delight. She came to us when the girls were tiny. We all adored her. Mama was a good-natured, ample lady with a generous smile and off she waddled.

"What will you make?" asked Magda.

"Goulash. What else is here?"

"But I don't want goulash," pouted Zsa Zsa. "I want chicken with *nockerl*."

"Well, you're going to get goulash," I said.

"But it's my birthday," she complained.

"So, in that case you can have two portions," I said, rolling up my sleeves. "The origin of goulash goes back one thousand years to the Magyar migration across the Great Plains. The herdsmen gathered around an open camp fire in the evenings and for their meal combined meat and vegetables in huge kettles, and that's how our national dish, goulash, or herdsmen's meat, was born."

"So what?" answered Zsa Zsa not unreasonably.

I bought enough meat to feed the Hungarian army. We had a woodburning stove and I could not regulate the temperature. I kept tasting the meat every few minutes.

"That's not the way Mama makes it," announced an unhappy Zsa Zsa.

"It happens there is no standard method for making goulash. The only thing important is that you stick in enough paprika and that I'm doing," I answered shaking in enough to drown the meat, the fat, the onions, and the whole damned gravy.

The only trouble is that the bits of meat stayed like pieces of stone. They never seemed to soften even though I kept tasting them. I tasted so much that there was only enough left for one portion at the end of the cooking. The children did not get any, and I had to give the servants money to go out and feed themselves because there wasn't even any for them.

"The meat is raw and hard," complained Eva, who was lucky enough to spear one piece.

"And it's my birthday," wailed Zsa Zsa.

But at least I tried, I thought to myself, remembering that great saying, "It is not enough to be Hungarian. You have to work, too!"

I was determined not to send my children to college. I didn't want them to be doctors, lawyers, or scientists. I didn't think it was necessary for the life I was preparing for them that they learn higher mathematics. To use a checkbook they did not need geometry or algebra. It was my plan to send them to finishing school to learn to play music and be elegant accomplished ladies with good manners and obviously good upbringing. I wanted them to be actresses and they are. They're not so talented like me but they are actresses.

"I do not wish to send our daughters to Switzerland," Vilmos announced to me.

"And why not?" I replied, putting on perfume in my dressing room one evening in preparation for another of the parties which I adored.

"It is too expensive. The Swiss franc is up very high."

"Nonetheless, Vilmos, they must go to a *pensionate*, a finishing school . . ."

"All they teach there is cooking, needlepoint, etiquette, piano . . ."

"Miss Rigot, their piano teacher, says they need more advanced instruction."

"How can you give them more instruction than you already give them?" demanded Vilmos. "You keep them so busy now as it is. You are compulsive with them. You regiment their day to exhaustion. Breakfast at seven, school eight to one. Then while Magda studies with Miss Rigot at one piano, Zsa Zsa is doing her studies at another, and Eva is doing her homework, then Eva gets Miss Rigot and Magda does homework and then it's dancing lessons, fencing lessons, riding lessons. By the time dinner is announced they have already collapsed."

"My daughters must know all the social sports that make for a good life. Not too much can they do any of them, but at least they can do them a little in order to be charming companions to their men someday."

The maid arrived in answer to my ring. "And who is this one?" asked Vilmos when a bony-looking frightened face appeared.

"I don't know. She replaced our English chambermaid the other day." And then I said to her, "Please make sure all the chandeliers are turned on and inform me when our guests arrive."

"Couldn't we have two consecutive nights with the house quiet and without people," grumbled Vilmos, putting on his tie.

"When I divorce you the house can be quiet and without people. Meantime, I must talk to you about our children going to Switzerland. Look here, Vilmos, I don't want that my daughters' men take your money. I want to give them a good bringing up and not money. We will never pay dowry for our daughters. Who needs a man who wants a dowry? I will take the dowry money and put it into a Swiss school."

"Why can they not go to a university here?"

"Because they are not boys, they are girls. I will send them to finishing schools to learn grace and poise. They will be well educated but in languages, social sports, and social graces. They will learn what is important—how to be agreeable to a man, so they can make glamorous rich marriages. Anyway, you know I always get what I want, so why not say *yes* immediately instead of aggravating me?"

I surveyed myself in the mirror. I liked what I saw. I was the first woman in all Budapest to have bobbed hair.

"Very well," he replied gruffly, "I will look into it."

I brushed my bobbed hair and watched with pleasure how it sprang right back to its little neat waves. "You don't have to because I have already enrolled Magda at Madame Subilia's. Madame Subilia is about fifty and she is very strict. The girls wear uniforms and hats and black stockings. They pray before lunch and they sing religious songs before dinner, and they are in bed by ten. It is a very high moral school."

The sounds of the doorbell, the sounds of laughter, the sounds of my musicians starting up broke in on the conversation. "Very well," sighed Vilmos heavily. "Madame Subilia's it is."

When I took Magda to Madame Subilia's, I went with Janette, who had a daughter, Ila, the same age as Magda. We decided to take the two girls to Lausanne together. Janette and I checked in at the Beau Rivage and we were so happy. We had freedom. Janette didn't need it as much as I since her husband wasn't so jealous. The truth is he didn't have that much to be jealous about. But in any case we were ready to have fun. So, we deposited Ila and Magda at school on our first day and went out shopping. That first night right away Madame Subilia called because Magda was crying all night. "I don't know what to do about your daughter," she said. "The child is so homesick that she cries and cries."

I was delighted. I quick called Vilmos and announced I'd have to stay. I was so happy for any reason to be away from Vilmos. The next day Magda went swimming and suffered a minor accident. There was a trampoline in the pool and she hurt her leg. She hit it against the side of the trampoline and they took her away to the hospital. This was followed with the big drama of her not wanting me to leave. I built the little crack on her knee up to huge proportions with Vilmos so that I could stay a few more days. I had to stop short of an amputation because then he would have come out there to see for himself and that I didn't need. Anyhow, the finale was I left her and came home.

The following year Zsa Zsa went. Her enrollment shows what a different girl she is and how self-sufficient. When Zsa Zsa went I didn't go and neither did her aunt or cousin. She accompanied some other girls who only went with her as far as Vienna and the rest of the way she made alone. She didn't cry. She wasn't lonely. She wasn't homesick. Whereas Magda came back for every Easter and Christmas and holiday because she was so homesick, Zsa Zsa was there for one-and-a-half years. My girls were growing up. In between letters from Magda saying she was dying to come home from school, she sent one very personal letter to me, making me promise to destroy it. She wanted a garter belt and was frightened her father would see it. I went to meet Magda when she came from school. I looked terrific when I went to the train. Maybe even I was a little bit overdressed, I don't know. Anyway, I wore a hat with a feather and a veil and my freshly bobbed hair and I was perfumed and jeweled.

I came rushing to meet my glorious foreign-educated beauty as she came off the train and to sweep her majestically up in my arms. My beauty came off the train with pockets of fat hanging off her plus red freckles, red pigtails, red eyebrows and I said to Vilmos, "What are we going to do with this ugly girl?"

I realized I had a problem on my hands so I did the only intelligent thing. I proceeded to make her over overnight. I dragged her immediately that same afternoon into the cosmetologist. She even had red eyelashes, so I made the cosmetologist tint her brows and lashes and fix her hair and bleach her skin and I gave her private fencing lessons. I didn't care if she ever became the Fourth Musketeer or not. I wanted only that she lost weight. In a few weeks she became pretty. I always said to myself, "Jancsika, maybe you are nothing but at least you will make the girls something."

Zsa Zsa was also beginning to grow up. She was in trouble at the school for trying to climb out of her window late at night and for disrupting classwork. She was not a great student though she painted nice paintings and wrote disrespectful poems, but she was excellent at making trouble.

When Magda was home from school she went into a millinery shop on the Váczi Utcza with Eva. Magda was big and tall and showed her age. Eva was diminutive. The high-class owner gushed to Magda, "Oh, Mrs. Gabor, I have heard about you and your beautiful daughters and I didn't believe they were so grown up." She had thought Eva was Magda's daughter. Magda stormed out crying.

I always dressed the three girls strikingly. They would wear the same dainty white shoes, the same exquisite organdy or silk or velvet frocks, even the same ribbons in their hair. They were starched, gloved, beribboned, and each with little bouquets of violets in their hands. I would do the same now with them if I could. They hated to be the same.

The fact is they were all totally different. Magda was the lady. Quiet, restrained, always reading. She was the grand duchess. Eva was fluffy, giggly, and single-minded about being an actress. Zsa Zsa was at first not so pretty and a little bit fat and a tomboy who accompanied her father to the wrestling matches. Then she changed into the *femme fatale*. Zsa Zsa was the one who was always special.

Zsa Zsa I worried about. When she was nine years old, a muscular young man, his face blackened with soot, came to our house to bring coal for a fire. Zsa Zsika wandered into the kitchen and while the other children were afraid of this man, she flirted with him. She heaved her little breasts up and down and pirouetted in front of him. When he went away, I said, "Zsa Zsa, how could it be you were smiling at him?" And she said, "Yes. I have decided that every man must die for me. I am sure that now he will think of me the rest of the night." How could I be angry with her? I had been like this and I was sure she inherited it from me.

We never discussed sex with the children. With prudish Vilmos I was afraid even to mention the word in the house. He had them so frightened that they believed that from a kiss they could get pregnant. I always told my actresses, Eva and Zsa Zsa, "Take care that you do not lose your virginity" but I never told them how they could lose it. I never taught them anything. I imagine they learned from their friends.

When Zsa Zsa plucked her eyebrows to a pencil line and appeared at the dinner table with nails painted jade, across the dinner table with his breath reheating the chicken paprika came Vilmos' shout, "I won't have my daughters growing up to be bad women. It's your fault," he glared at me. "Because you're not raising them to be normal human beings. You always want them to be so damned glamorous!"

I yearned to help them in their little love affairs. Although I didn't become stupid enough to neglect my own life, I tried to help them in every way. I tried to lie for them and cover for them.

By this time we had moved to a glorious villa on Stephanie Ut, a street of embassies and private mansions. We had a garden of acacia trees walled in by a high grilled iron fence. Somewhere on a trip home from school, Zsa Zsa managed to stick her hand through that fence and into the hot, wet palm of someone named Philip from the Rumanian Embassy. She sneaked back into the house about 6:30 one November evening. It was still light, but Vilmos had a knife in his hand and raved at her. "It is already very late. Zsa Zsa, I will cut your throat if you don't explain."

I quickly came in, "She has been out taking her riding lessons."

"In a party dress?"

"They were taking pictures with the horses," I said and quickly drew Zsa Zsa into the bedroom and safety.

Our villa in Stephanie Ut, which is a little like the Bois de Boulogne, had a street leading up to the skating rink. It was only a half mile from the house and on the same street as our house. In between, the streets were lined with trees and lovers would sit there when it grew dark. Vilmos' hobby was to drive up the street and shine the spotlight on the couples.

One night we were driving up to the rink to pick up the girls who were supposedly skating. Since this was the only area of coeducation, it was the spawning ground for timid hand-holdings. My beauties supposedly were there under the watchful eye of Fraulein, but Fraulein had gone into the heated room on the side of the rink to warm up for a few minutes and the girls had sneaked away. Eva by this time was madly in love with Pista. Pista was sixteen and had pimples.

Vilmos put his spotlight on the side of the street—an act I hated, by the way—and I saw my two youngest there. He did not see them. I nearly had a heart attack. Evika was with Pista and who Zsa Zsika was with I had no time to see. I knew instantly we could not go to the ice-skating rink to pick them up because they were not there.

I had quickly to think of something and stall for time. "Vilmos, I am cold. Let us stop for a cup of hot chocolate."

"They have a place for that at the rink and we'll get some there," he said.

"No, no," I cried.

He stared at me. "Why not?"

"Because they don't make good chocolate."

By then it was too late. He had driven into the rink; but I managed to waste about another fifteen minutes. The rink was under the bridge, and I took Vilmos' arm and said, "Come let us take a little stroll over the bridge together." Somehow the girls were back by then and we survived.

Knowing I was on their side, the children usually told me the truth. When Eva was about fifteen, she was insane for a handsome soldier, a lieutenant. He was so tall, once after a quarrel she pulled out a chair and climbed on top of it just so she could give him a slap. His name was Paul Yankovich. His father was a famous general. Eva used to tell me she often had to take a French lesson. It occurred to me she was taking so much French that she should be able to speak better soon than Madame du Barry, but I didn't bother about it until one afternoon when she was supposedly conjugating her verbs, I found her with this Yankovich in a confectionery shop eating sweets. They were like two birds; he was good-looking and his father was celebrated so I couldn't be angry.

The normal pattern of my abnormal life-style was changed one day when we learned Papa was sick. Mama was away on a trip and Papa invited the four children and their husbands to dinner at Gundel's, the best restaurant in the city. There was Janette and Harvey, Rozsika and Miklos, myself with Vilmos, and Dora and her second husband, Hugo.

We were all laughing and having fun. Harvey, Janette's jovial husband, teased Papa. "Tell me, Papa, in the thirty years you are married to Mama, did you not once ever cheat on her?"

Prim and proper Dora blushed. Janette repeated, "Come on, Papa, tell us. You ever cheat on Mama?"

Papa spoke only of Mama. She was his favorite subject. Lifting his wine glass, he said only, "She comes home in a few days."

Rozsika, roly-poly, blonde, and laughing and, as usual, finishing everyone's pastry said, "How could Papa cheat on Mama when she is the most beautiful woman in the world?"

"Well, children," smiled Papa expansively when the table was cleared and the men had lit their afterdinner smokes. "Once. I tried once."

Everybody set up a howl. Janette, who was hearty—the type who rose at five every morning, bathed in snow in the winter, and went on eight-hour hikes twice a week—exploded. "But if you had steak why would you want hamburger?"

"Well, I tell you," chuckled Papa, "once I was in a whorehouse in Austria."

"Where in Austria?" prompted Vilmos. "I want the address."

I gave him a proper slap on the wrist and Papa replied, "In Graz." And then in retrospect he added, "But only once and don't forget I'm fifty-one years old."

"And how old is Mama?" asked Dora's husband, Hugo.

"Forty-five," said Dorushka softly, sipping her *Kapuziner*, that's a small glass of coffee sweetened with milk.

"Look, children," explained Papa, "there is only one kind of sweet woman in the world like Mama. I would never have wanted to try this again in my entire life."

The next day Mama returned home. The day after that Papa became sick —his insides turned. Seven miles from Budapest was a spa and when Mama and Papa went there, all of us, the sons-in-law and the four sisters, came up immediately. They said he had a bad stomach and that he would be perfectly fine in a few days so we all had dinner together and prepared to go home. The taxis were ordered and one by one everybody said good-bye and "kiss the hand." I was the last to go and just at the precise instant that I was about to say good-bye, my taxi was honking and everybody was yelling, "C'mon, let's go," so I ran in to the taxi quickly. This was my great tragedy because I couldn't say good-bye to Papa and didn't even have the opportunity to say, "Kiss the hand." I never got over it. Not to this day.

I was in Lelle with Janette and Rozsika when we heard that Mama had taken Papa to Payor Sanatorium. Although we were assured he was all right and was coming along and would be out in a day or two, we three decided to come home immediately.

I took one last swim. In diving off the board, I hit something and cracked my ankle. I was carried on a stretcher back to the villa so I could not get home to the city to see Papa with the others. That night I dreamed Papa had died and when I went to the house, my sister, Dora, opened the door in a dark blue grenadine dress with a white collar. Somehow the white collar came off, and when Dora opened the door, she said to me, "Don't come in, because Mama will cry again."

I awoke in a pool of sweat. I grabbed the telephone and called Vilmos. "How is Papa?"

Vilmos answered slowly. "I just called and they told me he is much better."

At this point Papa was about to be operated on, but Vilmos and Harvey, who were good comrades, had agreed not to tell us. Janette, however, was on her way back to Budapest with Rozsie while I was still bedridden in Lelle.

"Did they say when Papa will be released from the sanatorium?"

"Yes. They said Sunday. So, don't worry," consoled Vilmos.

This was Thursday. Saturday Papa died. Sunday when I came back to Budapest I went to Mama's house. I couldn't stand it because, just as in my dream, Dora opened the door in the dark blue grenadine dress without the white collar. I gasped. Dora repeated the very same words she had uttered in my dream: "Don't come in because Mama will cry again."

It was ten days and Papa was dead. I wanted to die because I hadn't said good-bye and "Kiss the hand." I could not bear that pain. I opened my garden windows and I shouted loud and strong. I just shouted and shouted and screamed until my throat was hoarse and my chest was sore. I took to my bed and was physically ill for a year because of it.

At forty-five Mama was a widow. She lived alone in great style. She was the kind of grand woman who had an equipage—that's two horses. None of her daughters were exactly the kind to take a backseat and yet each of us involuntarily stood up when she entered a room. Perhaps it was because of her great wealth that unconsciously we respected her so much. I suppose if we had to support her it could be different. She had a maid, coachman, and cook. When her apartment was painted, she went to the Gellert Hotel, not to one of us to stay. We all begged her to stay with one of us but she wouldn't. She was like a queen who would never let any of us do anything for her. Once Mama had a servant problem. She said to me, "Maruska has left me and I have no chambermaid." Although it was for me a big sacrifice to send my Katie because she was my personal maid who dressed me and everything, I sent her over. I was pleased with my sacrifice. I thought to myself, "At last I am doing something for Mama!" But no. Mama sent her in a day back.

Mama wore black and went into mourning, but three years later she met a lawyer. Mama looked like thirty, and, like me, did what was best for love. She married him. At a dinner in my home all the sons-in-law were cynical about Mama marrying at this age. "You are all cheap, low-class women. When I die, Jancsi will do the same," bellowed Vilmos. "Why would anyone marry a forty-eight-year-old woman," sneered Harvey.

"Because a woman of forty-eight needs the same as a woman of twenty-eight, eh Rozsika?" taunted Rozsika's husband.

This was all very hard for us to hear.

"Why would a man of fifty marry a woman of forty-eight?" commented Harvey again.

"Because she is rich," put in Vilmos.

"Because she is beautiful," corrected Dora.

"Because she is sexy," laughed Harvey.

"He must need money," Miklos said cynically.

"Mama can have any man she wants," I insisted.

Mama and her lawyer went on their honeymoon to Abbazia, which is 699 kilometers from Budapest. In the sleeping car on the way, he asked his bride, "Francesca, darling, I have some debts and will you pay them?" Mama was fearfully angry. With her magnificent home and servants she was not concerned about the money. With Mama it was the principle of the thing. She could not believe this could happen to her, the spoiled, pampered Mrs. Tilleman.

"It happens to be a big sum of debts and, my angel, will you pay for me?" asked the lawyer.

Mama controlled her anger and answered very softly, "Oh, I will, of course. Why not?"

Then she excused herself and said she was going to the ladies' room. She left her luggage, her new clothes and everything and took only her train case with her. She never came back to him.

The newspapers wrote about Mrs. Tilleman of the famous Diamond House, and how she "escaped" just before her honeymoon.

When it was all over, Mama gave the four daughters this story: "In a vision, your father, my one and only true love, appeared before me. In this vision I suddenly realized that I could not go through with this. I could not be unfaithful to your father in my life." To me, Mama was a saint and it was a sufficient explanation. Again the four sons-in-law called a meeting. They concluded, according to my vulgar Vilmos, that saintly, beloved, adored Mama must have left him because he was impotent. Oh, it was a big scandal.

Every Sunday when Mama lived alone she would have a big luncheon. Most of the time we were not invited. She would invite generals, ambassadors, and the elite of the church, such as Cardinal Mindszenty. She sometimes asked Dora, who was a fine lady, and sometimes me or Rozsie, who had such a great sense of humor, but never would she ever include Janette.

Janette was rapidly becoming the black sheep. She was a revolutionary. She spoke filthy language, which was then considered quite modern. She had become a little bit of a bohemian. She wore sweaters, trousers, flat shoes. She was very ahead of her time. As my eldest sister, she had taken over the Diamond House, which was making a fortune, and looked like a bohemian.

Janette was a widow at thirty. She never married again, but she had a consuming love affair which ended poorly. This bad love affair is what changed her whole outlook. She threw away all luxuries. She had with her husband a magnificent bed with carved swans on it which she covered up with newspapers. She also covered up all attempts at being pretty. She was not very good-looking anymore, and so now she let her black hair go gray and uncombed and she became quite masculine.

Her lover was a train conductor; at least he was the chief conductor. His main contribution to her life was to let her travel without a ticket. This affair went on for many years, and it was then that Janette became coarse. The dirtiest jokes were what she gave to a party. Mama was ashamed of her.

Mama's third husband came about when she decided to take the big luxury boat, the *Saturnia*, from Genoa to the U.S. No woman was going to America alone in those days, but Mama was!

Despite the storm of protest which her daughters and sons-in-law whipped up around her departure, Mama went. When she came back she had a new hairdo and a new man. The hair was short. The man not so short, but he was fifty-six. He had all of his teeth and was good-looking, but he was bald. On the other hand, he was an "Excellency."

The first Tuesday she was back, Mama made a formal dinner for the ten of us. Mama at the head of the table, this man at the foot, we four girls plus Manci, the wife of my brother, Sebastyen, along one side of the table, and on the opposite side sat the four sons-in-law plus Sebi.

"I am Dr. Miksa Kenda." The guest of honor introduced himself to each of us and shook our hands solemnly. At the table champagne was poured by the butler and we all lifted our glasses. "To Mama," we chorused.

"To my beautiful Francesca and her family," toasted Dr. Kenda, gazing at Mama adoringly.

Over the rim of his champagne glass Vilmos caught Harvey's eye, and the glance they exchanged said more than a thousand words.

"This reminds me of a joke about the widow who . . ." began Janette.

"Now behave," warned Mama as the servants passed gooseliver paté to go along with the caraway soup.

Dora cleared her throat nervously. "Your new short coiffure looks very attractive, Mama."

"It's the newest fashion in America," replied Mama.

"She would look heavenly no matter what she did," said Dr. Kenda, smiling widely and I noticed anew how gleaming were his teeth.

"Only prostitutes bob their hair," whispered Vilmos to Harvey. I kicked him hard under the table.

I was so nervous that I not only drank my champagne to the bottom in one gulp, but I spilled the glass next to me.

"Look at Jancsi," cried Manci, whom I had never liked. "She is becoming a drunk." Everybody turned to stare at me and I in turn stared at Manci. I stared at her mousy brown hair, her thin lips, and her dull, dull clothes and wondered what my precious brother Sebika could have ever seen in her.

To make conversation I asked, "And how, sir, do you come by your title?"

"I am a medical doctor," said Kenda, "I am an internist to the Royal Family of Hapsburg."

"It is for this honor that he has been awarded the title *Excellency,*" added Mama proudly.

"However," added Dr. Kenda as he professionally carved the goose, "I do not like to use the title. It always seems a bit presumptuous."

"Mama tells us you are a very famous man," said Rozsika.

"He is an intellectual," said Mama, beaming across the huge centerpiece of flowers. "He is not only intelligent and successful and greatly honored for his work, but he also speaks nine languages."

"And do you play cards, Your Excellency?" I asked, simply because I could not think of anything else to ask.

Dr. Miksa Kenda looked up, "Cards? That is only for people who are bored with one another," and then he glanced over at Mother adoringly.

It came therefore as no great surprise when Dr. Kenda and Mama were married. As with all of us, the wedding ceremony was held right in Mama's living room.

Mama was ecstatic when she became "Her Excellency." She wanted to be always bigger and bigger than she was and it was from her that I inherited this yearning.

On his part, Dr. Kenda was supremely happy. He immediately retired, spending his afternoons at matinees and movies and spending the evening hours worshiping Mama.

At another of our regular Tuesday night dinners at Mama's Stephanie Ut house, I asked her privately, "Is this marriage truly such a good one as it seems?"

"He has made me unbelievably happy," said Mama.

"I don't understand. It is your house, your car, your cook, your chauffeur, your . . ."

"The doctor gives 500 pengös a month toward expenses. I don't need his money and I am satisfied as long as I have him."

"Isn't it true?" I persisted, "that you have to spend 2,500 pengös for every 500 pengös he spends?"

"Even if he would not give one pengö I would not mind. I take the money from my beautiful Miksa not because I need it, but because he is good enough to offer it. It is important only for him to offer it. It is important for a woman's ego."

My ego was also in need of nurturing. My marriage was growing staler and staler. The years were piling up and I was no nearer happiness nor a divorce nor a deep abiding love for some man nor a career nor any of the things for which my soul cried out.

The house was empty. It was Easter and the girls weren't home. I sat in my pink canopied bed feeling sorry for myself. Suddenly I had only Vilmos. I remembered Easters of old with Zsa Zsa cracking walnuts, Eva cutting orange and lemon rinds into thin strips and Magda dicing the many fruits into cubes and dumping them into the huge kettle. To this we added pounds of honey, dozens of wafers made from eggs and flour, light and dark raisins, a healthy dash of brandy. It cooked slowly for hours and hours with each girl taking a turn stirring it with a long-handled wooden spoon.

"Mama," the cook, made a delicate dough, chopped it into squares, then pressed each into a cut-glass design. We all held our breath while it baked in a very slow oven. How I wished we would all be together again to make this delectable holiday fruit dessert.

I took into consideration that my girls were not only growing up, but that at some point they would grow away. I thought to myself, "I don't yet know how, but I do know that I will yet lead my own life. I will not be dependent on them. I will not give them all of me and end up with no life of my own."

This decision was made during a summer holiday in Abbazia. I had rented a whole floor right on the shoreline in a house belonging to a Count and Countess Keglovits. Janette, who came with me, had another floor with her boy and girl.

All of us had breakfast together the first morning at nine and then the youngsters skipped down to the beach. My three headed into the ocean. "Take care," hollered Janette. "Three yards from shore the water gets very deep."

"*Nucika* will watch us," called Eva as she plunged toward the deep water.

"No, *Nucika* will not watch you," I called back. "I have not the time to mother you every minute. You must learn to care for yourselves even in deep water."

Eva swam back to the shore so she could speak with me without shouting against the noise of the surf.

"But why can you not watch us?" she pouted.

Vilmos was not with me and I was so happy to be without him that I was almost wild. I did not tell her that there were a couple of attractive men with whom I was flirting back on the shore. I said only, shaking my finger at her, "Evika, I have an appointment up on the high beach with the adults. So you have no choice but to take care and learn to swim in the heavy surf."

"But mothers are supposed to watch children," whimpered Eva. "We could drown."

"Then give for me a message to your sisters when you catch up to them. Tell them I order them not to drown. Tell them also if they drown *Nuci* will survive. I will cry three months. Your papa will cry two months . . . no, maybe one month . . . but we will both survive."

As I started back up the beach I turned to a wide-eyed Eva and added, "And remember, if you do not drown, I promise that you will all be rich and famous and marry kings!"

That night I was going to dinner and I put on a long gown and enormous feather boa. Zsa Zsa brought out my silver shoes and Magda laid out my evening bag and Eva, fussing over me, said, "We will wait until we grow up and then we will do all the same things as you and wear all the same thing as you."

"And we will all look the same as *Nuci*," said Zsa Zsa, "except me, of course, because I am the prettiest of everybody!"

I had long ago come to terms with the fact that I was no more going to be on the stage and I developed my own personality. I became the life of every party. I was invited everywhere. I became part of the jet set of Hungary. One year I was voted the Best Dressed Woman.

Another year Vilmos gave me a gray Mercedes car upholstered in red leather. Forty years ago we were only six ladies in all of Budapest who had our own personal cars and drove them ourselves. One was Mrs. Daimler. Another was an American Vanderbilt lady married to Count Szecenyi, a third was a famous actress, I was the fourth. This made me feel very important. I would drive down Andrassy Ut with a red sports outfit to match the upholstery and with a matching red straw sailor hat. Lady, our dog, was on the front seat alongside me with a bright red bow and my three beauties in the back, identical as dolls in matching gray coats to match the car's exterior. They were brushed, polished and they shone like the chrome. I was determined to make everyday life a stage for myself in a spectacular in which I alone was the star.

Although I had won a prize at the Grand Concours d'Élégance driving my gray Mercedes in a matching gray gown, unfortunately I was not quite so brilliant a driver. I was en route home from a hard-fought tennis tournament which I'd won at snobbish Margaret Island and I was alone in my car. On the bridge I saw an old flame, André Zalabondy, a movie director born in Fiume. The top was open on my touring car and I called, "Hey, Zala, I will take you where you're going."

"Thanks, I'd love to," he called back.

I pulled over and in starting to find my place back in traffic I was so busy speaking to Zala that I had a little accident. I accidentally pushed another car in front of me, which accidentally ended up in his denting his front fender and me pleating both his back fenders ever so slightly. The final result was we were compelled to go to the police station nearby.

As I rolled up alongside the police station I nudged Zala. "Quick, my dear friend, go. Disappear . . . disappear. Make yourself scarce."

Zala readjusted the sweater which was tied over his shoulders by the arms and made as though to deliberately snuggle back into the upholstery. "Ever since the collision . . . but I mean from the very instant of this unimportant tragedy," he teased, "you have been trying to get me to get out of here."

I looked around wildly. "Yes, Bondy, please . . . go away . . . go away."

"I won't." He folded his arms. "I won't go away."

The street was busy and I was fearful of being recognized sitting there with him. "Please, Bondy, please go away. Vilmos will find out you were with me and I am afraid of that."

He put his hand on my arm. "But Jancsika, I want to help you."

"No, not now, Bondy. Please. If Vilmos finds this out, I am afraid of what he will do. Bad enough I had this tragedy and I'm at the police station like a common criminal, but if he knows you were in the car with me it will be a disaster."

"Jancsika, my beautiful one," pleaded Zala. "Please don't send me away. You know how I've had a mad crush on you for years. Now is the time I can finally be of help to you. How manly will it look if in your moment of need I leave you?"

"I beg of you, Bondy." I was beginning to perspire from nerves and took out my handkerchief to hide my face in it as though that would protect me —one of the six women in all Budapest who drove a car! "I thank you for your grand manner, but you know that Vilmos is very jealous of you."

"Yes," he grinned like the rogue he was. "Remember the time Vilmos and you were in the Mercedes with the chauffeur and you invited me to join you on the way home from the opera and just as I began to get in, Vilmos slammed the door in my face?"

"Father was our friend but Mama we worshiped. I considered myself honored if I could just lace up her boots because she had everything and needed nothing."

"Get again pregnant," said Vilmos. "Give me a son and I will let you go."

One more still to come. . .

"I wanted them to experience *everything*. Once, on a rainy afternoon, I even made them all have a fight — a real fight with their little fists."

"I took them to both the opera and the theatre each week to stick stardust and showbusiness into their veins early."

The kids froze while their mother melted the heart of a new-found admirer.

"I gave them ballet lessons, tennis lessons, riding lessons. The Gabor children would be the most glamorous, most elegant, most beautiful, most talented, most pursued of any human beings. And why not? Hadn't their mother denied herself her career for them?"

"But mothers are supposed to watch children—they could drown," whimpered Eva. "Then give for me a message to your sisters," I told her. "Tell them I order them not to drown."

Budapest's first Mercedes touring car, a birthday present for Jansci (taking a rare back seat)
from Vilmos (piloting). Running-board riders:
Eva and Zsa Zsa.

"I was maybe 34 or 35. The most I could have been was 36. Okay, so 37, but not an hour older."

Photo·Manassé·, Wien

SÁRI GÁBOR

The apple-biting temptress, though she lost
out in a "Miss Hungary" contest because she
was underage, did win the part of a soubrette in
a Viennese operetta. Her stage name was her
real one, Sari, though everyone called her
Zsa Zsa. ("Miss Austria," that same year, was
a nineteen-year-old named Hedy Lamarr.)

The Gellert Hegy villa: when it was time to split up, there were 25 Oriental rugs to divide between them ("Vilmos knew I really meant divorce when I packed the crocheted Richelieu tablecloth").

I laughed in spite of my predicament. "That was the night we both went to the theatre and by prearrangement you were also there hiding behind black glasses and sitting in the mezzanine smiling down at me."

"Yes," laughed Zala out loud. "And what a romance you and I are really having! I don't think anybody in the whole world, including Vilmos, would ever believe that this love affair of ours is purely platonic!"

"You're right that Vilmos would never believe this. The time you sent me those roses, just that morning Vilmos had bought an armoire for the servants who were complaining they needed another closet. That same day before lunch you had sent me a bouquet of about four dozen long-stemmed roses . . ."

"Fifty. There were fifty exactly."

"Okay, fifty long-stemmed roses. They arrived with your card in them and two seconds later Vilmos arrived for lunch. I quickly stuck this huge box of fifty roses into the servants' room because never ever does Vilmos visit the servants' quarters. I didn't think he even knew where it was. Suddenly, in walked Vilmos and right to the servants' room to ask 'How is the armoire?' Then he looked around and he barked, 'Who sent such roses? They're for you!' he screamed at me."

"Why did I ever send them?" Zala moaned, holding his head.

"I didn't have time to destroy the card. In fact, I hadn't even seen the card yet. Naturally Vilmos pounced on it and bellowed, 'A man sends such flowers only for after lovemaking!' "

"It should only have happened," mumbled Zala.

I then spied two policemen coming toward us. "Go. Please go. I kill myself if he knows you were with me."

Zala kissed my hands and disappeared. I went to the police station all alone, in tennis clothes and bright blonde hair. I faced this young police officer at the desk. "It seems I had a little accident," I began, smiling as charmingly as I could while still retaining as helpless a look as I could.

"Oh, I certainly am sorry about that, Miss," he replied.

"Not Miss—Madame," I corrected him and then, fearful that he'd make me too old, I hastily added, "But only brand new married."

"I certainly am sorry about that, Madame," he smiled again, looking down from the high desk.

"Could you not come down from that throne, sir?" I said. "I can not see you up so high."

He obligingly climbed down. "There, is that better?"

"Oh, yes, much better, Captain," I said, and proceeded to give him a quick outline of what happened.

"Unfortunately," he explained, "I do not have the power to take care of this business. I am not the captain."

My smile became a bit thinner when I realized I might be wasting it; but since he was the only one there, I thought it couldn't hurt so I started up again. "But can you not help me anyway?"

I was sure he was so flabbergasted with my beauty and my perfume that he could not resist. "Can you not say," I suggested, "that you were looking out the window when the accident happened and you saw that I was alone in the car and nobody else was there? Please, if my husband finds out what I have done, he will kill me. If anybody finds out what you have done, you can only be arrested." I put my right hand on his arm and then I thought if one would be good then two would be better and so I put both my hands on his arm. Please?"

"Okay," he sighed. "But I can really be arrested for swearing falsely."

Oh, I was so happy. The newspapers came out with a story that the beautiful Mrs. Gabor had a little car mishap and the mysterious man with her disappeared as though by magic and that a police officer swore she was alone and was held for questioning, but was freed when nobody could actually prove Mrs. Gabor had anyone else with her in the car at the time of the incident.

I went home and again I was lucky. I caught a sore throat. Late that night after Vilmos read the papers he stormed at me, "I will wait until you are better because, after all, you are the mother of my children and I cannot kill you now with this sore throat. But when you are well I plan not only to kill you but also your mother, your sisters, your brothers-in-law and your nieces and nephews. It is going to be genocide."

I kept the sore throat as long as I could and, somehow, I survived the experience. The next time I heard about Zala, who was a sort of crookish kind of fellow, was the day the newspapers wrote that $100,000 had been smuggled out of Hungary and how police were on the trail of a suspect, a man called André Zalabondy, who had also disappeared at the same time. I was not to see him again for many years.

I believe, now that I look back, that it was in these years when I was trying to find my own personality that I first became aware of my vanity. About six o'clock one evening I went out of the house to walk our Scottie dog. Unfortunately I didn't have a leash but Lolita was never on a leash. This beautiful little Scottish terrier always trotted right after me. A policeman, from the mounted regiment, sort of a commanding officer with braid and all, chastised me on the street. "You don't have that dog on the leash and that is against the law, ma'am," he said gazing down at me from horseback. He was very good-looking with just the slightest scar on his cheek. It probably was that he nicked himself with the razor but in my romantic mind it was a sabre cut and it made him even more attractive.

"I apologize," I apologized, "but I just this minute took the leash off."

"Madame, may I have your identification?" He took his riding glove off and reached all the way down.

I had my driver's license on me and I was very proud of such a possession. Grandly, I handed it to him. I was fined five pengös for the misdeed, but this didn't bother me. Later I kept hitting my head and saying to myself, "Stupid. How could you show your license to a strange man? Your age is plainly written out as thirty-two. Why didn't you say you don't have any identification and let him think you're only twenty-five! Stupid, stupid." I realized then how vain I had become. But to my way of thinking women have to be vain. I no longer apologize for my vanity. I accept it.

I had grown tired of Lelle with its quietness, so I begged Vilmos to let us sublet for one season in Siófok, which was where the fun-loving jet set went. I don't know how he even considered it; but the reason I gave was that Siófok was twenty kilometers closer to Budapest and he could get there quicker when he came out. Therefore he allowed me to go and look for a place.

Naturally he didn't let me go alone. He selected my brother's wife, who was dull. He knew he could trust Manci—because not too many men would be willing to go to bed with her.

So to find a place for the following summer Manci and I went to Siófok in the middle of December. The real estate agent gave us a key to an empty house for us to stay overnight and see if we wanted to rent it for the coming season. So, Manci and I were sleeping at the end of a long, black, silent block, all alone. It was a deserted area because in the dead of winter everybody is gone except the few people who take care of the houses. We didn't see a soul and we were very afraid to be alone. It was so deserted that even we were afraid to put the light out.

I blinked at mousy Manci in her long flannel nightie and to shut out the sight of her, I quickly jumped into bed and pulled the covers up over my head. "Don't you want a hairnet?" said Manci. "How can you sleep without one?"

From under the quilts I mumbled, "No, I never want a hairnet. It kills a woman. Who wears a hairnet?"

"I do."

This I had to see. I rolled the covers off my face and there she was with the flannel nightie, bear grease or whatever it was all over her face, and a hairnet which flattened her out completely. "Here I have one for you," she said, handing me also a hairnet.

"All right," I sighed. I figured it was one way to shut her up.

"Since I'm wearing one, too, this way we'll look like sisters instead of sisters-in-law."

I wanted to take it right off after that, but she turned off the small lamp and we went to bed. Maybe fifteen minutes later as we lay still in deep blackness I heard something. "Do you hear something?" I whispered to Manci.

"Yes, it sounds like two people," she whispered. "Like two men."

We lay there rigid, scarcely daring to breathe.

There was a beat then a very small very low, "Me, too."

I rolled over next to her and we hugged one another very close. I hated her, but I went very near to her in the bed and we clung together. "You're right," I said into her ear. "It is two people stepping."

We were afraid to death and quaking and just when I heard the steps the loudest and figured sure they were going to break into the room, I quick took my hand out from under the covers and grabbed off my hairnet. I was facing death, yet I knew I wanted to face it without a hairnet.

After the rustling sounds of me scratching around in bed taking off my hairnet, the house became still again. The two men or whoever they were disappeared.

When we were safe in my warm cozy home the next night, Manci told to Vilmos, "We were sure we have to die. Jancsi only took off her hairnet and fluffed up her hair."

I am like that. If I am sure I have to die, then I will die pretty.

I admit also something else, and that is that I always knew I would become famous, I knew something incredible would happen with my daughters. I did not believe from such a bitter marriage I could bring forth three such unbelievable daughters without something would happen.

The next time Zsa Zsa came home from Madame Subilia's she was much more grown up than when she'd left nine months earlier. When I'd kissed her good-bye she had been a pretty child but still in that nondescript, lumpy state which mothers lovingly label baby fat. In other words what she had were lumps not curves.

She arrived on a Saturday morning and Vilmos and I were at the train station in Budapest. Although she was in a heavy sweater and a pleated skirt, it was obvious she had improved.

I nudged Vilmos as she stepped onto the platform. "Look, many changes have taken place."

As she rushed towards us, he stared. "Is she wearing makeup? There is a smoother complexion than I remember."

Zsa Zsa hugged us and kissed us and there was a sophistication about her, a new sparkle in her eyes, a new tweezed arch to her eyebrow and my prayers had been answered—the bump in the back of the pleated skirt and the lumps in the front of the sweater had all eased into curves.

I could not contain my excitement. "Vilmos," I exclaimed, "she is now a beauty." He hugged her. "Naturally. She is my daughter isn't she?" He smiled, then quickly added, "But now the problem is she was expelled from school . . ."

"Not expelled," I corrected him as I directed the porter to put the baggage into our Mercedes. "Asked to leave, yes, but expelled, no."

"It is not that I wasn't intelligent, Papa," put in Zsa Zsa. "I had a flair for languages and learned to speak English, German, and French without having to work too hard."

"Then why did Madame Subilia ask you to leave?"

"It was so much discipline and convention and psalm singing," I explained. "Too much for our little beauty."

"Yes," added Vilmos. "And Zsa Zsa was only advanced in such courses as sneaking out and going to parties, reading grown-up books, and wearing pretty clothes."

"But Papa," pleaded Zsa Zsa, "you must become more modern. Eyebrow plucking, cosmetics, and dates are considered normal for a teen-age girl. Papa, you are very behind the times."

"Enough of this talk," Vilmos climbed into the car. "I will not have my daughter acting as a loose woman!"

"Loose? I am fifteen and I have never even had my first date with a boy!"

"Don't worry," I consoled her, "there is plenty of time for that." An idea was formulating in my mind. My Zsa Zsa was going to take my place in the world. Was she not almost as beautiful as I had been at this same age?

Driving home I felt a warm glow. I no longer resented my years with Vilmos. I knew now what I had to do. Aloud I said, "You will become an actress, we'll make it happen."

"Oh, yes, Mama," breathed Zsa Zsa rapturously. "In Switzerland everybody said I should be a film star because I was so beautiful."

"An actress," spat Vilmos. "Again with the desire to be an actress."

"Oh, but Papa," begged Zsa Zsa putting her arms around his neck in the car, "I want desperately to be in the theatre and show business."

"And so you will," I said firmly with the plan already evolving in my mind.

When we pulled up to the house, my younger sister was waiting for us. "How pretty Zsa Zsika has become," mused Rozsie.

I pulled Rozsie into my bedroom and shut the door. "Rozsie, darling," I began, "have you been reading *Theatrical Life?*"

"Of course," she said, taking a bonbon from the box of chocolates at my nighttable.

"Did you read about the 'Miss Hungary' contest which is now going on?"

"Of course. All of Budapest is waiting to find out the results of the contest."

I took a deep breath. "I am going to enter Zsa Zsa in the competition."

Rozsie nearly choked on the chocolate. "That is impossible, Jancsika. The contest has been going on for weeks and is almost over. Tomorrow is the finals."

"It is not my fault that Zsa Zsa has been out of the country and unable to enter earlier."

"But you cannot just enter her at the last minute."

"I am going to."

She knew I was serious. She sat down on the edge of my chaise longue, folded her hands in her lap, and asked me quietly, "How, Jancsika?"

"I will figure out a way."

"Two years before you tried with Magda and didn't make it."

"Magda at least made the top five."

"Ten, you mean. The top ten she made."

"Five."

"Ten."

"All right, so it was ten. But she was not talented and not even interested. Zsa Zsika is *interested*," I said.

"Very well." Rozsie stood up. "Let us enter her and see what the little monkey can do."

I ran to the telephone and called the man running the contest, Incze Sandor. I explained to him that my daughter had just arrived. "I can't help that," was his whole comment. "The contestants all sent their photographs months ago!" I decided not to let this little rebuff put me off. "Come, Zsa Zsika," I announced, "we are off to the hairdresser."

"For what, *Nuci?*" asked Zsa Zsa, who had no inkling of why she was being shoved into a beauty parlor for the first time in her life. A mixture of egg and lemon made her dark blonde hair lighter; a style Zsa Zsa liked from a movie magazine completed her head. She got the works. A facial, eyebrows reshaped, nail polish with an exotic name.

Between applications of face packs, she stared at me. "Don't be afraid. Leave everything to me," I said and kissed her.

The next problem was what to wear. Grabbing my new star by the hand, I dragged her to Magda's closet. "When Magda tried out for this contest two years ago she wore a long black rose print taffeta dress with a big skirt and a tight waist."

With the mirrored reflection of this fitting dress which hung on her a little like a nightgown, Zsa Zsa was overcome by fear. "Oh, *Nucika* . . . I don't know. . . ."

I called Fraulein. "Make the skirt a little shorter," I ordered her.

Fraulein got down on her knees and began pinning it around.

"Shoes," I muttered. I dug into Magda's closet again and found the matching high heels. My child the star put on her first pair of black satin high heels.

I sat on the floor surveying her from afar. "Okay, now. Walk." Bravely, Zsa Zsa struggled to keep her balance.

"Back and forth across the room. Walk. Go." And back and forth dutifully marched my child star while I coached her from the sidelines on how to walk gracefully and smile even though her feet hurt.

With her head, her face, her nails, her eyebrows, her body, and her feet all alert, I told her to put her mind to rest. "Okay, now, go to bed and sleep quickly because we have a lot of things to do tomorrow. Tomorrow morning you are going to compete in the Miss Hungary contest. The judging will be in the Grand Ballroom of the Hotel Royal at eleven o'clock."

"In the morning? Sunday morning?"

"Yes, but you will have plenty of time because I will wake you at six. Now don't give it a thought. Go to sleep."

"Oh, but *Nuci,*" she whimpered. "I am afraid . . . I don't think that I. . . ."

"Nonsense, Zsa Zsika. It is just that you have just come back from Madame Subilia's and you aren't yet adjusted to glamor and excitement. You just think about what you will win. It is advertised that when somebody wins they will get the chance to go for the larger Miss Europe crown. Now you just think about that . . . and go to sleep. . . ."

"But, *Nuci,* how can I think about that and go to sleep at the same time?"

I turned around as I was about to shut the door. "In that case I will think about it and you go to sleep."

That evening after everyone was asleep, I crawled out of bed since my eyes were wide open. Over a glass of warm milk and a plate of sausage, I tried to figure out the best way to handle the situation. Vilmos woke up and came looking for me, grumbling because I had disturbed his sleep. He sat down in the kitchen with me and, in between grumbles, finished my plate of sausage.

"I will not have my daughter put on display," he growled. "This whole idea is foolish. I read in the newspapers that contestants have to be at least sixteen. Zsa Zsa is only fifteen."

I waved aside his objections. "Please, despite these technicalities I feel this is the beginning of an exciting life for my daughter. Let us understand, Vilmos, that while you have denied me my life of stardom you cannot stand in the way of my attempts to see that our girls get a chance."

Poor Vilmos. He gave in out of sheer tiredness.

When we arrived at the hotel ballroom the next morning, the finals were already down to the last five. "Oh, *Nuci,*" trembled Zsa Zsa, teetering nervously on her high heels. "I am so very afraid of this contest."

I could not then worry about Zsa Zsa's nervousness. I had enough of my own. I pulled her off into a corner, smeared a little rouge on her cheeks and instructed her. "Now, remember you are more beautiful than any of those girls out there. And do not forget that you are a Gabor. Walk slowly and keep your head to the judges and smile. Keep smiling. Always smiling. Even if you are falling—smile!"

I left Zsa Zsa propped up in the corner on her high heels and rushed up to a man and woman who looked as if they were in charge. "Please," I said, "you have to put my daughter on stage for the contest."

They glared at me as if I were crazy. "Impossible," they said. Another man lounging in the wings took a look and yawned, "Oh, what's the difference. Put her on."

Buoyed by this I quickly grabbed a card on a table with a crayoned number on it: 146. I pinned it onto my daughter's shoulder, pulled her to the entrance of the stage where she nearly fell because of those damn high heels, and while she was still in her daze I pushed her into the middle of a line of nervous, tittering girls. It was the last second. How I had the nerve I don't know. I stood backstage and watched my radiant daughter, with the mass of newly tinted red-gold hair tumbling around her face, parading on stage in front of judges wearing purple sashes. Before I knew it there were only three contestants left.

The room was only half full because the judging was strictly for the trade and press people. I wanted not to be hiding myself behind the curtain. I wanted to go out front and mingle with the people and start the applause for my child, but I could not because there were no private people present. There were only judges out front. Everytime I caught Zsa Zsa's eye I would beam encouragement and stage whisper, "Smile. . . ."

Everything happened very rapidly. Now they must choose between three girls . . . big applause for Zsa Zsa . . . now they must choose between the two who are left, Zsa Zsa and another girl. I was wringing my hands anxiously backstage waiting for the results and trembling when someone rushed up, grabbed my hand, and cried excitedly, "Congratulations, Mrs. Gabor." Another announced, "Your daughter just won first prize."

"You mean my daughter has been selected 'Miss Hungary'?" I asked.

"Yes, and as the winner she gets the thousand dollar prize plus ten beautiful dresses."

"What about the voyage?" I said nervously. "Does she get the voyage?" That's what I wanted most—the chance for excitement, the chance to be in show business, the chance to get away from Vilmos.

"Yes, she will go to France with a chaperone to enter the Miss Europe contest," called back whoever it was rushing off.

I couldn't believe it. I cannot tell you how I felt. I hardly had time to wipe the tears of joy from my face before Incze Sandor, the magazine contest organizer, his face set in a hard look, marched directly up to me. "I am very sorry, Mrs. Gabor. Your daughter did not win. She is the first runner-up."

"But why?" I lost my poise entirely. "She is the most beautiful. A blind man could see that!"

"Mrs. Gabor," he said coolly, "your daughter came in second. That's that. Your method of entering the contest was highly unorthodox. Not only that but we have discovered your daughter is also underage."

People were rushing up to me and shaking my hand and hugging me. "Congratulations . . . your daughter is the queen . . . best of luck . . . Sari Gabor is the new Miss Hungary. . . ."

"No she is *not*," snapped Sandor. "However, we will give you a consolation prize of a bottle of perfume."

I saw my Zsa Zsa, a teen-ager, the most beautiful in Hungary, standing off to a corner, totally bewildered, with photographers snapping her picture. Others were hollering, "No, no, it is the other one" and everything was swirling around her.

"Big deal," I spat.

"What more do you want?" angrily demanded Sandor, standing nose to nose with me against a wall. "She wasn't even legitimately entered and we are willing to declare her a runner-up."

I glared at the tall, dark-eyed girl who was now declared the winner. I was beside myself with anger. "There is no doubt that my daughter should have won. She got the biggest applause, the judges voted for her, the press is on her side because they are still even now taking pictures of her so it is obvious *they* want her."

"She is first runner-up," he said icily. "A consolation prize of a bottle of perfume."

I hollered at him, "I don't want the perfume and neither does she. I want *everything* for her. You have cheated me. I will never forgive you."

I broke down in tears. Again I had lost a career.

By morning the whole episode had made the front pages. There were articles about how Zsa Zsa's beautiful mother was upset. There were pictures of Zsa Zsa and the winner, a girl named Klarika, whose mother was an actress, which made the whole thing an even worse pain for me. Most of the reporters were on our side. One commented this was the first time in history that a girl was unhappy because she was not older! Another talked about the vicious rumors circulating backstage that I had used bribery. That the judges had been reached. That they had all been at a party at my mother's home the night before and hobnobbed with the society of Budapest and were therefore influenced. Everyone agreed Zsa Zsa was the most beautiful and should have won.

I learned later that Incze Sandor had not wanted Zsa Zsa to win. His was not a very large magazine and didn't have so very much money. The winners had to travel to France with a chaperone. He had selected a writer named Guti Borske as the chaperone to accompany Klarika because Borske was a well-known journalist and her own magazine was going to pay her expenses. With Zsa Zsa, he knew I would have insisted on going, which I certainly would have, and he would have had to pay that money and he didn't have it.

The following Saturday after the contest, I was strolling along Rákóczi Ut. As I passed the big movie house, the Urania, a friend of mine, the director of the movie house, called to me, "How is the mother of the runner-up Miss Hungary?"

I walked nearer to be friendly and he said, "I called to you because I thought you might like to know that we are going to be having a big talent contest on our stage and the winners will go on to compete in Vienna."

Here was another opportunity. "When is this contest?"

"Tomorrow. I thought maybe you'd like to bring your daughter here and let her enter the contest. If her talent is as outstanding as her beauty she's sure to win."

"Oh, thank you, thank you," I pumped his hand up and down. "Thank you." I ran down the street like a mad woman. Such an opportunity could not be lost. This was the chance Zsa Zsa needed. How could I do this by tomorrow? But of course I had to do this by tomorrow.

My mind was a whirl. I passed one of the sidewalk cafés and sat down to have a drink of *fekete*, black coffee, to think over the situation. Suddenly my heart stopped. I had been so excited I really hadn't given much thought to exactly what the director had said to me. "If Zsa Zsa's talent is as outstanding as her beauty she is sure to be a winner."

Talent? What talent? Zsa Zsa couldn't sing. She couldn't dance. She had never acted. She could barely walk. To say the least, she was not an accomplished pianist. My God! What could she *do?*

I ordered another *fekete* and took hold of myself. I remembered a movie a few weeks before in which the leading lady who was not noted for her ability but rather for her personality had done a little song and dance dressed in a soldier's outfit. So if Zsa Zsa is not a great artist, she will be a personality! She will look sweet on the stage, perform a little number, and surely enchant the judges. I left the café and went looking for a shop where they sold costumes and uniforms. There was nothing frivolous and pretty and gay you could not get in Budapest.

Thirty minutes later, I had for Zsa Zsa a toy soldier suit. Carrying this big box under my arm, I entered our house and in a trance walked right past Vilmos. I put the box in the girls' room and went to look for Zsa Zsa. Vilmos just stood and stared. He knew me well enough to know something was brewing. I found Zsa Zsa in the back of the house talking with Eva. Taking her by the hand, I led her to my room and shut the door behind me.

"Zsa Zsika, I have wonderful news for you. Tomorrow at the movie house they are having a very big talent contest. The top winners get a trip to Vienna to compete in the Austrian-Hungarian contest. Isn't that thrilling?"

"But, *Nuci*, what would I *do?*"

"There is nothing to it," I answered. "I have it all worked out. First of all, I brought you a darling costume and tonight I will teach you a little song and dance. By tomorrow you will be a sensation!"

"*Nuci*, I am afraid. I cannot do anything."

"You will sing."

"I cannot."

"I will teach you."

"I am afraid."

"I am not. I am confident. Besides, this is important to me. Another besides is that you are pretty so why should they not adore you. You will do the march of the toy soldiers because it is perfect for someone who does not have too much talent. It is just a little movement."

"All right, *Nuci,*" she said softly, "show me what I must do and I will try."

I got the soldier's uniform and put it on her. She looked marvelous.

"Do not worry," I told her. "We have plenty of time. I have one whole night to put you into shape."

I was the whole night dancing and singing. I sat at the piano with my poor child. Her entire future career was to depend strictly on what she learned from my piano playing. Zsa Zsa had picked out the notes of the song she was to sing. She learned rapidly but couldn't carry a tune very well. After she memorized the song, I showed her the dance steps I remembered from the movie and what I did not remember I made up. Long after she had finished rehearsing and had gone to bed, I sat up worrying. She wasn't very good, this I knew.

The next morning, I quick rushed over to a voice teacher. "In the short time allotted to us all I can do is give her one fast voice lesson." said the teacher.

"Okay," I said. "I figure she needs so much help that how can it hurt?" During the lesson I closed my eyes and visualized her on stage looking beautiful and singing. If not all on key, at least sweetly. The whole picture was so charming it removed all doubts.

That evening there were several winners. Two won for poetry. One for drama. Two got bronze badges for singing. The audience gave Zsa Zsa a nice round of applause. And the judges told me how pretty she was and when the final results were in Zsa Zsa had won nothing. She had come in, as I remember, in eleventh place. They gave her a piece of paper signifying she had been a contestant plus a consolation prize of a wooden plaque. The winner of Zsa Zsa's category, an illegitimate child who is now a 200-pound hausfrau, had won the trip to Vienna and my beauty had a wooden plaque.

One of the judges was Joe Pasternak, who later became a famous Hollywood producer. Even in those days Pasternak knew talent and *no* talent when he saw it. "Your daughter," he told me privately, "is beautiful. Nothing more."

The judges had voted her out of the winners' circle, but they had not seen the last of my little girl! As we drove home from the contest I talked to Zsa Zsa calmly and encouragingly. I did not want her to feel I was disappointed. She had done her best. She had tried. I could not expect any more. So I couldn't make a Sarah Bernhardt out of her, there was no use getting upset!

"There will be other contests, *Nuci,*" she said. Then taking my hand in hers she squeezed it. *My daughter was trying to console me!* She had courage, I saw that. No matter what the future held, she would never be defeated, this I saw too.

The top three winners of the talent contest were to leave Budapest for Vienna the following week to compete against winning talent from Austria. The morning after the contest, while my husband was trying to drink his coffee in peace, I interrupted the silence. "Vilmos, I think I will take a little trip to Vienna this weekend. Since Zsa Zsa is not in school, she might as well come along."

Vilmos put down his cup and looked at me. During our married life I was never permitted to travel alone.

"Jancsi, there is absolutely no reason for you to go to Vienna. If you want to go shopping, I'll give you extra money and you can go to stores here. Vienna is definitely out."

I controlled myself by stirring honey and thick sweet cream into my bowl of kasha. Without looking up at him I said firmly, "Vilmos, I cannot wait. I am going to Vienna *this* weekend to enter Zsa Zsa in the talent contest. The biggest producers and directors from all over Europe will be there. I have a feeling something good will happen. I am sure some very important person will discover Zsa Zsa. We have to give her this chance."

Vilmos was in a hurry to leave for his office. At the front door, he turned and said, "All right, Jancsi, you and Zsa Zsa can go. But you must promise me if she does not do well this time, you will stop trying to make her something that maybe she is not meant to be."

All week long I prepared for our trip. It never once dawned on me we would be unwanted! The only difference between my daughter and those who had won the contest was that they got their way paid to Vienna while we had to pay for ourselves. I spent the next day and night with the dressmaker to get a few gowns to add to Zsa Zsa's not very exciting wardrobe.

In Budapest everything was done on a leisurely basis. A lady of fashion didn't order a dress and expect to get it in a few days. The ritual was to look through the latest magazines from Paris, then rip pages out, then take them to the favored seamstress, saying, "I want the neckline of this with the skirt of this with the sleeve of that."

This time there was no time. Within 72 hours I had ordered, selected, and brought home three new dresses for Zsa Zsa.

Zsa Zsa and I and our many pieces of luggage climbed into my Mercedes and started off for what I thought was going to be a little weekend in Vienna.

3 Vienna is only around a hundred miles from Budapest, but it's another world, another culture, another kind of excitement. Many times before I'd made the trip by river steamer. This time, I drove. It was early July when we left, a bit warm, but we were too excited to care. What difference did temperature make when one was surrounded by the beauty of Hungary's mountains, purple with flowers and trees? Who paid attention to such a trivial thing as heat when one could drive along the banks of the Danube and watch the lights from tiny villages begin peeping through like baby stars? When we arrived at the outskirts of Vienna, once again I breathed deeply to get my fill of the scent of the pines mixed with the fragrance of blossoms and I looked, awed as always, at the magnificence of the Vienna Woods.

Vienna had its own unique magical quality. Vienna, with its many outdoor cafés and elegant shops, its museums, its theatres, its magnificent opera house. Vienna, the city where my Mother was born and spent her girlhood. Vienna, the city where the waltz was born, where there was enchantment in every breath of air and delicacies on every table. Is it any wonder I looked to this city for a sign that my daughter's future would be bright?

At the Grand Hotel I sent Zsa Zsa's soldier suit out to be pressed. Although the soldier routine had not been an overwhelming success in Budapest, perhaps in Vienna it would bring us luck. Really I didn't have much choice. Zsa Zsa knew that routine by heart and there was no time to prepare anything else.

We had dinner sent up, then I made phone calls to check on the details of the contest. The final round, I learned, was scheduled for the following morning. I ran hot water in the tub, sprinkled in an extra quantity of bath oil, and told Zsa Zsa to lie down in the warm water and relax. I did everything to keep her calm, which she already was, while I raced around like a wounded chicken. While Zsa Zsa was complaining on the outside that she couldn't sing, she was excited on the inside. I had purposely tried to make it so not wanting her to see how important all of this had become to me. After her bath, I helped set her hair and then, tucking her into bed, I turned off the lights. She fell asleep almost immediately, while I paced up and down the other room thinking about the events of the following day.

92

Well, my daughter the star was not good in the contest in Budapest and she was not good in the contest in Vienna. Again the audience applauded her warmly. Again the judges told me how lovely she looked. There were two differences. In Budapest, Zsa Zsa was given a wooden plaque. In Vienna, Zsa Zsa came in twelfth and was given only a piece of paper.

She was crying because she hadn't won and I would never let on how badly I felt so I bubbled, "Come on Zsa Zsika, dry your tears. We will go to the party. Going up in the elevator early this morning before you woke up I overheard some people talking about a party to be given in honor of the contest winners later tonight."

"But I am not a winner." The tears began again.

"So what? You were not even supposed to be a contestant."

"How can we go to a party if it is only for the girls who won?"

"Take a nap," I said, "because we have a big evening ahead of us. I have heard that every important director and producer not only from Vienna but from as far away as Berlin has been invited."

"In that case I will take my nap."

I reached for the phone and called one of the contest officials. "I wish to thank you for being so sweet to my daughter and myself, Herr Direktor," I began.

"It was my pleasure, Frau Gabor," he replied.

"I know my daughter did not win anything, Herr Direktor, but I understand everybody is going to a big celebration this evening. Could you be so kind as to send us an invitation so we may join in congratulating the winners, too?"

"Of course, my dear lady. How could a request like that be refused?"

An hour later a messenger came to our door bringing a personal invitation from the contest committee. Before Zsa Zsa woke from her nap I had already been down to the desk to arrange for hiring a carriage. I told the concierge, "Money is no object. You must find for me an especially beautiful coach." I wanted us to make a grand entrance in the back of a carriage drawn by a horse decorated in gold braid.

I didn't know how this was going to help Zsa Zsa's career but I knew I wanted it. Fortunately I had money to pay for it, too.

The party was in a wonderful little Viennese suburb called Grinzing, a village famous for its vineyards. The tiny town was one of the biggest wine-making centers in Austria. Throughout the village were little places where one went to eat and drink *Heurige,* the new wine. The cafés were gaily decorated. Waiters and waitresses were dressed in colorful peasant outfits.

Dressed to the teeth, Zsa Zsa and I entered our fancy hired carriage and started off for Grinzing. At the café where the party was being held, there were people everywhere laughing, singing, eating, drinking. Also, I think there was a little gambling going on in one of the side rooms. Zsa Zsa and I sat down at a table. She couldn't turn her head fast enough looking at the goings-on.

I, too, glanced around. Everyone at the other tables looked important. I had no idea who anyone was but I did recognize one person. She was the nineteen-year-old beauty queen of Austria and she wore a diamond tiara and she was the most beautiful thing I'd ever seen. Her name was Hedy Lamarr. After we had been there for about an hour, the strolling quartet took time out for a glass of wine. The men I'd noticed running back and forth to a side room with heaps of shiny coins in their hands even sat down and forgot the gaming tables for the moment. There seemed to be a lull in the activities. The time was ripe!

"Zsa Zsa," I whispered, "Get up and start singing and dancing. Quickly!"

She looked at me in protest. I jabbed her in the rib with my elbow. "Zsa Zsa, this minute! Get up and sing that song I taught you."

Zsa Zsa stood up. I pushed the chair in front of her, boosted her onto it and then helped her climb to the top of the table.

Her voice wasn't very loud so I started singing along with her. Actually I was doing most of the singing for her. I had a good voice and I loved to sing and I had to face the fact that while my child the star looked like an angel her voice was not too good. A hush came over the café. Everybody was watching Zsa Zsa. I was too excited to be embarrassed.

I sat singing and clapping my hands in rhythm to Zsa Zsa's little dance steps. Perhaps I sang and clapped extra loud to encourage my daughter, who I could now honestly tell friends had appeared professionally at the Grinzing in Vienna but, whatever the cause, for the first time I saw a new side of Zsa Zsa. Her fright had disappeared as she sang and whirled on the tabletop.

While Zsa Zsa was still "entertaining" on the table, two men came towards us. I looked at them and almost fainted. I recognized the one with the black hair and the widow's peak as the most famous opera singer of the day, Richard Tauber. Coming over to where I was sitting they bowed from the waist and introduced themselves. The other gentleman turned out to be Hubert Mariska, one of Vienna's most illustrious theatrical producers and directors. Following closely behind them was another whose face seemed familiar, too. He kissed my hand and said, "How do you do, Madame. I am Franz Lehár."

The blood rose in my cheeks. No wonder his face was familiar. His picture had been in papers and magazines for years. Franz Lehár of *The Merry Widow* was one of the world's most famous composers. I couldn't believe my eyes. Surely I was dreaming that these three men were standing quietly, all watching Zsa Zsa dancing and singing on top of the table. My young daughter, unaware of the importance of her audience, calmly finished her routine and then, forgetting to act grown-up, jumped off the table and onto the floor and plopped herself into her chair with as much poise as a three-year-old.

I heard Herr Kammersänger Tauber, in his gentle, musical voice said to Mr. Lehár, "My God, Franz, this is the girl we've been looking for! This is Violetta."

Lehár nodded.

Tauber then turned to Mariska and said, "Hubert, look at this girl. She's so exciting, so animated, so full of life. Our troubles are over!"

Mr. Mariska nodded.

Tauber continued, "Gentlemen, we have found our little soubrette!"

Then they ordered tall, thin tumblers of heavy wine, sat down at our table and everyone started talking at once. Mr. Tauber explained, "I have recently composed an operetta called *The Singing Dream.* It is being prepared for production and, of course, I will play the lead."

"I have been helping my friend Tauber with the musical scoring and also making casting suggestions," said Mr. Lehár. Mr. Mariska said, "I am to direct the production which will be staged at the famous Theatre an der Wien."

"The whole show is ready to go into rehearsal except," smiled Mr. Tauber, "that we have been searching for weeks for the right female to be the soubrette. The part is an important one. In the play the girl is the sixteen-year-old daughter of an American millionaire who has come to Europe with her family. She is to arrive on her family yacht just in time to complicate the plot. . . ."

In the midst of the discussion, Joe Pasternak came over with his protégé, who had been one of the top winners in both the Budapest and Vienna talent contests. She was not only pretty, she was also an outstanding singer. Her, I didn't need. I also didn't need Pasternak because he recalled Zsa Zsa's "performance" in Budapest. Aghast that my daughter was being considered for this part in a production with the country's most important stars, Mr. Pasternak pushed for his protégé.

As the evening wore on and my smile wore on, the Messrs. Tauber, Lehár and Mariska became more and more convinced Zsa Zsa was the girl they were looking for. I almost died right at the table when Mr. Mariska finally said, "Mrs. Gabor, please bring your daughter to the Theatre an der Wien tomorrow morning at eleven."

I gulped. "Of course."

Tauber, a monocle glittering in his right eye like a German officer, peered intently at his new star. "What is your name?" he asked her.

"Zsa Zsa," I answered for her because my new star was licking her dry lips from nervousness. "Her real name is Sari but the Hungarian actress Sari Fedak was always called Zsa Zsa, so I decided I would call also my Sari by the name Zsa Zsa, too."

"I think I prefer the name Sari," said Tauber.

"We shall have to go through the formality of an audition tomorrow with

Fraulein Sari Gabor," said Mr. Mariska, "after which we shall immediately sit down and discuss terms."

Numbed by it all, I could only mumble, "Thank you. Thank you very much. Thank you. Tomorrow morning at eleven."

On the way to the hotel the clip-clop of my fancy, gold-braided horse's shoes on the cobblestone streets was a much more spirited rhythm than it had been on the trip from the hotel earlier. I cradled Zsa Zsa in my arms, breathed in the heavenly perfume of the night, and said, "Listen, Zsa Zsika, even the horse is happy for us! Listen to him prancing down the street. Even he understands from tomorrow on a new life will begin for you."

Fraulein Sari Gabor was sleepy. Even the excitement could not keep her eyelids from closing. All the rest of the way I sat back in the carriage thinking, "My daughter will be a star. Let those who are jealous say Zsa Zsa Gabor has no talent—*she will be a star!*"

Suddenly all these unbelievably wonderful thoughts drained me. The excitement of the day had been too overwhelming. Sitting in the carriage, as the horse trotted through the outskirts of Vienna, my daughter asleep in my arms, I looked up at a moonlight sky and began to cry. I cried because I was happy. I cried because I was grateful to God that He gave me the courage not to give up. Perhaps, too, some of my tears were for a memory. The memory of a girl named Jancsi Tilleman, who had seen a play at the age of twelve and had vowed that one day she too would be up on a stage.

The theater was dark and totally empty for the audition. The production was to be in German and Zsa Zsa sang one of the three German songs she was to sing. She was not good. A dance instructor coached her for ten minutes and then she stumbled through the routine. I kept applauding and encouraging her. Herr Tauber and Herr Mariska sat there like death. The rest of the cast and the choreographer looked about the same. I couldn't believe it when Tauber said, "I think she'll do, but she certainly needs work, work, work."

They gave us a three-year contract with not much money and not a star billing but we were thrilled. Within an hour I hired dancing, singing, and dramatic instructors and I called Vilmos. He raged at me, "Zsa Zsa on the stage? Are you mad?"

"It is not anymore Zsa Zsa. It is now Sari."

"Zsa Zsa or Sari, I don't give a damn. I want her out of there. Wasn't that beauty contest enough? Now the stage? Jancsi, she's just a schoolgirl!"

It was too late. Sari Gabor was launched and so was I. I put Zsa Zsa in a *pensione* and sent Cuki over to live with her, and the papers in Vienna wrote that there is a Fraulein coming from Budapest to act as special chaperone for this newest star of the Theatre an der Wien. There was my Zsa Zsa already all over the newspapers and she was only sixteen!

August was the rehearsal. Three weeks later in September was to be the opening. The middle of the second week came a call from Vienna. *"Nuci,"* cried Zsa Zsa. "I fall out from the part."

"But you cannot."

"But I did."

"But you have a contract."

"But they said they will let me out very easily."

"But they can't do this to you."

"But they did."

"I come immediately to Vienna."

At the theater I saw my star sitting with her legs around a chair backwards like a man. Her chin was on the back of the chair and she was staring at the stage watching a professional actress who really knew something about singing and dancing. "They have brought over another girl to be my replacement," said Zsa Zsa sadly, never taking her eyes off the girl longer than it took to acknowledge me. "Already, everything is being made in twos. One for me and one for the new actress who is supposedly replacing one. They have half a dozen women sewing right now—right here in the theater making dresses for the other girl."

"What is that?" I kicked a half bottle of red wine at the foot of her chair.

"I think that this calms me down. I know when Hungarians are unhappy they drink wine so I am doing it too."

"Come." I took her by the hand. I found Mariska, the producer, in his office. "We have a three-year contract so what do we do?" I asked.

"I cannot help it," he replied heavily. "She can't sing, she can't dance, she can't act and she can't speak German."

He might have been right on the first three but on the last one he got me angry. "But she speaks perfect German," I retorted sharply.

"Yes, but not Viennese German."

"You did not hire her because she was Viennese but because she was gorgeous."

"Madame," he sighed, "we will make her an understudy. Look, it's no use," he stated flatly. "I know how hard Sari's been working but she needs more time, more stage experience."

At this point the star herself burst into tears. "Even if they want me now I can't go through with it."

I grabbed her and shook her. "Yes you can. If I can get them to take you back you will go back."

Mariska dismissed me. Then I spied Zsa Zsa's partner in the operetta, a comedian named Fritz Steiner, so I said to him, "Well, what happens now?" I didn't know he was not overly crazy about her.

"Look," he snapped, "I'm twenty years an actor. I have been hungry most of these twenty years. I have been hungry more times than I have not been hungry. I have earned this role, this show, this position. How can some rich young girl with no experience be my partner?"

I had a terrible fight with him and everything was very bitter.

The night before dress rehearsal when she was to make her big appearance side by side with the other girl for them to make their decision, I put her in a gorgeous white garden party dress with polka dots and an organza picture hat. They had been made in Budapest and she had brought both with her when she came to Vienna. I put a highlight in her hair with a special rinse. I supervised her makeup. I sprayed perfume over her and I gave her a glass of champagne to make her loose.

When we came to rehearsals the director said, "Oh, beautiful Mrs. Gabor. I see how you sing for her and fix for her. I wish she was as talented as you."

With his nose in the air the choreographer sniffed. "The perfume and the dress are nice but it won't help. The girl has to act, too!"

But you know what? It did help! Mariska whispered to his wife, Lily Kartzog, who was quite a famous lady, "The other girl is so plain next to Sari —the difference is tremendous."

"Sari is unbelievably beautiful," agreed Lily Kartzog. "She takes your breath away."

"Look at my daughter," I crowed, "look at her. Can you imagine her on that stage tomorrow night? The audience will gasp when she comes out."

"Well," shrugged Mariska, "she can't sing and she can't dance and she can't act but at least if she'll keep that pretty face of hers to the audience . . ."

Lily, who was on Zsa Zsa's side, said, "Violetta is a millionaire's daughter and Sari looks it."

I went into my act. "Please Mr. Mariska, let Sari play the part in dress rehearsal tomorrow night. It's only fair. Herr Tauber and you put this entire idea into her head. You can't break her heart now. Give her another chance at dress rehearsal."

"Okay," he sighed. "Tomorrow night. Dress rehearsal."

I put all my energy and my smartness into getting this for Zsa Zsa. I was very extra good to Fritz Steiner, the lousy comedian. Zsa Zsa was an obvious virgin so he let her alone but he propositioned me: "If you go to bed with me I will help her." I wasn't about to lose any help anywhere so I let him kiss me a little and feel me a little and I promised also to go to bed with him a little —but only after the premiere. Meanwhile, I also offered him a two-carat diamond for his pinky and he was not so overcome with his passion for me that he did not accept it.

All the staff and the cast and the experts were deciding between Zsa Zsa and the other one so I worked like a dog. I paid Herr Dr. Schmidt, the cranky conductor who hated Zsa Zsa, 100 Viennese schillings per hour to teach her to sing better. I wanted everyone on my side. I even gave some poor beggar woman whom I didn't know five schillings just to make her happy so all good luck could come to my side. I bribed everyone. I thought my whole life depends on this.

In my room at the Hotel Grand, I worked with her all night. All night Zsa Zsa cried, "But, *Nuci*, I am sure they want the other girl," and I would answer all night, "But you must try. Even in the Bible it says you must try for what you want."

When we finally lay down for a couple of hours I couldn't trust myself to sleep. I stayed awake praying. During rehearsals the next day, I went out and bought bananas and fed them to Zsa Zsa because bananas bring you strength. At the break in rehearsals, I dragged Zsa Zsa backstage. In her dressing room she lay down exhausted while I personally rehearsed her. I was dancing and pirouetting and teaching her and showing her. Mariska went by and stopped to watch at the door which was slightly open. Then he applauded and said to me, "Madame, if only you were fifteen years younger!"

There is a saying that "Az isten is Janos" meaning "God Himself is a Hungarian." At dress rehearsal I finally believed it. In one scene Zsa Zsa was to walk across the stage dragging Steiner, but this particular time she tripped near the end. For some reason Lily Kartzog thought this was cute. She clapped her hands in glee, "But this is adorable. It is so cute," she said. Zsa Zsa got the role.

At sixteen, Sari Gabor was a star—at least in Vienna. The Vienna *Neue Presse* wrote: "And extremely amusing was the charming Sari Gabor." Dr. Rudolf Bolzer in the *Wiener Zeitung* said "Miss Sari Gabor, who played Violetta, bears great promise for the future." They recognized her on the streets. They shouted, "Sari! Sari!"

Opening night she was thronged. When the matinee idol of Europe, that greatest handsome operatic tenor of the world, Richard Tauber, tried to leave backstage with his leading lady, Mary Losseff, with whom he was having a big affair, and he said, "Please make way for us," someone said, "Richard, that big crowd of people is not for you. It's for Sari." She was the biggest thing in town. There were stories of her in the press and stage door johnnies out front and crowds of people lined up backstage.

Even Hungary's head of state, Miklós Horthy, talked about Hungary's newest star. Even Hungary's newest star's father resigned himself reluctantly and ungraciously to her fame.

I came home. But I was restless. Vienna had been elixir to me. Home meant Vilmos.

The outside world was gaiety, excitement, adventure, life. The Vilmos world was death—death to my romantic soul, death to my youth. Vilmos had nobody but me. His mother died early in our marriage. He had not a father or at least I never heard of one anywhere.

Vilmos wanted to cover me, to hide me, to smother me. He was rude. He was domineering. He was heavy-handed. But he gave me everything. I guess I hated him and made everything so hard for myself because I felt cheated.

Although I didn't ever have a lover I did think about one all the time. A woman who has no work must have a lover to take up her extra hours. In my beautiful apartment with my silks and satins I would lie on the chaise longue all afternoon while Vilmos was working and I would die for a lover. I would kiss the pillows. I would rub against the arms. There was too much time on my hands to think. I never had anything to do. A woman who is rich and has nothing to do and is young it is normal that she is restless and she wants love. With the husband she cannot make love in the afternoon and as

101

I later learned afternoon love is the best . . . if only because it is not with the husband!

Thus, I wanted my children always to have romance and always to have men at their feet. When Zsa Zsa was thirteen I had taken her to Pörtschach, a resort in Austria. Some foreign king's mistress, who was about thirty-two and devastatingly gorgeous, was also there. She had a big Rolls-Royce, minks and chinchillas and an enormous 50-carat yellow diamond and because she was the girl friend of this Ahmed Zugu or whatever his name was she was treated as though she were a princess. Only on her table were flowers.

With all this she was alone. She would come to the restaurant and sit all alone to have dinner. The people I was with there were nobody. We were just people from Budapest but my table was gay and laughing and she always looked over enviously.

I had one very good-looking man at my table. He was a nothing, a druggist in Budapest, but he looked good so I teased him, "Go and ask her for a dance."

"Oh, no," he shrank. "I dare not."

I urged him, "You are beautiful looking so you can get away with it. She is very lonely, I'll bet, and she'll be more than happy. Go and try."

She accepted eagerly. And after drinking in the gaiety around me she complimented me. "Madame, when you come into a room you bring life. This whole room was sitting like sticks and stones until you came in." Then she said about Zsa Zsa, "This girl will be one of the most beautiful women in the world someday."

I told her, "I only hope my daughter grows up to be like you."

"Do not envy me," she said softly, "I am very much alone. You were very right to take pity on me. I am a poor, lonely, unhappy person."

Again I told Zsa Zsa. "Never be in a position where you are stuck with someone just because he will take care of you. Better to be successful and independent and take care of yourself!"

Budapest was then the center of Eastern European and Oriental intrigue. There were Gypsies, there were Turks, there were Austrians. The ancient city in which I lived was made for romance. Lovers drank Tokay by the river, spent their passion to fiery tzigane music and embraced to sighing violins. I so yearned to be part of that.

Suddenly, I felt very old. I thought my life is over and now I must just give up and wait for the end. One experience I had brought this to my mind vividly. I went with Magda to Abbazia, which was then a very fashionable resort. We were at the hotel on the ocean. I loved it because there were always shows and music and flirting and entertainment. I was the star of the whole place. Everyone came to my table. "May I have a dance, Jancsi?" "Oh, Madame Gabor, how pretty you look," and so on and so on. I was maybe thirty-three or thirty-four. The most I could have been was thirty-four. Okay, so thirty-five, but not an hour older.

This man, a movie producer, came over to my table. "My name is Fodor," he bowed. I smiled up graciously, "Of course, Mr. Fodor, what may I do for you?" He asked, "May I ask your daughter to dance?"

Oh, I was so hurt. I cannot tell you how hurt I was. Abbazia I had loved always. I decided I would not bring my girls along because they steal the show from me. All right, so maybe this shows I was a bad mother. I only know this was a deep hurt.

Abbazia was such a fashionable place at the time and so popular. I went upstairs that night sick with pain. Every room had a terrace and overlooked the ocean. My terrace was next to that of a beautiful German girl from Graz, whom I had noticed earlier whirling around the dance floor with a blond, beautiful god. They were not married and I was so jealous.

Because her terrace door was open I could hear the knock. "Who is it?" she called. A voice answered, "Kurt, *mein Liebchen.*" *Liebchen* he had called her. I stood there with my ear to the thin glass partition on the terrace. The sound of the door unlatching and then his footsteps and then the sound of the bolt again being thrown. I couldn't stand it.

She had had a lot to drink and she didn't feel well. "How do you feel?" he asked. "*Schlecht,*" she kept repeating in German, "*schlecht . . .* bad."

I heard again the voice of the beautiful blond Kurt, "Here, take this. You'll feel better."

There was no talking for a few minutes and then distinctly came her fuzzy German. "Oh, no. No, I can't. I can't do nothing." Another minute and then, "Oh, I have to vomit."

I could not believe such a waste of so beautiful a blond god and while I was leaning impatiently against my side of the terrace partition, I heard sounds of her going to the toilet. So unromantic, I thought.

The next noise was the bed creaking as she got into it or he got onto it or they both got into each other, and he said, "You must not have so much to drink next time."

From her all I heard was the familiar repeat, "Oy, *schlecht . . .*"

It was very fashionable for a woman to go away alone for a few days. She would go supposedly for her health, for the salt air or the sea breeze or whatever, but really it was to have a change of scenery to hold her until the next time. I was so jealous.

Just as I wondered what was happening I heard a rhythmic rocking and then animal sounds and then her moan, "Ohhh, seventh heaven is nothing compared to this."

I nearly killed myself because of the hurt I had experienced earlier and because I had nobody to make beautiful love with. I wanted romance so badly I cried myself to sleep.

I think perhaps the beginning of the end of my marriage came with my great illness and that all began—as so many other events in my life began—following a bitter evening with Vilmos.

It was the night of the annual Anna Ball at Lake Balaton. For one reason or another I had never been to the Anna Ball before. I was excited about going and by telephone to Budapest told Vilmos about it. "Now, don't disappoint me," I pleaded.

"No, I promise, I will be up on Friday, the night of the ball, and we will go."

I bought a stunning dress in light pink and stockings that were also light pink and were shiny like a mirror since that was the fashion then. I tried the ensemble on ten times before he arrived that weekend.

He arrived late that Friday evening and I was already dressed up in my girdle and bra, high heels, shiny pink stockings. My hair was perfectly coiffed and I was bathed, powdered, and made up.

In came Vilmos with only one idea in his head—to make love. If I refused I was sure it would displease him and he wouldn't take me to the ball. So I took off my girdle, stockings, messed up my hair and my face and went to bed with him. Afterwards he was so tired that he just rolled over and went to sleep. He never took me to the ball.

I sat there and cried. I just stared at his back as he lay sleeping and I wanted to put a knife between those shoulder blades. I thought, "It is worth five years in jail to kill him," but then I was afraid maybe it would turn out to be eight years and that much I didn't want to spend in jail.

All my frustration, my resentment, my hostility, my cheated dreams welled up inside me and I hated him.

The icy chill that developed between us ended up with me suffering a heavy cold. I added to that a sore throat. When the cold finally disappeared I was left with a hoarseness that I couldn't shake. I was also tense and disgusted with my married life. I was a mess.

Reichenhal was a place that smelled of pine and one went there for inhalation. I wanted the air and, also, I wanted to get away from my husband. Janette, who had the idea for me to go, agreed to accompany me. I don't remember how we worked this out but we went just the two of us alone. I remember that I announced to Vilmos late in the night, "I am going to Reichenhal."

"You are asking me or you are telling me?" Vilmos inquired of me.

"I don't care what I am doing with or without your permission. I *am going.*"

Although Janette supported my going to Reichenhal, which, by the way was where Mad King Ludwig of Bavaria killed himself, she warned against my becoming too independent. "I tell you the true story of a friend of mine," she began when we were seated on the train. "This friend, Basha, is very beautiful. She is like you. She was married to a husband who was very jealous."

"Like Vilmos," I muttered.

"One day Basha asked her husband on her knees please let her go with her girl friend to the Italian resort place, Cortina d'Ampezzo, and the husband's friends all said, 'Let her go. Don't show that you die from her.'"

"How long was she there?"

"Two weeks. And she had a marvelous time."

"Lucky thing."

Janette stared out the window. "So she begged him to give her another week. It came about that she was away for four weeks. The first week he called her three times a day. The second week only two times a day. By the fourth week only once a day and then sometimes he would skip one day."

I turned to Janette with my whole body. "What happened?"

"When the calls fell down, she decided it is better to come home and she thought that she would surprise him. Jancsi, this is the worst! Never surprise a lover or a husband!"

"Why?"

"She was the one who got the surprise. She caught him with another woman. Right in the bed he merely said to her calmly, 'Darling, don't make a scandal. We will divorce.' The wife wanted to make suicide but there was nothing she could do. He got a divorce and he married the other woman."

"Is she now happy?"

"Jancsika, you know that in Budapest when a man divorces he has only to give a very little. Remember, Basha was a beautiful, spoiled woman. She had her own house and her own car, and now she has nothing."

"And you say she had been very sure of her husband's love for her."

"Very. But perhaps a woman should never be too sure."

I understood, but the ache inside me was growing nonetheless.

At Reichenhal, the day I checked in I spied a very handsome fellow. "Who is he?" I asked my dining room waiter.

"He is German, but he lives in America. He has come over only to claim his inheritance," said the waiter bending low over my plate.

"He drinks champagne for lunch," I noted.

"He is a millionaire, Madame," said the waiter.

"And so handsome," I sighed.

"I have seen many beautiful women and even two film stars follow in his wake trying to conquer him since he's been here. The other day a society lady came from Graz to try to conquer him."

I didn't dream that I could ever even speak to this god king but the next day I stepped into the elevator and he was the only other passenger in it. Thank God it was an old elevator and creaked down to the lobby very tantalizingly slowly. As the silence built up inside the tiny cage for two floors, he addressed me. "Didn't I meet you in Paris?"

Such an old line, but I was thrilled. By the time we reached the ground floor he had invited me to an outdoor festival that was being held nearby. "I have a sister," I said.

"By all means bring her, Madame," he said.

I went immediately back upstairs floating on air and I told Janette about our invitation. Despite Janette's masculinity and flat shoes he was to her very gallant. The following day, we played cards together and I lost fifty marks. "But suppose I don't have the fifty marks," I teased.

"Then you must shoot yourself in the head," he teased back. He made only a small joke but I would have died for him I was so in love.

The next days we were always together. He told me I was pretty, I was extraordinarily feminine, he kissed my hand but nothing happened. The third afternoon we went for a drive in his sports car. It was very warm and I became hot. Afterwards, we went to this exact town which was made famous by Mad King Ludwig of Bavaria. Part of the scenic sights to see was a salt mine which was deeply far down in the ground and icy cold. I caught a chill or something and I began to feel a little pain within a couple of hours, but I was so overcome with happiness that I put it out of my head.

The fourth day he sent me a short sable coat because I had been chilled. Stunned, I stammered, "I cannot take this." He waved me off. "Then do with it what you will. I've paid for it."

That same day he whispered to me, "Tonight after dinner we will meet in the garden." I knew what this implied and I wanted it so much. I thought, after dinner, I will put on a black peignoir for him and be all ready with perfume in every one of the best places. I planned to float upstairs directly after dinner and change from my street clothes into this peignoir. I had the most elaborate plans carefully laid.

I was just proceeding out the door to dinner when the phone rang and the concierge told me my husband was downstairs. I was wild with disappointment. I looked at Janette, who grabbed the sable off my shoulders and threw it into her room. "If he sees the sable we'll tell him we won it at the Casino," she said. I barely heard her. I was so upset I had turned to stone.

Before dinner I managed to run out quickly and call my god king. I told him hurriedly that I could not see him afterwards because my husband had just arrived. He was angry. He answered only, "Thank you," and put down the phone.

Later that night I saw him at dinner with an English girl who was also a guest. She had a society background, was coolly beautiful and she was only eighteen. Besides that she had a horse of her own. The following morning I was standing at the entrance to the hotel smelling the pine trees and the two galloped by on their horses. They rode so close by me that they almost ran me over and they didn't even greet me. They ignored me totally and they were laughing. He didn't even glance in my direction. This was very bitter for me.

Four days later, when Vilmos had to leave, I was badly suffering rheumatic pains. But I had an even greater pain than the rheumatism. I was truly sick at heart.

It was such an agony to me and to my vanity never to have tasted romantic love that I just kept building it in my mind. I was suffering such pain inside me from the rejection and the loss of what might have become my first love affair that I could not even stand up long enough to dress. Janette dressed me, put my clothes in my suitcase, and she gave the sable to the concierge with instructions to return it. On the train back she read me a newspaper which had a love-story novelette in it. I was crying as she read this. My heart hurt me more than my rheumatism. Janette was even crying. In between her own tears she tried to comfort me. "Please, Jancsika, don't cry . . . don't cry . . ."

Four days earlier, I had been beautiful. I had been in love. Now they carried me off the train in a stretcher.

Vilmos took me to a sanitarium in Budapest. It was very private and very costly. They could no nothing. Then he had me admitted to another one. Nothing. Then another and another and another. I was constantly full of morphine. For one or two hours the morphine would take the pain away but at no time could I admit to being cured.

It was only the searing physical pain which killed the other. So, finally, this mental cancer was burned out of my mind. Vilmos was distraught about my condition. He ran around the streets of the city sobbing and asking everybody, "Can you help my beautiful wife?" Through a business acquaintance he met a dentist who said he had an old doctor friend by the name of Novack who was seventy-five and was, he thought, retired. However, the dentist said, if he wasn't retired and if he was still taking any cases at all, he was positive that this doctor would be the one to help.

My condition was such that I had been dismissed by the last sanitarium because they could do nothing more for me. Day by day my life was spent lying in my own house on my stomach and in such excruciating pain that when the nurses made my bed they would move me on the sheet.

In sheer desperation and not wanting to leave any possibility untried, Vilmos found this old doctor and begged him to attend me. The man came to the house and he gave to me an injection from a very very long needle. It was a needle like for a horse. What it was I don't know but later blessed warmth crept over my body and the pain subsided. With his injections it subsequently went away—and stayed away.

With it went the intensity of the emotions I had toward Vilmos. I no longer hated him. I no longer wished to hurt him. I just knew that I could no longer live with him.

It was along about this time that Vilmos sat upright in bed in the middle of the night. Sitting erect as though there was a poker in his back, he said loudly, "Zsa Zsa—I know suddenly . . . this very night, Zsa Zsa has lost her virginity!"

"Zsa Zsa is well taken care of in Vienna. She has her chaperone. She also has her daily classes at dramatic school. She. . . ."

"I know that this very night," he repeated wildly, "Zsa Zsa is no longer a virgin!"

I heard Zsa Zsa had developed a technique for dropping sleeping pills into her chaperone's nightcap so she could enjoy life a little more. However, I did not argue with Vilmos because I didn't know.

I naturally found out about this love affair with Willi. I heard he was an animalistic, very male-looking Asian with black eyes, gray hair and Eastern features. This was a one-sided love. An older man in his forties and a seventeen-year-old girl with her first crush.

During those few hours when she wasn't with Willi, Zsa Zsa was attending to her career. After *The Singing Dream*, she went to work as Mistress of Ceremonies at a nightclub called Femina in Vienna. She didn't sing. No, really, the truth is she *couldn't* sing. She came out in beautiful dresses and announced the next act.

Alexander Korda, the Hungarian-born film producer, meanwhile wanted her for a play in England. The difficulty was that the British government would not issue a working permit for her. As an outraged mother, I did the only intelligent thing. I sent a letter to King George himself. I also put her photograph in the letter and I said to him, "Dear King, does England want to deny Sari Gabor the right to make a brilliant career? Please answer right away!"

His staff send word back thank you very much but His Majesty the King is a little too busy to worry about things like this right now.

Zsa Zsa was very bitter about this. Also her love affair with Willi wasn't too fulfilling at this moment due to the fact that Willi, who was a little bit married, had gone back to his wife.

Since there was nothing else in view, Zsa Zsa decided very wisely that she might as well get married. The only question was, to whom?

109

Enter into her life Burhan Belge, the diplomat from Ankara who was then Director of Press for the government of Turkey. At my noble Mama's parties were always generals and diplomats. At a party she had given a year earlier she had introduced Zsa Zsa to Burhan. He had been on a mission to Germany and broke his return trip to Istanbul with an overnight stop in Budapest. He was staying at the Turkish Embassy and the Ambassador, Mama's friend, brought him to the party. At that time Zsa Zsa was terribly young and he had jokingly said, "When you grow up I will marry you." Later he saw her onstage in Vienna and noticed she had grown up considerably.

We wanted Zsa Zsa back in Budapest after Vienna and there Kismet threw them together again.

I liked His Excellency. He was my same age. Not too attractive—dark, slight, a little sour-looking—but polished, suave, important, a very smart man. He was a best friend of Hitler. When Burhan came from Ankara to Germany he was a bigshot. He was personally received at the train by Hitler. I saw a photograph of Hitler with all his ministers, with Goering and everybody, and I also saw Burhan there. At this time in 1937 I didn't think Hitler was so bad and so bitter and would kill six million Jews.

Zsa Zsa was not so insanely in love with the Turk, no. She respected him and she knew if she got away from Vilmos, she would then be allowed more in life and so she married him. I told to Zsa Zsa, "Look, my darling, if you marry to Burhan it does not have to be forever. You can always come back to me if you don't like him."

The Turk was a great woman expert. Before Zsa Zsa he had three wives. Zsa Zsa claims she was fifteen when she married him. She was not exactly fifteen. She was more like seventeen. Let's say she was a *good* seventeen!

While Zsa Zsa was partying with the Turk, Magda was marrying the Pole. Oh, Mama was so impressed with me and what I'd made out of my two oldest girls. One was already an Excellency and the other was becoming a Countess.

Magda met Count Jan de Bichovsky through her schoolmate, Sylvia. After graduation from Madame Subilia's, Sylvia was for six months our houseguest. She was an English girl from London and when she went home she then did me the favor of taking Magda along with her for the next six months. On a vacation with Sylvia and another girl friend, Magda met Bichovsky. With none of my children did I exactly have difficulty finding them a husband. Each one made it quick and I was like my mother. She gave dowries fast because she wanted to be free. Instead of dowries I gave my blessings but also just as fast, I, too, wanted to be free.

Magda brought Bichovsky home with her. He was nice looking. He was an aristocrat. She liked him—so okay. They had a brief ceremony at the City Hall and the wedding reception was in our home. I always make our weddings in our home. When I hear mothers make marriages for $12,000 in the Waldorf Astoria, I say to them, "Are you crazy? In half a year she could come back. Better you should buy furniture than to spend money on a wedding that won't last!"

I sent Magda for a wedding present two trucks of antiques. Not $5,000 antiques. $500 antiques. Good copies. The reason I sent them beautiful furnishings is because I'd heard that Count de Bichovsky's castle had been robbed and he was now refurbishing. I also heard that he was a very important count but not such a very rich one.

Six months later, I went to visit them. My first and last visit to Poland. The day I arrived, it was cold. I came down from the plane in Warsaw with a mink coat and a flowered hat with a dotted veil. I had rearranged my hat and my hair for an hour before we landed so I could impress them because I knew Bichovsky's sister and relatives, many old ladies from fine families, would be at the airport.

Deliberately, I was the last off the plane so I could strike a dramatic pose and wave grandly before proceeding down the steps. My veil was thick and long and there was a slight breeze. I struck the dramatic pose all right. I waved grandly and I proceeded down the steps all right. It's just that I didn't get very far. The stewardess, since I was the last one off, had slammed the door of the plane but the wind had blown my veil back through the door so she slammed it on the veil. I walked. My veil stood still. My hat flopped off. My hair blew all over. Ugh, so embarrassing!

In honor of this great glamorous lady who had arrived so grandly, my hotel room was full of pink carnations. It looked like everybody in the family had ordered the same bouquet. I said to Magda, "Now I must send gifts back to everybody."

"What will you send?" she asked.

"Flowers. Pink carnations. I will send the exact bouquets back. I think it would be very economical, no?"

"No," shuddered Magda. "You can't. They will recognize them." It occurred to me my brand new Countess had a very grand standard even if she didn't have such big money.

Eva, who had attended Forstner Girls Institute in Budapest, now announced she was going to put all her education into becoming an actress. Naturally, I liked the idea since it looked to me like the other two were now not going to be actresses any more.

Along came a theatre director who saw this fluffy, creamy-looking angel with the big brown eyes and the platinum hair and told to me, "This beautiful girl must be a star."

"All right," I told him. "When you take over Eva then you can make from her a star."

"Excellent," he beamed. "I will be more than pleased to take her in my hands."

The only problem was that he seemed to want to take her into his hands only at night. When Vilmos heard that Eva can only learn her acting lessons from this man after dark he roared, "No! Absolutely not. The only kind of acting he will be teaching her will be you know what. She must be in by six o'clock every night."

Vilmos was so against it that Eva's theatrical stardom had to be postponed.

Meanwhile, Zsa Zsa called me to say she was coming to Budapest for the big flying day party.

"What is that?" I asked.

"Regent Horthy's three flamboyant, attractive sons have arranged a flying day party."

"What means 'flying day party'?"

"This means that from all over the world VIPs, special guests, celebrities, aristocrats and the Corps Diplomatique are coming in by private planes for this one famous day."

"And you are going?"

"Of course. Don't forget I am now Her Excellency," she giggled. "Burhan is coming, too. The whole world will be celebrating in the magnificent gardens of the King's Palace right in Budapest."

"Not the whole world," I grumbled. "I was not invited. I guess I am not such a big shot. I am only big with doctors and lawyers and wealthy merchants."

"Oh, *Nuci.*" Her voice was husky on the phone. "I wish I could invite you but I have nothing to do with it. There will be the Italian Ambassador, the French Ambassador, Prince Pignatelli . . ."

"What will you wear?"

"There is nothing in this godforsaken Ankara to buy. No good dressmakers and no *haute couture.* So order me a dress for a garden party. I want to wear it with a big white hat."

In the middle of the night of the party Zsa Zsa called: "*Nuci,* we are still at the garden party and afterwards most of the people are going to the Ritz Hotel for supper and the show. *Nuci,* I found the most beautiful young man you ever saw. He's like a Swedish prince. He's tall, maybe six foot four. In the whole world he's the most beautiful man you ever saw. And he has blue eyes and he's blond and . . ."

"So for who is this man?" I interrupted. "For you, for me, for who?"

"Eva," Her Excellency shouted on the phone. "For Eva. You told me she has nobody so tell her to get dressed and go to the Ritz Hotel and stand there and when we come in I can maybe move her in. I want her to meet this guy."

"Is he for a husband or for a date?"

"He will not marry Eva because he is a Swedish doctor from Hollywood but this is good for Eva. She can use a young man to date right now."

Eva was undressed. She had creamed her face and hands and settled into bed with a plate of salami and scallions and a radio blaring dance music.

I put Eva in a beautiful dress, a long Biedermeier dress with a bonnet. I was dying with excitement. I thought, Hollywood! A tall, blue-eyed prince!

"I feel in my bones something big will happen with this, Evika," I said excitedly. "Now, remember, you are just to accidentally 'bump' into Zsa Zsa and her prince."

"How do I do that?" she asked.

"I don't know. You want to be an actress? So—act!"

When we came outside, a neighbor stared at Eva and commented, "She is a little overdressed, no? In the bonnet and long dress she looks a little like a fake porcelain doll."

"So what is wrong in this?" I asked as I hurried away.

Just two days before I had bought Eva this little red German car, a Steyr. It cost 5,000 pengős and looked like a little insect. *Poloska* in Hungarian means "bedbug" and that's what we called it because it was so small. I put her in the car. She was not a good driver. She didn't even have a license so I drove her almost to the door of the Ritz and then I instructed her, "Go slow the next few feet right up to the Ritz. When you get there you sit in the car right at the entrance to the hotel. Don't leave."

"But I am so afraid to do this," Eva wailed. "What will I do if they send me away from the hotel?"

"Don't go," I ordered, giving her the best motherly advice I could.

Sure enough at the Ritz the doorman wanted to take the car away but very smartly Eva spoke up. She told, "No, I am waiting for someone, to pick him up."

I was not the type to stand there and watch. Once I had her all propped up I left. I know the rest of the story by heart though because this I was told a hundred times by Zsa Zsa and another hundred by Eva.

It was all like a fantasy. Zsa Zsa came and saw her sister in the car and ushered her sister into the majestic Ritz lobby, which was full with symphonic music. Zsa Zsa introduced Eva to Dr. Erik Drimmer. The unfoldment was as though it was a dream. They sat down together opposite one another. They didn't say "Hello . . . How are you? . . ." but they were holding hands.

Burhan stared at them. He asked his wife, "Do they know each other from before?"

Zsa Zsa could only shake her head no. She was so ashamed. She stared at her sister and her Swedish doctor. Tears were streaming down both faces. It was love at first sight.

Dr. Erik Drimmer was not rich. He was not then a full doctor. He was a boy studying to be an osteopath. A chiropractor who had taken his training in Hollywood, he was at the party because a millionaire patient had brought him.

This became a big, big love. For the whole three days he was in Budapest they were together. When all the other guests departed he, too, left. They sent letters to one another for a whole year and then he came back.

It was to be a small marriage at the City Hall with the reception in my brother Sebastyen's country place, six miles from Budapest. It was only sixteen people. Sebi's wife, Manci, brought some hearts from the bakery and that was her whole party. The guests went with veils and flowers and I wore orchids and everybody met at City Hall. The only thing is there was no wedding. It didn't go through. They are very particular about things like papers in Budapest and Erik's papers weren't proper.

Oh, such a tragedy. Oh, they were so unhappy. Eva was crying. Not just little crying—she was bitter crying. The finale was there was nothing to do so we still all of us went to the reception at Sebi and Manci's. It was then that Eva lost her virginity. Not at Sebi and Manci's but right after because they were both so unhappy and had been counting the hours until everything would be legal. At least, I think that's when she lost her virginity. I don't know. I know only for sure that somewhere along the line Eva definitely lost it someplace.

Erik could not wait longer so he left for London without marrying her. He had a big job with a wealthy British Jewish couple who had two paralyzed children. His duty was to work with these handicapped youngsters and his payment was $2,500 a month clear because he lived with them. Six months later he telephoned to say all formalities had been completed, he had taken a little apartment, and Eva should come over and they will be married in London.

When Dr. and Mrs. Drimmer stood up to dance at the Savoy Hotel everybody slowly moved off the floor just to admire them. Total strangers clustered about gaping because never had they seen such a good-looking couple. He was blond. She was blonde. He was 6 feet 4 inches, she was 5 feet one. They were so beautiful that tears came to my eyes.

For me it was a time of great rejoicing. It was now 1939 and I was finished with the girls. They were all out of my house. I had one daughter married to a diplomat in Ankara, one daughter married to a count in Warsaw, and one daughter married to a doctor in London.

The moment for me had arrived.

9 I always wanted a divorce but I didn't have money. One reason it had been possible for my husband to keep me chained down was that in my own name I didn't have a penny. Any money I had was only what I saved from what Vilmos gave.

He was smart. He knew that if ever I had money I would leave. It isn't that I *suddenly* wanted a divorce. It's that I ALWAYS wanted a divorce but always I couldn't get one because always I didn't have money.

I so envied my divorced friends and in these days I forever pumped them with leading questions. I met my friend Sonja with my sister Janette and as we shared a Magyar dessert I asked Sonja enviously, "You are newly divorced. You are enjoying your freedom, yes?"

"Yes." Sonja had purple nails and an onyx cigarette holder. I considered Sonja ultrasophisticated.

"How is it with another man?"

"When you have legally your freedom you lose the glamor, the value, the excitement," said Sonja with the smoke curling up around her nostrils. I thought I had never seen any woman as sophisticated as Sonja. "Physical love is good with another man only when you must steal it and test the excitement."

Gray smoke came out again. I was not so very impressed with Sonja anymore. Her smoke was ruining my dessert. "Jancsika," said Janette, putting her arm around me. "I love you. I love also Vilmos. I love the children you have made and the life you have made. I only know that I have seen in your house a huge calendar and I have watched you every day tear off a page and with a big sigh say, 'Oh, one day less to live again with Vilmos.' Only you can make the decision."

An elderly longtime friend came to me with a proposition to invest in a motion picture operation. This meant many trips to Paris with her which I adored because I loved showbusiness, I loved leaving Vilmos and I loved the idea of making money. For my share I had to invest $30,000. Vilmos had five houses. He sold one and gave me the money against his better judgment. I convinced him this would bring in big earnings.

I was six weeks into the business when my psychic sense began working. My father came to me in my dreams and told me this is not a good deal. "Get

117

out of it," commanded Papa. Sure enough I was hit with debts for rental of film, distribution money, hiring of equipment, publicity, and so on.

Vilmos was not too upset because he had laid his half off on a partner. I was upset, though. I had wanted very much a business. I had wanted a means of establishing a little life on my own and earning money.

At the age of forty, I realized I cannot anymore be an actress so . . . what to do with my life. I knew only the jewelry business because my whole family was in it including uncles and cousins and my brother, who was the proprietor of a shop on Andrassy Ut.

I finally threatened Vilmos. "I don't stay with you if you don't give me money for a shop of my own."

There were the usual arguments but Vilmos saw that this was a new me. A determined me. He bought me the shop, decorated it beautifully with mirror and mahogany, and paid everything including the rental at Number 4 Kigyó Utca off Budapest's Madison Avenue. *Utcza* means "street" and this was the most fashionable, the most elegant *utcza* in Budapest. It was situated between Váczi Utcza and Kosut Lajos and I named the shop "Jolie." "Jolie" was written out on white marble and gold.

There were not tables in my shop. Only counters. The gold and crystal objects inside were antiques. Elegant. Expensive. I had twelve girls standing in there selling always.

At Christmas I would maybe increase to fifteen. Jolie's became the most successful jewelry shop in the city. I manufactured and I sold. I produced costume jewelry handmade with the same artistic talent associated with priceless antique gems. My costume pieces were copied after the old court jewels of Hungary.

My shop became a gold mine. Just like Bulgari is known in Rome, that's how well-known I was in Budapest. Jolie's did so well that at holiday time they were standing outside in line waiting until somebody goes out from the inside. So, I hired a policeman for eight pengös to take care that the line was always orderly. It wasn't exactly a line for six blocks but when I put a policeman to the small line the line always grew from four people to fifty. I instructed him, "Bring me in the customers two by two." When there were only four people it was a little difficult for him to have a permanent job, but when people see police they think you're giving things away free and usually this created mobs who flocked over to see why police were there and then even more people came. Everybody said, "Oh, that Jolie is so smart."

My shop did so well I could not believe it. At Christmas I made enough for a year almost. I made so much money that every time I had a large excess I bought a house. Once when I didn't know what to do with the money I bought two houses at one time. I owned five houses in Budapest. I opened another shop around the corner called Crystello and it sold fine crystals and porcelain.

My shops made me rich. The wonderful part of it was that taxes were strictly on the basis of how you lived or what the tax people saw. Somehow I managed to pay very little. When the tax people came to inspect they saw my solitaire from Vilmos and they clucked, "But, Mme. Gabor, you will have to pay extra taxes because we see you have such big diamonds."

"Oh, but this is glass," I said to them. "It is very good imitation."

"You have also servants."

"Oh, but for thirty pengös."

"You have also a Mercedes-Benz."

"Oh, but an old one." I was so charming and so pretty and so smelling good and I always took out my handkerchief drenched with perfume and waved it around so that they were eager to get rid of doing business with me.

Finally, finally, finally, Vilmos consented to a divorce. Why did he finally? Maybe he sensed the inevitable. Maybe he knew it had to happen sooner or later. Maybe he was tired of my unhappiness because I was not a good wife to him ever. Maybe it's that I had become so successful on my own that he knew he couldn't stop me. Maybe it was the morning that I went out and actually rented another apartment and he began to see this was for real.

"Vilmos," I said to him gently that evening. "Vilmos, we will be always good friends after the divorce."

I think it was at this moment that he understood and conceded.

"All right, Jolie," he sighed heavily. From the day my shop opened he and all my friends had begun calling me "Jolie." "I always knew that if you ever had your own money this would happen."

"I know that your secretary Magda has been in love with you for years so now maybe you can be happy with her."

"I will not be happy with my secretary Magda or anybody else ever because I don't love Magda or anybody else ever."

This I could understand because Magda was ugly but didn't mention it because I didn't want to upset anything.

"But why, Jolie? Why do you leave me when you are almost forty? Not anymore a young girl? You will divorce me and where will you go?"

"Don't worry about me. I will have a career and you can go to your secretary Magda."

Vilmos cleared his throat. "Suppose I let you go away and live away but you don't get a legal divorce."

I did not wish to upset him. I needed him.

"Vilmuska, with the divorce we will be always good friends. I will see you for lunch. I will eat with you many nights dinner."

I looked at the man I had lived with for twenty-two years. The fight was gone out of him. He sat there quietly, his eyes brimming with tears. "All right, Jolika. I give you the divorce."

Separating was painful. We had twenty-five Oriental rugs—even on the sofa, on the table, across the bed—to divide. It is so terrible to boil down a whole lifetime with a man to the disposition of a pile of carpets . . . this red one belongs to you, this blue and gray Bukhara with the fringe is mine, this small Turkoman is the one you bought . . . it's terrible.

I took a little three-room apartment with a terrace near the Elizabeth Bridge. It had belonged to a famous actress before and it was on the Veress Pal Utcza in Pest. I was on the fifth floor and my windows all looked out on a garrison where the soldiers live. It was very pretty even though so small I could barely get my brocaded chaise into the bedroom and all my crystal cocktail and liquor sets and golden demitasse cups from Crystello into my salon.

Vilmos with his butler took an apartment on the Rákóczi Ut and it was the last night we were eating dinner together in our old apartment. Over our dining room table hung a big antique chandelier which in the division of property belonged to me. The moving men arrived as we were sitting at opposite ends of this enormous dining room table. The children were gone, the piano teacher and her daughter were gone, the tutor was gone, Fraulein was gone, the friends were gone. It was just the two of us silently at opposite ends of this gigantic table.

Bitterly but very elegantly as he lifted his knife and fork, Vilmos directed them. "The chandelier belongs to my wife and is to be delivered to her address. You may take it down now."

The chandelier was dismantled around us as we ate in silence. My lip quivered. "Is not this awful after twenty-two years? I feel so terrible." I started to cry.

Vilmos said softly, "You have not to cry, my darling. Stay with me."

That was the most dreadful moment of all. After that everything was easier. It was this painting goes to her . . . this mirror goes to me. . . . All twenty-five of the carpets had been sent out to be cleaned. Fifteen belonged to me and ten to him. The cleaner didn't know anything so he sent the whole twenty-five back to our old apartment. They were all rolled up and Vilmos was happy. He wanted me to come and check them and see which ones were mine. He wanted me to come over every single day and make my selections. He was so happy to have another reason to get me over. He wanted me to remove them rug by rug.

The day Vilmos knew it was finally and forever over between us was when I packed up my crocheted Richelieu tablecloth. It had cost 700 pengös and I loved it. Once, when I was flirting in Abbazia and Vilmos didn't find this cloth in the dining room, he said to the children, "The Richelieu cloth is not here. That means she is not coming back. You have no more mother." The girls were crying. He was raving. At that time it was only being laundered. Now when I really took it with me he knew I wasn't coming back.

The day of the divorce we arrived separately at the courthouse but left together. Driving home after we were granted the papers, Vilmos said to me, "Let us have dinner together tonight."

"Good idea."

Magda, our chief witness, was sitting in the back of the car. "How can you two go together for dinner tonight when you are now divorced?" she demanded.

I blushed. "I am now free to do what I want, am I not?"

"Yes," she nodded.

"In that case what I want is to go to dinner with your Papa."

He was very generous to me and after the divorce I loved him more. We became good friends. With my one maid in my bachelor apartment I didn't make anything in the kitchen. I always gave her money to go out for food and I had at Vilmos' apartment almost every day lunch because he called me every day at 12 o'clock. "Come, Jolika. You know I have the best gooseliver in town and it is your favorite so come for lunch."

"No, I don't go," I would start the same way each day. "You want only to make me old and fat. I don't go."

One o'clock came the next call. "I have everything what you like. Come, Jolika."

And then I became hungry and at two o'clock I would appear and eat my head off because he always prepared like for twelve people even though it was just us.

Vilmos had the bigger apartment but whenever any of the girls came in they would always live with me and I would bring them along to the lunch. At those times Papa was happy because he was eating like the old days. There was a weekend when all three of them were in Budapest and I was busy with a designer redecorating my shop. I told the three, "You go alone. I have no time."

The three went over and in half an hour they came back crying. They found me sitting outside at a sidewalk café with this wonderful little Jewish boy whom I loved and who was my designer. I was just in the middle of my meal when the girls came in starving. "What is it? What has happened?" I asked. "The lunch was not good?"

Magda, with tears in her eyes, sniffed, "Papa threw us out. He shouted at us, 'Not without your mother! Without Mama I don't want you!'"

"He wouldn't let us eat," complained Zsa Zsa.

I shook my head. "Oy, here I am with a Countess and an Excellency and I am only a poor businesswoman and I must pay for everything. So, sit down and eat."

They sat down. Again I shook my head. "Always you bastards cost me money!" But I loved that they wanted to be with me.

After the divorce we not only had lunch together but Vilmos would take me to the theatre and he would take me to dinner and then he would escort me home and sometimes we would even sleep together a little bit and then he would tip the concierge for the after-hours care. After we were divorced I was happy with him for the first time. I now enjoyed to be with him and I am almost ashamed to admit that a little bit I liked very much to sleep on his shoulder, in the crook of his arm. He always smelled so good.

From 1940 to 1941 I saw my divorced husband nearly every day. And then Paul came into my life.

BOOK THREE

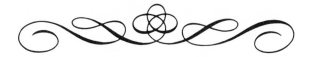

Jolie Gabor

I was forty, I was free, and I wanted the whole world. I was at the Hotel Cristallo Palace in Cortina d'Ampezzo, a skiing resort. There were four men who were eager for me but I wasn't satisfied with one. I wanted to conquer all four. At least I wanted to know that all four were dying for me.

The consequence was if I went with one the other three were watching and would ask where am I going. I ended up never having an affair with any of them.

At night back in Budapest I would walk with a friend along an avenue where there were rows of coffeehouses and strolling violinists. It must have been the fifth month after my divorce that I was promenading along this avenue with a gentleman and from the corner of my eye I spied Vilmos behind me. I turned to look and there he stood, absolutely still like a stick, shaking his fist at me!

When I finally had another man besides Vilmos it wasn't so terrific. I thought all my life that I must have this, that I die for this and so I had this and . . . nothing. I thought to myself this is not so out of the world now that I have it.

Magda and Eva escorted me to the train to Lido for my first vacation alone. Magda was driving the small German car I had bought for Eva. She was in front with Magda and I was in back and we had open the roof of the car and it was sunny and beautiful. We passed a flower market. "You must arrive with flowers," said Magda. "I will go out and get some for you." She went out. I reached out to gather up my silk dress so the door would not slam on it. As I did, Magda slammed the door and the tip of the middle finger on my right hand was cut off.

I was taken right to the hospital. What I had wanted to save was my silk dress and what I lost was my finger. All this was for the sake of a little flower. My nature is to always go with the sunshine and so I consoled myself that it could have been worse.

Naturally, I never got to Lido. Instead, I found Paul. I think that maybe God wanted me not to go to Lido and to have this experience—I don't mean with the finger, I mean with Paul. If ever I come face to face with God, I am going to ask Him only one question—"Why?"

125

In Győr, which is a little town between Vienna and Budapest, I had a chic friend, Elsa Hollas, a lawyer's wife of about twenty-eight, who adored me. I had opened a branch of Jolie's on Main Street in Győr. She wanted to run it so we agreed that she would manage it and have an option to buy at a future date.

When it was clear I would not continue on my way to a vacation in Lido, I went to Győr to complete this negotiation.

There I met a man. He was thirty-six. He had never been married. He had snow-white hair and blue eyes. He was also the most cruel man I ever knew. As good as Vilmos was to me that's how cruel this man was to me. His name was Paul Savosdy. Most other lovers I have long since forgotten. Paul Savosdy I will remember always.

Paul lived with his sister and brother-in-law 20 miles from Győr in a castle that once belonged to Prince Esterházy. After we had dated a few times he invited me to stay over in his castle. I was perfumed and made up and I waited all night but . . . nothing. Here I was naked and eager and only a few doors away in the same damn castle and he wouldn't touch me. "Not in the family house," he said. He wouldn't sleep with me in his beautiful castle, the bastard.

Then when I had to go to Vienna to buy goods for my shop, he went with me and we spent two days together. First we went to a nightclub. I was so glamorous in a short black velvet coat with poufed sleeves and a white ermine collar. I had also a black velvet hat trimmed in ermine with a feather and a real diamond brooch on the hat. It was the first time in my life in a real nightclub with a strange man alone. We drank champagne.

On the way back to the Grand Hotel we passed a little old lady who sold flowers on the street. She had maybe fifty roses in a basket. He bought the whole lot for me and I had to pinch myself that this happiness cannot really be. I walked along carrying this armful of huge red flowers. I felt that if I were to die after this it would be worthwhile because here I was actually going to go to bed with a man I adored. I was counting the minutes but he made me wait. When he finally got around to it, it wasn't bad. In fact, it was pretty good. It could only have been better if it had been in the castle! He had to be so goddamn noble that he wouldn't sleep with me there.

Paul was occasionally good to me but mainly he was sadistic. His parents exported Tokay wine to the United States. Their lands were in the wine-growing area of Tapolca. He had gone to school in Vienna to learn agriculture but had drifted into the food business. He worked for Mendel, the international meat packer. Mendel, this tycoon, wanted to make a meat manufactury in Pápa near Győr and Paul's family had a farm with 2,000 cows. As soon as Mendel saw this property and this aristocratic family he quick offered him an executive job with this large meat firm and Paul left the vines to become a vice-president.

Paul came to Budapest every ten days, so for the nine days he was away

I worked like a maniac in my shop. I slaved. I took no sleep. On the tenth day when he was coming I rested. I bathed in bubble bath for two hours. I went to the hairdresser, the cosmetician. I got all perfumed. I bought special hostess gowns and frilly diaphanous nightgowns. I waited for him like a king. When the doorbell rang I added more perfume in the seven necessary spots. The greatest sacrifice of all I gave to him: I gave up eating *kolbász* for fear it would give me a garlic smell.

We were divorced a half a year and still I had difficulty being with Paul. I was accustomed to being afraid that Vilmos would find it out. This was a hard habit to break. I was so afraid that in the very early days when Paul came to my apartment, I would call Vilmos' butler. I would ask, "Sandor, tell me, where is Mr. Gabor?" If he would tell me, "He is just now stepping into his bath, Madame," I would then relax. Otherwise I could not relax in or out of bed.

I was nine days dreaming of Paul, waiting for him, and making myself beautiful for him. He stayed over in my apartment and we made love. We made love all over—on the floor (this is the best) and, he reminded me years later, we did it even in a closet. This I don't remember.

I do remember his cruelty. I do remember the night we sat down to dinner with my beautifully set table and flowers. It was a long table.

"You will sit at one end of the table and I at the other," he ordered.

"But *why?*"

"Why?" he smiled coldly. "Because I enjoy grandeur and elegance."

I thought to myself, "Yes, but it's *my* grandeur and elegance." Aloud I said only, "I know and that's why I have decorated this whole long table for just the two of us to have dinner. But why can't we sit near to one another? Maybe we could even hold hands."

"No, Jolie, this is the proper way for well-bred people to dine."

"But I made this whole long table only to flabbergast you, not to deny me!"

I walked over to where he stood at the foot of the table and I kissed him. An impatient look crossed his handsome face and he waved me off, the bastard!

The meal progressed in silence although I could not eat for the hurt.

"Why do you not eat, Jolika?"

"I can't help it, I cannot eat."

"I am upset that you cannot eat."

"I am also upset but I cannot eat. I am eating my heart out. That is enough for me to eat."

"Oh, by the way, darling," he said, tossing up and down his own private key to my apartment, "don't mind but after dinner I must go to Countess Sasha's apartment for . . . a little bit."

"The Countess? But she is a *kurva*. She will *baszni* with anybody for money and you will leave me tonight to go and see her?"

"Darling," he sighed as he drank my wine and wiped his lips delicately with my linen napkin, "do not be such a jealous person." He stood up. "You must try to control yourself."

"Only of you I am jealous, Paul. Please don't leave me. Please don't go to her."

"Try to eat something, Jolie."

"I can't. I won't. I will kill myself if you go," I screamed as the door slammed shut behind him.

I sat with my head in my hands maybe three minutes. I thought I was so in love with him that even if it should ever happen that he would want to marry me I would be afraid to marry him. He could not have been a husband to me. Only a lover. This was a love of pain.

And then I picked myself up and began to eat. I ate and I ate, I even ate what he left over. I stuffed myself.

I only lived for that one overnight period every ten days. I couldn't wait to be with Paul. The hair on my head tingled. I was so happy in the beginning that I pinched myself. The beginning was gorgeous. He loved me—everybody said he must have loved me because he was always with me—but I loved him better.

Paul gave me money. I had two in help behind the scenes in my shop. My secretary's name was Sari and my accountant was Tibor. Our second Christmas together he gave my secretary 100,000 pengös with the instruction, "Tell your lady to buy more gold and diamonds and more merchandise so that she can make an even bigger business than she already has." But it was only a loan. After the holidays I gave it back to him.

So, he was good to me in his way but he gave me much pain. I know he loved me. Friends swore he loved me. But he was a sadist. I recall the evening he let himself in with his key after his nine days away. I was wild for him. We made love all over. We came out and went to the table and there lying open on the table was a letter. It was a woman's handwriting. It said, "I love you. I adore you."

That letter hadn't been there when we had gone in to make love. He had taken it out of his pocket and left it there deliberately just to aggravate me. Just so I could see it and eat myself up alive. This was unbearable cruelty. He loved me, yes. But I suffered like a dog.

Suffering is part of the game of love. In any relationship between a man and a woman, one is always more in love than the other. One always suffers more than the other. I enjoy to suffer. I enjoy to beat my breast when the telephone call doesn't come or when the present isn't good enough.

Paul and I were together five years. On our third anniversary I was expecting perfume, flowers, jewelry. You know what this meat executive brought me? Ten pounds of *kolbász!* It was a great gift because there was a shortage of this and friends said, "Oh, Jolie, how wonderful for you!" For me it wasn't so wonderful. I thought, "Salami! How romantic!"

I know that when you do *not* suffer, at least sometimes, you are not in love. It is just that with Paul I suffered too much. We all must suffer *first* to appreciate what we then get. What we have easy we don't appreciate. I guess . . . I don't know. I only know that from Paul I became a little bit sick.

Because of Paul I went to a psychiatrist. The psychiatrist said, "Your problem is that your husband was always so much in love with you that now you are really drawn to the opposite. You want some man with whom you do not feel so secure. You could never love your husband in the way that he loved you. Now it is in reverse—you are in love with a man you are not sure of."

I agreed but it didn't help me any. "For a change, Doctor," I said, "I do not want to be the one to be loved. I want to be the one who is doing the loving. *I* want to be in love." For twenty-two years I dreamed of loving a man.

"So you have what you want but now it is not bringing you happiness."

"Always I cry because Paul cheats me. He loves me, he says, but maybe that's not true. Maybe he just *acts* that way. So, I think to myself, 'If this is supposed to be happiness and I am miserable what the hell is happiness?' I mean, OK, so I have a big happiness . . . so???" Little did I know then that I was just in love with love.

I think also Paul was afraid of my three daughters and their glamor. He was afraid we were all a little too much for him. I used to tell to him, "This is only the beginning for my children. They will become somebodies much more even than they are now."

Sometimes I also became a little frightened of them, like the Easter-time all three were with me in my tiny apartment. I slept in the bedroom under my sexy pink silk sheets and in my lacy, seductive, light blue silk nightgown. In the dining room I opened a cot for Her Excellency. A chaise longue was in the hall for the Countess. Eva was on the couch. Somehow Zsa Zsa and Magda had a fight and Zsa Zsa threw a book at Magda. Some hours later they made up and we went to sleep. In the middle of the night all was quiet and, then, suddenly I heard a big crash.

Everybody was up. "What is it . . . what happened . . . what . . . ?" It was Magda. She had thrown a glass against the far wall of the foyer.

I was very angry. "Why did you do this?" I demanded.

Standing in the middle of the hall with her hands on her hips, Magda stormed, "I got angry all over again."

"But we were all asleep!" I said.

"She's crazy," announced Zsa Zsa.

I looked at the silk wall in the foyer. It was ripped where she had thrown the glass. "I have just decorated this apartment and put silk up on the walls. Magda, are you crazy?"

"In the middle of the night I woke up and thought about Zsa Zsa throwing the book at my head," answered Magda. "Do you know that one more inch and it would have hit me in the head and I would be dead? I thought about it all of a sudden and that's why I got mad again."

"Do me a favor, darling," I said to Magda as I swept up the broken glass. "You go back to Warsaw with your Pole. And you," I turned to Zsa Zsa, "you, Excellency, you go back to your Turk and leave me alone to go back to sleep."

Magda went back. The others I took to St. Moritz for a vacation. In advance of their coming I had ordered them identical gowns. One set was white brocade with lilacs on the skirt and our first night in St. Moritz I insisted they put them on. "But we don't want to wear alike," complained Eva. "We hate to look the same and wear the same."

Zsa Zsa kicked her dress away with her foot. "No, I don't wear this. We are not anymore children. Who ever heard of grown-up women dressed alike? Everybody will think we're mad."

"Maybe, but it will create a sensation and this I love," I said. In the end they put them on to please me. When they came in to dinner in the hotel dining room it caused a revolution!

This vacation in St. Moritz was to be my treat and I paid for everything. The girls hadn't brought any money and I didn't have enough yet we didn't want to leave. "If our two rooms and two baths here in the Palace Hotel is going to be so expensive," said Zsa Zsa, "suppose we all try to get into one room and then we can save."

"No, better we get out of this glamorous hotel altogether," I said. "There is a cheaper chalet right nearby."

"But it is not such an elegant crowd there," sulked Eva.

"All right," said Zsa Zsa, "so we will come here for mealtimes."

Our first night in the Chalet, the girls dressed in another of their matching gowns—silver décolleté lined with turquoise plus furs and jewels and when the bill came Eva murmured, "What shall we do? We can't sign because we don't live here and we have not any more Swiss francs."

"Don't worry, children," I said, and I wrenched off a huge 18-karat gold medallion from my bracelet and gave it to the concierge for payment.

Another evening we were invited over to the Palace for drinks. They gave us champagne. We hadn't eaten any lunch and Her High-class Excellency Mme. Belge whispered to me, "I wish instead they would give us a frankfurter." That night a friend of mine who lived at the Palace made a package of food and smuggled it to us. On our last day we laughed so much we couldn't stand it. I said to Zsa Zsa, "Today either we go to the hairdresser or we have lunch."

Although they created a sensation and although I adored them, I was very happy when they went back to their Pole, their Turk, and their Swede because they created a little too much excitement for me. For instance, Zsa Zsa and Katie. I had only one servant in these days and Zsa Zsa wanted to take her from me.

"But Zsa Zsaika," I pleaded. "You are an Excellency. You have many servants. I have only this one. This Katie is my life. Katie knows my clothes, she knows which shoes to which bag to which hat. She manages for me everything. Katie is my life."

"But, *Nucika,*" she argued. "You cannot be selfish. I would not take her if I did not need. The servants in Turkey are terrible and I must have Katie."

Like I would always do for my daughters, I gave in. Always I end up doing what they want. "Zsa Zsaika," I said as she packed up to leave for Ankara with her three suitcases and my one maid, "Katie is only twenty-four. She is plump. She has a nice rosy pink face. You must treat her gently."

In six months Katie came back. I couldn't recognize her. She was pale. She was skinny. "Her Excellency is too difficult to work with," she trembled. "When I bow down she strikes me on the head. Even at midnight when she comes home she wants me to get up and put away her clothes for her."

Sometimes I thought maybe that Paul was right in being afraid of my daughters. They were growing up to be a little too much to handle even for me!

As I try to get my thoughts together for this book and I think about my life, I cannot believe I loved Paul Savosdy so much—but I did. It is long since over but even now when I think about it I vividly remember the agony I suffered. Aaaahhh, I loved him so! I had many loves in my life and they were all pleasant and when it was time to go out I went out and it was easy and right. But Paul Savosdy was my one heartache. Maybe it was because he was the first man in my life after Vilmos. Maybe . . . I don't know.

2 War broke out on September 1, 1939, with Germany's invasion of Poland. Not long after, Burhan came to me. "Jolie," he said, "go out from this country. Go to America. Go to Mexico. Go anywhere but get out of here."

"I am not political. What has Hitler to do with me?" I said. "I know you are a brilliant politician, Burhan, but also you are a little bit of a jealous son-in-law. I think, maybe, that is why you want me to go away."

"It is true only that I once complained you influence my wife too much. I mean, I don't think we could even have a baby unless you first agreed."

"You're right," I said, patting him on the knee, "I'm too young to be a grandmother."

"Jolie," he smiled, "you know I have great affection for you."

"Yes, I know. And I like you, too, very much. I like you even though you are jealous of me. Even though you once said to Zsa Zsa, 'You would be better if you were married to your mother.' "

"That is only because whenever we have any difficulty Zsa Zsa always wants to run home to you in Budapest."

"I admit," I said, "that my three girls hang on me like a Christmas tree but is that a reason for you to come here especially to Hungary to tell me to go away?"

Burhan pulled up his chair even closer to mine. "Jolie, it is only beginning. All of Europe will burn. Everyone will be killed. The Jewish intellectuals will be massacred by the Nazis. The Christian aristocrats will be massacred by the Reds."

"I know that these are critical days," I replied slowly. "I have heard that the future of all of us is uncertain. I can not believe, though, because Budapest is gay."

"Hungarians," he said wryly, "hate to face reality. You Hungarians are creatures of moods, capable of dizzying heights of joy and dismal dregs of despair. I applaud the Hungarian temperament but I do not now have the luxury of coping with it. I tell you, Jolie, leave Hungary. Immediately. Today."

We faced each other silently for a few moments in the twilight that was fast settling over my apartment.

"I am grateful that I have already smuggled out my best jewelry . . . my children. They are all married to foreigners. I have gotten all my children out."

"Zsa Zsa will always be safe because of me," he said. "She will be protected by a diplomatic passport."

"I have none of them living in Budapest so I have nothing to fear from the Nazis."

I looked into the inside room. My secretary who had been nice enough to sacrifice her Sunday afternoon was answering my letters. In the mirror on the wall I saw the day-old effects of my Antoine hairdo with the light blue velvet ribbon still in it. In the salon where we were sitting, my eyes touched on a brand new radio-victrola which I had just gotten plus a stack of new records, mostly hot tangos and love songs. On my baroque bar table sat an assortment of divine liqueurs, Gerbeaud bonbons which Paul had brought, and two vases of flowers. That night Mama, who was still as beautiful as ever, was having in her house fifteen people for a sit-down dinner. I could not see what I had to fear.

There were many others, however, who *could* see what they had to fear. One was my stepfather for twelve years. Dr. Miksa Kenda was a churchgoer but he came from Jewish blood. Because of the position of his son-in-law who was a big shot in Parliament he was afraid of his faraway Jewish parentage. There was not Nazism in Budapest as yet. Still he was terrified. He injected himself with poison. Nobody understood why he made suicide. Later we understood.

Others who could see what they had to fear were the parents of Paul Savosdy. His father and his mother were both Jewish but when Paul was five years old the whole family became Catholic.

When the talk about Hitler and the Jews became daily conversation, I discussed this with Paul. "In every room in your castle there is a cross. Not even the Pope lives in such a very Catholic place. If you are of Jewish origin, how is it possible you can be such a good Christian?"

"This happened when I was a very little boy. My elegant mother's friends were princes, counts, priests, the finest most respected people in Europe. Mother herself was brought up in the most aristocratic atmosphere of Germany. She was raised in Dresden. Her friends always called her 'The Princess.' Still, there was a pogrom. My Jewish mother and father suffered greatly. It lasted only two days but Mother decided *never again!* And now we are Christians." I was to remember that remark in days to come.

The situation in Europe was heating up. I had once to go to Berlin and Leipzig for jewelry. In Leipzig there was a blackout and I remember going through the streets with a lamp hearing Nazis shouting, "Death to the Jews . . . death to the Jews . . ." Everybody told, "Jolie is crazy to go now to Berlin and Leipzig for jewelry." I never went again.

In Warsaw, of course, the war was even worse. Magda's Bichovsky had gone to London and joined the British Army. So Magda came back home. She wanted to come back anyway, even after the first few months because already she was tired of this Pole. She did not stay with him very long—maybe only a few months.

Poland fell, so, within a very short time Magda was not anymore the Countess of Warsaw. Whatever happened to the Count after that, I really don't know. He disappeared and who appeared in his place was the Portuguese Ambassador.

3 For Magda's Portuguese Ambassador I thank God. It was this man who saved my life.

Magda had lived in the Ritz Hotel with her husband, where this Ambassador Sanpayo also lived. They had been formally introduced. When I learned this I asked her, "Magduska, who is this man?"

"He is the Portuguese Ambassador and he has asked me to be his secretary."

"Take the job," I replied. "Your husband is gone and working will keep you busy."

While my first-born was developing the Portuguese Ambassador, my last-born was leaving for America. She and Dr. Erik Drimmer had been in London one year and he had decided that 1940 was now the time to get out of Europe. I went to London for the round of farewell parties.

"Oh, *Nuci*," cried Eva when I arrived, "you must give me that red hat you are wearing. It makes you look like Madame du Barry and I want it to do the same for me when I arrive in Hollywood."

"But you are going on a boat," I said as we sat in her little London apartment packing. "On a boat you cannot have such a big red hat with feathers."

She tried it on in front of the mirror. "Please, *Nuci*, I want it as my farewell gift," she begged.

"Evika, you will look ridiculous in this. It is for a taller, bigger, older woman. It is not for you. Besides, it is the first time I am wearing it. Anyway, I am thinking to visit you in America in six months and I will bring it over for you and give it to you then."

I was so selfish that I didn't even wait until she sailed away on the boat. I went instead to Deauville. Magda was there and she had called me. "Come, *Nuci*. It is very close to England and it is now high season and everybody is here."

"But Eva leaves in three days," I said on the phone.

"It is not so far by plane. You can fly back when she sails," reasoned practical Magda. "We can only be here another three days. So, come, *Nuci*."

"I am so impulsive and I want so much the good life," I answered her, "that I think I am not a good mother. Should I not stay and be with Eva until she goes?"

"I am also your daughter," she said, "so you will be still being a good mother if you come to me." Always each of the girls tried to tear me into pieces for herself but this time I knew in my heart I wasn't going for Magda. I wanted to go to Deauville because it was the good life. Besides, I was unhappy in London. It had been raining every day and from terrible awful weather, my feet were aching. I had only high-heeled shoes and I couldn't find a comfortable pair to fit me. I told to Eva, "I don't feel good here. I am uncomfortable and I don't want to spend here another three days but I come back from Deauville for your sailing."

Eva was bitterly unhappy. "Please, *Nuci*, stay. I am going to the United States in three days."

I told Eva good-bye and God bless you and I went to Deauville. When I arrived there was a telegram from Eva saying, "You will be sorry that you didn't give me the hat and stay to put me on the boat." Eva had been bitterly unhappy. From her unhappiness I became unhappy.

"Instead of laughing and having a good time you are crying the whole three days," complained Magda, who now also was unhappy with me. "You are no good to me here so call Eva. Fly back to Eva."

I tried for one whole day to get through to Eva by telephone but I couldn't. There was trouble with her phone. I learned later that I could not reach her because they had taken Drimmer's phone away. He was not a rich doctor just a beginner chiropractor and he had taken his phone out two days early so he didn't have to pay another month's charges.

I was frantic because I didn't know the name of the boat or the day or the time of the sailing or anything. This became very bitter for me. I didn't wait with her, I didn't go to the boat, I didn't give her the red hat, I didn't catch her again even by telephone, and I didn't go over to visit in six months. I couldn't. A little thing like a war came in between.

Months later from Hollywood she wrote that she was sick from homesickness and loneliness and how terrible it was that I had not even waited to see her off on the boat, but that she would love me even though I had hurt her.

The guilt that I am a bad mother and the punishment of my pain came in on me like a flood. The years passed but always my heart bled because of Eva. My agony was such that even my lover, Paul Savosdy, was affected. "Don't eat up your heart about this," he used to tell me. My panic was that maybe something could happen with the Nazis and maybe never would I see Eva again.

I nearly didn't.

It was now Zsa Zsa's turn to command my attention. Sir Percy Loren, who was the English Ambassador to Turkey, adored Zsa Zsa. He had an oldness about him so I don't think they had anything together. I judged him about fifty-two. Sir Percy was repeatedly good to Zsa Zsa. He always gave her advice and it was he who told her, "My dear, you are not for Ankara."

She naturally agreed and when Eva married Drimmer, Sir Percy arranged for their Excellencies Burhan and Mme. Belge to be received officially in London by Anthony Eden. They were treated like royalty. The Turkish flags were flying. Anthony Eden himself came to the train. At least I think he did. I don't remember. Well, if he didn't it wasn't because he didn't want to.

It happened that Zsa Zsa took over the papers. The newspapers wrote that the world's most beautiful woman arrived to London. They wrote what she wore by day, for coffee, for lunch, for cocktails and always they referred to her as Zsa Zsa. Even then she was just plain Zsa Zsa. The conservative British papers actually reported that Anthony Eden is giving a reception for Zsa Zsa—they didn't even mention Burhan.

All of this crept into her head and stayed there. She knew she should be somebody and when she realized that Eva was going to Hollywood it gave her the idea that it was really she who was created for this life. Zsa Zsa was born to publicity. Newspapers and cameras and press and reporters are a miracle for her.

Zsa Zsa came to visit me in Budapest. Just the two of us. "I am very unhappy in Ankara," she began late one night.

"I think maybe it has something to do with the fact that Eva is now in Hollywood, yes?" I said.

"*Nucika*, are you not of the opinion that it is I who is the actress in the family and not Eva? And are you not of the opinion, therefore, that it does not seem exactly right for my younger sister who is not an actress to be beating me to Hollywood?"

For the moment each of us was busy with her own thoughts. "I can not bear it," she admitted softly. "I am desperate to get to Hollywood."

"I think also you are desperate to get rid of Burhan," I commented over my shoulder as I went to the kitchen to pour us both a cup of coffee.

She waited until I returned and snuggled down into bed. "Burhan and I have been together already a couple of years and I am bored to death with him."

I gazed at her adoringly. I always thought Zsa Zsa was the most beautiful of my daughters. Many people can't decide but for me it was always Zsa Zsa. "Is that what this visit is for? To tell me this?" I asked.

"This is not a visit. This is my jumping off place. I plan to leave Burhan and to go to America." Watching me carefully and seeing that I did not flinch, she gathered momentum. "I know that Ankara is not anymore a life for me. Therefore my first move was to get out of Ankara. I told Burhan I was coming for a visit to you in Budapest."

I put my coffee down and turned to face her in the bed. "You knew before you left that you were never going back."

"Yes. In New York I have a friend, John King, a retired businessman whom Burhan and I entertained in Turkey. I'm sure he will take care of us."

I was excited at the possibility. "But it is difficult at this time to arrange visas. How can we do?"

"Look, *Nucika,*" she said eagerly. "I can get mine because of a diplomatic passport and I can manage to get yours. We can get our tickets and our passports together in a very short while and we can both go to America."

Tears came to my eyes. "I cannot go, Zsa Zsika," I said. "Suppose I go and something happens and I cannot get back here because of the war?"

"For what must you come back in such a big hurry?"

I was too ashamed to answer her but she read my thoughts instantly.

"Paul! Is it that you are so much in love with Paul Savosdy that you are afraid to leave him?"

I could not face her. "Yes," I said.

She stared at me wild-eyed. "You *must* come. You have the money, the opportunity, and I will arrange the visas. When you arrive, Eva will forget that you didn't give her the red hat and your heart will finally be at rest."

I shook my head wordlessly.

My daughter crawled across the bed and threw her arms around me. We both started to weep. "But, *Nuci,* you know how much I love you. I cannot leave here to go to the United States without you." In those days she had a big hot love for me and she pleaded, "Please . . . please . . . *Nuci* . . . please come with me."

Tears rolled down my cheeks. I was so torn. "I cannot. I am too in love with Paul."

"But he is a nothing," she said stunned at my decision.

"He is more than that," I said. "He is no good, but he is in my blood and I cannot help it."

Again we didn't speak for a few moments and the silence hung heavily. "How will you be for money?" I asked.

"I have some from Burhan. I also have from grandmother plus the 12-carat ring which grandmother gave me plus some other little bits of jewelry like the ruby necklace Papa gave me for the wedding present."

I stroked her beautiful hair. "What will you do about your Turk?"

"I will divorce him in America. I don't think it will be too difficult because when he finds out I have run away to America I think he will want the divorce."

I reached out and held her hand tightly. "Zsa Zsika," I said. "Please don't run into another marriage quickly. But if you must, then make it a hotel director."

For the first time she smiled. "Why a hotel director?"

"Because a friend to me has married in America, in Carmel, California. She married a hotel director and she sent me her picture under the umbrella and near to the ocean and she tells 'Oh, this is the best life in the world.' She tells that with him the food is good and the service is good and the accommodations are good and there is so much courtesy and so many parties. She said it makes for a good life. So remember this."

It was the spring of 1941. One year later Zsa Zsa did, indeed, remember this.

4 After Pearl Harbor the Allies closed their embassies in Hungary and all the business was being conducted through the neutral Portuguese legation, which made Magda's friend the Ambassador one of the most powerful men in Budapest.

Month rolled into month and Burhan's prophesy was coming true. Europe was indeed burning. War and the fear of war were all around us. We were still relatively unharmed in Budapest but everyone knew it was just a matter of time.

Every Tuesday from middle 1942 to middle 1943, just before the war struck us personally, somebody else in our family would give a dinner party only for the family. We had so much in common to tell one another that we would speak in 400 speed. I usually had the most to tell because of my daughters. How that Zsa Zsa had begun washing her dark blonde hair with henna because Eva complained, "We can't both be Hungarian blondes" and how Zsa Zsa was bored with Eva's life and wrote me how Eva, now with Paramount Pictures, bleached her hair blonde, plucked her eyebrows, and dieted at lunch on cottage cheese and half a canned pear.

Some of our rapid-fire compulsive talking was from nerves. Things were happening around us and we clutched onto one another for strength. I was very family-conscious. I was driven with the desire to keep the family together until the last possible second. Maybe most of all I was responsible for us getting together every Tuesday.

It came again a Tuesday and Rozsika said, "I can't come because I have tickets for the theatre."

"Don't tell you can't come," I lashed out at her. "I feel the time is approaching when we can't always be together so don't let anything be in your way on a Tuesday night. It is at Mama's house this week."

Then Janette also called, "I cannot go. I have an important meeting and I must attend."

I pleaded with them to please come. They didn't. I was angry. "How do you know?" I said, "but that this might be the very last night we can be together?"

Sebika, who had been educated in a military academy in Berlin since the age of fourteen and had many Germans for his friends, was optimistic. "Oh, nothing will happen and if it does nothing can ever touch us."

140

So the few of us who could make it that Tuesday did. I had a sixth sense working overtime. I was nervous. While we were speaking I drank my champagne then I drank Dora's champagne then Sebi's champagne and finally Manci—naturally—complained: "Mama, we don't have champagne. Jancsi drank everybody's glass."

This is over thirty years ago and I see even that silly thing of drinking the others' champagne, like it would be yesterday. My intuition turned out to be correct. It was the very last Tuesday that we ever again were to be together as a family.

At 5 o'clock on a Sunday morning in March, 1944, the Nazis marched in. Quietly, with perfect planning, they met no resistance and passed the city's outskirts while the city was still asleep. By noon storm troopers occupied Budapest without firing a shot.

The wonderful, delicious Jewish boy who was my decorator and whom I loved, lost all his fingers at the hands of the Nazis and afterwards they killed him. That couple I admired—the pretty singer and her Jewish piano-player husband who owned the Arizona nightclub—were threatened with a firing squad and tortured and then three Nazis came into the Arizona. "Give us all your money and your nightclub and we'll take you to safety in Switzerland." They did as they were told. They got into the plane flown and provided by the Nazis and when they were 20,000 feet up the Nazis pushed them out.

The reason I don't like much to return to Budapest even for a short visit is because the memories are not good. Early one morning I heard a commotion. The Nazis had rounded up all the Jewish lawyers as their first targets. One thousand of these Jewish lawyers were stood up along the banks of the Duna and shot!

To me, even worse than the Nazis were the Christian Hungarian traitors. Paul's queenly mother and his father who had been a diplomat before going into business had adopted a Christian orphan and raised him from infancy. This Christian orphan became governor to Tapolca. When Paul's brother and sister were dragged off to concentration camps in the middle of the night the family called this governor. Even a power as great as his could not save them. I always considered the Christians of Hungary worse than the Nazis.

Because of Magda I had a radio and could hear some news. I learned that Paul's mother and father were taken to a concentration camp. It was a crushing blow to the mind to recognize that the Princess had been forcibly pulled out of her magnificent, lavish Esterházy castle, kicked and beaten and thrown into a ghetto where they made her lie on the floor on a mattress until she was deported in a death train. I still cannot stand to believe it.

Everybody was afraid. Nobody could trust nobody. There was no food, no water. Things were pitiful. A young gentle mother whom I knew and her little child were in the shelter. The child was so weak from lack of food that this precious mother cut her wrists and gave the daughter her own blood to drink. She had managed to secrete on her body a solitaire. To keep herself and her baby alive, she gave that diamond of ten carats for one skinny stale piece of bread which normally would not even have cost five cents. She later got out alive, I heard, and married one of the wealthiest men in Paris. That's the way it was. Some died like rats. Others became something.

It became apparent that we, too, were in danger. Vilmos was in difficulty because he was a known anti-Nazi. Magda was marked because by then she was working for the underground. Everybody was afraid in those days.

At 9:00 A.M. on what looked like any other average Sunday, Magda's friend, Ambassador Carlos de Sanpayo Garrido of the Portuguese Embassy sent his car for us with instructions to get in quickly and present ourselves at the Embassy. The driver locked the doors behind us, unfurled the official Portuguese flag, and rushed us through the streets.

It was Magda's friend who saved our lives. He secreted us safely on neutral Portuguese ground in the legation's summer house in Galgagyörk, thirty miles away. The legation was in a castle set on ten acres and surrounded by gardens. Inside we were catered to by butlers and chambermaids. Vilmos and I, at first, had our own separate quarters but one by one and two by two and week after week more and more people came. Even the aide of Regent Miklos Horthy arrived one day and we all had to make do. In this rambling old ugly Tahy castle there were thirty persons under the protection of the Portuguese. We spent our days walking in the garden. And I was spending sleepless nights worrying about Paul.

I'd heard the Nazis found out that he was of Jewish birth. They did not kill him because they needed him. Paul was a food expert. His firm, Mendel's, sent hams all over Europe, Australia, Canada, America. They brought him to a special deportation camp where Paul was put in charge of feeding 5,000 people. They were Jewish VIPs who couldn't be immediately slaughtered because their cooperation was needed. They were princesses, countesses, ministers, excellencies, collaborators—all sorts of people who could render assistance. They cleaned their beds, washed their own clothes, mopped the floors. Eventually they, too, would be killed but, meanwhile, they had to be kept alive. As soon as there was no more need for the Jewish VIPs, there would be no more need for the Jewish meat expert who was feeding them.

Then one day Ambassador Sanpayo was recalled to Lisbon. He had been heavily involved in the underground and his life was no longer safe. He was leaving for Portugal and Magda, who was listed as his secretary, planned to go with him. They begged me to go with them and they would register me as the cook of their legation. Me, a cook, can you imagine?

Vilmos pleaded with me not to go, "Jolika, if you leave me then I am *kaput.* I will die here. Who will watch out for me?"

So, I said, "Okay, even though you are not longer my husband I will not leave you." But honestly, it was because Paul was still there and in danger. He

A painting by Paul Fried which was reproduced in newspapers throughout the world.

Gems in the family diadem: the business card of
the Jolie Gabor pearl salon.

"Magda and Tony Gallucci lived in a town-house in Manhattan plus a castle in Southhampton, an actual castle . . . . they used to ask 300 people to their parties. Tony's problem was he drank. Once Magda beat him with a whip: she cracked a glass of Scotch right out of his hand. She didn't really hurt him too much because he managed to stay alive another twenty years."

Zsa Zsa's TV talk-show career was launched with just one line: "Oh, these? These, dahlingk, are just my *working* diamonds."

A Hollywood agent said Eva was such a great beauty that she went to Paramount for a screen test and they gave her a contract immediately.

Goulash is good, but "*Kolbasz* is the long, skinny, smelly Hungarian salami without which none of us can exist."

In her shop; Bimba Beck in the background:
"I had arrived professionally. Letters from
abroad addressed just to 'Jolie Gabor, America'
reached me."

The Clark Gables at one of Jolie's Western
parties.

had treated me so badly that my heart fell out but I remained so crazy in love with him that not even my life mattered as much to me.

The Communists took Budapest in January of '45. I lost my houses, my belongings, everything. They robbed and raped and stole, so if they were supposed to help us I didn't see it.

For that moment when we would need it, many of us had put our money in platinum and gold and diamonds. In Galgagyörk it was a rule that everybody must give in their valuables when they arrived. So everybody did. And everything was taken.

Armed robbers wearing black face masks ordered us outside with the Ambassador, who was still in residence, and they put in a car all our valuables. They threatened us with bodily harm if we didn't keep quiet. Immediately afterwards they disappeared and a short while later another group came to us. This second group in civilian dress said, "We are the Hungarian police. We heard there was a robbery and we have come to save you and we will take you now to police headquarters."

My heart sank. To be taken from the protection of the Embassy compound on a pretext could mean death. We said we would forget everything and we insisted it wasn't necessary to go to the police station. They insisted it *was* necessary and that they had to make a full report. Their attitude made it plain we had no choice.

They herded us out of our safe neutral ground, repeating over and over, "We are here to protect your life and to get back your jewelry." We couldn't be sure who they were—whether they were police or what. We did not see the faces of the original robbers since they were masked but I felt uneasy. I smelled danger. At the police station, Count Mylot and I recognized the boots of this second group of men as having been those that were on the masked bandits. In other words, both groups of men were the same—they had made for us a stage play!

We knew instantly the plan was to get rid of us. The way Nazis took care of people they didn't like was to first bring them to the police station for questioning. Afterwards they were taken to Schwabhedge, which was a section of Budapest, a big area up in the hills that goes around the Duna. Once they were unloaded at the Schwabhedge they were forced to dig graves for "other people." The next step was to shoot them at the edge of these graves so that they themselves could fall right in.

We were terribly nervous. It was sure we have to die. We were all braced that at any moment they would transport us to Schwabhedge. You could sense they wanted to. It was only the presence at the police station of the Portuguese Ambassador that saved us.

I thought, "Jolie, this is the end of your life. Thank God you have your other girls in America or they, too, would be *kaput.*"

The Hungarian police, acting under the orders of the Gestapo, who obviously had engineered this project to trick us out of the legation, had made the error of taking along the Portuguese Ambassador. At the station Ambassador Sanpayo demanded a telephone and promptly called the Foreign Office. He knew that his colleagues would be outraged to learn that the Gestapo had arrested him no matter under what pretext or mistake.

Immediately, other outraged ambassadors came to his rescue: "You can't hold an envoy of a neutral country," they said. "We will file immediate complaints with our governments." The Portuguese Ambassador then took his stand in relation to us. "You cannot touch these people. They are in my charge and I will not go free without them since they are under my protection." The police tried to make the Ambassador leave us. He would not. "I do not leave alone," he said. The other diplomats argued, "You cannot lay a hand on the Portuguese Ambassador. Nor can you touch his charges."

The day had begun at five in the morning. We were in nightgowns with robes over us and I had added a huge fur hat. Vilmos had on pajamas and riding boots, the Ambassador wore a dressing gown, trousers, and bedroom slippers. At six o'clock that evening the stupid Hungarian police grudgingly gave us our freedom. It was only Magda's relationship with the Portuguese Ambassador that saved our lives.

We sped back to the Portuguese legation. Over dinner it was discussed that Sanpayo had to leave quickly because he was now in even greater peril. "I wish to take you out, too, Jolie," he urged.

"I have not the heart to leave Vilmos," I said. "He does not yet have a visa."

Vilmos' eyes implored me. "I know the children adore you and they want you and you will get out safely but without you I will be lost. The children die for you. They adore only you. But they have their lives. I have only you. When you will be gone I will be lost."

This was true. It was also true that I had unfinished business in Hungary. My accountant, Tibor, had sent me a telegram in code to Galgagyörk saying, "Paul has pneumonia and is dying." Since everything was being censored this meant his life is in danger.

With Magda and her Ambassador en route to Lisbon I turned my thoughts to the one other refugee I had to save—Paul Savosdy.

There was a young Portuguese Chargé d'affaires with a young wife who were now in charge of the two legations—the one at the Ritz Hotel in Budapest and the summer one, the huge castle in Galgagyörk. They were nothings, but in the Ambassador's absence they were trying to be frightfully chic and social and fit into the continental international society.

The Chargé and his wife came every weekend to Galgagyörk with a shiny car. They were very good to me because I was the mother of Magda, who was on very close terms with the Ambassador. I begged the Chargé to save Paul's life. He was willing for several reasons. He was eager to do a favor for Magda's mother and two, he thought Paul could be useful with his connections in terms of food, since at this point we were all subsisting on horsemeat and three, I gave the wife a diamond ring. She said, "Oh, Madame Gabor, we don't do this for your ring," but she took it quick. "Okay," agreed the Chargé. "We will grant this Savosdy fellow asylum but in order to get him out of the country with you, the only way is for you to marry him."

This idea frightened me. I was literally afraid to be married to him. I saw that when he is my husband he will kill me because he was for me a disease. For me this was not a happy love affair. There were two days when I heard a false alarm that Paul was killed and would you believe I was actually glad that the torment was over. As long as he didn't belong to someone else I could bear the fact that he no longer would belong to me and I felt relief.

I no sooner had Paul safe when I lost Mama. My mother, who was also housed in Galgagyörk, wouldn't stay. She said, "My three other daughters and my son are in Budapest and what is good for them is good for me. I must be where the largest part of my family is." Meanwhile Sebika had been trying to get refuge for Manci in Galgagyörk but there was no more room. When Mama left I was the only one who said, "We will take Manci in here."

Seby didn't worry for himself. Luckily, his former schoolmates in the military academy in Germany helped him. He became a chauffeur for the Nazis and felt with his friends he was in no danger. He came only to see Mama in the legation but wouldn't stay even though I begged him. To this day I will never believe I could have done something so stupid as to bring Manci and her twelve-year-old daughter into the Portuguese legation.

Meanwhile, word came to me that Paul was safely under the wing of the Portuguese Chargé at the Ritz Hotel. Paul, who had money from the Mendel business, cleverly brought the Chargé and his wife wines and gourmet food packages and he entertained them handsomely in their own legation. They fell in love with him. Exactly at this time when they were falling in love with Paul I was in Galgagyörk fighting with Manci.

Once she was safely inside the walls of the castle she began fighting for the lives of her mother and father. She and I fought each other bitterly because she said, "You fight for your lover and I fight for my parents."

As soon as I knew Paul was safe, however, I stopped battling with Manci. There was too much danger everywhere. We were not only worried about the Nazis but we were terrified for the Red Armies because they were after the aristocrats and here we were in a castle with VIPs and we were also frightened for the Americans because we had to escape constantly to the cellar for refuge from the U.S. bombs. I had received news that my apartment near the Elizabeth Bridge had suffered a direct hit and was totally destroyed. I, who had gotten hysterical if a maid dropped a plate, now didn't care that my whole house—paintings, china, crystal—was demolished. It didn't touch me. Nothing but my love for Paul was real to me in those days.

Manci was dull and plain. She never wore beautiful clothes nor did her hair nor smelled beautiful nor perfected her makeup nor put on jewelry. Sebi loved lovemaking and when Manci married Sebi she always gave the excuse to him that she was sick with female trouble so she couldn't make sex. She confided to me, "Every day at six I would have an appointment to go to the doctor for my so-called female trouble and Sebi believed it."

I remembered that every day at six she did actually leave her home and go to this doctor's office. What I didn't know and what Sebi didn't know and what Manci confided to me as we spent endless aimless hours in Galgagyörk was, "The doctor left his office every day promptly at six o'clock and at 6:05 every day his brother, the engineer who was my lover arrived. Every single evening we would make great love and I would be home the latest by 9:00 P.M." I looked at this gray mouse astounded. She looked like a nun and she gave off that same aroma. And here I had never ever had a lover in all my twenty-two years and she had had one every night.

Manci was the only woman at the legation who was related to me and we were two lonely, frightened women and so we talked. Crouched side by side in the black cellar an afternoon when bombs were whistling overhead, I told her about Paul. "I want to go out from Paul's love affair but cannot," I told her. I told her everything. I told her my whole heart.

The following weekend the Chargé brought Paul out. I'm the one who had begged for his life. I'm the one who had personally fought for his survival. I'm the one responsible for his being safely under the protection of the Portuguese. Still he was not terrific to me. Among the thirty in Galgagyörk was a handsome young girl, the mistress of an anti-Nazi. When I awoke in the morning he and this girl were walking in the garden. I thought I would slash my wrists. Everybody there knew how I felt about him—Vilmos, Manci and her daughter, the Chargé and his wife—I was humiliated.

I was burning so badly inside my stomach that I showed too much my pain and my love. When he saw me there, my face flushed and strained, he called to me, "Oh, Jolie, you are up so early."

The girl looked at me. I looked at her. To pierce the silence he greeted me again, "I didn't expect you are up so early."

I was up so early because this was the first time I had seen him in weeks and I could not waste one second of seeing him. On his part he was still in love with me but the way he was in love was not the way I was in love. He began to promenade with me and he said, "The Chargé tells me we should marry."

"And what is your opinion?" I asked.

"Let us do so," he replied quickly. "I am for it. Why not?"

I felt he only wanted security. "We have time," I said. "Let's see what happens."

"Look," said Paul as we paused a moment under the shade of a tree that was just beginning to put on its green spring coat. "I know you are worried because you are four years older. You don't have to be ashamed. I don't mind."

"I must admit," I smiled wryly, "that your request for my hand is not exactly in the way that is a woman's dream. It's for sure yours is not the most romantic proposal a girl ever had."

"But you know that I care for you, Jolika," he reasoned. "After all, I am willing to marry you."

"Yes, I repeated, "I know that you are willing."

"It is you who are afraid."

"I see you as only for me an expensive pleasure for which I must pay a high price." I allowed myself a small smile. "Perhaps I will only permit you to be my lover. Perhaps if I marry you it will be for me a life of pain." I allowed myself another small smile. "We will wait . . . we shall see . . ."

I had earlier come to grips with the fact that I was in love with love, which was my subconscious reason for having wanted to be an actress. I thought this way a hundred men would be at my feet and I had realized even without the psychiatrist that everything I did, I did for love. With Paul it was a passion so deep as to be almost unbearable. It was a sickness, but I could not say it was a real genuine love. It was a love affair not a love.

He was willing to marry and come to America with me as his passport to freedom except I knew that it would not be an easy life with him. I was afraid. But stronger even than this fear was my fear of losing him.

His morning walk with the young handsome mistress of the anti-Nazi thwarted, he spent the afternoon flirting with Manci. Manci! I was a queen in feathers and marabou and beautiful hats and perfume. They called me Mme. du Barry. Yet he had left me to eat my guts out while he fastened those precious blue eyes on Manci, the mouse. Manci! From my window I could see his snow-white head and Manci's nondescript brown head bowed together laughing over something. Manci! Flirting with Manci to whom I had confided my heart! Manci who knew I would die for him!

It happened that the Chargé's wife was not well and had a bad stomach. Manci tells, "I am a good cook. You take me to the Ritz Hotel and I will cook for you. I know how to make special diet foods." First, Manci wanted to be in Budapest, safe under the protection of the Portuguese legation at the Ritz Hotel. She did not like the Portuguese country safety of Galgagyörk and she did like Paul whose duties caused him to live in the city at the Ritz. Also, she wanted to get in close with the Chargé and his wife because she wanted them to save her parents.

The first night she was in the Ritz she had an affair with Paul. It was only a six-room suite and everybody who was there knew everything. That first night, I heard, she was in pajamas and she fixed up her hair fluffy and pretty and she brought Paul cognac on a silver tray. He was in bed in his room and she volunteered to bring him a nightcap that he never ordered. She ended up giving him an even bigger nightcap.

Manci's daughter Annette was jealous of her mother. When they came back up for the weekend, the daughter sidled up to me, "Oh, Auntie Jolie, my mother takes such good care of Paul that I'm sure you'd be interested to know this." She said it in a way that you knew she was deliberately dropping you a hint.

But still I didn't sense any danger. I thought maybe there was some pitchy-potchy but nothing really. How could I believe such gossip? I was witty and gorgeous and she was the type who would scrub his shorts!

Slowly, you hear things. Slowly you begin to put pieces together. You can imagine how I felt. Manci, whom I had saved, was in bed with my Paul, whom I had saved. Little Manci had suddenly become a power. I had said "Sebika's wife must be saved" only because I adored Sebi. So it was I who had saved her life—and for what? So she could take my lover away from me!

Sometimes women fall for a man whom they wouldn't believe they could love because they like only tall and handsome and he's short and not good-looking. As I stared at Paul, I thought that nobody can give advice as to the tricks between a man and a woman.

God knows I had done all the right things. All the tricks I knew I had used with Paul. I always waited for him well-groomed and perfumed. Even an ugly female when she has a good smell is enticing. The only thing is, for an ugly female she has to use a little more perfume so she smells from ten inches not just from eight. Another help is a beautiful hostess robe and a fluffy nightgown. Even when Paul didn't want me so much he went crazy when I waited for him in a frilly nightgown with feathers. This is guaranteed to work.

Another trick I knew instinctively and always practiced is that I never tell my troubles. This kills a man. I tried, too, when he was a little stupid to shut up my mouth. I looked at him as though he would be the smartest. It's the little things that count.

It is very easy for a woman when she is rich and can afford the finer things to show off an elegant dinner. When a woman is poor it is more difficult. She must do extra things to attract him. Like Manci did. She washed Paul's socks.

Well, Manci's way was working. I even knew that the greatest magnet to win him back would be jealousy but with Paul I had no powers to make him jealous.

I didn't believe that he didn't love me. I couldn't believe that I could have saved him only for another woman—and my own brother's wife! It was

Sebastyen himself who had told me that he didn't love Manci. That she had absolutely nothing for him. That she was a prude. Sebi was like me. He was handsome, fun-loving, exciting, successful, full of life. Sebi only began to notice Manci when he learned that she was having an affair with a man she took away from me.

When I mentioned the rumors, Paul put me off with, "How can you compare yourself to Manci? One is a queen. The other is a mouse."

And so, on a bitterly cold day, we all left Hungary. It was snowing and the U.S. bombs were falling and Mama and Sebika risked their lives to come say goodbye to us in the Ritz Hotel. Sebi was an angel, He wanted his wife and daughter out but he adored Mother and he didn't want to leave her and no matter how much I pleaded she wouldn't leave her other three children. "I will be all right," she assured me. "I will go back and hide in my own house with the concierge. He has a good place to hide."

"Never mind the concierge, Mama. I insist you stay here in the underground shelter of the Portuguese legation."

"But the concierge has been a friend of mine for many years and I trust him."

"No. If you go out from here then I don't leave this country. I stay here."

So Mama finally agreed to stay. She and Sebika said good-bye to me. It was a hurried good-bye, scarcely enough to last you the rest of your life. I was never to see either of them again.

I had in my lap a small box of $200,000 worth of diamonds and platinum, all I had left in the world. At this point the entire legation of Portuguese officials was in danger so they were coming out with us. A Hungarian count took over as chief of the legation so to him I gave this box to deposit in the National Bank in the name of the Portuguese Delegation. I thought, "Let God just save me and sometime, somewhere, someday, somehow I will retrieve it."

There was block-to-block, hand-to-hand fighting. The Nazis were killing the Jews and the Communists were killing the Nazis. There was fire in the streets, there were people being hauled off to ovens, American bombs were falling from the sky. It was slaughter in the streets, bombs in your neighbors' living rooms, friends trembling under yellow badges and mothers begging passers-by to take their babies. There was danger everywhere.

It was arranged for us to go in four cars. The Chargé and his wife, me with Vilmos, Paul, Manci, Manci's daughter Annette, Count Mylot, two high generals, and Baron Gudman with his son and daughter-in-law. In the lead car, in the Chargés personal car, on our way out of Hungary in the escape which I engineered and in which he owed me his life, Paul whispered to me, "Jolie, I like you very much but I am not in love with you." He kissed me, he clung to me, he hugged me, he patted me but that was it.

And like this I left Hungary.

We went from Budapest to Vienna. En route to Austria through Germany we saw burned-out cars on the highway. For Germany the war was mostly over but in Hungary where it came late, it was still going on. It was near the end, though, because Berlin was falling.

We were terrified to go through Germany and we drove during the blackout. Nobody ever checked my belongings anywhere we went. I'd left all those jewels in Budapest because I was afraid they'd be confiscated and I was so disgusted when nobody ever asked me what we have in the car. At one point we were told the car is too overloaded. I had to throw out my bags because I had more luggage than anybody else. Everybody complained, "Jolie has too much. Make her throw out." So I tossed it out without a backward glance and all I had left in the world was the old mink coat I was wearing and my hand baggage.

From Germany we were going into Switzerland but the problem was we couldn't get a Swiss visa. We were afraid we'd be left in Germany. I had tried very hard to negotiate with the authorities. I owned half of a five-floor house on the Váczi Utcza, and I told my Budapest lawyer that for a Swiss visa for Vilmos, myself, and Paul I would give my part of the house. The answer came, "No." But he also told me "You have not to worry. There is a little bridge between Switzerland and Germany. You have to run maybe two minutes. It's the length of a block."

"Where is this bridge?" I had asked.

"At Sankt Margrethen, which is on the border."

"Santa Margaretta is a resort, no?"

"Yes," he replied, "but it's a border town situated between Switzerland and Germany and connected by this little bridge. If the authorities ask for your visa, get out of the car and say, 'I have it but I don't know where' and then run. Once you get halfway they can't throw you out. And don't worry. It's really only a few steps."

I steeled myself for this run. The Chargé, who drove our car arrived at the Sankt Margrethen border police. He spoke with them for two hours. He pleaded diplomatic immunity. He demanded they let us through but they wouldn't. He finally succeeded in setting us up in a small hotel in Sankt Margrethen while he went to formally arrange for our visas.

We were placed in the charge of two Swiss policemen who stood guard over us with their guns. We couldn't do anything. We just sat under heavy guard and heavy hearts, terrified that somehow things wouldn't be smoothed out. None of us really could understand why the Portuguese were so committed to delivering us out of occupied Europe to freedom. We couldn't figure why but we didn't ask. We were just grateful and worried that at any moment this magic would stop.

We were hungry. Vilmos had 80,000 pengös on him and I had 100,000. Formerly for fifty pengös you could eat for a week in Hungary. Now as we traveled we found that one piece of bread cost 500 pengös. One cup of coffee was 200. One little chicken cost us 10,000. The pengö had no more value anymore. "We will eat up all our money in one week," fretted Vilmos. "Our fortune is worth nothing." We figured in three days we would be completely without a cent.

You know at the exact moment that I knew Paul had really and truly fallen in love with Manci? We were all hungry and Paul had in his luggage Hungarian salami. He cut Manci a thicker piece than he cut me. When I saw that her salami was fatter than mine I knew he loved her for sure.

As we were sitting at the table in this little hotel in Sankt Margrethen the telephone rang. The waiter walked straight to me and said "Madame Gabor, you are wanted on the telephone." I stared at him. I couldn't believe there would be a call for me.

"From whom?" I asked incredulously. "How? Who knows that I am in Sankt Margrethen?"

"Maybe even here Madame Gabor is a big shot," said Manci, her face full of the salami I should have been eating.

"Jancsi . . . Jancsi . . . it's Zala," I heard over the crackly long-distance phone.

"Zala? Zalabondy? My Zalabondy, who I haven't seen in fifteen years?" I gasped when I could find my voice.

"Yes . . . yes . . . it's me, Zala," he crackled impatiently.

"From where do you speak?" I asked him.

"Now just be quiet and listen. From now on your group are all my guests. When you arrive in Berne you will have $5,000 waiting for you."

I couldn't believe what I was hearing. "Five thousand dollars when I arrive in Berne?"

"This must be part of the money he stole from Hungary," hissed Vilmos, who had gotten up and walked closer to the phone.

"Now, look," said Zala, "do as I say and collect this money at the Portuguese legation in Berne. I will contact you again." And he disconnected.

I repeated the instruction to Vilmos. "This is like the Count of Monte Cristo," he marveled. "I don't believe it."

"Vilmos," I exclaimed, "do you remember two years ago when we first suffered such a shortage of foods in Budapest and one day a 20-pound bag of coffee was mysteriously delivered to us and it had on it only the name 'Zalabondy'?"

He grunted. "I guess I should feel a little ashamed of the way I used to treat him. . . ."

We could never stop for long in our flight to safety because we were always warned it was not safe. The next morning we got into Switzerland. On the Swiss side of the border the Portuguese legation met us, authorized our papers, which said we were Portuguese citizens, and we were passed through.

When the war was only beginning to break out, I was in St. Moritz with my girls—the time they wore the same clothes—and the manager at the Palace Hotel had then told me, "Why don't you leave your furs and jewels here, Mrs. Gabor? There are rumors that things may be happening poorly in Europe. I will put the jewels in a safety deposit box and they will be here in case you ever need them." Impulsively, quickly, I had done just that.

I'd heard many stories about things that were never found and were mysteriously lost so I had no security they would still be there.

They were such decent people that when that manager left the hotel's employ, he informed his successor of my valuables that were in his safekeeping and so all these years later the new director handed them right over to me. There were two coats missing—my nutria and my silver fox, but who cared? I was so grateful that I gave a diamond bracelet to the new manager's wife.

In Berne, Zala's $5,000 was waiting for us and so was another phone call. "When you pass from France to Spain," said Zala, "you will be taken care of at the border. From that point on you will be my personal guests."

Again Vilmos and I couldn't believe it. We didn't even understand why the Portuguese were taking such special care of us, how could we even begin to understand why Zala was? There were so many things we didn't understand.

Zurich is where Paul with Manci and her daughter got off. Some others also stayed in Switzerland. It was a hard parting. You become very close with human beings when you flee to safety together and you live and eat and tremble with fear together. In the case of Paul it was for me great anguish that he was leaving me—and with Manci yet!

I was heartbroken over him. This last night when we were to part ways he made me a gift.

"You may come to my room tonight," he whispered at the dinner table.

"Thank you for this favor," I whispered back sarcastically—but I was grateful. I would take even crumbs from him.

He stroked me tenderly as I lay in his arms for what I knew would be the last time.

He prevented any conversation with kisses. This was my farewell present from Paul Savosdy.

All my life I thought that when I have finally a romance, I will soar with ecstasy on the wings of an angel. Well, I had it and I was no angel and I did not soar anyplace. I was so unhappy that I knew never ever could I love like that again.

France was blue with smoke as we drove through. The smell of fire and burned bodies hung everywhere. Dead people lay piled up on the highways and burned-out cars littered the roads. We stayed at a little hotel in a village. There were steps leading down from the door. I lost my footing and banged my head on the iron gate and suffered a gash across my forehead. Vilmos rushed to my rescue. "Come to Papa," he soothed and as always he lay my head on his chest. He stroked me and comforted me, "I'll help you," he said stroking my hair. He was so sweet and so dear and that night I slept in the crook of his arm. "I'll help you," he kept repeating. "Do not care anymore for this butcher." He meant Paul. "Forget this butcher." The physical pain was so intense that it blotted out the emotional pain and I was over Paul.

At all borders our stomachs would tighten from nerves and we would be mortally afraid. But at the border of Spain we were met by the police bearing chocolates and flowers! A uniformed escort ushered us to a magnificent hotel. Here we were received like kings. The police actually bowed to us and informed us that Alberto, the Director of the Hotel, would personally be awaiting us courtesy of Mr. Zalabondy.

Zalabondy again!

In Barcelona everybody, all of those traveling with us, had rooms reserved at the Ritz in their names. Me, I had an extra room and mine was filled with pink roses. Me, in my shabby clothes, I was like the Dowager Empress. I couldn't understand it. I couldn't understand anything. Over and over Vilmos kept repeating, "He is like the Count of Monte Cristo, who came back rich after so many years." And over and over I kept repeating, "I wonder what he wants from me."

Early the next morning Zala met us for breakfast. He had not changed too much—a little older, a little heavier, a lot more sure of himself. "How did you find me? How did you know where I was?" I asked.

"Magda told me," he said, patting my hand.

"Where did you find Magda?" I asked him.

"I didn't. Magda found me when she got to Spain with that Portuguese Ambassador of hers."

"Oh," I said, "that Magda is so smart. She found him and then she found you."

Zala didn't like Magda. He considered her too aggressive and not nearly grateful enough. "Why is she so smart? She just opened the phone book and found me. I'm a pretty important man around Spain, you know."

I *did* know. That is, I knew he was now the best friend of Franco but

I didn't know how. "Zala," I lowered my voice and leaned across the table toward him, "last I heard you were in trouble in Hungary and then you went to the U.S. and you became broke and so how is it you are now here and rich?"

"Jolika," he smiled, patting my hand again, "you ask too many questions. Right now I have to go to Casablanca on business. I will be back for dinner."

"Yesterday when we arrived and I asked for you they told me also that you were away for the day. They tell me you fly away someplace every day and come back every night for dinner."

Another smile then, "Yes."

"Zala, I think you are on one side an angel and on the other side a crook. What do you really do?"

"I am an importer of sardines."

"And from sardines you can be a friend to Franco? I think you are a very mysterious person."

He stood up. "I must leave for Casablanca. What do you want for dinner?"

"Fish," I said. "I want fish."

When we were ready for dinner that night the waiter brought in a huge fish.

The next morning a Hungarian who was an executive with the hotel greeted us with a bow so low his forehead buffed my shoes. "Mr. Zalabondy begs you to understand he was taken away on business. In fact, he had to fly to America for the weekend. He says he will see you on Monday. Meanwhile, you are to be assured that everything is arranged for you."

There were fresh flowers on the table. A complete set of matching luggage was delivered to my room with my name on it and Zala's card attached. I gasped to Vilmos, "After Budapest this is like a dream."

"But why?" asked Vilmos.

"Basically it is that he adores me," I preened in front of the mirror, deciding that now that I had a rich and powerful beau I definitely had to take off another ten pounds. At least eight. Five for sure. "But," I continued, "it is more than that. Maybe a little he wants to show me what he has become. Remember, you humiliated him so now he wants to show to us he is a Croesus, an emperor."

"Still," Vilmos said slowly, "there is something not kosher."

Magda and I cried and screamed and wept and shouted on the phone —she in Portugal and me in Spain. "Nucika," she finally got out after she calmed down. "Nucika . . . oh, Nuci . . . I don't believe it, Nuci I have lost my hair from nerves. I haven't slept one moment until I got you out of Hungary and on your way into Portugal. Oh, Nuci, not one word did I hear from you all the time you were traveling from Budapest to Spain. . . . oh, Nuci."

We both broke down crying again. For a few moments neither of us could speak. *"Nucika,"* she said finally, "you don't know how hard we all worked to get you and Papa out of Hungary. Zsa Zsa and Eva arranged to get to Cordell Hull, who is a superimportant man in Washington. He is Secretary of State of America. Mr. Hull himself sent a telegram to the Portuguese government who are acting as emissaries for the Allied powers to help save the Gabor family. I will tell you all about that when I see you but, anyway, I was working from Portugal and Zsa Zsa and Eva were working from America."

"Oh," I said, "No wonder there was such care taken for us."

"Zsa Zsa and Eva are doing very well," Magda reported.

In April of 1942, when Zsa Zsa married Conrad Hilton, I was still in Budapest so the telegram came through the Portuguese legation. She had said: "He is not a hotel director as you told me I should get, but he is the most beautiful man and I love him and he is a hotel owner." Her telegram ended: "Connie marrying me has made me almost the happiest woman in the world but I cannot yet be the happiest without you."

"So, is Zsa Zsa today so happy with Hilton?" I asked Magda.

"Well, yes, but it's a little bit less the happiness than it was. Still she is married to him. Eva's new husband, Charles Isaacs, is also very rich and powerful."

"The last letter I got from Eva after the divorce from her Dr. Drimmer told how homesick in California she was even for one familiar face, and she said that the only one she saw from home was Bundy Solt. The last time I ever heard from him he asked me for five dollars. At least I sent him $50, and when I arrived in America he was making $5,000 a week. A famous Hollywood screenwriter, that's what he's doing."

"And Evika, is she happy with Charles Isaacs?"

"Yes, Zsa Zsa was responsible for finding Charles just as she was responsible for getting rid of Drimmer."

"Yes, Zsa Zsa wrote me that she broke up the whole marriage. She said Eva was already a little unhappy with him, though, because he always went to the homes of big film stars like Signe Hasso and Greta Garbo to give his treatments and she was very jealous."

"Well, but after a while she wasn't so jealous because she lived with Erik in a tiny $65-a-month apartment with one bedroom and a little living room and that was it. When Zsa Zsa found Hilton and moved into a big house, they found this Charles Isaacs for Eva and he's a millionaire."

"What kind of a millionaire?" I asked.

"A *real* one. A handsome young real estate broker from a good family, but right now a member of the Coast Guard. When Zsa Zsa arrived in Hollywood and she found Hilton she told to Eva, 'Forget Erik. He only makes maybe $100 a week. You must have a rich husband. Get rid of him.' But anyhow it was not good anymore. Zsa Zsa tells me Eva had nothing."

The operator cut in to see if we wanted still to talk longer. Of course we wanted to talk longer.

"But Eva sent always to me pictures of herself in a swimsuit at a swimming pool."

"Maybe it was Bette Davis' swimming pool."

"But she always sent to me and to Mama pictures of herself in fluffy white dresses with notes saying she was going here and there. I showed all these to my friends and we all thought she is another Garbo and so if Garbo makes $10,000 a week then she has at least to be making $5,000."

"Not even 5,000 pengös. She had as a starlet only $120 a week. When Zsa Zsa got there Zsa Zsa didn't want to be a starlet. Zsa Zsa wants to be a film star so Eva began to be unhappy. As Eva told me, when she arrived, Hollywood was looking for beauties so they took her. Actually, they did try to make her into a star. They put her in a Hawaii beachparty film but nothing happened."

"It is better I only know this now," I said, "because I always told to my friends that my daughter is a big star."

Magda chuckled.

"Only once did I realize Eva wasn't too successful, maybe," I said. "She wrote me she needed money for a few thousand dollars worth of work on her teeth. So I sent with bitter difficulty the $2,000 to make the teeth."

"That's really how her agent found her. A Hollywood woman agent named Olga Lee saw her there and said she is such a great beauty that she took her to Paramount for a screen test. They gave her the contract immediately."

"After all with my teeth, why not?" I joked. I was feeling so good and so safe now that my sense of humor had returned.

"And did you hear, *Nuci*, how she went to the screen test in a black satin dress and her mink coat from Budapest?"

"But this must have been very impressive."

"At eight o'clock in the morning on a hot summer day in July?"

"Oh, well, in this case it is a little too impressive!" It felt so good to make fun.

Then we began to speak a little about Zalabondy. "He will be very good to you in Spain," she said, "but he will never go with you to Portugal. We are only forty-five minutes away by plane and yet Zala cannot come into this country. He's not allowed in. I don't know what exactly he does. I know he spent some time in Washington a while back. Seems he wanted to convert a battleship into a fishing ship with a hospital on it . . . sort of like a floating city for the fish industry. But it never came about. There are times when he can't seem to get into America, either."

"You mean he is in bad with the whole country of Portugal?"

"He can't even pass the border."

"He has been so good to me," I said. "One of those who escaped with us was Baron Gudman. The Baron fell ill and it was decided that he needed fast an operation. When we got to Barcelona he was admitted to the hospital and he died there. Zala paid for the funeral and all the hospital expenses."

"No," said Magda, who knew everything. "Don't you believe it. The debts are still outstanding. He paid for nothing. I know because the Chargé and his wife, who were with you as far as Spain, are now back here and they have told the true story."

"So what does he want from me, Zala?"

There was a low chuckle, then, "Hilton. He wants contacts with Hilton. He desperately wants to meet Hilton."

Zala's Rolls-Royce was at the entrance to the Ritz and he took Vilmos and me to his mansion. It was lush, built around a garden, wood paneling throughout, antiques, many servants. Over *gazpacho* he showed me a newspaper clipping which said that Hilton and Zsa Zsa were having troubles and that Hilton will have to give her $10 million in alimony.

This was never anywhere near true but this is what impressed Zala as a businessman. "You know, Jolika," he said when the meal had progressed to the *paella*, "I think it would be very nice if when you get to America you could arrange for me a meeting with your son-in-law."

"Well, come with us tomorrow to Portugal and we will arrange it." I was eager to see how he would handle this.

"No, I must leave for the United States," replied Zala, "and I will be there waiting for you when you arrive."

We arrived at a little Portuguese border town and without Zala's influence they weren't so nice to us there. We were just other refugees. They stopped us, searched us, and a little stared at us. I, a penniless emigré from wartorn Hungary, arrived from sunny Spain like visiting royalty, with the blue fox coat and matching hat I had retrieved in St. Moritz, brand-new luggage from Zala, an armful of pink roses from Zala, too. Vilmos was a little like a king himself, with his coat lined in mink left over from the old days.

Magda met us at the station half laughing and half crying. Nervous and visibly worn, much of her hair had fallen out. She was bone thin and her face was drawn.

After the hugging and the kissing and the tears, Magda told us, "We are going to the resort town of Estoril, which is only a half hour outside of Lisbon. This is the nicest part of Portugal."

As we drove under a cloudless powder blue sky along the ribbon of road that paralleled the white sandy beaches and emerald green ocean of the Portuguese Riviera, I asked, "When do we leave for America?"

"We don't. We cannot leave here until the war is over, and since we don't know how long it takes we are going to live at the Hotel Palacio. The Palacio is the best hotel and Estoril is the nicest atmosphere."

I gazed admiringly at the white and pastel pink, yellow and green villas along the way and thought that I have not exactly to have a hardship living here. "But, Magduska," I said, "Papa and I have no money."

"First of all Portugal is inexpensive," she explained as we drove slowly along this exquisite portion of the world, which seemed not to know things like Nazis. "One hundred escudos is four dollars. For four dollars per day you have a suite overlooking the ocean. Butlers and waiters and chambermaids will bring things on silver trays and you can live like royalty."

"Yes, but so far," said Vilmos, "we don't even have the four dollars to change into the 100 escudos."

"It is agreed that Eva and Zsa Zsa will each contribute $500 a month while you are here. For $1,000 per month you can have 25,000 escudos and here that is the height of luxury."

I saw that they had gambling in Estoril. "In that case Vilmos can go to sleep early and I will take nightly ten dollars—250 escudos—and I will gamble and be a very *grande dame*. As a matter of fact, if Zsa Zsa is going to get ten million, I can afford to gamble more than that!"

"But I don't want to go to sleep early," put in Vilmos, but his ex-wife and daughter were too excited to pay any attention to him.

They gave Vilmos and me one bedroom. "How can anyone live in one bedroom with an ex-husband?" I complained to Magda. "This is uncivilized."

"It is their only suite," she answered.

"I cannot share one bathroom and one bedroom with *Papuska*. You must do something. You are excellent in languages. In one month you speak anything. I know already you speak perfect English and since you couldn't make romance with the Portuguese Ambassador every single moment, I assume you must have spent some time talking, so you must also be excellent in Portuguese. Therefore, in one language or the other go and complain to the hotel director. I am very unhappy."

An hour later she came back up distraught. The answer was no. I nagged her. "Go down again. Be angry with him. Look at this one room with the two narrow twin beds separated by the skinny night table. Please . . . Magda . . . do something."

"All right," she sighed. "Do the best for tonight. Tomorrow I will manage something."

Several days later, Magda came in, bursting with happiness, to say, "Congratulations, I have managed to get you an extra bedroom"—and she found only one narrow twin bed had been slept in. I had been homesick so I went to Vilmos' shoulder for consolation and put my head on his chest, as I always did and, anyhow, he was being kind to me in these days and he stroked me and it made me feel better.

Magda began to scream, "I stand like a fool arguing with the hotel director and you're sleeping with Papa!"

Later, from my new bedroom, I spoke to Zsa Zsa and Eva. It was the first time we had actually heard one another's voices in five years. When Zsa Zsa and I caught our breaths and stopped our hysteria at hearing each other's voices, she told me what they had done to get us out of Budapest: "Every day at five o'clock I would visit Eva and discuss what we must do and try to find ways of getting you out. Every month there were fewer letters from you. Finally Connie let me go to Washington and Charles did the same for Eva and we flew there to talk to all our friends. We spoke to Dr. Vasco Garrin . . ."

"Who's he?" I asked.

"First Secretary of the Portuguese Embassy. The big problem was that Portugal accepted war refugees only if the United States guaranteed their admission into this country but this was impossible in the case of an enemy alien, which is what you are."

"But Magda said something about the Secretary of State helping."

"Yes. Eva and I called on all our diplomatic friends including those I knew from Turkey like Dr. Munir Ertegun, the Turkish Ambassador to the United States. Eventually a ten-minute meeting was set up for us with Cordell Hull. Eva and I were both nervous because this was the one man who *could* help. He promised nothing because he said everything depended on your papers. But he did say he'd try. The result was a high-level telegram to the Portuguese government to use their offices to help the Gabor family. That meant you and *Papuska* and your sisters and Uncle Sebi. The code was worded to say that the Portuguese must save twelve people."

I was thinking of Baron Gudman and Paul and Manci and the others. "Who exactly were the twelve?"

"I don't know and it didn't matter. It had to be to save more than just the Gabors because there would be too much difficulty in explanation otherwise, so the word went out to save twelve at Galgagyörk. This way it looked OK as though a whole group of VIPs were to be saved."

I thought to myself that Manci making love with my ex-lover in some bed somewhere in Zurich at this very moment probably had no idea that her whole life was due solely to the courtesy of the U.S. Secretary of State.

Realizing now what a VIP I was, I ate like royalty the next morning. Vilmos and I had room service, breakfast served by three slaves who brought for us chocolate, tea, toast, fruit, and buns.

We went for a walk through the town. Vilmos tried desperately to speak but Magda and I chattered endlessly. "You must learn Portuguese," she said.

"No, I learn English. I am not interested to learn Portuguese. I don't intend to live in Estoril all my life. I will live in America."

"But you must speak at least a few words."

"I can speak the word *amanha*, which means the same as Spain's *mañana* and that's the way they do everything here I have already learned. Everything I asked the cleaning lady to do she answered *amanha*—tomorrow. It is enough I understand this. I don't learn more."

The walk took all morning. We arrived back after noon. Still Vilmos kept interrupting.

"What is it?" Magda finally asked him.

"Yes," I scolded irritably. "You keep interrupting like you want to say something."

"I have been trying to tell you from the breakfast time but still you do not bother to ask me what I want."

"Okay, we ask now," I said. "What do you want?"

"I want to tell Magda to tell the room service breakfast waiter not to give me coffee, to give me tea."

"Oh, poor *Papuska*," soothed Magda. "He speaks only Hungarian."

Poor *Papushka*, indeed. His hair had turned white. His stomach had turned flabby. He was in a foreign country without friends, without power. He was lost.

Despite the luxury around me I couldn't eat well or sleep well or enjoy myself. In the first month I swam only once in the pool. I had no heart for these things while my precious mother, Sebi, and my sisters were still in Hungary. I had no way of knowing what happened to them. In my mind I saw Rozsie struggling in the arms of soldiers—were they Nazis? Were they Russians? I saw Janette tortured, Mama fleeing, Sebi hunted.

In a prearranged code I ultimately devised a plan. I wrote out a telegram ordering the Portuguese officials still in Budapest to save them. The message read to "immediately put the Tilleman sisters together with their husbands in the hospital." The "hospital" meant the Portuguese legation where my mother already was. The "Tilleman sisters" meant Dora, Rozsika, Janette and Sebi. I personally went to the post office to send this and I forged His Excellency Carlos de Sanpayo's name on it.

The clerk at the post office balked at sending it. "Who are you?" he asked suspiciously.

"I was asked by the Portuguese Ambassador to Hungary to send this for him," I replied.

He looked it over again carefully. "But where is the official stamp?" I looked back at him blankly. "The official stamp from the Ministry. I cannot send internationally a message from an Ambassador without his official stamp."

So I went by myself to the Ambassador and begged him to give his official stamp. He could not. I went back to the Palacio and cried myself to sleep.

My next stop was the hospital in Lisbon. I developed a pain in my kidney and one night it was so bad that I screamed in agony. Ultimately the pain subsided and I was released. The odd part was that at dinner that night I thought I would celebrate with one sip of white wine. "No," said Vilmos firmly. "You cannot have anything to drink." The next morning I said, "I think I will take a swim." Tears welling in her eyes, Magda picked up my hand wordlessly and kissed it. "Take care," she said huskily.

Vilmos and Magda were too good to me. I didn't understand it. When I was brought to the hospital for my second set of X rays I didn't want to go. "But why?" I asked. "I feel all right. I am not sick anymore." That's when I learned they had mixed up the X rays and mistakenly labeled mine as belonging to a man who was nearly *kaput*. He had one kidney gone and the other nearly gone. The doctor had originally said to Magda and Vilmos, "I am sorry but there is no help for this." That man actually died four days later and that's when they learned they had mixed up the X rays. Instantly I was over being sentenced to death, Magda and Vilmos were not quite so much adoring me.

I was blue. I was homesick. I missed Zsa Zsa and Eva. I missed my family whom I didn't know if I would ever see. I was not functioning emotionally. At least that's the only explanation I can now give for having allowed myself to be picked up.

A handsome blond man at the Palacio bar was very after me. He was much younger than me. "I will give you the best evening of your life," he said.

"Okay," I said, "so give it to me."

I was proud that he wanted to take me out. I was happy that I was still desirable to a man. My marriage was over. My love affair had gone badly. It was nice that such a good looking creature would want me. A woman likes to know if she's worthwhile and still desirable. I thought he would just take me to a nightclub. In any case, I was despondent and didn't really care that much.

In his red car we drove to Lisbon. I was a little tipsy after our few drinks at the nightclub and he checked us into a hotel and I took off my clothes and went to bed with him—as unglamorous as that. It was a small hotel. That's the part that I remember. Him I have almost forgotten. All that stays in my memory is that I gave myself.

I don't remember how I came back. I know I left him and made it home to Estoril alone. Never again was I so impulsive or feeling so low. Never again did I give myself to a man I didn't like. I was so ashamed of what I had done that I sat in my bathtub for one hour trying to wash off the dirt.

There is one theory that rattles around in the hearts of my people and that is *Mindenki Magyar*—everybody is Hungarian. It was on a Sunday. I had just returned from the neighboring town of Cascais and was sitting on the verandah when an ordinary-looking but very flamboyantly dressed man addressed me—in Hungarian. His name was Leo Ritter. He was a millionaire furrier. While I was talking to him another man came over and addressed me —in Hungarian. This man, a well-known maker of automobiles, was something like the Ford of Hungary. Now, in Ritter's early youth he had shovelled shit at this car manufactury and had read much about the glamorous Gabor family. With the fortunes of war, the glamorous Mme. Gabor and the Ford superexecutive of Hungary were refugees and the janitor was the millionaire from America! Fantastic! "Just think," said Ritter, "now I can shake hands with this man who had where I was once a janitor."

As the war ground to a halt, I prepared myself for the trip to America. I had one American friend, the wife of a clerk in the Embassy. Much later I learned she was a poor proletarian who washed and cleaned and cooked and lived in a lousy two-room apartment in Washington. However, with her husband's $400-a-month salary in Portugal she was *très nouveau riche.* She was a great lady with a villa at the seashore plus two servants and a French *mademoiselle* for her two-year-old son. She came always to call with long green silk gloves, so I thought they dressed like that in America because, after all, she was from the Embassy. I was so impressed with her. She gave me copies of the American *Vogue* and told me, "When you buy a cheap dress in America, then everybody you see on the street has the same."

I thought this is so because she told it to me. Now I know I can buy a *shmatteh* for $80 and never see it on another soul! I not only know it but I do it! She also showed me an evening gown in *Vogue* which cost $600. So I thought a good evening dress costs this much in America because she never bothered to tell me they don't *all* cost that. As a result I decided with my last money I will make all my dresses for America in Portugal—for $100 apiece —and I will put myself together so that when I come into America my daughters have not to be ashamed.

I had dozens of cheap Portuguese dresses made. I found a store where I could get lace and crocheted things for $100 so I bought out all of Lisbon. With my extra money I bought for the children black lace underwear and they told me when they saw it that only *kurvas* wear this. They were combination chemises. Then I bought red alligator shoes. Everything was terrible—but what did I know? Thanks to this clerk's wife advising me I bought all this. And I thought America will never have seen something so great!

On December 1, 1945, I boarded the *Mirandello,* the oldest Portuguese freighter alive. There was no place for Vilmos because most of the place was taken with its cargo of cork. I wanted very much to travel to America with Vilmos together to show the girls that their Papa and I are on good terms, but I could not wait. I thought this is the fulfillment of my whole life to see my daughters in the United States.

The reason I took the S.S. *Mirandello,* which carried more cargo than passengers, is because in those days the diplomats and big shots had priority on the planes. I could not wait even an hour for a plane or a better ship which was leaving a week later because for me the most important was to be on my way. And this smelly old freighter was the first ship bound for the United States. Its destination was Philadelphia.

The boat was in Lisbon for fourteen days loading. The baggage-loading men were so poor that they ate only fish and their pay per day was sixty cents. The voyage took thirty days and we were three women and seven men—eleven passengers in all if you count Migna the cow. The men aboard were very sad. They were German Jews, all great patriots from Germany, but because they were Jewish they had emigrated to London. All had been in England as soldiers and all had lost everything and everybody. One was a doctor who had escaped from a concentration camp and had served in the British army.

Another, an ex-lawyer, showed me a Parisian nightgown he was bringing for the wife he had never seen. It was marriage by mail as so many of them were doing since it was the only way they could come in and be United States citizens. In the old country he had witnessed the deaths of his children, his wife, his mother, and his father.

I had a cabin with three women. I was unhappy with the two others so I gave my gold watch to the steward and he somehow managed to move out some cork and find me a private cabin. It was small like a closet but it was all for myself and I was very happy.

I was so happy that I didn't even mind the bad weather. There was such roughness that everybody but me was throwing up. Because I was so happy to be going to America to see Zsa Zsa and Eva, I could feel nothing else. This boat was way up on its side for most of the voyage and every single person but me was dying.

Because all the others were vomiting, the last night I was alone with the Captain, who liked me. There was no big romance . . . just a very little. Just some kissing. This Commander also had an eye for the pretty chambermaid on board.

I was the queen of this junky cork-carrier. The crew pencilled on my door "Madame du Barry" because I came down dressed in a floor length caftan every evening. With a broken, yellowed mirror the size of a book and my lighting strictly one unshaded light bulb, which hung from the ceiling nowhere near the mirror, I bleached my hair by myself the best I could. I think the inside roots were a little dark but at least around the edges I was very blonde so I guess I must have looked okay. I only know everyone kissed my hand and the Commander said this was the very nicest holiday crossing he'd ever had.

We celebrated Christmas dinner on the ship and we were six people at the Captain's table. The entertainment was a boiler-roomworker with a guitar which he never much used before. The refreshment was a case of champagne they had dragged out of the cellar or wherever it had been under lock and key. The crew afterwards told me such a shipboard Christmas had never before happened.

December 31, 1945, dawned cold and damp. I paced back and forth across my small cabin. After five years of separation only hours remained before Zsa Zsa, Eva, and I would be together again. I was worried, a little sensitive: after all, I hadn't seen Eva since 1940 and Zsa Zsa since 1941. They were changed. They had to be changed. They had learned to live without me. The question was, how changed were they?

When it was still black outside I began getting ready. I had hours but I wanted my high-class daughters to be proud of how I looked when I walked down the gangplank. I shampooed my hair. I sprayed from my arms to my toes with perfume.

Wanting very much to impress, I had my special arrival outfit pressed. It was all over dark wine-colored everything: high turban, dress made in Lisbon with one hundred scallops on the hem and cuff, same wine-colored shoes, bag, and gloves. I was wearing a mink coat, which was a big thing, I thought, because in whole of Budapest they had maybe only eleven mink coats.

When I came to the railing I thought I was so damned elegant that America will faint when she sees me. Well, maybe America didn't faint but the two girls did. The first thing they said to me was, "You are not at all elegant. Too much wine color."

But I am getting ahead of my story. It was still only about three in the morning and I was all dressed. For me that night dragged like a heavy chain. Unable to bear it a moment longer, I went outside and stood on the deck, eager for my first glimpse of this golden land.

I couldn't see anything. The fog was thick like goulash. Nonetheless, nothing could dampen my enthusiasm. I had been in Estoril one whole year. I'd dreamed of this moment a million times.

It was five o'clock on New Year's Eve morning when the old hulk of a boat came to rest alongside the dock at Philadelphia's harbor. To me even a canoe would have looked beautiful if it had carried me safely across the ocean to the daughters I'd been separated from.

I had butterflies in my stomach. I checked my two trunks. I had brought everything with me because I didn't want to depend on my children. I had bought out all the junk I could find in Portugal—plates, bric-a-brac, porcelain, everything. All $500 worth of stuff when I unpacked it came broken in little pieces.

I looked out in the gloom and by the lights of the pier I could see Zsa Zsa and Eva and two strange men dressed in overcoats, hats, and gloves. The man in the Stetson and boots, I presumed, was my son-in-law Conrad Hilton. The tall, dark, and handsome one with his arm protectively around a shivering Eva had to be my new son-in-law Charles Isaacs. And there . . . in the flickering half light . . . I saw another man. Just as he had promised he would be, he was waiting for me when I arrived. Zala—It was Zala!

As the gangplank lowered I strained to catch a better glimpse of Zsa Zsa and Eva. They were weighed down with luxurious mink. The temperature was freezing but my girls were in high, slim heels, thin nylon stockings, heads bare, hair combed out long and so much jewelry that they sparkled like Christmas trees. I thought to myself, "Well, they probably put on everything they owned just to impress me." And I, by God, was going to impress them!

I waved good-bye to my nine fellow passengers, the ship's captain, the crew, Migna the cow and flew down the wooden ramp into the thick fog, to the arms of my daughters and my new life. Mama had arrived!

BOOK FOUR

Mrs.
Peter Christman

We kissed, we hugged, we cried. I was beside myself—I didn't know what to do or say first. We stood, jabbering in Hungarian, crying and clutching each other for dear life. Zsa Zsika . . . Evika . . . *Nucika* . . . five years. . . . It had been five years . . .

I looked at those two beautiful faces streaked with tears.

I looked at those two luxurious mink coats rippling in the breeze. I looked at those two millionaire husbands waiting discreetly off at a distance. I was a little scared. I thought, "Jolie, look at your little girls. They're rich. They're real millionaires. And what have you got—nothing but a hundred dollars left to your name." But in my heart I really am an actress. I quickly said to myself, "No! You don't play second fiddle to anyone—not even your rich, successful, glamorous daughters!"

I whipped open my bag, pulled out the one and only last hundred dollar bill I had. "This is all I own," I laughed. "This is what I bring into the New World. Tell me, my beauties, what will a hundred dollars buy in America?"

"Oh, about two hats," laughed Zsa Zsa.

"Hats I don't need," I said, and promptly turned around and ran back up the gangplank. "Here," I said, shoving my entire fortune into the hand of the stunned Captain. Please distribute this among the crew."

Maybe I was penniless but for sure I had impressed the girls! I walked back to my daughters and their husbands, head high, pockets empty. I was starting life all over again.

And where would a penniless immigrant fresh from the Old Country with nothing but the clothes on her back and a son-in-law who owns hotels stay her first night in America? Well, where else but the Royal Suite of the Hotel Plaza.

I was escorted by a fleet of bellboys—to turn on the steam heat, to open the window, to take the bags, to show me the closet, to point out the three bathrooms. I couldn't believe it. I told to Conrad Hilton, "But I cannot live all by myself in three bedrooms and three bathrooms even if you own this hotel. I have lived in one closet on a freighter for a month. I am not more accustomed to such splendor."

"Well, nothing's too good for my mother-in-law," he winked at Zsa Zsa.

169

"But I don't like to live in the Royal Suite when I am so poor," I explained to Conrad. "I like better a small suite."

"I can't help you, little lady," he grinned, "I'm not the manager—only the president. From what I understand this is the only vacancy and, anyhow, there is no royalty in town at the moment so the place is yours."

"It is very sweet of you," I said, smoothing my hand over the brocaded chairs, "but it is ridiculous."

"You can stay here for as long as you like. You're my guest," he said graciously.

I was thrilled when Zsa Zsa and Eva told me we were going to a big fancy party that evening. "How sweet of you," I said, "to make such a fuss over me!"

Eva giggled and informed me that the party wasn't exactly in my honor. In all the excitement I'd forgotten it was New Year's Eve!

"Fantastic," I kept saying over and over when we arrived at the party. "I'm in America only a few hours and I'm wearing an evening dress, drinking iced champagne in a ballroom crowded with the most beautiful people in New York wrapped in dinner clothes, satin gowns, lush furs, exotic perfumes, exquisite jewels and fancy titles. I can't believe it."

"The same happened to me," said Zsa Zsa, not to be outdone. "I arrived in New York on June 3, 1941, at nine o'clock in the morning. At noon I was lunching at a famous restaurant called 'Twenty-one' with the one American friend I had."

"But I'm doing better than you," I gloated. "I'm staying at the Royal Suite!"

Late in the night or, rather, early in the morning when I finally got back to my suite and settled down, I found I was very unsettled. I couldn't sleep. I walked around and around counting the different stars from the different windows. I tried going to sleep, but the sound of voices and laughter filled my ears. I got up again and stood at the salon window. Below me a sea of happy people rushed by, blowing horns, throwing bits of confetti in the air, hugging one another, singing at the top of their lungs, all filled with the good cheer of the holiday.

Hours later I crawled into my soft bed between sheets as fine as silk and I pulled the satin quilt up around me. The dawn of a new day was breaking. It was January 1, 1946. I was beginning a new life in a new world on a new year.

"Jolie Gabor," I said to myself, "You have come a long way."

I was in the Royal Suite with the three telephones and the three toilets but I didn't dare order a cup of coffee. I told the desk not to send the messages to my room. There was a cable downstairs from Magda confirming that she and Vilmos were arriving by plane in three weeks. There were flowers from Zala and a phone message from Eva. I told the desk clerk, "Don't send anything up to my room because I myself will pick up everything."

"Even the flowers, Madame?" asked the astounded clerk. "Yes, even the flowers," I said.

I went down and personally picked up the flowers, the cable, and the phone message and brought them to my high-class Royal Suite. I didn't have even twenty-five cents to give to a bellhop.

The next few days are rich with memories: My afternoon activity was strictly watching the little old blue-haired ladies in their flowered hats and skinny chokers sitting in the ultra respectable lobby eyeing everybody—that is, when their heads weren't nodding. I thought, "I will live in this hotel with a little dog and I will go out from my room and sleep in the lobby as they do." But I didn't like the idea.

My second day, Zsa Zsa took me to the Plaza movie theatre two blocks from the hotel. I adore movies and this *Love Letters* was a love story starring Jennifer Jones. In the darkness I slipped off my old brown mink from Budapest and folded it on my lap. "Why are you doing that?" whispered Zsa Zsa.

"Because it is warm in here," I whispered back.

"No, I mean, why do you keep it on your lap? It will be uncomfortable. Put it on the empty seat next to you."

"Zsa Zsa," I said, "Maybe now you are so rich that to you to lose a mink coat doesn't mean so much. This is my only remaining souvenir from Budapest and, besides, it's my only mink coat. This is my only bit of luxury left. I don't want it to be stolen. I'm not insured."

"I have a great idea," she said, slipping off her silver gray mink. "This is one of the only two platinum mink coats in the country—Delores del Rio has the other—and I hate it. It cost Connie $20,000 but, naturally, I have it insured for $25,000."

"Naturally," I muttered, trying to pay some attention to Jennifer Jones too. "So?"

"So I will lay my coat over yours and if anybody is looking to steal a mink coat they can have mine. It will be a favor to me."

She balled my coat up inside out and put it on the seat next to her, then folded hers with the fur showing and laid it neatly on top of mine.

We were absorbed in *Love Letters* and when finally Jennifer got the guy we looked over to the seat next to Zsa Zsa. My old Budapest mink coat had been stolen and her brand new one was still there!

Zsa Zsa was upset for me. I think maybe because she was afraid she would have to buy me a new one. In any case, now it was final. I was really flat broke. One of the policemen who came gave me his coat and, hugging it to me as we walked back across the street to the hotel, I commented to Zsa Zsa, "Good. Now I have absolutely nothing. I must really make a new start."

(Twenty years later I walked into the same theatre with the same little cashier still there and when she saw me she said, "Oh, Mrs. Gabor, did you ever find your mink coat?")

That night was the turning point of my whole life. There was a cocktail party in the three-room suite of this Mr. Leo Ritter, whom I had met in Estoril. On a round coffee table he had a spread of hors d'oeuvres. In the center of the food stood a round silver tray piled high with Christmas and New Year's greetings. He showed them off proudly. He even had a Happy New Year's card from some prince which he grandly pointed out. I was admiring them all and I saw holiday greetings in Magda's handwriting. I picked it up to read it and I nearly died. She had written, "Take care that Mama doesn't see this. I worry very much about what will happen when she hears that her mother and her beloved Sebi were both killed by a bomb."

I let out a scream and the girls came running over. "What is it . . . what happened . . . what's the matter . . . ?"

I couldn't speak. I thought only that I would die.

"Look . . . look," I gasped.

Eva grabbed the card and accosted Ritter angrily. "You left this card lying around along with all the others?"

Zsa Zsa ran after me because like a wild animal I had raced out the door. Upstairs in my own apartment I punched the bed and shrieked and buried my head in the pillow. "I will kill myself," I cried in a frenzy of pain, racked with sobs. "I will kill myself."

"Please, *Nuci*," Zsa Zsa soothed, "Please. Eva and I were waiting so anxiously for you all these years and now you arrive and we will have the hell of life. We are so unhappy about sweet Uncle Sebastyen and Grandmother but we knew about it for months. Now we are so very unhappy for you—and for us."

"Sebi used to tell me," I wept, " 'Jancsika, I will also divorce and we will take a house together. We are two bohemians and we will live together.' "

Eva took my hand in both hers and kissed it. *"Nucika,* listen. We are your two children, Zsa Zsa and me. We have been waiting all this time for you to arrive to make us happy. Please, we also loved Uncle Sebastyen and Grandmother Francesca but we don't want this happy reunion ruined with such bad memories. Please, *Nuci,* think not just of them. Think of us."

"Killed by a bomb. They were killed by a bomb," I sobbed, beating my pillow.

"Nuci, please," begged Zsa Zsa on her knees at the bedside, stroking my shoulders as I wept. "There is such tragedy here in this room where a few hours ago there was such happiness. Finally, after so long waiting, we have you and instead of this being a happy occasion for us our lives are now ruined."

"Sebi had said we will both be divorced and we will live in America and you will have lovers and I will have lovers. Now neither of us will ever have anything. I also want to die."

Zsa Zsa and Eva turned me around in the bed. Both sat alongside me and Zsa Zsa pleaded with me, *"Nucika,* this didn't just happen. We have known this for over ten months, but we didn't tell you. Magda has known it for a year and so has Papa but they wouldn't tell you. They were afraid what would happen if they told you this. They were afraid you would kill yourself."

"During the whole year you were in Portugal Magda didn't tell you," explained Zsa Zsa slowly and softly. "She wrote us how scared she was that you'd meet some friend in Portugal from Hungary who would tell you."

And from this *devil* Ritter . . . from him, I thought, I have to learn this.

Zsa Zsa went on, "Grandmother and Uncle Sebi were trapped with others including Manci's mother inside the Portuguese legation. The U.S. bombs were falling and there was a direct hit. Everybody died."

"Sebika and my sweet, sweet mother," I moaned. "It's my fault. I blame myself. She stayed where I insisted she'd be safe. She wanted to hide with her concierge and it's my fault that she was killed. I made her go to the legation."

"Uncle Sebi was visiting her that day," continued Zsa Zsa. "It was a direct hit and they were both killed."

"Sebika a millionaire. A handsome boy of thirty-three." I moaned, wringing my hands and rocking back and forth on the bed. "I can't stand it. And Mama. She was only sixty-nine. My fault . . . it's my fault!"

Eva and Zsa Zsa looked at each other. They had not been so devoted to one another before I arrived and this was bringing them closer.

"Can you imagine," I continued talking almost to myself, "if I had gotten the official stamp from the Ambassador for my telegram and had gotten my sisters taken to the same legation? That's what I wanted because I felt they'd be safer there than in their homes. If I had gotten that signature then all my sisters would have been killed along with Sebi and Mama. My sisters are alive by accident. If I had done what I wanted to do I would have killed them all."

"Nuci . . . please . . ." began Eva.

"I nearly killed them all."

"Nuci, stop," cried Eva, unable to bear it any more. "Please do not make our lives miserable. You are making us more unhappy than we were before you came. Please, *Nuci . . ."*

Tears rolled down Zsa Zsa's cheeks. "Magda will die when she hears it was her card to Ritter that gave you the story."

"Please, *Nuci,"* whispered Eva, "we have been waiting for you to bring us again happiness. Don't ruin your life and our lives . . ."

The Royal Suite was on the highest floor. Late in the night when the girls had left I went to jump. The problem was I couldn't make a neat suicide. The windows were too small and immediately underneath them was a narrow terrace so I thought all that will happen is I will bang my head and be very messy and not only won't I die but I will disgrace and embarrass the family.

I had heard of the Empire State Building. I knew it was the highest building. Since I had decided to do away with myself I went there early in the morning. I don't know why but I came out on the seventeenth floor. I think I took a wrong elevator and that's where I ended up. The seventeenth floor isn't as high as the building but it certainly is high enough to die. I looked around for a window but the one I had access to wouldn't open. I kept trying to tug it open. Meanwhile, the elevator man was going up and down and stopping for passengers and each time I seemed more and more suspicious to him because I was hanging around doing nothing but looking agitated.

He called to me, "Lady, would you like to come up or go down or what?" I was so ashamed that I got in.

It was at that moment that I decided to do something constructive. I would go to work. "You must get over this," I said to myself. "You must forget. You either have to be or not to be. Your mother and brother are dead so either you die, too, or you live—and if you live then you must do it with happiness and a full heart. When you live you must live happy. Either die or live happily."

I decided instantly to go under the sunshine. That was seventy-two hours after my arrival in the New World.

3 My girls also helped me to make an about face. They were different. Before they had always been for Mama, for *Nuci*. By the time I arrived this big hot love had gone a little. They found they could exist without Mama. Not so well, maybe, because Zsa Zsa and Eva were not happy with each other. Zsa Zsa lived in New York, Eva in California and neither came to see the other often enough and they were a little separated.

They had become a little tough. They had made it on their own without me and they showed it. When I said to them, "All right, children, life is now over for me . . . I am in my forties. I gave my marriage of twenty-two years to you and now it is finished for me . . ." There was bitterness and unhappiness. They weren't so thrilled with me here. I was to them a burden, an added responsibility. I didn't fit any place. They didn't know what to do with me.

No more did they eat out of my hands like little birdies. They didn't believe I could make a fresh life and they weren't anxious to change theirs to accommodate mine. They wanted only to impress me with what they had done without me and I wanted only to show them what I could do without them. But what could I do? I had nothing. Except I had one thing. I had sensitivity. A typically sensitive mother. A little too much they neglected me for their own lives right at the beginning. Eva immediately went back to California. Okay, she had seen me. She kissed me, hugged me. Enough! Back to her world. So I said to myself, "All right, Jolie, before when you were something they respected you. You must become again something. When you become something on your own, they will become nicer to you."

Because I was penniless, the girls agreed to give me an allowance. Zsa Zsa sat me down. "Look, *Nuci*, Eva and I have discussed it and we will each give you $300 a month."

"Look," I said, "I don't want you to send every month and then, maybe, one month you forget and I have to come to you and remind you and like this I will be sensitive and ashamed. If I cannot be independent I would rather go back to Budapest. I must be something. I cannot be nothing. Not in any country."

I took a deep breath. "I don't want to come to you every thirty days for a handout. If you give $300 a month that will be for the year $3,600. You give me in one check your support for the year and Eva the same. In two checks give me the whole $7,200."

"What will you do with it?"

"I will be an independent somebody. I want again to be a queen with big money and a big shop and big jewels."

Impatiently Zsa Zsa said, "But you cannot become a big something so fast. This is America. It is not Hungary, which is only the size of Indiana. Eva and I will give you $600 a month. Besides, we will furnish you with a nice apartment in the Plaza or a little house somewhere and you can live nicely."

"Never. I will never be dependent on my children. Advance me that year's money in one sum." I remembered a sign I read somewhere that said, "It is not enough to be a Hungarian. You have to be talented, too." I stood up and faced Zsa Zsa squarely. "I will open a shop."

I had a good nose. I walked the city for two days straight. I spoke already a little English. I talked to people. I came to the conclusion that Madison Avenue or, secondly, Fifth Avenue would be good.

However, I looked and looked but I couldn't find any available space. The war was over and it was the biggest real estate boom in the last twenty years. People were spending money and there was no place to be found. Nobody was vacating. Besides, I was picky yet about what area I would even consider.

I asked Zala—this friend who threaded himself through my entire life and who had already by this time had met Hilton and so was ready to do me more favors—to please place for me an ad in the newspapers. The ad said I wanted to take over a shop on Madison Avenue. The following morning I received a call from a French couple. "We have a Madison Avenue shop," they said, "but very tiny."

It was between 62nd and 63rd Streets, which in those days was pretty far uptown. It was a very very little jewelry shop right on the Avenue but they couldn't make a living from it. The rent was only $126 a month but even for that small space I had to give $3,000 for the key.

The next problem was merchandise. I told Zsa Zsa, "Somebody told me about a showroom on Fifth Avenue where you can buy good costume jewelry. Will you go with me?"

"Yes," she said.

"I called the showroom already," I told her, "and explained who we were, and a very smart boy said he would personally escort us through but first he offered to buy lunch."

Lunch was at the Monte Carlo restaurant with two very gentlemanly, handsome men. "To christen your new business," said the sandyhaired one, "we will order champagne."

"Oh, no," I said. "I would like first to see what you have before I drink champagne because I am very anxious to discuss immediately the business."

But the champagne came. "The biggest thing in America today is costume jewelry," began the tall one with the crew cut. "We have the best costume jewelry, not expensive but beautiful."

More champagne and the result was I went to the showroom and bought for the whole sum I had left which was $3,600. I bought six dozen Negro heads and swords for $15 a piece. In business you pay only after thirty days but Zsa Zsa was also drunk after this little lunch so she gave this man a check for the whole amount.

I had no room for showcases. I put the stuff in mirrored cabinets on the wall. The shop was so small that my table was a stool and when I had a customer I actually had to leave the door open. I sat on a stool that I painted silver and I had another stool for the customer. For the first few months there was no business at all. Even for the small amount of rent I fell behind one month and it was Zala who gave me the money.

I thought, "Well, this is not for me. Better to go back to Budapest. Better to give this up."

A Hungarian couple came over and they said they would take it from me. They were bargaining so inventorying was like hell every single night and into the early hours of the morning. The Hungarian couple weren't married. They were lovers. She was a cosmetician and he was a salesman. When I was all finished with the inventory they gave me only the money for the merchandise. They wouldn't pay me the $3,000 I had paid for the key.

The brother of the owner of the building was a lawyer so I went to his office and we made the arrangement that they would pay me every month $500. The lawyer said to me, "Look, this contract that I am drawing up will cost you $300 but I am telling you not to do this. I don't want to work on it and I don't want your business."

I looked at him. "Why?"

"Because you are a very naive woman and I don't like the idea that you will be hurt. They will never live up to their guarantee. They don't have it. So, my free advice to you is to save your $300. If you couldn't make a business here they cannot make a business."

In a few months I was already out of money. I was blue and depressed and didn't know what to do and Eva called, "Come, I invite you to Hollywood. Come out and enjoy the sun for a while."

"Well, since there is no business I guess it won't matter if I go out from the business world for a while," I sighed. "But I don't want to just sit around out there. What can I do?"

"I don't know," she said, "Maybe I can figure out some way to pay you."

I closed down and went to California. I thought that I would just live with Eva because I didn't know where to turn. She was working in a theatre in Hollywood and every night her husband, Charles Isaacs, and I were alone because she would not come home until late. Charles adored me. When she went to the theatre he took me to dinner. I would put on one of the evening gowns I had made in Portugal which I had thought was so beautiful and which really was so terrible. He would say things to me like, "To live with you is such a pleasure because before Eva and I were not doing so well but since you've come you've made this a much more cheerful home."

The girls were not happy with their husbands and neither were they happy with each other. Eva's career was not great and she was bored with her marriage. Zsa Zsa and Hilton were not good together and there was friction between the two girls. With my arrival they laughed with each other, they lived with each other and they loved one another. Charles said to me, "Jolie, you bring happiness."

"Well, what else is a mother for?" I replied, glad that I had at least one thing I did not have to be blue about.

"These two were waiting a long time for you. They need you."

"I know. That's why I cannot walk around with a long face. For this reason I worked like a fool from eight in the morning until two in the morning. I was fanatic because I knew I had to kill my own personal pain. Therefore I have learned to smile even when my heart is breaking."

Charles knew that now again my heart was breaking because I couldn't find my way so he took me out constantly. He took me to meet his mother, who had money from real estate and she was like a princess in white ermine and diamonds. This old American woman had been brought up in Switzerland and lived in a house with three servants and a butler. She adored Eva. One Christmas she sent her other daughter-in-law a bottle of Miss Dior perfume and flowers but for Eva she gave a $20,000 diamond bracelet. She was proud of Eva because Eva was well educated and pretty and her sister was married to Hilton.

Mrs. Isaacs played bridge and gave formal parties with her elegant friends all in brand new, fabulous handmade gowns from America and I in my *fercrochta* Portuguese dress.

Charles even took me yachting. He had bought Jascha Heifetz' yacht. "Come with me," he would beg. "Eva is a bad wife. She won't go with me on the yacht. Only if you go she'll go." So I went and so did Eva and he was so happy.

"Didn't she ever go on the yacht before?" I asked.

He smiled wanly. "Only once and that was because she made me invite the whole cast of the show she's playing with."

Charles was so good to me that he even looked away when I stole from him. I saw that there was a big fortune in his magnificent mansion. Pea soup in cans, ham in cans, vegetables in cans. Since in Hungary they were starving, I stole a few each week and sent them home. I even stole Charles' shoes one time and mailed them to Budapest.

In return he showed me the glittery world of Hollywood: the white limousines with matching chauffeurs, the wall-to-wall girls who were all blonde, all skinny, and all smiling with capped teeth. And he showed me this beautiful thing called a cafeteria. I'd never seen anything like it. After years of wartime rationing I loaded my tray with everything I could squeeze on it. Such a variety of food!

Charles told me, "Jolie, in America we don't roll the *r*'s. You don't pronounce them as hard as you do back home." So when I went to the counter of the cafeteria to exchange my fork because the one I had been given was bent, I said to the man, "May I have a good fawk?" And the man grinned, "With pleasure, lady." After that I was afraid and I asked only for a spoon.

Zsa Zsa gave for me a party because I didn't know anybody. She invited the very biggest stars and she introduced them all to me. I was terribly excited. The French butler gave me a cocktail called a screwdriver. It was orangey and in a big glass and I was thirsty and didn't know what it was so I drank it all down fast like lemonade. The drink made me lightheaded and a superelegant English maid appeared from nowhere. Zsa Zsa had hired these caterers and extra staff who go from one star's party to the next. The maid, holding me up, said, "Madame, may I escort you upstairs so that you might fix your hair?"

I didn't want to go upstairs and of course my hair didn't need fixing but I was starting to black out so I went and ended up fast asleep. When it was already morning Zsa Zsa came up and I called to her, "Oh, I'll come back down in a minute," and she said, "But everyone has left. It's 4 A.M. It's a pity that you didn't come down because Reginald Gardner made a toast for you. He said, 'To Jolie Gabor, the Queen of Madison Avenue' and we all looked for you and you were sleeping."

My staying with Eva didn't work. She went to the theatre every night so what I would do to pretend I was needed was to give her a glass of milk and hand her her coat when she left. One evening I didn't get to it in time. "Where is my milk? Hurry up, *Nuci*," she called, tapping her foot. "You know I'm in a rush and I cannot wait about."

A bell went off in my head. I knew she didn't mean it unkindly, of course, but I thought, "Jolie, be careful, because in no time you will be just a servant." As she was leaving she called to me over her shoulder, "Tell the boy to make steak for dinner."

"Please make steak for dinner," I told the Filipino houseboy. He inclined his head ever so slightly and replied, "I take orders only from my Madame." Then he patted me on the behind and pattered off.

I knew that I must get out of there because otherwise I would become soon nothing. I moved the next day.

Charles was upset. "Jolie, I would give you everything to live with us. I will even build you a separate suite so that you can have your own little home."

"It's a temptation, Charles, but impossible. I must do something on my own. I must be somebody without my daughters. All mothers have the same feeling of extreme sensitivity when they're supported. They feel insulted. I must maintain my self-respect."

Charles understood. Eva didn't. "Darling," I said to her, "You have three Cadillacs. You have a raspberry-colored bathtub. You could have anything in this world yet you are still working in small parts for a few dollars and rushing off for tryouts and auditions and agent calls. Surely you can understand how I must do what I must do."

"But you are welcome here," she said unhappily.

"A mother can only keep the love and respect of her children by keeping away from them. Even a house as large as this is too small to hold us both. When a mother is in the position where her children have to keep her, she has reached the stage where she is a nuisance. I am here only a week and we are already both unhappy. I will go back to New York."

In New York there was nothing to go back to but debts and a shut-up shop. Back I went.

My shop windows were empty. I didn't want to waste time getting my merchandise out of inventory cartons. So quickly I dressed the window with my own cultured pearl bracelets, cultured pearl earrings and a few better Hungarian pieces I had brought with me. I just stuck my own personal pieces in any old way, all piled up, unshined and uncleaned, because I didn't have the heart to decorate. The first night I worked until one o'clock in the morning and a man and woman wandered by. Seeing me inside they knocked on the window and came in and bought a bracelet. It was my own bracelet. I was very nervous. But not too nervous to know what to charge. I just doubled what the piece had cost me and they paid it.

The next day was a second customer. She liked my Hungarian clasp, which was in real silver but studded with fake diamonds, rhinestones, and surrounded by real pearls in a copy of antique Austro-Hungarian crown jewels. It was this mixture of the real and the fake which eventually made me my fortune. Anyway, I saw that if I had less things out people could see them better. Also some "Going Out of Business" signs helped, too. Very quick I made a few hundred dollars. I didn't quite know what was happening but I thanked God for whatever it was. He loves me, I thought.

Magda and Vilmos had by now arrived. Vilmos went to visit Eva and Zsa Zsa in California.

Meanwhile, I was in my shop every morning at 7:30 to clean it. "Who wakes early finds gold" is an old Hungarian proverb. I thought seriously of looking for the old Hungarian who said it and shooting him in the head. I spent eighteen hours a day there and every night I would go home and all I would do was soak in the bathtub.

I would have put out more of my own pieces because they alone were selling but I didn't have more to sell. During that first week an open postcard arrived. Unsigned, it said only, "The valuables you sent to the Hungarian bank for safekeeping were stolen by the Russians." That was all I ever knew.

A customer came to my door. She waited outside and saw how I struggled to sell a woman a lousy fifteen-dollar piece. The shop was so tiny that when I had more than one customer they had to form a line. When this other lady left, she came in and introduced herself, "My name is Evelyn Sharpe."

As I learned later, Evelyn Sharpe was a young widow who had inherited two hotels. We became good friends and she gave me my start. This first day she said, "You are a nice, pretty woman. Why do you work so hard to sell this junk?"

"What *should* I sell?" I asked her as we huddled up stool-to-stool.

"I need two good cultured pearls for my ring. Buy these for me and forget about this fifteen-dollar junk."

"But I thought American women liked costume jewelry that was cheap."

"They like costume jewelry, yes," she replied, "but what you should sell is more of the kind of stuff you yourself are wearing. Sell fairly expensive pieces for fairly expensive women. And stick to this cultured pearl stuff."

I went to the Fifth Avenue store of Rosenthal, a well-known importer from the Orient, to place an order for cultured pearls. The owner was stunned when I walked in. "Are you Madame Gabor?" he asked.

I told, "Yes."

"You remember you bought from my Paris office pearls for your Budapest shop? Well, I will be very pleased to work with you here in New York."

"Yes, I too would like but you are very expensive," I said.

"We will give you thirty days' grace," he said.

I began to feature Rosenthal's cultured pearls until one rainy afternoon a small, plump man stood outside my shop window gazing at me through the glass. "You don't remember," he said when he came in, "that we met in Abbazia and we danced together."

"I would like to remember," I told him, "but I don't."

Closing the door behind him he leaned against it. "Remember the summer in Abbazia when there was a contest of best legs and best bosom?"

"And I wore a sweater and I won the contest!"

"Right," he laughed.

"Of course I recall," I said in happy remembrance, "but that was long ago. Tell me, who are you and what are you doing here so far away from Abbazia?"

"Well, my name is D'Elia. I'm from Italy but my business is cultured pearls."

"Sit down," I said to him.

We spoke for two hours. I told him about my business with Rosenthal, who gave me for thirty days and he said to me, "I will give you how much you want for how long you want for as long as you want. I will give you on consignment but not for thirty days and not for sixty days but for as long as you want it. I would like to help you. I remember very well meeting the beauteous Mme. Gabor years back in the old country and I would be pleased to be her slave now."

This D'Elia gave me for a very reasonable price, thousands of cultured pearls—ropes and ropes and ropes of them. Nothing designed, just miles of pearls, which I stuck in the window. A few olderly women attracted by the piles of pearls came in. The first had a quite expensive beige alligator handbag and was wearing matching shoes. She took off her gloves to finger the pearls and her solitaire blinded me. "You are a rich woman," I said. "You are wearing a $50,000 diamond ring on your hand but on your neck you are wearing cheap cheap pearls from Woolworth."

"Well, I must say you're outspoken," she said, but she seemed amused instead of angry. I grew bolder.

"With big diamonds on your fingers, how can you wear this awful 98-cent junk on your neck?"

She bought from me a cultured pearl choker for $200. Another lady whom I also insulted said, "I have a real pearl necklace for $30,000 in the vault but that I don't dare to wear. I'm afraid it will break. And, anyhow, it's small."

I brought out a pile of large-sized rough baroque pearls. "Look, with this you will have happiness. They're inexpensive and they're big and they're *real.*" She was just a customer off the street and I didn't know her but I said to her, "You will leave the expensive $30,000 pearl necklace in the vault without enjoying it and when you die your daughter-in-law will wear it."

"Oh, no," she exclaimed, "I hate her!"

I fastened a pinkish strand around her neck. "For $300 you can buy from me such a necklace as I have just put on you. It is really genuine, cultured pearls. And, anyhow your neck will look better."

I sold her and she bought loads of ropes of pearls and I had great mouth advertising. I think a little it was my bold way of speaking that helped make me a great success. Every woman told every friend and one, two, three, I made thousands and thousands of strands of pearls and sold them. Unfortunately I could not string the damned things myself. I am not handy in doing things.

My problem was where to stick my sewing ladies. They couldn't sit in the phone booth shop and make the necklaces with the clasps because there wasn't room. They had to come in after 7 P.M. to do the work. To make a success in your early days you need bluff and courage—and I had plenty of both.

I'd go there 7:30 in the morning to sweep and dust and open up. I had to place everything on the street to be able to make room to clean and I would slave straight through until midnight. I can not say that I enjoyed it in those days. I didn't.

When Vilmos came back to New York he didn't come into the shop the first time. He just stood outside my tiny window, the tears rolling down his cheeks. I said, "Vilmos, why do you cry?"

He said, "Because my wife in Budapest was such a queen and now she has to work like this."

I wanted to move from the Plaza because it was ridiculous. I went out every day from this floor-length Royal Suite to the shop, which was the size of my jewel case in Budapest and I mopped the floor myself. I said to Hilton, "I don't want this. Give me instead one single room in your hotel and I pay." I thought it cost maybe $80 a month.

He said, "Look, Jolie, as I told you before, I am only the president. I'll have to go to the manager, but if that's what you want, all right."

The manager showed me a single room and I swear you my servant in Budapest lived in one much better. And this one cost $300. I had made such a fuss about changing that now I had to, so I said, "Okay, I will move in for anyhow a few days."

Again I was lucky. A Hungarian came to my shop and she mentioned, "I live on East 80th Street but I go now back to Vienna."

I said, "In these days you cannot so easily find an apartment. Can you give over your apartment when you leave?" She appeared doubtful. "Well, it is not so very cheap. It is $59 a month."

I managed to cover my shock at this frightening high rent and I moved in. It was a furnished apartment, one room in a boarding house.

When I lived in my rich life I was wondering what would be the worst thing that could happen to me someday and I thought that it would be to have to live in one room. I thought then, "Oh, how terrible it must be to have no servants, to cook yourself, and to have windows that just look out on a court and not a beautiful view." Well, that's exactly what I had. I looked out on another building on 80th Street.

When I came to America not ever had I even washed a glass. In my little back room on East 80th Street I had a little bathroom with a gas range. I can maybe make an omelet but the point is I am not interested. I don't like doing it. If I have to cook then I lose my appetite, so I decided that if I am poor and if I must cook then I will not be hungry. This wasn't too bad because I lost weight which I didn't mind.

I was interested only in business. Mr. D'Elia, the pearl man, kept to his word. He had given me $50,000 worth of pearls on consignment and I had given him notes and the guarantee to pay. He in turn promised that when I cannot he would carry me but he never had to. I paid like a general. Sometimes

I gave him his money in installments or in coins or right from the cash register but I paid.

I was helped a little by my daughters—not by money anymore but by publicity. Zsa Zsa and Hilton were having big marriage troubles and this was in the papers and everybody thought my famous rich daughter was behind me so that's why the dealers took me on.

Zsa Zsa was unhappy with Conrad. "When I came to America I wanted to be a star," she told me, "but I married Hilton right away and then I couldn't be a star because I had to take care of this great marriage."

"Why could you not have a husband and a career like Eva does?" I asked.

"Because Charles and Eva are also not so well together and because Eva is also not such a star. Connie has gone around with Lana Turner and some of the biggest and it was more important that this VIP man should die for me than that I should be a big actress no matter how much I wanted it. This was no small achievement for me so I gave up all ideas of show business to take care of him. My friends told me that Lana Turner was dying for him and they said, "Don't even dream that Connie will marry you.' "

"So why did he?"

"Because I knew he was dying to go to bed with me but he is old-fashioned of German origin. This type if he goes to bed with you he will never marry you. Connie invited me for a weekend and I wouldn't go. The whole romance was maybe six to eight weeks and I never went to bed with him before."

"Oh, you're so smart," I marveled.

"You know something, *Nuci?* On our wedding night he talked to me about a hotel deal he was setting up. Now on the golf course he'll make a shot and while the ball is driving he'll say, 'Wonder if they'll give us the ten million we asked for.' He doesn't even know I'm around."

I was sorry my daughter was suffering but I was glad she was back confiding with me again as in the old days. "He is a very bad man, *Nuci.* He's a German. He left his young wife, who was maybe thirty-five, with their three sons and when I had my nervous breakdown during the time we were getting you out of Budapest, he didn't even go to see me. He's heartless."

"But he is to me very sweet. Although you and he were separated when I arrived in America, still he came to meet me. He was gracious and charming. "Even in Beverly Hills he gave for me a nice luncheon party."

"Well, why shouldn't he like you? You are fun and you ask nothing of him. He took an immediate liking to you and he and I began to see one another again only after you arrived. But it is not good."

On one of those times that Zsa Zsa and Connie "began to see one another" they must have done more than see because Zsa Zsa became pregnant. Still they maintained separate residences and, baby or not, Zsa Zsa had decided that under no circumstances would she go back to Conrad.

Zsa Zsa's lawyer said, "I will bring out ten million dollars from him." I was then so European that I said to her, "Don't work with that lawyer. He will drive you crazy with longtime fights in court."

Zsa Zsa argued, "But he says I can get a big fat settlement."

I told her, "Pay no attention to such a gangster lawyer. You have had troubles. You don't need mental pressures and big fights now. Get a nice lawyer and handle it politely and quickly."

So she got a lawyer from Claudette Colbert. He was so nice he was stupid. A jerk. Zsa Zsa got only $35,000 in cash plus alimony of $25,000 a year for ten years unless she remarried. She made a stupid stupid divorce. Not even a permanent suite for life at the Plaza. Not even 10 per cent discount on any suite anywhere in the world. Wherever Zsa Zsa goes, in a Hilton Hotel she must pay herself. Ridiculous.

Zsa Zsa's divorce from Hilton was in the newspapers and Eva was a film star—not so big a film star but some sort of a film star—so in this way they contributed to people coming to my shop. A big success was my handmade Hungarian clasp, a copy from Empress Maria Theresa's crown jewels. In those days I was the exclusive seller of this item and it made me big money.

Mrs. William Randolph Hearst, Jr., got the idea to add a pearl dangling at the end. This one pearl hanging off the bottom is what really made the look go. It took off and we even made from them earrings. With my $50,000 worth of ropes and my Hungarian clasps I started the fashion in this country of the cultured pearl necklace and, believe me, they were standing on the streets.

I wanted a bigger shop. Zala pleaded against it. "Jolika, stay where you are. As long as you are here you can always make a living. Stay in this miniature place because this will always take care of you."

"But I don't want to make just a living. I want to make an elegant success and I want to show my daughters that I can make it myself without them, without their husbands, without my husband, without anybody."

"You are going to kick your head in a big tree," he prophesied dourly.

"I don't need you to quote Hungarian proverbs to tell me I am biting off more than I can chew. I know it. But I will chew it anyway."

"But why are you not satisfied with what you have?" asked Zala.

"You are today a best friend of Conrad Hilton," I said to him. "His first international hotel, the Istanbul Hilton, is arranged by Zsa Zsa. His second hotel, the Castellana, will be built on your property in Madrid. Why did you wish to meet him? Why were you not satisfied with what you already had?"

"Okay, Jolie," sighed Zala.

The girls were also against. "There is no space anywhere. This is still what they call the postwar boom," Zsa Zsa insisted.

"Then I will try to make this place bigger."

"But this location is too high uptown. You should come down from the Sixties to the Forties where all businesses are."

"My instinct tells me in the future everything will move further up and the fashionable shopping center of the future will be in the Sixties and even the Seventies."

The shop right next to me was a ladies' hat shop and it was badly neglected so I went in and inquired, "Don't you want to sell this shop?"

The lady said, "Are you crazy? I make $50,000 a year in this place."

"I'm glad for you but sorry for me," I said. "It would be wonderful if I could have this next-door shop since there are no more stores to be found. However, I guess it's impossible if you're doing well."

"Yes, it's impossible. Forget it," said the lady.

I believe in hard work, I believe in resourcefulness, but I also believe in luck. A few weeks later a woman came into my shop. "I am the sister of the hat shop lady," she began. "I heard you want to buy it. Well, I want to tell you to please take it because we don't like anymore this shop."

I looked at her startled. "Your sister nearly threw me out when I suggested it."

"My sister had a stroke. She cannot speak," she said quietly. "And she is a young woman, only forty-five."

It is odd the way things fall into line for me. I reflected on this for one moment.

"How shall we do financially?"

"My sister wants $10,000."

"I don't have that," I answered. We talked a while and I bargained her down to $8,000, which I also didn't have and I guaranteed I would pay every month $1,000, which I also didn't have. I worked under the theory that to be big you must think big. So I thought big—how I was going to follow it up was a different question.

I was not a youngster. I was in a strange country. Despite the limitations nothing could frighten me off. I was like a schoolgirl—happy, anxious to get started. I knew America was made for me—I could not wait to get my fingers on it all. When you are nothing and you have nothing you have nothing to lose. Impulsiveness is then a luxury you can afford.

I sold everything that could be sold. I had years before given a Hungarian set of jewels to Zsa Zsa that she was tired of so she gave it back to me. A woman came in and bought it for $1,500, so that very first month I could pay my note to the hat-shop sister. I wanted to borrow from Zsa and Eva $2,000. They were sure I could never pay it back so they told me they didn't have it. Once I was refused I knew that never again would I go to them.

Meanwhile the rent in my $59-a-month apartment was raised. And do you know who raised it? Eva, that's who! I learned that this five-story brownstone in which I lived was for sale. I talked Eva into buying it. "But what do I need it for?" she asked.

"Because real estate is a good investment. I had always houses in Budapest. It is always a good investment. Anyhow, this one is cheap. It is only for $40,000 and you will be able to sell it for $60,000. For the best residential area in the world—80th Street between Fifth and Madison Avenues—the price I hear is very cheap."

She took my advice and bought the house without even seeing it. She forgot when she bought it that I was paying rent and somehow nobody remembered to tell me don't pay so I kept sending my $59 each month to the new owner of this little house, my daughter Eva. Shortly I received a notice that my rent would be upped to $64. I complained to Eva who said, "It's the lawyer's fault, not mine." I was so insulted that I stopped paying altogether.

But I did not want anything for nothing. Eva needed to replace two small diamonds which fell out from a ring. I set them back for her at a higher cost than I would have paid to her in the rent.

A customer told me she had seen Irene Dunne at a blacktie opening wearing my Hungarian earring with the fake emerald center and the dangling cultured pearl. I had the idea to send her a complete set—including necklace and matching bracelet with the identical clasp. I didn't know her. I had never met her. I enclosed the following note: "Dear Miss Dunne. If you like this please send me $2,000 which is the price of the set. If not, you may wear it a while with my compliments and then we will see." I waited two months and there was no reply. On the first day of the third month I received a check.

This gave me the idea to do the same with other celebrities. I met Hedda Hopper at a party and I sent my earrings to her but she said, "I can't wear them because Irene Dunne wears hers everywhere."

I always needed money and had so many holes to stick it in that when I got my hands on any I didn't know where to put it first. So, with this sudden windfall of $2,000 I did the only intelligent thing. I had my face lifted. I thought to myself, "I must look young for my business. I must be an ad for my jewelry."

All women must make the face. It is not worthwhile to buy an expensive dress when on the cheeks when it is sagging. If a person has not a good nose then she must make the nose. If she has not a good chin then she must make the chin. Make everything.

I moved into my big shop and I became like a crazy person. I met the famous socialite decorator, Ellen Lehman McCluskey, and I said, "I would like to decorate but how I can afford it?"

She said, "Don't worry. Leave it to me."

In one month she put a canopy in front and made the inside like a drawing room in dove gray and taupe. The shop is long and narrow. She placed individual, small gilt tables for two in the center of the floor. They were like dressing tables and the glass top served as the showcase with the jewelry reachable from the side where the salesperson sat. The customer, sitting across, faced a round, standing mirror. The lighting was subdued and definitely flattering. Side display cabinets in Louis the 15th period were full of jewelry. There were thick rugs and crystal chandeliers and Austrian curtains. And this is how it is still today.

I congratulated her, "Ellen, you have made my shop so fabulous. How much is it?"

She hugged me, "Only $32,000 for all the alterations and furnishings."

I screamed at her, "Ellen, are you crazy? I don't have any money. They will put me in prison because I have such debts."

"Look," she smiled, "I see you in action. I know that soon you'll have money because you're so damned smart and, anyway, I'll buy many pearls from you and spend the money back that way and like this we'll come together."

Thirty-two thousand dollars thirty years ago was pretty expensive for one room. "You know what?" I said to her. "I owe so much to everybody that I am not even nervous about this debt. Stupidly I am very happy. I am excited like a gambler."

Zsa Zsa then screamed at *me*, "You are crazy!"

"Don't worry for me," I said back to her. "You won't be responsible if this is what you're worrying about. My name is on everything, not yours. Anyway, somehow I am not afraid. Somehow something will happen."

"Okay, somehow something will happen," repeated Zsa Zsa impatiently, "but suppose somehow something doesn't happen. Then what?"

"Then, my darling daughter, I will escape. If I can't pay I will leave the shop and the business and the merchandise and I fly away back to Budapest."

Next Eva went to work on me. "How and when are you going to do the business to pay all these notes?"

"It is only September. Christmas I will do enough for the whole year like I always did in Budapest. Just wait for Christmas."

Somewhere along about this time Magda got married for a few minutes to something named William Rankin. He was a Hollywood writer who I think was only writing home for money. She got rid of him almost as quickly as she married him. She had met him through Liz Whitney who had invited her for a weekend to her home in the hunt country in Virginia.

She called me to tell me about it. "You never saw anything like the Whitneys' house," she said on the phone. "They have a drawbridge and a moat surrounding the house. When the drawbridge is down the horses come in and there are horses and horseshit in the living room. Liz has great friends, you know. She's a good friend of Aly Khan and also of a writer named William Rankin. Do you know him?"

"Aly Khan?"

"No. William Rankin."

"No."

"Well, William Rankin you'll get to know because I just married him."

Like her sisters, Magda also had gone right away to California when she arrived. She was a little bit jealous because Eva had a Hollywood husband and Zsa Zsa had a Hollywood husband so she wanted one, too. She had nobody else so she married Rankin.

Magda called me every day from Hollywood where they lived and I said, "Magda, can you afford this?"

"Oh, *Nuci,*" she rhapsodized, "I can afford everything. I can even afford to talk very long in the afternoon when the rates are up."

"Is it that this new husband has so much money?"

"I don't know. I know only that he's good to me. He made me charges at all the stores. He bought me a mink coat and a red car."

This was all very nice until only two months later the bills for the mink coat and the red car came to me. Of all the marriages in the Gabor family I would say that this was not one of the best. When he asked to borrow money from Magda she threw him out for good.

Now that Zsa Zsa had gotten rid of her second husband and Magda had gotten rid of her second husband, Eva decided that she, too, would get rid of her second husband.

I didn't mind when the girls divorced. Only when Eva told me she wanted to divorce Charles Isaacs was I emotional because I knew he adored her. The doctor sentenced him to death when he was just thirty-six. The doctor said he had cancer and could only live one more year. Eva could have ended up with six million dollars if she had not divorced Charles Isaacs because he died five months later. Several weeks after the divorce Charles was sitting with Eva one afternoon. He was so weak that his chauffeur had to carry him out to the car. He had come just to pay Eva a friendly visit and wish her well. Eva knew he was going to die very soon. She could have stayed with him for his inheritance, but she didn't. I think maybe she was in love with another man but anyhow it didn't work out and she regretted it.

Eva was so unhappy that she came back to *Nuci* like in the old days and slept in my bed with me. She even put on my nightie. I said, "I will give you a fresh nightie" and she told, "No. It is my only consolation to be very near you. I want to smell you. I want to cuddle into you. I need you."

Meanwhile, pregnant Zsa Zsa spent her days waiting, reading, painting, walking in Central Park, going to the theatre, and making the move from a Madison Avenue hotel to this penthouse she was furnishing expensively in French antiques and all in gray and red and white and gold. One night we two went to a nearby movie to see Somerset Maugham's *The Moon and Sixpence* starring George Sanders and Hedy Lamarr. In it he was a bastard —and he beat up Hedy Lamarr. Zsa Zsa turned to me in the dark and whispered, "This is the man for me."

"Shhh," I hissed to her.

"I like a man who beats me. I want such a strong man."

"Zsa Zsa, please," I whispered as the people began turning around in front of us.

"*Nuci*," she whispered back, both hands resting on her swollen belly, "this is the man I will next marry!"

When she did finally meet Sanders her first excited words to him were, "Oh, Mr. Sanders, I'm madly in love with you."

He looked down on her and in his bored way drawled, "Mrs. Hilton, how well I understand that."

While Zsa Zsa was busy having a baby and a romance at the same time, Eva was pursuing a career. Richard Rodgers had seen her at 20th-Century Fox in Hollywood and invited her to read for the role of Mignonette in Rodgers' and Hammerstein's Broadway production of *The Happy Time*. She was to make her Broadway debut.

Meanwhile, Magda was working for me and she asked $200-a-week salary. This was very expensive but I was happy to have her.

Magda was publicity-minded. She made for me fashion shows in the Waldorf and articles in the papers about how "good jewelry is the best accomplice glamor ever had." The first time a TV station called me to make a television interview I was terrified. "Magduska," I quaked, "I cannot do this. I must refuse."

"You cannot refuse. They want you and we need the publicity and you will tell them things like how *V*-neck dresses call for large pins at the base of the *V*, strapless gowns call for drop earrings, plus the never-nevers such as: never wear a choker with long earrings together, never a daytime watch with evening clothes, and so forth. And you will say how every costume and every occasion offer exciting jewelry opportunities and it is important that women take advantage of them."

"I know all that. I told it to you," I said, "but still I haven't done this before and I don't speak English so good. You speak back and forth five languages and you are well in English so you come with me."

"It is not necessary. Listen to me, you will say things like, 'Pearls give a softness and a glow that no other stone imparts.' "

"Magduska, I *know* that—it is from me you got all this thinking. If this was in Hungarian I would also tell them that pins may be used imaginatively even on black velvet cocktail shoes or on a belt or on a hat. I know all this. The thing is that I am nervous to speak in English on television."

"You are never nervous to speak in anything on anywhere."

Still I forced her to accompany me for security sake. In the cab going over I said, "Magduska, I will give you $100, which as you know I cannot afford, just for you to go instead of me."

"No. I refuse."

"Please, darling, let me go out of the cab. I will give you $200 because I will be so tongue-tied and afraid of the microphone that I will disgrace both of us."

"No."

We got there and Magda opened her mouth to say only, "hello" and "good-bye." I never shut my mouth. Immediately the lights went on I was an actress. I took over. I interrupted the host. I would still now be talking if the program wasn't over.

My big shop was an immediate success. There were customers right from the beginning. Zsa Zsa's hold-up also helped. Early one morning a tall robber in dark glasses, gray suit, fedora, and pigskin gloves took from her $250,000 worth of jewels, which the papers wrote as being $500,000 and which was only insured by Lloyd's for $185,000. This was a page-one splash with headlines and photographs and all of it was good for my shop.

I had been in America over a year. Businesswise I had made progress but my personal life was miserable. I felt terribly alone. In her pursuit of George Sanders, Zsa Zsa was commuting back and forth between coasts, in pursuit of her career Eva was doing the same and with Magda just in pursuit of life I was very much by myself. In the evenings I would return alone to my empty little apartment. It was a very blue period. Nobody worried about me. Nobody cared about me. I was lost. I had no one to love and nobody who loved me.

I was so desperate that one night I went to a movie by myself. The theatre wasn't full and there were many empty seats yet in the middle of the picture a man sat down next to me. After a few minutes he placed his hand on mine. Do you know what? I let it stay there. He squeezed my hand a little and I squeezed back. I was so grateful for human warmth and companionship that I didn't so much care how I got it.

After the movie he asked me for a drink. I went. I did not go to bed with him or even to his place. He was a nothing, just a working-man, but I was grateful for his company even if it was just for that time.

Across from my place of business was a little eatery with a counter called "Hamburger Heaven," one of an inexpensive chain located throughout Manhattan. I went there to have breakfast before opening each morning. A tall, nice-looking, distinguished, typically American man used to come in about the same time. One morning as I was finishing my coffee he asked, "May I pay your bill?"

"Oh, please," I protested. "It is only 99 cents. I don't mind to pay it myself."

"Please," he said sincerely, "I would consider it a favor."

He seemed very gentlemanly and not at all as one trying to be fresh. "All right," I smiled, "thank you."

Sliding onto the stool next to me at the counter he said, "I would like to finally admit to you that I have been watching you for the past few weeks. I have even peeked in at you through the windows of your shop."

"Oh, then you know who I am?"

"Oh, yes," he said and went behind the counter to bring us each a second cup of coffee.

"And who are you?" I asked, not at all wanting the second cup of coffee but not wanting to hurt the feelings of this nice man.

"I am the manager here. Actually, I manage three of the Hamburger Heavens. They are owned by one woman."

"I see."

"I come in to work about the same time each morning as you. While you are having your breakfast I am checking the register, bringing in cash, and more or less looking over the situation. I confess," he said shyly, "that you are one of the situations I have been looking over."

"Since we are trading confessions then I confess I have also been watching you."

"Thank you," he smiled shyly. "My name is Peter Howard Christman." He gathered courage. "You . . . you sort of seem to be so lonely having breakfast by yourself." Then he stammered out, "I wondered if perhaps sometime when you are free and maybe not too busy . . . er . . . perhaps we could see one another sometime . . . say, of an evening . . . like for dinner . . . I know I would like it very much if I could see you sometime after you are finished work . . . or something."

I just nodded agreement and said "Perhaps."

The Lord knows I wanted to but I thought, "Oh, he is just a worker in a hamburger place. It is not very chic." And then I thought, "But neither are you so chic. You are just a lonely unknown saleslady of jewelry whom nobody else wants to take out."

The next morning in Hamburger Heaven we chatted again. I found him pleasant. I told him my problem of an expiring visitor's visa and my worries about being able to stay in this country even if I could become a success financially. He seemed totally interested but did not again bring up the subject of dinner.

Some days later I received a letter from him. He explained, "I am unfortunately shy and despite my being able to talk with you in the restaurant when it comes to actually asking for a definite date it is difficult for me to do. Therefore I take this opportunity to invite you by letter to have dinner with me. If your answer is yes, please call me." He wrote his phone number at the bottom.

I was quite ready and willing to go out on a date. I telephoned him. "Thank you, Peter, for your kind invitation and I will be very happy to accept for next Monday night, March 10th, 8:00 P.M."

That weekend Zsa Zsa went into Doctors Hospital to await the birth of her child. Monday night she called at 7:40: "I think the baby is coming. Come over."

"Right away," I answered.

I did not think to call Peter. I flew out and laughed and cried and blew my nose over Francesca, who was named for my mother. Zsa Zsa's room was filled with flowers, there was a telegram from Conrad, telephone calls poured in, Eva and Magda and Vilmos and a half a dozen Hungarian friends arrived from I don't know where and I came home late in the night.

Only the next morning did it dawn on me I had not even left poor Peter Christman a note. He'd most likely come for me, found me out, and had gone away thinking all sorts of awful things. I was upset but I didn't know exactly what to do so I did nothing.

Some days passed, then Peter telephoned. Coldly angry, he said, "I am forty-eight years old. I have never been married. Now I can see how really lucky I've been not to get involved with women, particularly foreign women like you, who make a date, then run off without the courtesy of even contacting."

I couldn't explain over the telephone so I said I would see him the following morning. "I am embarrassed to tell you the real reason I didn't keep our date," I began over my toasted English muffin with marmalade. "You see, I am afraid that when you hear you maybe will not want anymore to take me out."

He was all ears but his face was so wounded that I thought it better to harm myself by admitting I am now a grandmother than to hurt him by not giving him the legitimate explanation. "You see," I began hesitantly, "I am now a grandmother. My daughter gave birth to a girl that very Monday night, March 10th."

"In that case," came the large smile of relief, "I forgive you."

"It is just because you are so nice that I am telling you the absolute truth of why I didn't keep our date." I wiped the marmalade off my sticky fingers and lightly rested my hand on his arm. "Look, now that I am a grandmother, I am sure you wouldn't want to take me out."

"But why wouldn't I want to take you out now?" He lifted his coffee cup and clinked it against mine. "I think it's wonderful. Of course, I want to see you."

I was very happy. We made an appointment for that evening and I suggested we stop by the hospital and see Zsa Zsa and Francie before going to dinner. As we walked down the maternity floor the nurse who knew me came rushing up. "Oh, Mrs. Gabor, how nice to see that you brought Mr. Gabor."

Peter blushed and the nurse rattled on. "You know, Mr. Gabor, the baby looks just like you. She's the image of her granddaddy."

Peter laughed. After we got to the room and Zsa Zsa showed us this red and so ugly baby, all shriveled and bald, he stopped laughing. He even stopped smiling. "Just like me this thing looks?" he asked.

Then Zsa Zsa started to laugh. "If she looks like anybody," Zsa Zsa said, "it's a shriveled old man like Nick Schenck!"

Peter and I began seeing each other regularly. He earned about $95 a week in take home pay. Once a week he took me out to a Third Avenue Hungarian restaurant where it was six dollars for dinner, and then to a movie. I was happy that at least now I had someone to eat with.

He had an old $500 beatup Packard convertible and took me also for rides or out visiting his friends. Though he had no money, he was genteel, well-spoken, and a championship golfer, so he knew rich people and had chic friends. He took me originally as a guest of the Du Ponts to the Southampton Beach Club.

"This is the most swanky club in America," he said to me. "It's very blue blood. Only if you come over with the Pilgrims can you belong." I looked around. "To me it looks like a nothing," I sniffed. "The place is so underdone that it's shabby. And the women are so casual that they look poor."

"Look, that's the way it is with the top people. Because of my golfing I'm close with some Rockefellers and I have friends like the Greek Ambassador and a lot of the so-called high-class people in this town and that's the way they are."

"If this is such an elegant club how come they let you in here?" I teased.

Sundays we would drive to Atlantic City and walk the Boardwalk. My eyes looked only at the shops and the jewelry. Peter was annoyed. "Darling," he chided me, "why don't you look at the moon?"

"Peter," I said to him, "I am romantic and I like the moon but I also like money. I must pay rent."

The second trip I brought a rare Hungarian necklace with me to put on consignment in a shop on the Boardwalk. It was handmade and very elaborate. They didn't want it, but I argued, "It doesn't cost you nothing. Only I lose if you don't pay me so why don't you do it?" They did and I made a few thousand dollars.

In Atlantic City we had only one room. This was my first adventure in America. I didn't know what to expect. I didn't know did they do it the same in America as they did in Hungary? I learned in one night that they did.

Peter Howard Christman was a nice clean-cut man. When I first went with him it was because I was lonely and I thought even if I don't have sex

195

it is all right because I will at least have company. However, it came out that he was a very sexy man.

Every day he drank an entire bottle of whiskey, but he never got drunk. Years earlier he had suffered a bad case of pneumonia and the doctor prescribed a bottle of whiskey daily. Each morning he'd start with a few sips in the bathroom before breakfast, but always he was gentlemanly and nice to me.

Slowly this friendship ripened. Zsa Zsa was busy with the baby and Sanders. Eva was busy with her love life and her career. Magda was busy with what looked like the makings of another husband, a lawyer named Sidney. I realized with a jolt how alone I was from the girls when Zsa Zsa wanted to go to Europe with Sanders and she begged me, "*Nuci*, it is now hot summer and you have no airconditioning in your little room and my bedroom with the antique mirrored walls and the apple-green velvet upholstery and hangings is so cool. Do me a favor, *Nuci*, stay in my house while I am gone."

"I will do anything you wish, Zsa Zsika, but I don't baby-sit."

"But you can sleep in my golden bed. All I want is for you to take care of my house and look in on my Francie."

I realized I had to make this point once and for all. Taking a deep breath I sat down in her living room. "Zsa Zsika, I will tell you and I will teach you for always. I refuse to be a baby-sitter. I am a mother but not a martyr. I didn't put my own daughters on my lap and cootchy coo with them and I won't do it with my granddaughter."

"But, *Nuci*, I ask from you a favor. How can you be so selfish?"

"If you must think of me as a selfish mother rather than a sweet baby-sitter, that's okay with me."

"*Nuci*, I must go with George to Europe and I have here a new nurse. Please you sleep here because it's a new setup and I am afraid to leave my baby for fear something will happen."

"Don't be afraid," I said. "Nothing will happen. The nurse won't drop or kill the infant. And please do not think of *me* as a baby-sitter. I want to put a stop to that before it ever starts. Besides, if you are so afraid then don't go with George. Stay here with your baby."

"Never again will I ask you. Only this once. I am having with George such a big hot love affair that I cannot let him go without me. Please just this one and only time and never again. Lulu, my Finnish maid, will even bring you breakfast in bed. Okay, so don't baby-sit. Just look in on Francie and stay in the house."

Against my will I agreed. Three days before she left, she said to me, "You cannot come and stay in my house, *Nuci.*"

"Why?" I asked surprised because I had already packed up some things.

"Because Lulu and her husband, John the butler, don't want that they should have the care of the baby plus the house plus the mother of the madame. They say it is too much responsibility."

"All right," I sighed. "I understand. But don't worry, I will look in on everything."

Zsa Zsa with Sanders left for Paris. I opened the big shop every morning by 8:00. I took a taxi which came to one dollar. While Zsa Zsa was in Europe I got up extra early at 6:30 and had the taxi stop at Zsa Zsa's and wait. It was all arranged that Lulu would bring me a big mug, a *Krügel* of steaming coffee with milk and saccarin. The baby would be there at 7:30 promptly when I ran in and while the taxi waited I would drink my coffee, play with the baby and ask Lulu, "How is everything?"

I spent fifteen minutes at the house. My taxi cost me $2.25 because he waited and then took me to my shop. It was all timed well.

This one morning I arrived like always and I saw Lulu fixing a big tray with everything on it to take upstairs.

I said to Lulu, "Please, darling, please whatever you are doing stop and quick give me my coffee or I will be late." Never had I waited for my coffee before. It was always the moment I arrived because I stayed only fifteen minutes.

Just as I said this Zsa Zsa ran downstairs and her first words of greeting to me were, "Oh, Mother, Lulu is so busy. How can you bother her to give you coffee?"

"But . . ." I began.

"Drink it in a coffee shop. There is one opposite your store or why don't you drink it in your shop? Please don't bother Lulu, she is busy."

I ran out of the house crying. My secretary, Riza, a woman who was my friend from Budapest, soothed me. "Jolika, you are too sensitive."

"She makes me feel that she is such a big something and I am such a big nothing. I can't take her words to me."

"She will apologize," said wise Riza. "She always does."

One hour later came red roses with a note saying "Seretlek, I love you."

"Riza," I said, "I will pour all my strength and my love into my shop. I would rather be a professional businesswoman than a professional mother. It is not worth it to sacrifice your life for your children."

Peter's friendship began to mean more and more to me. During this time I discovered my visa would be expiring and I was in danger of being sent back. There was only one way to stay—marry an American citizen. It was not the fact that the visa was expiring so much as the fact that I was terribly lonely which drew me closer and closer to Peter. He supplied the devotion and companionship I was used to, the affection I so desperately missed. The more we saw each other, the more I felt in my heart I wanted to marry him.

The next weekend in Atlantic City I proposed to him. Gabors always do the proposing. If we meet a man we like we say so and if he is too shy to ask us then we ask him. Peter seemed pleased but he quickly began to warn me.

"Look, Jolie, I have been a bachelor all my life. I have never been married before. I have decided that I will never marry."

With that he kissed me. He was still very romantic. After togetherness in the bed, he continued the subject I had broached earlier. "Jolie, you know I am not the marrying type. I like whiskey and I like golf and only then do I like women. I am quite set in my ways."

Three days later, Peter said, "I think maybe that I am in love with you. And I think we could have a very beautiful life together. The truth is I am already Gaborized and I am very happy for your proposal and I accept it."

We went to Maryland to the town where you can get married right away. When I looked into the stores instead of his eyes he was hurt. "Maybe I will not marry you," he said.

"Oh, yes, you will," I teased. "I want desperately my citizenship and secondly I want you."

"I will marry you then," he teased back, "only because I am afraid you can be thrown out of this country."

"Thank you," I curtseyed.

We went through town in our lousy Packard and priests came up to inquire are we interested in marriage. What a business this is in Maryland. So who says the Gabors always marry for money? The first day out of Maryland my brand-new groom said, "All the money I make I will have to spend on myself because that's what I'm used to and there isn't too much of it anyway."

"That's all right with me," I assured him.

Many of the qualities he admired in me when we were keeping company became baffling to him when he became my husband. He couldn't understand my drive and ambition. He kept saying to me, "Jolie, relax, enjoy life, don't work so hard."

"Peter, you have only $110 to your name each week and I promise you I will take care of you. I know you are not dying in love with me and I know that you married me because I don't have legitimate papers; I have opened a shop and I don't even have a green card."

"A little of that's true, Jolie," he admitted. "I do feel sorry for you because at any moment they can come and take you on Ellis Island and you're put out."

"Okay, so I am grateful to you because I know that your marrying me will help me. I ask only that you do not try to stop me from wanting to make the best out of myself."

In the evenings after his day at Hamburger Heaven Peter helped me with the books and taxes. I can not add, but I can take one glance and estimate correctly. I am not so good either with multiplying or subtracting or dividing but I can look at a pile of merchandise and guess how much it is to the last rhinestone.

I had my own primitive sort of bookkeeping. When the merchandise came in and when it was returned, when it was sold and for how much. A professional bookkeeper came in at one point and was horrified. "But, Mrs. Gabor," she humphed, "this is not the way to keep books."

"But it is my way, if I knew so much as you and I knew what is my overhead I would never go into business and so I would never become successful and I would be just like you working for someone. I would rather try to be successful than smart."

Under my shop I had a tiny basement office so Peter helped sort things out for me, particularly when we had a 20 percent luxury tax on everything and I could afford neither the time, the space, the money, nor the patience for a professional bookkeeper. He was really a very decent guy.

I married him because I wanted a friend. The friend, unfortunately, wanted to instill in me his brand of philosophy which was slowly to drain all ambition from me. After a hard day's work if I wanted to go someplace and was willing to pay for the treat, Peter would squelch it with, "No, darling, we'll stay home and have a little dinner. After that we can spend the evening listening to Guy Lombardo on the radio. He's on tonight."

I didn't even know what a Guy Lombardo was! "But Peter," I said, "to spend the evening listening to the radio is not exactly my idea of fun."

"My darling, you are so European that you must learn the American way of life which is to listen to Lombardo on the radio."

"How can I convince you that there are other things in life in terms of exciting evening entertainment? I mean, this can't be my future!"

I wanted to have everything. I wanted a house in the country. I wanted a bigger apartment. I wanted the world. He wanted to listen to Guy Lombardo music.

"I think you are not happy with your little apartment and your little shop and the little pleasures of listening to a Guy Lombardo on the air," he told me.

I didn't even know Lombardo and already I hated him!

"The woman who owns the Hamburger Heavens wanted to marry me but I refused," he said. "If I did marry her I could have been better than manager but I said no. I didn't basically want to marry anybody until you just overwhelmed and beguiled me and now I don't basically want to do and be and accomplish more than I am."

Twice I had Peter and Vilmos together. The first time I told Peter to invite Vilmos to Tavern on the Green restaurant and I gave Peter $30 to pay the check. The following time I gave $50 to Vilmos to do the same to Peter. Vilmos was so very elegant but by then he had no money. In my old life if he only *thought* of a man telephoning me he would kill him. Now he was having dinner with my new husband. I looked from one to the other. The whole thing was incredible.

My poor Vilmos could not adjust to any changes. He himself had changed so much that I wanted to die from unhappiness whenever I looked at him. Vilmos became another person. I saw a man, once so powerful, who had lost everything, a man who now lived on the goodness of his family, uncertain of himself because he could not speak English and stubbornly refusing to learn it. No more did he roar and thunder. Now he inquired, he asked, he looked beseechingly. My poor Vilmos was lost. He belonged in whatever was left of the old world he had known.

I remember taking my silverhaired Vilmos to the plane for the trip home. I kissed him good-bye and we hugged silently. *"Isten veled,"* I said. A marvelous Hungarian good-bye which means, "God take care of you . . . all be well with you." I waved him off.

At this phase of my life I was losing a husband right and left. Peter's hours had been shifted from five in the evening until midnight. I told him I didn't get married not to have a husband. I wanted him there when I got home.

Things did not get a chance to grow colder between us because of Peter's illness. He had pneumonia which left a weakness in his chest and he hungered for a climate drier than New York. By coincidence, a member of his family passed away in Arizona. He fell heir to a little house and a restaurant in a small town near Phoenix. He begged me to go West with him to help run the restaurant. The thought of becoming a waitress amongst the cactus—this I couldn't take.

He pleaded. I refused. The last thing Peter said before he left was, "I will come back to you when you lose everything in your big shop. Then you will see I was right!"

The Jolie Gabor pearl salon at 699 Madison Avenue—where it still is—was a specialty house, an unusual thing in the jewelry business. Nowhere else could anyone find such a selection of cultured pearl pins, bracelets, ropes, and earrings costing anywhere from five dollars to $5,000. For instance, I designed earrings using the best pearls, platinum, and real diamonds. The price was $1,000. I copied them in rhinestones, silver, and less expensive pearls for $39. Then I made a good copy of those in metal for five dollars. I had something for everyone.

I used Eva in a layout featuring an interchangeable set which, clasped together, could form one opera-length necklace with two jeweled clasps or a triple strand choker or three individual bracelets. These were very popular.

I used Zsa Zsa in a display featuring my pretend emerald. A good emerald costs maybe $40,000. A bad one with flaws costs maybe $2,000. I designed a pretend emerald with deliberate flaws cut by a diamond cutter which appeared so real it looked like it should cost $2,000. I sold it for $115—and I didn't lose money.

A page ad for Valentine's Day featured the four of us wearing that famous clip-on drop earring of rhinestone clusters, edged with cultured pearls, and centered by the "emerald." Everyone wore that. It became my signature. When Nicky Hilton married Elizabeth Taylor, he could afford any wedding present from Paris, London, or anywhere. He gave his bride my earrings.

When Elizabeth came into my shop she was so incredibly beautiful that it was not to be believed. You were blinded when you looked at those bluish-purple eyes and that black black hair. She was about eighteen and she unbuttoned her blouse to try on a necklace and you could see that full bust—not so full as it is now—and nobody could take their eyes off of her. But she was a little unhappy that she had to buy costume jewelry. "This is very nice," she sniffed, "but it's not such great value. It's not real diamonds." I told her, "Don't worry, darling, you are young. Wait a little bit. You will have yet all kinds of real diamonds!"

With my copies of copies of copies I not only had rich customers but I had poor women who wanted to look like rich women. Thanks to Hungarian workmanship, my pieces had the custom look of real jewelry and always contained some real stone.

My idea was to put a few good things such as real pearls around a rhinestone pin. Fashionwise it became beautiful. Businesswise it became fantastic. There is a 100 per cent write-up because with your own ideas you can set any markup you like. Surrounding real pearls with European rhinestones and other junk, setting the whole thing in real gold made my shop just that —a gold mine.

I was honest. Too honest, maybe. Like I would tell a lady, "Oh, for your fat neck you must make your pearls high so buy a choker." I would say to a customer, "Darling, you don't need Jolie Gabor's earrings. You need a face lift."

They were flabbergasted rather than angry. This extravagant flavor is something that is part of me. I cannot help it.

I know that I exaggerate. A little bit I think it is a Hungarian trait. Zsa Zsa does everything double. She maybe paid $300 for a gown but she will say $600. She tells me, *"Nuci,* I am sending you a ten-page letter." It turns out to be only five pages. Zsa Zsa doubles everything but her age. I, too, exaggerate. If someone is beautiful I say they are the most beautiful in the whole world. If someone is a millionaire I say multimillionaire. But there is one American trait I don't have. I don't say a person looks good when she doesn't. I cannot lie so I don't. Either I tell or I don't tell. I have no inhibitions. I am outspoken like a child.

My honesty put me into troubles sometimes. A tall skinny lady with a neck like a chicken came to buy a necklace. My assistant showed her one for $3,000. The lady loved the necklace. My assistant loved the commission. I did not like the pearls. "Madame," I said, "the color is too pink for you and the length makes your neck even longer and skinnier. Everything is wrong." I fished out a necklace for $500. "Here, this is for you." She was thrilled that Mme. Gabor herself had personally preferred to lose $2,500 rather than sell what was wrong for the customer. Okay, but my assistant nearly died. She had spent an hour making this sale and I killed it in one moment. I never did that again. At least I don't think I did.

One of my famous experiences was this fat little woman with a short neck, she looked like a madam from a bordello, who waddled into my shop. I thought to myself, "Oh, this is a big customer," because she was full of emeralds and bracelets. She blazed with jewelry. She made my salesgirl confused and crazy. She wanted the trays of rings, she looked at the imitation emerald earrings, she fingered the brooches. She tried on everything. "I want to see Mme. Gabor," she bellowed after an hour. "I wish to know what Mme. Gabor personally thinks I should buy." So I came out from my little office. "I have for you a very special newly arrived three-strand pearl necklace with a diamond clasp," I said. "You have to have this. It is my absolutely best piece and the price is $2,500." I personally fastened this around her short, fat neck. "This is the best for you," I said. "It makes your neck longer."

"But I can't decide, Mme. Gabor," she said, looking in the mirror.

"So, all right, go for a little walk and think about it."

"Okay," she agreed, "Maybe I have first my lunch and then I decide."

"All right," I told, "this is the best. You go."

I sent her out with my very best piece. She put on her stole and she didn't buy nothing and she went out with the $2,500 necklace around her fat neck. She never came back and we weren't insured. My salesgirl said to me, "And you had to personally come down to wait on her yet! We really needed you to make this big deal sale for free!"

The chicest society names wanted to work for me. The sales force numbered a German baroness, a French countess, and a princess from Hungary. The only commoner there was me.

Mine became known as the aristocratic shop. All these society salesladies were really hard-sell types, but of course they knew nothing. They were all new at working. A little they thought it was chic to work there because they liked the name and glamor of Jolie Gabor. It became for these women an adventure. They all wore black to show off the jewelry. By day they'd be in my store pushing pearls and by night they'd be in El Morocco wearing them.

The exception was the small, dark Jewish girl, who is with me to this day. A friend invited me one night for a game of canasta. There were four tables. The hostess introduced the others to me. "This is Mrs. Soandso, this is Whoeversheis, this is Bimba Beck . . ." That was nearly a quarter of a century ago. Bimba Beck is still with me. Today she manages the shop.

Bimbuska and I had two desks opposite each other. She was maybe six weeks with me and I ordered her, "Look me up the number of Nat King in one of my three handwritten telephone books and call him."

"Yes, ma'am," said Bimba, reaching for the books. She opened to *K*. "It's not here," she said.

"So look in the other books."

She looked. Nothing. "My dear," I snapped impatiently, "if you can't find a simple telephone number, you're stupid."

Nervously Bimba began looking under *N*. Nothing. "Oh," I slapped the desk with great irritation. "What do I have working for me? I thought you were an intelligent girl."

"I am intelligent, Mrs. Gabor. I have looked through three books under *K* and *N* and it is not there."

I glared at her across the desk. "So look under *S.*"

"*S?*"

"Yes, *S.*"

"Why *S?*"

"Because in my telephone books all men are listed under *szerelem.*"

"*Szerelem?*"

"That's the Hungarian word for love.? Every man who came near to me or called me or took me to the theatre or with whom I had a little liason even if I didn't sleep with him I put under *szerelem.* How can I remember all their names? I cannot. So this is my system. Look under *S.*"

In those days the girls did nothing to help me. In fact, sometimes I got unhappy from them. Eva was on a television interview program wearing a choker with earrings I had given her that day for a Christmas present. When the interviewer asked her what she got for Christmas she took out a gold comb which costs maybe $24 and she said to the interviewer, "This I have from Van Cleef!" Then she took out something from Cartier, but never did she mention my present. She didn't even mention that Mama gave to her the jewelry she was wearing. This made me very unhappy—not only for the publicity and not only for the money but for the unfairness. It was not the only time she did this to me. So, after the show I said to her, "How can you do this to me?"

She said, "I don't always think of everything."

"How could you be so cruel?" I said. "For a friend you would do it. Plain simple customers say it. Why not my own daughter?"

"You know that when you are on TV you are so tense that you don't always know what to answer," she apologized.

"Never mind. Forget it," I said, but I was very hurt.

The time had come, I thought, for a good place to live.

On 63rd Street between Madison and Fifth Avenues I passed a brownstone house and stopped to read where it was written out, "House for Sale." An old man hobbled up, "You want to buy this house?"

He cupped his ear at me so I guessed he was hard of hearing.

"I couldn't but thank you anyhow," I said very loud. "I am looking only for an apartment."

"A what? Oh, well, maybe I know of an apartment and maybe not. Maybe there isn't anything for you at all. How much do you want to pay?"

"Maybe a few hundred a month," I shouted.

"For $600 a month you can pay the mortgage on this house."

"Mortgage? I don't know what is mortgage. I know only I am just looking for an apartment for renting in the neighborhood because I have this shop, Jolie Gabor's down the street."

"Ohhh," he said surveying me closely, "When you have this beautiful shop then you can afford also to have this beautiful house. Come, I show it to you."

In this moment I was making money and some days I would actually take in $1,000, but I didn't have any overage. I had to pay out every month $1,000 to the hat shop plus my rent plus my inventory plus my help plus my fee to Ellen McCluskey plus I had to live myself. Money was running in so I knew I could spend for a nice apartment even though I didn't have anything in the bank and I still owed everybody.

"You need only maybe $5,000 to pay down," said the man.

"It's nice," I said directly into his cupped ear. "Such a nice location."

"They're asking $55,000 for the house."

"Try to have it for fifty," I said to him. I was impulsive because I was not sure about anything. I didn't feel any foundation under me. I was without money and yet I was trying everything—in business, in places to live, in marriage, everything. There is a Hungarian saying, "When you are poor and you have not so it is the same."

"Oh, Magduska," I said back in the shop, "I saw a house that is so magnificent. I give every month $600 but this is the mortgage and like this I can buy it."

"*Nuci,* isn't it enough that we are poor?" she said irritated. "Is it necessary for us to be *meshugga,* crazy, too?"

"It is 16 East 63rd Street, in the swanky Sixties right off Fifth Avenue very close to the shop. I can not afford good rent anyplace so I have decided to buy a whole house because it will be cheaper in the end."

"Where will you get the money?"

"Look, darling, I have my one big diamond ring so I will pawn it." I went to a pawn shop on Madison Avenue. This was my first experience. They were very impressed with me. A small bald man with a brown suit saw me as I approached the shop and he came outside and took my elbow to guide me into the rear entrance.

"Don't put me through the back door," I told him. "Don't hide me. I am not ashamed. I am proud that I have such a diamond to pawn!"

The next day Zsa Zsa started on me. "*Nuci,* you are crazy."

I said, "Don't worry, my darling daughter. You don't have to give a guarantee for me. I do it myself. Don't be so afraid for what I am doing."

"But $55,000, *Nuci.*"

"Look, Zsa Zsika, you cannot make a big success if you act small. Anyway, I told the caretaker in charge of the house when he showed it to me to try for $50,000."

The next day I discovered that the caretaker, because he was hard of hearing, didn't hear me right. "I am sorry I cannot get it for the $40,000 you suggested," he said to me. "The best they'll do is $42,000." So God help me this is the absolute truth. I nearly dropped dead.

I always rely on my special little angel. I always work under the theory that "something will happen" and something does happen—always. I am anyhow a fatalist. I could not seem to be worried the way everybody else was worried for me. I gave 10 per cent, $4,200 for a down payment, and it was mine.

The brownstone house was thirty-five years old and had been built for one family. The whole first floor was a ballroom. Now that I had it I couldn't see how I could live in that whole place all by myself. My friend the Duke di San Miniati said, "Jolie, make this a boarding house."

"But this will cost me a fortune."

"No, because if you make from this house lots of little apartments the tenants will pay you rent and help pay the mortgage for you. With tenants you can live for nothing."

"Yes, this is a good idea," I agreed. "Even if I must spend money to convert each floor into one apartment, I will live there rent free and at the same time I get an income from the rest of the building. Yes, this is good business."

I had to redo everything. It was awful. From where there was a closet there came a bathroom. From where there was one large salon there came a bedroom and a living room. From where there was a hall there came a kitchen. It was after the war and there was such a demand for equipment that I had to wait forever for everything. I had to wait nine months for bathroom color tiles. And how did I pay? I sold some big pieces and when I had the money I paid it.

Magda was my first tenant. Unfortunately, I was not so thrilled with her for a tenant. For a whole year she didn't pay me nothing. "You must pay," I said to her. "When you make from me $900 a month working in my shop and you always come in late, you can pay."

"But you are my mother and I am your daughter so why must I pay?" she asked.

"Because you are accustomed to a rich mother," I said, "so you think it is always the same way. It is not the same way. I am not rich now."

Finally she paid, but she was very offended. It is really impossible to live with Magda. She is a difficult case. Zsa Zsa the same. They are strong like Vilmos.

I had some famous tenants: the society genius Earl Blackwell and Bob Schuler, who is now married to singer Patrice Munsel. Bob had two rooms on the top floor for $150 a month. One night he threw a party for 75 people so he dumped gravel on the roof without checking with the housing authorities. The whole building could have collapsed. The head it would have collapsed on belonged to the famous designer, Jacques Fath, who had the apartment beneath. I was underneath Jacques, Magda under me, and in the basement was a composer who gave singing lessons. It was a kooky, marvelous house.

Except that I was the landlady, the whole house was one great big family. Everyone knew everyone else socially and whenever anyone had a party all the apartments were thrown open. It was totally unique and un-New York-like. How I paid for this most expensive real estate in the world I still don't know.

I couldn't believe my success. I was a big bluff. I only had the looks of money but I didn't ever have any. I would bluff everybody. I lived like a millionaire but I never had a dime.

I am lucky. Twice the ceiling came down in my new house. The first time, I was in Florida on a little vacation and I saw a picture in a newspaper. "Oh," I said, "in this picture I see what looks like my curtains." I look closely and it's a shot of Magda and underneath is written, "Jolie Gabor's ceiling falls down." If I had been there I would have been dead. It caved in right onto my red velvet bed.

Another time I came down the staircase and just before my nose I could feel a little dust. Right two inches from my face fell down the whole staircase ceiling.

Another time a waterpipe broke on the fourth floor at midnight and the house was flooded. There was water all over the place and the damage was very high. The rugs on the stairs were ruined, the fallen plaster had marred my furniture, the house was a shambles, the repairs were assessed at $25,000. The next morning at 9:30 Bimba rushed over and she found me playing the piano and singing Hungarian songs. Her eyes went up into her head when she surveyed the house and me.

"I have realized there is nothing for me to do so I am doing this," I said in answer to the unasked question.

"How lucky I am that I know a person like you," said Bimba, staring at me with her hands on her hips.

The phone rang. It was Eva. I spoke to her all the while playing piano.

Her voice rose sharply, "What is it you are doing?"

I said calmly, "I am playing the piano."

"Under the circumstances," said Eva, "don't you think this is a bit ridiculous?"

"Evika, darling," I explained sweetly. "I have no time. I must get dressed and get to my shop and take care of this trouble so this is the only time I have to play my Hungarian songs. Bye, bye."

7 I had a great desire to live the way I had in Budapest. Nearly everything I did was designed to impress my daughters, to prove that I could make it myself without their help. The next step was to hire a butler.

Harry was black. He was also a fairy. Harry had worked formerly for a rich man and a little bit he looked down on me. Harry really knew how to serve and how to live and he had great style. When he went to the supermarket with $10 and we both knew he only spent $5 he never gave me what was left over. When I'd ask for the change he'd say, "Mrs. Gabor . . . !" The way he accented those two little words plainly implied that he was absolutely shocked at my lack of class.

There was a time I was angry with him and I shouted, "Lincoln should never have freed you," and he put me down calmly with, "You have no right to say such a thing. You're not even a citizen!"

It took nine months to complete the house. The tenth month I told my girls to give me a guest list for my first party. Zsa Zsa had already introduced me to the President of General Motors, society writer Constance Collier, who wanted to write a book on my life, some Vanderbilts, some princes. I had nothing but I somehow attracted the high society people with me and the theatrical people too.

I sent invitations on special cards imprinted with the girls' pictures. I had a box fashioned on the first floor and in it I put Gypsy violins. I had an all-Hungarian buffet with waitresses in peasant dresses, butlers in Hungarian uniforms. The goulash only cost me $200 but the bill from Louis Sherry's who catered the party was $4,000 because they sent flowers and servants and two people just to take coats to the basement. For $12 I rented a long red velvet carpet and spread it from the sidewalk to my house. I had 250 people including Errol Flynn, Laurence Harvey, Paula Laurence, Orin Lehman, Betty Furness, Margaret Leighton, Clark Gable and the one thing that got all the conversation was the red carpet. Dorothy Kilgallen, who was a top Broadway columnist, talked only about that on her radio program. For a week she wrote about this in her column. She wrote, "Jolie Gabor has to come to America to show us how a party should be."

I jammed everyone into my apartment and when they couldn't squeeze in anymore I announced, "Dinner is served downstairs in Magda's place."

Frank Sinatra, who was not invited, appeared very unhappy. He walked around with his hands behind his back. Since he was not anyhow invited I said to him, "Frank, you had to come here to be unhappy?" The swimming star Eleanor Holm arrived in a great rush of people with Elaine Stritch, Ted Straeter, Betsy von Furstenburg, Nina Pattersen and Victor Borge and they met on the ground floor. Eleanor was wearing a diamond choker and her husband Billy Rose's greeting to her was, "That diamond necklace was a collar not a choker. Where's the rest of it?" And her return greeting was, "I sold it." Then Billy said to me—and I could have killed him because so many times I heard people say it—"I don't know why you work so hard when you have such rich children." I was making up my mind what to answer when he added, "You have wonderful children if they let you live in such a big, beautiful house as this." So I told him off. Even *now* my daughters need me. I must fly to them when they are in trouble and everything.

Igor Cassini wrote that Jolie gets ten percent of everything Zsa Zsa does. I was furious and I wrote him a letter which must have been a good one because not one word did he take out and he ran the whole thing in his society column which then was in the New York *Journal American*. He headlined it: "Jolie's letter to me."

Zsa Zsa came late because she had to go do a TV interview show. I had just given her a beautiful lavaliere necklace and she was wearing it on the show and the host said, "This is such a beautiful necklace. Did you get it from your mother's shop?" And Zsa Zsa said, "No, it was a gift from an admirer." I was so angry that when I saw her walk in I said to her, "Zsa Zsa, I don't want to see you. Please don't come to the party. How dare you be so fresh about my jewelry? This is how I make my living. You don't support me. When you told, 'This jewelry is from an admirer' you could have said that he bought it from your mother's shop."

She cried and she was so unhappy. "Nothing—not the fame, the parties, the TV interviews—not even the life is worth it without you," she said.

So finally I said, "All right, I will let you in." What can a mother do?

The girls were close but competitive. If one got something, the others wanted to know why they hadn't gotten it. They coveted each other's accomplishments so that night Zsa Zsa, who was wearing a divine Dior of red satin and velvet, was a little unhappy because she didn't like that also Eva was there plus me plus Magda as though she was part of a team. She considered that she was the most famous one and she likes to be the only celebrity.

In front of the press, Joan Fontaine, Brian Aherne, Joey Adams, Cecil Beaton, and Paul Lukas, who were standing together, somebody asked me, "Who paid for this party?"

I was offended. I said, "I did."

"Oh," she said, "it's a beautiful party. I thought you promoted it like

Cobina Wright always does. Cobina gives parties but she doesn't lay out the money herself. She gets someone to subsidize it." At that point I didn't know that you could get other people to pay for your parties because you were a celebrity and invited celebrities. I said to her very hurt, "I paid for it all myself." Of course I did not add that all I had to my name was $400 and I didn't know how long it was going to take me to pay it off. I didn't figure that was her business.

Today even the youngest people invite me and need me. They throw parties in my name because they meet important people through me. Of course they also like me on their own.

This was an after-theatre supper that I gave and it was black tie. I even refused entrance to famous couturiere Ceil Chapman because she wasn't sufficiently dressed. "Go home and change, Ceil," I told her. "I invited you because I thought you are a fashion plate and you will make the party."

"You mean I am not elegant enough for you?" asked Ceil.

"No," I told. So she went home and changed.

Hope Hampton came with her long yellow blonde hair flowing to her shoulders, and her usual floor-length gown of sequins and bugle beads and winking and blinking with jewels was eating Hungarian salami with her fingers and almost wiping her hands on Hermione Gingold's dress or Denise Darcel's cape or Walter Slezak's tuxedo because they were all so jammed in together. I said to Hope, "Darling, you would be even prettier without that teen-age hairdo," and linking her arm with the young boy escort she always has she said, "Darling, this is my trademark."

Bobo Rockefeller came with Mimi Bass, the mother of lawyer Norton Bass, who got the six million dollars alimony for Bobo. Mimi was a good friend to Bobo, who was a good friend to me. Mimi had come into my shop through Bobo and bought a big amount of my jewelry and never paid for it. I asked her many times to pay. She never paid. I sent her bills. She didn't pay. She called when she heard I was having a party. "Jolie, dear," she cooed, "can I come to your party?" So I told to her, "When you bring me a check you can come." She came uninvited and without a check.

Another of my guests was Aly Khan. Aly called me "The Queen of Madison Avenue." We would go to El Morocco and dance until the early hours. He was a regular guy. I brought him to an Off-Broadway show where they called him, "Mr. Cohen." One time, when I was with some other people and I wanted a frank or a hamburger and we came to a little frankfurter shop, they said, "Oh, Jolie, you cannot go in there." Then through the glass I saw Prince Aly sitting there all alone eating his hot dog and sauerkraut.

That night at my party Prince Aly "Cohen" was seated on the floor surrounded by Anita Loos, Geraldine Page, Lily Pons, Charlie Feldman, and Betty and Jane Kean and he had taken from my buffet two plates. One was piled high with Székely goulash and finger rolls. The other plate on the floor had assorted strudel plus a cup of hot coffee plus a glass of champagne. I always served champagne. "This is the most delicious goulash I ever tasted," he grinned. "You know something, Jolie, of all of them you're the best Gabor." Then, noticing a man who was obviously paying Magda very close attention, Prince Aly asked, "Who's he?"

"That's Magda's boyfriend," I answered, "for the time being."

The time being was very short because Magda soon became engaged to New York attorney Sidney Warren, whom she had met when she needed someone to straighten out her affairs after her divorce.

"You know I am the quiet, serious one in the family and Sidney, too, likes books and the simple things in life. He is the type for me," Magda told me.

"But I can see that you are not so madly in love with him," I said to her.

"Well, but it will grow."

"All right," I told her, "so marry him. It will be good to have a lawyer in the family."

Shortly after their marriage somebody asked me, "Do you think everything will be calm now in the lives of your daughters?" and I replied, "What a quaint fancy."

It didn't take Magda long to get rid of her latest quaint fancy. She did it by going to Harry, my butler, and saying, "Take Mr. Warren's suitcases out!"

Magda was always strong. "How can you do this?" I asked her, thinking of this baldish man who would come home only to find himself out on the street.

"Harry," she ordered, "after you pack up Mr. Warren's things, change the lock."

She absolutely wouldn't let him in and I saw him hanging around outside. We had a downstairs door which you had to open before you could get inside to your apartment door. Both locks had been changed. Sidney went to a public pay telephone and called me. At first I really wanted to help. I consoled him. Then I reasoned with Magda. That was when I found out he was not such a good guy and had done some deals that were not so 100 per cent kosher and so that was the end of Sidney Warren, Magda's third husband.

I threw many parties and went out a lot in these days. I began to learn about escorts. Hope Hampton told me, "I will never marry again because of the alimony so what I do is take young escorts. I give them money for the entertainment and at the end of the evening I take the change back because I will not pay for a man."

In those days there was the Stork Club and Sherman Billingsley, the owner, had an evening TV show from there. I was to be the hostess one week and I needed an escort. I wanted to have a big name for the evening so I decided to call the Archduke Franz Joseph. "I want your husband for the evening," I said to Princess Martha. "I want him to escort me."

"Oh, I *am* sorry," she murmured, "but we are both engaged for the evening."

"You may keep your engagement," I said. "I don't really need you. Just him."

"Excuse me," she stammered. "but are you referring to the Archduke Franz Joseph?"

"Yes of course," I said. "Put him in a dinner jacket because I need him."

"Madame," and the voice had turned cold, "that is quite impossible."

"Okay, if you don't then I say to everybody on television that you are a bad designer. You and your husband design apartments, don't you? You do big decorations, don't you? You also want good publicity, don't you?"

"Okay," she sighed.

"Okay with me, too," I said. "Now I say you are the best designers in the whole world."

Right after the TV show I put Archduke Franz Joseph in a taxi and sent him home to Martha.

Perhaps ten nights later I was invited to a party at Billy Reed's Little Club, which was then popular. I called that evening Prince Hanover, the brother of Queen Frederika of Greece and the grandson of Kaiser Wilhelm. There was maybe twenty-five years difference between us. He was young, blond, blue-eyed and tall. He said, "Oh, I wish you had told me earlier. I have a date."

"Okay," I said, "I find somebody else."

"Wait," quickly put in the Prince. "Give me a few minutes."

Ten minutes later he called back. "I go with you. I broke my date with a 21-year-old model who is the belle of New York."

"But why did you do that?" I asked.

"Because, my dear Jolie, I find you infinitely more entertaining."

I went everywhere every night. I was living like a bachelor girl and I had incredible energy. I could work ten hours and afterwards dress myself and go to the Waldorf Astoria for a party until 2 A.M. I had vitality, I had buoyancy and except for the fact that this was a new country my whole world was Budapest again. My house blazed with lights, parties were being given, people were dropping in, there were invitations to dinners, old friends arriving on every boat, new friends ringing my telephone at all hours . . . even when I didn't know them.

Late one afternoon I had a call from Texas, Dallas. "You don't know me," a man said. "I am a total stranger but I have heard a lot about you and I have read about you and I would like to know if you would have dinner with me when I am in New York next week."

"Certainly not," I said.

"I'll take you to an elegant respectable place," he said. "I'll take you to El Morocco."

"I am very sorry," I said. "I am not a call girl," and I put down the phone.

I was becoming a bit of a celebrity who could and did say outlandish things and get away with it. Wherever I went in a foreign city there were headlines. I went to Montreal and the front page featured my picture with the caption, "Jolie Gabor's first time in Canada." I went to Philadelphia for a showing of my jewelry and they did a double page spread on me.

Then I was in Texas and a newspaper wrote a whole column about "the fiftyish Mrs. Gabor." I went to bed with a compress on my head and a plaster on my chest. Years later I was in my late sixties and a journalist wrote, "She looks like the very late fifties" and I was again a wreck for two days. I wanted only to look like I was in my thirties.

Even when you are up in years any woman who is outgoing and, of course, has a successful shop and a townhouse and surrounds herself with glamor can have a man. Only those women who have to ask something of the man don't have a man. You have always an escort when you are the invited one and when you take him out to a party and it costs him nothing. This way is easy. I never lacked for escorts.

I even gave away some of my extras. Like for instance Count Dorelis, who was married to a society rich lady named Dolly O'Brien, who was later adored by Clark Gable. Count Dorelis escorted me several months and then Dr. Ilona Gero, a rich Hungarian lady friend of mine who had many corporations, wanted him. When we were in Florida she phoned me, "Jolika, I have much money but it does me no good. I have no escorts. Can I borrow a little bit yours?"

"Well, I have two these days," I said. "I have Prince Jupescu and Count Dorelis. So which one do you want?"

"I want the Count."

"Dorelis? Why Dorelis?"

"Because he has an Eldorado Cadillac."

I thought a moment. "Well, I must admit I don't particularly care about Dorelis. He is handy to have around but there is really no romance there so maybe I will give him to you."

"Oh, thank you, Jolika," she said, "thank you."

"What will you give me for him?"

"What do you mean?"

"Well," I said thoughtfully, thinking aloud, "I don't really want him but I have no need to give him up either . . . however, if I can get something for him then maybe . . ."

"What do you want?"

In those days there was a stunning swimsuit that sold for $100, so, since

I was not too interested in him and I was very interested in the swimsuit, I said, "You buy me that rhinestone swimsuit, all right?"

She said, "Okay, it's a deal."

So I sold Count Dorelis for a rhinestone bathing suit and she delivered on her promise. The Count found out and was offended. He said, "I surely thought I was worth more than a bathing suit." He was right, too. She should have thrown in a cap.

Most escorts no matter who they were adored me. Only one didn't. That was the one selected for me by Zsa Zsa. We were going to a movie opening and she asked, "You have somebody?"

I told, "No. But people always have a good time with me. Even the big film stars I have had as escorts have had fun with me so you get me somebody."

The man, a producer, came for me at Zsa Zsa's house in Beverly Hills and he was a terrible sourpuss. I was very displeased at such a man and he looked to be even more displeased with me. At intermission I said, "You are not very happy to me. You don't even speak a word."

He cleared his throat. "Well, it's just that I'm a little disappointed. They told me I'd be with Marilyn Monroe."

"You mean Zsa Zsa promised you that your date for the evening would be Marilyn Monroe?"

He nodded his head up and down. "Oh, my God, you have all the right to be disappointed," I said. "Oh, you poor, poor man. I feel so sorry for you."

He managed a small smile and it seemed he was starting to like me a little because I felt so terrible for him.

"What can I do?" I asked him. "You want me to leave and you can then sit with nobody?"

"Oh, no, please," he insisted. "Stay. Please stay. It's just that it was a shock when I came to the house and Zsa Zsa said, 'I would like you to meet my mother.'"

"I see what you mean," I agreed. "Nobody would be enchanting to you in this case."

We became the best of friends and later he called and said, "Would you allow me to invite you to dinner tonight? Now I would very much like to go out with *you!*"

I was never insulted and I never felt badly when I had nobody. I would just call Riza, a Hungarian who worked for me, and we would go out and even without a man I was happy. We went to a roulette game at Montauk, Long Island once and I put on her my white silk gown and I introduced her as "Countess Riza." She looked like royalty with my beautiful imitation jewelry and I addressed her all night as "Countess." The men thought everything on her was real and they swarmed all over. We died laughing and we had a gorgeous time.

Always I was going and running. One Sunday I was dying of tiredness.

I was so weary with the shop and the house and the payments that I wanted only to stay in bed the whole day. That morning I got a call from Eva from Beverly Hills. *"Nuci,"* she said, "I arrive tonight from Hollywood with Bundy Solt so why don't you make dinner in your house and we both see you later."

"Bundy now makes $5,000 a week as a screenwriter, is that right?"

"Yes."

"So let him take us out. I have no servant Sunday."

"No, it is better if we have a Hungarian dinner home quietly with you. See you later."

I had to make the bed and clean up the house. Then I telephoned a nearby Hungarian restaurant. The restaurateur, a Mrs. Terhes, was our cook in Budapest. She said, "But, Mrs. Gabor, we have 200 people in our restaurant now and there is nobody to send over with the food."

"Okay, never mind," I sighed. "I'll get dressed and come over by taxi." So I brought the dinner to the house, set the table, went to a florist for flowers for the table and my only consolation was that Bundy said, "Evika, can you appreciate what your mother did for you tonight?"

I am convinced that never can my children say I was not a good mother. I was and I am and that is the truth. They may be too busy for me but I am never too busy for them.

For a weekend of relaxation I was invited to Southampton, which I had been told is the most swanky place in the East.

There was a small jewelry shop in Southampton run by two boys who had lived together for a dozen years. In their shop window they had nice things such as beaded bags for $200 and I was interested in their wholesalers so I put my card under the locked door and I wrote, "Come and see me."

They were in the late thirties. Their names were Robert and Sheldon and they were very nice. When next they visited me they saw an emerald ring in my shop for $800. I had paid $600. I sold it to them cheap. I didn't make very much on it. "It's from Europe, isn't it?" asked Sheldon.

"Of course," I replied. Actually, I had gotten it from one of the wholesalers they put me onto but I didn't tell them that.

These two were very social. They introduced me to elegant people and told me to get a house in Southampton. "It's good for your business to be seen there," they said.

We had gone to a big party at a gambling casino in Montauk, twenty-five miles from Southampton. On the way back Sheldon said, "There is a brand new house for sale not far from ours in the most elegant, most desirable section. It's on the sea on Cooper Neck Lane."

"And I happen to know you can make a good buy," chimed in Robert.

I laughed. "Oh, you two are crazy. I need a summer house like I need an attack of malaria."

The gate was open so we drove up and with the headlights of the car shining I looked in the windows. There were two floors without even a chair anywhere. Downstairs was a big living room, a little dining room, a pantry. The second floor I couldn't see but I learned later it had three guest rooms and baths.

They moved the car so the headlights would reflect at a different angle. The house stood on the water and there was a lake with swans. It was everything I loved.

"Okay, I try," I said to my friends, taking down the advertised phone number. "I'm sure it won't work because I have nothing but I try anyway mainly because I like Southampton for the weekend and I can't afford the hotel."

I called the number and the agent said, "The asking price for the house is $35,000."

"Okay, so that's the asking," I said, "what's the taking?"

"$35,000 is what I want for the house."

"I understand," I said, "but what will you take?"

"Well, at least $30,000. Not a cent less than thirty."

"Twenty-eight I give you."

"Thank you, Mme. Gabor," he said icily, "but I'm not interested." And he pushed down the phone.

Three weeks later I was working in the shop at midnight and the phone rang.

It was this man. He gave his name but I didn't remember it. By this time I had forgotten the whole idea of a house. He said, "You called *me*. You wanted to buy my house, remember?"

"Oh, yes, so?"

"All right, $28,000," he said. "The reason I have decided to give this to you so cheaply is because the man who owned this built it for his mistress and now the mistress is *kaput.*"

I thought to myself, "This is the same story every real estate man tells every buyer," but I didn't say anything.

"When he threw out the mistress there was no reason for this house so this is now a very big bargain."

I wanted very much this place because in my 63rd Street house I had originally decided to furnish apartments and I had gone to a big exhibition sale of furniture and I had bought many sofas, lamps, and huge junky things for five apartments. Then Duce San Miniati told me, "This is the worst thing you can do because when you rent a furnished apartment people can stay two months then move out, but when they furnish their own place and spend the money and go to the trouble then they will stay maybe three years at a time." So I really needed a house immediately to stick all this furniture which the auction place would not hold for me any longer.

"So," said the man, "is it agreed that we have a deal?"

I told him, "Yes."

"$28,000?"

I knew I would have to put 10 per cent down and I didn't have $2,800. I didn't even have $2,000. "The most I can pay now is $22,000."

"But," he sputtered. "This is the best location in Southampton. The house is brand new. And we agreed $28,000."

"But that was before. Now I don't have the money."

We argued back and forth and finally it was agreed. "I will move in immediately," I announced.

"But this is only September. We are going into the winter and this is a summer house," he argued. "And, anyway, you can't possibly move in because the house will be in escrow until the official closing."

"Look, I don't understand escrow and closing. I take this house only when I can take it immediately."

"But, Mrs. Gabor," said the voice patiently, "it is a law that when you buy a house it is first in escrow and then you can't take it until there is a closing."

"I move in immediately or I don't take this house."

"This is impossible," he said.

"Well, I'm very sorry then I can't move in."

"No house can be taken immediately," he explained, "because it must go through examination before you can take title."

"You don't trust me?"

"I trust you but I don't trust me. Maybe we made some mistake. Maybe I don't know just how big the land is you are entitled to have. That must all be checked."

"Look," I said, "I have $500. I will give it you immediately and furnish your empty house and make it a showplace. I need it fast because I have a lot of furniture and I must put it someplace and your Southampton house is perfect."

He was obviously upset with the way I did business because he muttered something I didn't understand. I think it was a curse. "By the way," I said, "how is it that you call me at midnight?"

"Because I called your apartment and it didn't answer so I am not stupid so I tried your shop."

"Okay, so if you are not stupid then take my offer. After Christmas I give you the balance of the down payment. If I don't come through with the rest of the money in December then I lose my $500 plus everything that is in the house—all the furnishings and everything. Is that agreed?"

"Well, let me think about it."

The next day he came to my shop, saw that it was a showplace and he agreed. So can you imagine? For $500 I had September through December and Thanksgiving and Christmas in my own country house in Southampton! How I ever had the nerve to do these things I can't imagine today.

One big problem came up when I had my Southampton house—how to get there. I needed a car and, as usual, did not allow the fact that I had no money stand in my way. I bought a Packard. This Packard was the last lemon ever made. The salesman had a powder blue jacket and silver-colored hair and it all went so well together and he was so handsome that this is why I bought it.

I said to him, "You will teach me to drive in the United States."

He replied, "Every day, my dear lady, I will personally come for you." Unfortunately every day he also personally came for a Hungarian friend of mine who didn't buy a Packard from him so I lost him and what I ended up with was that lemon of a car. I had to pay $400 down. When I was ready to get rid of it I couldn't get more than $500 for it so I gave it for a gift to my cosmetician, Rozsie Poganyi. She is also a Hungarian so it was all right.

Later on I also had for an escort a high executive of Packard by the name of Graham Wheeler. Somehow I thought that evened the score.

I had little bits of difficulties with my car. I was given a summons for reckless driving on the highway after they insisted I cut off a police car. I didn't really cut off the police car. It was just that I missed the turnoff and so I pulled suddenly to the side of the road and the police car was on my right. I didn't see him or I wouldn't have cut him off as I explained to the judge.

Another day I was approaching the Triboro Bridge and I made a small mistake which resulted in my smacking a little into the bridge—but only a very little—so they gave me a ticket and I had to appear in the suburbs somewhere to answer it. I was so busy so I wrote a letter. "Dear darling Judge. Please be so kind as to forgive me and I will never do it again. The bridge came to me not I came to the bridge. You see, I drived and it was slippery and I went a little near to where I shouldn't go so near. It wasn't that I meant to really bang into the bridge so please excuse me." It was such a sweet letter that the judge said, "All right. When you send me a picture you don't have to appear." So that's what I did.

Eight months later Peter turned up again. My shop was thriving. People were buying jewelry by the pound. My friend, Mrs. Evelyn Sharpe, who always mimicked my accent, told me, "You alvays said to me, 'Dahlingk, I vill be famose someday.' "

That was true. I did always say that and it was happening. "Someday" was already here.

Peter walked around in a daze. He couldn't believe. "All you had was a tiny hole-in-the-wall shop and one room in a boarding house. Now you have a gorgeous big decorated shop, a townhouse off Fifth Avenue. . . ."

"With twenty people still working in it to finish off the tile bathrooms," I laughed.

"And a country home in Southampton and a Packard car."

"But no money," I put in quick. I was thrilled at the way he walked around shaking his head and looking at me in amazement.

"But how were you able to do all this, Jolie?" he asked. "In three generations people cannot amass what you have. Why do you work so hard and dash about buying houses all over the place? Why can you not relax, take it easy, sit down and listen to the radio?"

I understood that we were from two worlds but Magda encouraged me to try and patch things up. "He's a nice man," she argued. "He's sweet, he's kind, he's a presentable escort, he's a companion, and he's a good bookkeeper too. You need someone to help you with all you're doing. With him at least you could have some help in managing the business. Tell him to come back and come to work for you. Pay him the same weekly salary he's been getting in Arizona."

I did as she suggested. Very gently he replied, "Jolie, I am still not over the first pain you caused me by refusing to come to Arizona. We can still be friends and see each other occasionally but I don't know whether I could come back."

"Why don't you take a few days to make the decision?" I suggested.

Three days passed and he came to me. "Maybe we could get back together again but I think we should do it gradually," he said. "Tonight let's just have dinner together and spend the evening."

I agreed. For a week he came by for me, we had dinner and then went back to my house. It was working out nicely and it appeared we might be able to begin life together again.

Then Zsa Zsa invited Eva, Magda, Bundy Solt, Peter, and me to lunch at her house. Naturally we spoke Hungarian. Peter said not a word. Zsa Zsa finally said, "Peter, why don't you speak?" and Peter said, "How can I?"

It is true that when we get together we speak at 400 speed. Hungarians always flock together and talk over everything and everybody while paying not too much attention to what anybody else is saying. When the girls and I get together, I admit it is murder for any outsider.

The late Dorothy Kilgallen who was syndicated daily in the late New York *Journal American* gave a party for the four Gabors. We never have enough time together and when we see one another we all race like trains on a speeding track to speak. Kilgallen had many famous people at this party and there we four co-hostesses found one another and hid ourselves in a bathroom. We spent the evening, two sitting on the edge of the tub, one on the toilet seat, one on a little stool—all in big ballgowns—talking the whole night. Oh, was she angry. She was furious! "How dare you," she shouted at us. "I give a party for you and you spend the whole night in a toilet. You don't even appear!"

After Peter and I left Zsa Zsa's luncheon that day he said to me quietly, "Perhaps you had a good time, Jolie, but it was very boring for me."

So I understood. However, I couldn't change. We just couldn't make it fit. This marriage business was a side of life I could not seem to manage. When I married a rich man he wanted to run me. When I married a poor one he wouldn't let me run him. What is a woman to do?

We were together off and on for a couple of weeks. He had moved some clothes into 63rd Street. There was no burning love between us but I think we both wanted sincerely to make a go of our marriage.

At the end of our trial period, just before we were going to get back together on a permanent basis, Peter called at the shop on Friday afternoon. "Let us go out for dinner tonight. We'll go to your favorite Hungarian restaurant."

"I'd love it," I said, "and I accept the invitation."

"Pick you up around eight," he said.

Some friends of mine from Paris arrived that afternoon en route to Houston for the opening of Sophie Tucker at a fabulous hotel, the Shamrock. "Come along with us for the weekend," they begged. "We invite you as our guest."

I had worked hard for so many years that this seemed like an unbelievable pleasure. There was no time to delay so, without telling Peter because the one second I had to call he wasn't in, I flew to Texas.

From Houston I phoned several times but he wasn't in. I left messages everywhere and finally, when I did get him, he was coldly angry.

I was always a something and a somebody compared to him but I knew that I had become too much for him. However, he had nobody and he loved me and I felt sorry for him. Also Magda insisted, "You have to have him back because you are so busy you don't know what to do. You need him. You're up to your ears in business. Try to get him to stay."

So again I asked him, "Would you like to come back to me?"

He was such a decent man. He said, "Could I have an hour to think about it?"

He sat on a bench all by himself in Central Park the whole day and thought it over. When he walked into my shop I said, "Well, did you think it over?"

"Yes," he said.

"What is your answer?"

"No."

"No?"

"No. I want you instead to go back to Arizona with me."

"But that is impossible," I said.

"Why do you make such a quick decision? Why don't you at least say you'll think it over as I did?"

"Okay," I sighed just to put an end to the discussion. "I'll think it over." This was a Saturday afternoon about five o'clock. That night I had a big party to go to. "Why don't you go and get into your tuxedo," I suggested, "because I will be home soon and we can then go to this party."

He nodded and I watched him disappear slowly down the street, his shoulders sloping sadly. That evening there was nothing of his left in the closet —just an old gray coat hanging all alone with the note: "This is for your poor Hungarians." Every month I sent a parcel of food, money, clothing, and special delicacies like chocolates to Hungary.

There was also a friendly, diplomatic letter waiting for me on the piano. Six handwritten pages on yellow paper, it began, "You are an adorable sweet kid. You want the whole world. I am going to Arizona for my health. I'll keep in touch with you."

The gist of the other five pages was that he did not want to resume our marriage because while I was wonderful I was also unreliable. We would always be good friends, he assured me, but he felt we had no basis for a marriage.

I had no pain and no remorse. I wasn't happy when he left me but I wasn't unhappy either. The whole episode had been less than a year and once more I was without a husband. That night I just called up another gentleman I knew for an escort.

Eight months later on a Friday afternoon I received a government letter informing me that exactly three weeks from this date, I was to appear at the Immigration Office, take their test and, if all went well, be sworn in as a full-fledged American citizen.

I was overjoyed. I began making preparations. I went up to a little spa in Rye and shut myself up for a week. Day and night I memorized from a little book about thirty-three presidents of the United States. I studied the amendments to the Constitution.

Becoming a citizen consumed me. I was nervous about it since I had once before come up for immigration and a letter had come from some bastard— they never told me who—saying that I was a dangerous Nazi who should not be given citizenship. Because of that it was denied me and I know this is a fact because the immigration agent told it to me himself.

When Zsa Zsa's Francie was four years old she had said to me, "*Nuci*, Mommy's friends are so glittering."

So I said to her, "Francesca, what is this word *glittering?*"

She said, "It means 'sparkling.' "

"You are only in this country four years. I am here five years," I said, "how is it you are this intelligent about English?" Francesca was so smart. She said, "It is because I am an American citizen." She had always heard that Grandma wants to become a citizen and she knew enough even at that age to tease me about it.

The letter from the Immigration Office informed me I was to bring my papers and my lawyer informed me, "You are in trouble."

"Why am I in trouble?" I asked.

"Because you must take your husband as a witness."

"But I have no idea where Peter is. I haven't heard from him since he left."

"The only way you have been able to apply for your papers was because of your marriage to an American. So this American husband must be present in person at the Immigration Office to testify for you."

I drummed my fingers on the glass table top in my shop. "I have also as witnesses you who can speak the truth for me plus coming down with me is a Hungarian friend who is an American citizen."

"You must have Peter," repeated the lawyer, "or some proof that you are actually married to an American. Other witnesses will prove nothing in this case."

Thursday, the day before I was due at the Immigration Office, I didn't know what to do. It looked hopeless. I was in my shop tearing my hair out with dismay and wondering how I would pull off this maneuver when the postman came in with some mail. Among the bills and letters was a pretty picture postcard from Phoenix. When I read it my heart stopped:

"Dearest Jolie. You are a good kid and I was thinking of you and I thought I would drop you a few words to send my love to you and the girls. If you would be interested in reaching me here is my box number. . . ." Then, "Please write me. All my love, Peter."

I was so excited I called my lawyer, and read it to him immediately. "I will ask Peter for help."

"How?" he exploded. "You don't have a telephone number nor an address. All you have is a box number."

"I will send him a telegram. It is three hours earlier in Arizona."

"Jolie," he said, "people with box numbers come maybe once a week or once a month to pick up their mail. He isn't going to have this wire in time to be of any help to you."

"Maybe this will be the one day in three weeks that he is going to pick up his mail. Since Fate sent me this postcard the day before I am to appear I feel Fate will take me all the way."

I sent my wire: "Peter, my darling, I need you badly. I could become citizen tomorrow if you could be here to help me. All my love, Jolie."

That night I called my attorney and my Hungarian friend and said to each, "Look, please, I beg of you come with me anyway because in any case I am going to keep my nine o'clock appointment at the Immigration Office. I just know that something will happen."

The following morning we three together took a taxi from my house. We walked into the little office and sat down on a bench. I was highly nervous. My witnesses just slumped on the bench.

I was in my very best dress. And I had drenched myself and my chiffon handkerchief in Arpege. After forty-five minutes the door to one of the cubicles opened. A man in shirtsleeves came out. "Mrs. Peter Howard Christman, would you step this way, please?"

I stood up. The attorney rose to go with me, but I waved him off. "No, first I will go alone. Just me, my handkerchief and my Arpege."

I floated into the office, followed by the gentleman. As I passed him I waved the chiffon hanky with a little fluttering gesture. It had such a good smell that right away he put on his jacket.

Before he could ask me anything I went right into my big story laying it on thick. "My husband adores me and he is so sad that he can't be with me here this day. We adore one another but my husband has only one lung and so he is in Arizona," I rambled on. Then I pulled the postcard from my purse. "You see my husband is away now and he writes to me every day. Look, see, he really loves me." I stretched my hand with the card in it over the desk to give it to him and I also waved my handkerchief around a little.

Finally, I think just to shut me up, the clerk said, "Look, don't knock your brains out. I need your husband. If I don't have him then I need his birth certificate to make sure he's born in America. I don't care if you hate each other as long as he's an American."

I got very upset inside but outwardly I remained very cool. I didn't know what to do so I stalled for time until maybe I could think of what to do. Also, I wanted to give the perfume time to work. I leaned across the desk and fluttered my hanky around him.

He said, "Please, Mrs. Christman, I like the odor very much but I'm not sure that my wife will."

"I'd be pleased to get my husband's birth certificate," I said, "but I don't know to do that."

The gentleman smiled very nicely and softened. "What you have to do," he explained, "is to go to the City Hall to the Hall of Records and you have to look up the birth records for that year that he was born."

"Oh, of course, that's exactly what I'll do," I beamed.

"All right, then in that case I'll give you an extra three days. If you have the birth certificate in your possession by then you may come back to this office and become a citizen."

"Oh, I thank you so very much," I gushed, "because I know how very long it takes to get a second appointment."

I kept yakking until there was no way to prolong the discussion. I rose and was just thanking him when the door opened.

I thought I was dreaming. It was Peter. "I am Peter Christman," he said. "I came here for my sweet wife."

He kissed me, he hugged me, he held my hand, then he turned to the Inspector. "I hope I have arrived in time. Nobody deserves to be a citizen more than my wife. She loves this country and she will be a great asset to America."

Oh, what an unbelievable happy ending. In the space of one heartbeat we signed a few papers and I was raising my right hand and swearing. I was officially an American citizen.

I quickly telephoned my butler, "Quick," I told Harry, "put up the picture of Mr. Christman in the living room. Stick one on my night table, too."

"The only photographs we have left are lying around the bottom of some closet somewhere—that is, if I can still scratch them up," he clucked. "And, besides, we don't have a frame anymore for him. You threw out the silver one he gave you for Christmas and his soldier suit pictures are extra large sizes."

"So throw out my small oil painting and stick Peter in that frame and prop him up against a vase. Oh, and Harry, run quick and buy champagne and caviar."

"You have champagne in the refrigerator."

"Okay, so just get caviar. I'm bringing Mr. Christman home with me now."

As we walked into the house, I said to him, "Last time you asked me to have dinner and I did not keep our date. This time *I* ask *you* to have dinner."

After dinner, we put on records and listened to romantic music. Then

I sat down and played the piano and we sang. We were a little high on champagne and Peter wanted to sleep with me. "Impossible," I said.

"Why?" he asked. "I am your wedded husband."

"So okay," I said.

"I am going to stay with you from now on. I love you. We will begin all over again." I was hungering for a man so we had a very hot night between us. Therefore, in the night I loved him but in the morning I didn't love him anymore. And I knew it was over.

Over a cup of coffee he asked, "Do you love me?"

I said, in a very matter of fact tone, "Oh, I don't know."

He jumped up from the table. "I thought last night we talked about a big reconciliation—you told me you loved me."

I said, "You said you loved me so I said also the same. But that was in the night. This is now in the day. In the morning it isn't so very much that I love you."

I suppose it's my hard luck that I'm too honest and sincere. Peter flew from Arizona and helped me and I felt close to him because of what he had done for me. However, gratitude and love are two different things. So I paid his fare back to Arizona and gave him $3,000 as a small settlement and that was the end of Peter Howard Christman.

BOOK FIVE

Jolie

I called George Sanders "The Deep Freeze" because he was so cold. When Zsa Zsa married him and they lived in California I went there for three days. They had a long black mirror table in the dining room. On one end sat Zsa Zsa and way at the other sat the Deep Freeze and in the middle there was me. Francesca had dinner with her nanny elsewhere but she wanted to stay up as children do so she came to the table and bothered her mother. George didn't like it when Francesca was around to annoy him so Zsa Zsa shoved her away. "Okay . . . okay . . . Francie . . . bye bye Francie . . ."

To do anything rather than be gotten rid of, Francie then kissed her mother's face and hands and she kissed me all over, too. "How are you, *Nuci?* . . . How long do you stay, *Nuci?*" Not that she really cared but only to delay another minute so she didn't have to go to sleep.

At the far end throughout all this sat King George, stony, like an emperor. Shyly she skipped over to him. In a burst of affection she hugged him with, "Georgie, Georgie, I love you. . . ."

Without looking up from his plate George said icily, "Goodnight."

With her nanny behind her she bolted. At the doorway she turned to him and shouted, "You Russian!" George was born in Russia. Then Francie ran out. That George Sanders was cold as an icebox. Only a Hungarian could have done something with a fellow like that.

I went out always with my friends, not with Zsa Zsa or George, because they went nowhere and did nothing. Their wedding night they spent playing chess, which I'm sure Zsa Zsa didn't mind because it's all full of kings, queens, and castles. Their excitement was to paint their house themselves with spray guns or to repair the plumbing and electrical wiring themselves. I'm not sure whether George was a great do-it-yourselfer or he was cheap. I think it was both.

George hated big parties so they never went. I arrived in Los Angeles at 10 P.M. and phoned eager to go out and have supper and I found them fast asleep. They lived the quietest life. Every night they went to bed at nine and watched wrestling matches or movies on TV. Zsa Zsa, who in those days preferred being home with George to being taken around the world by anyone else, used to tell me, "You know, *Nucika*, television is getting much better!"

229

When I stayed with them I went out every night. George didn't respect me too much and when a friend came for me George would say to me coldly, "That is your life and this is our life." My friends took me to Mocambo or Ciro's and at night I would creep in very quietly and Zsa Zsa was so jealous because she was also accustomed to this good life.

However, George had wanted a hausfrau and that's what my glamorous daughter became. She brought his slippers to him. She rubbed his back, she flattered his ego. George always said, "I'm helpless. I need someone to mother me." When Zsa Zsa heard his car, she would run to the bar and prepare his vodka then drop to her knees and he'd pat her head like a dog and say, "Are you a good girl?"

For Christmas he only bought her chocolate. "But this is fattening. How could he do this?" I asked. "Darling, chocolate is not good for you."

She said to me angrily, "You are always so material. The chief thing is he bought me a present!"

"And what did you buy him?"

"Oh, what's the difference," she said. "It's the thought that counts." I knew she didn't want to tell me.

I nagged her, "Tell me."

"I bought him a grand piano."

What more could I say to her?

One year she bought him a solid gold cigarette case and he allowed her to keep it filled. The house they lived in was her house. The furniture was her furniture. When he went to the movies he never had small money. He only had a check and Zsa Zsa paid or I paid. George never put his hand in his pocket for anything. Never once did he pay for me anything.

The first time Zsa Zsa saw him on screen, she said, "There's the man for me" and she never changed. George was fourteen years her senior. Their romance was hectic—I was forever bringing her to the airport or picking her up from the airport. When George left her in New York and took off for Hollywood without asking her she would follow next day like a slave and I would take her to the airport. Three days later, when he treated her poorly again after she cooked for him, made breakfast for him, served him, she would fly back and I would fetch her again at the airport. I said, "I see ahead of me years of taking you and fetching you."

"Oh *Nuci*," she wept, "I love him but I can't endure a man who does this to me."

She was dating Stuart Barthelmess, Count John de Benden, the Prince of Hanover, Franchot Tone, Jack Kennedy, and Bob Topping, but she only died for George. "I will throw away all my alimony for him," she cried when he wouldn't marry her. "I am dying in love with him," she would say, "but with him it is nothing. He doesn't show emotion. He doesn't look. He doesn't give."

George was a bitter, mixed-up man. His first marriage had failed. His wife, Elsie, was ill and he blamed himself for her condition. Zsa Zsa cheered him up but you needed a derrick to lift George. That's how heavy he was.

Still, just as she asked Burhan and Hilton to marry her she asked George Sanders also to marry her. She begged him. Like Hilton, Sanders didn't also want so much to marry Zsa Zsa. He wanted to be an American citizen and Zsa Zsa was also not an American citizen so if they married it would not help either of them. But Zsa Zsa persisted and in the end George married her.

I nearly changed George Sanders' life. Again I was a houseguest for two days. George was so in love with the piano Zsa Zsa had given him that he had taken up singing. Zsa Zsa was so in love with him that she got angry even when I mumbled to her, "It's the piano *you* bought that he's playing on." Instead she would say only aloud in front of him, "Look, *Nuci*, George is at the piano singing 'Some Enchanted Evening.' Isn't that wonderful?"

"At this time everybody's singing 'Some Enchanted Evening,'" I said. "What's so wonderful about this?"

"Tell him what a beautiful voice he has," she whispered, nudging me in the ribs. "After all, you are a houseguest."

"Oh, George," I said, "you have a very beautiful voice. I will tell everybody in New York what a wonderful voice you have. Maybe then you can get a part on Broadway. Maybe you could even get the job to replace Ezio Pinza, who is leaving the *South Pacific* show."

"Yes, that's right," encouraged Zsa Zsa. "He would be truly marvelous."

We both stood there in the background while George played and sang and paid us no attention. Finally he deigned to notice us. "Don't you dare tell anyone in New York that I am a singer, Jolie," he said sharply. "You will ruin my career. I am a great dramatic actor. I am not a musical comedy person."

Zsa Zsa kept encouraging me and urging him to consider the possibilities. Suddenly, before I knew it, I was twisted into the position of being an agent for a talent I didn't know if I could even sell and who didn't want me to sell him even if I could!

I was leaving early the following morning and before I was up and dressed, George slipped into my room and he said, "Well, if you really want to mention it to your friends in New York go ahead."

"I am not a theatrical agent," I said to George. "All I can do is tell Mr. Rodgers of Rodgers and Hammerstein how good your singing is."

Sitting on the edge of the bed he said to me, "I told Eva that I would call Mr. Rodgers for this very same reason and she said it was impossible because you must wait two months for an appointment with him."

When I left for the airport Zsa Zsa again pressed me to get this thing done for her. "Please, *Nuci*, try. I want it so badly for him."

When I came home I had my secretary phone Dick Rodgers and tell him that Mme. Gabor wishes to speak with him. Ten minutes later he called back personally. Secretly I thanked God that I knew elegant people at least well enough to get them on the phone. "When would you like to see me?" he asked on the phone.

"Right away," I said. "It is very important that I see you."

"Come over now," he said. Another ten minutes and I was in his office.

"I have a wonderful idea," I said to him across the desk. "My son-in-law, George Sanders, has a better voice than Pinza and I think it would be sensational for this great dramatic actor to replace Pinza in the show. This would be such great publicity for *South Pacific.*"

When I sell I sell. Rodgers was impressed. "I love the idea," he enthused. "Let's see how good Sanders is. Tell him to send me a record."

I called immediately George and he sent a record, then Mr. Rodgers wanted to see George so again I called him up and Zsa Zsa and George came to New York. In a few days George had been given a contract for $5,000 a week.

Zsa Zsa was so thrilled because she wanted to stay in New York and dress every night and go to the theatre. "Oh, let's celebrate," said Zsa Zsa happily. "Let's have a party."

It was to be a small sit-down dinner at my house. I invited Sylvia and Clark Gable. That very afternoon Clark Gable came into my shop carrying a small bunch of violets. The women inside nearly died. He came up to me to ask, like a little humble boy, "Is it black tie?"

I told, "Yes."

The shop was loaded and he was afraid to stay because the women were adoring him madly so he left immediately.

The party was small but chic. George and Zsa Zsa, Clark and Sylvia Gable and me and my escort, Prince Odeskalsky. After dinner Zsa Zsa and Sylvia Gable wanted to go to El Morocco. I must also pay for the El Morocco. Isn't that incredible? You can't expect Gable, who is your guest, to pay and you can't expect Sanders, who doesn't pay for anything, to pay, so again it was me.

Clark and George, however, didn't want to go. They wanted to stay in my house so we compromised. I took them to a little Hungarian supper club in the West Forties, where a protégé of mine, Anny Kapitany, was singing. It was a terrible little place. Nobody was there but us.

After all this George changed his mind. He basically hated people. He just wanted to do movies and see no one and talk to no one and stay at home. From this episode he did, however, get something good. He ended up doing the film version of *Call Me Madam* with Ethel Merman. I wonder who paid for *that* celebration.

One day I got a tearful telephone call. *"Nuci,* can you imagine? George left me here in my house which I bought with my money and went to London to work in a film. I begged him to take me and the baby but he wouldn't."

"Maybe he doesn't want the baby when he is so nervous with the picture and everything. Why don't you leave Francie home?"

"Because I have also big trouble here. The nanny wants to go away. Oh, I am in such big trouble. With all this problem George went and left me and is in London and I cannot live without him. I will kill myself. You must come out here and make order in my life."

"You have not to die," I told her. "I will come. Only I have two protégés in Hollywood who must be with me."

"*Nucika*, darling," she cried, "Whatever you want is okay. Whoever you bring is all right. Just come. I tell you what, from happiness that you are coming, I will give a big party."

"All right," I said, "You may give for me a party but you must invite who I want not just who you want. I want every Hungarian who is something in Hollywood."

"You mean like Mike Curtiz, Charles Vidor, Gabriel Pascal, Joe Pasternak . . ."

"Not Pasternak. I don't like him."

Zsa Zsa laughed. "All right, so I invite your Hungarians for your party if you promise to come out and arrange my life. If you come then I know everything will be all right. It's because you bring me luck that I will even send you the ticket."

I said immediately, "Yes, please, that would help." (Naturally she didn't send it. She forgot. Always she forgets such things.)

"*Nuci,*" she whimpered at the end of this phone call, "You must help me. I am dying for George because he is different from all the others who are dying for me. He is suave, cool, aristocratic."

"Okay, I come to California," I said.

It was at this big party that George Sanders' actor brother, Tom Conway, invited Zsa Zsa to be a guest on a TV panel show. This whole party, which was given in my honor, was the very start of Zsa Zsa's career.

Tom urged, "Come with me, Zsa Zsa. Go on this panel show with me. It's a new program called 'Bachelors' Haven' and you answer questions about men and husbands and it's something you could do so easily. They're looking for the wife of a celebrity, so I suggested you."

"How can I go on a panel show when I don't know what to say," she shrugged.

Conway turned to me, "Jolie, tell her to come."

"Zsa Zsika, I come here to bring order out of chaos in your life and you always say I bring you luck so maybe this is a lucky thing to do. At least it will make you stop thinking about George. It will give you something glamorous to tell him and tease him about. Do it."

"I have no dresses for television," she said.

Inside she wanted to come and she needed my support. I told her, "Look, when the guests leave we will try on every dress until we find one which suits you very well."

"I don't even look beautiful," she whined, and her beautiful eyes clouded. "George has left me two days already and he is in England and I am crying my eyes out and that isn't helping my face."

"Forget about my rotten brother," grinned Tom, who was as warm and outgoing as George was cold and not caring, "and remember that yours is the most beautiful face around. You'll be terrific."

Zsa Zsa finished her glass of white wine. "But I have now such big trouble and now you invite me on a panel show?"

"Zsa Zsika," I said softly, "are you not tired of being a hausfrau? Are you not jealous of Eva's triumph in the Broadway play? Well, this is a big opportunity for you. You have no reputation to worry about because nobody knows you. Even if you are not so marvelous you cannot be harmed."

After the last guest had gone, I said, "Come, we will try on dresses." We found a simple off-the-shoulder black Balenciaga, which set off her jewels.

When the TV emcee commented on the air, "Wow, look at those diamonds," and Zsa Zsa answered, "Oh, these are just my working diamonds," and the audience laughed, from then on she was made.

She became a permanent member of the panel. Telegrams poured in from all over. Friends like James and Pamela Mason called to say she was magnificent. The trade papers labeled her the newest hottest find on television. *Variety* said: "A star is born." Within a couple of months she had a manager, a public relations organization, a cover on *Life* magazine, a dramatic coach and a part in Mervyn Le Roy's MGM musical, *Lovely to Look At.* I am sure if not for me right there giving her support she would never be a famous theatrical personality on her own today. I had talked her into the whole thing. I had accompanied her to the show and she took off like a rocket. For just being herself my Zsa Zsa was finally a star!

The luck I brought Zsa Zsa was not yet finished. I even helped her find someone for her child. Walking along Fifth Avenue not long after I bumped into another Hungarian refugee, a composer. "Remember me—Brodsky?" he said. "I heard you were here and I wanted to call you."

"Oh, Brodsky," I said, "I have now so much trouble with Zsa Zsa. She has become a success but she cannot go out to enjoy it because she has nobody to look after the child."

"Wait," he exclaimed, "I know a Hungarian woman who might do you."

So I told Zsa Zsa and she said, "Ugh, better nobody than a Hungarian!"

Well, this Hungarian whom she did not want is still with her almost a quarter of a century later. Even today Zsa Zsa says to me, "If I wouldn't have Elizabeth I would die!"

At the Plaza Hotel, where I spent my first night in America, where Zsa Zsa arrived the summer of '41 as Mrs. Burhan Belge, where she reigned as Mrs. Conrad Hilton, where she cried herself to sleep very often as Mrs. George Sanders, she met Porfirio Rubirosa.

Rubirosa was the opposite of Sanders. Whereas George was icy calm, Rubirosa was insanely jealous. Rubi was a spender. Rubi loved to do night-clubs. For Zsa Zsa, with George in America and Rubi in Europe, it was a perfect setup. These were incredible days. Rubi taking Zsa Zsa to the airport in Paris, George waiting for her at the airport in New York. The telegrams, trans-Atlantic calls, the pledges of love Rubi made, their meetings every few months, their fights (with Zsa Zsa packing her bags), their reunions (with the expensive presents), their fights again (with Rubi packing his bags).

There was Rubi's career which, as a diplomat/playboy of the Dominican Republic, took him all over the world; Zsa Zsa's career, which had blossomed into fifty television shows, six films, thirty-two magazine covers; George's career; my career; Rubi's marriage meanwhile to Barbara Hutton; Zsa Zsa's divorce meantime from George Sanders. With Rubi life was hectic.

Now with Zsa Zsa the star and Rubi the lover everything was big drama. There was the Christmas in Las Vegas, where all three daughters were to appear onstage together. The hotel wanted me on the stage, too, but the girls did not let me. They said, "You are not an actress." Such actresses like they are, *I* am!

Zsa Zsa was upset. Because of Rubi she had alienated George, whom she still loved. Rubi was pressuring her. He followed her in his private plane to Vegas. "Marry me or I marry Barbara Hutton," he shouted at her in a passionate rage while she was getting ready for opening night. Zsa Zsa was nervous about the opening, nervous about George, and she told him to get away. They fought physically. Rubi gave Zsa Zsa a black eye. She screamed and fell into the door hitting her head. They called me in my room. I came running and Zsa Zsa screamed to me, "He'll marry Barbara."

"So let him," I screamed back.

Rubi raced out in a rage. In one hour one hundred red roses filled Zsa Zsa's suite. She could only see them out of her one unblackened eye. With it came a note from Rubi saying, "Good-bye." Oh, such drama.

After the opening night I came back to New York. Two mornings later, at 9 A.M. my phone rang. "It's me, Rubi," said the familiar voice.

I hung up. He called back. "I am at the Pierre with Barbara. I have just married her," he said quietly.

"I don't believe this," I answered, terrified that Barbara Hutton would pick up the phone. "Are you mad? Can Barbara hear you? She will kill you and me!"

"No," he said softly, "she cannot hear me. We have several rooms."

"But you are married only for two days and how can you call me like this?"

"Oh, Jolie," he moaned. "I die for Zsa Zsa. I cannot live without her. I cannot stand to be away from her. I must see Zsa Zsa."

"But this is too terrible for Zsa Zsa," I said. "She has ruined her own marriage to George Sanders for you."

"Please, Jolie, help me," he pleaded.

I hung up and called Zsa Zsa.

"Rubi is for me like a disease," she said. "On account of him I have lost George, whom I really love. I've always loved George and I'll always love George. With Rubi it is different. I guess it takes a psychologist to explain. Rubi is a disease of the blood. I cannot be without him. Now I have lost them both." She cried bitterly. I cried. More big drama.

Seventy-two days Rubi stayed married to Barbara Hutton. When he separated from her I was in Miami.

I was asleep when the phone rang. "It's Rubi," said the well-known voice. "I am coming over."

"But I am in bed," I said to him.

"I cannot help it," he said. "I am in town at the airport where I parked my private plane, the one I got from Barbara, and I will come over in a taxi to see you while they put gas in my plane."

So, up I got and dressed again I got and Rubi arrived. He had been drinking. "Zsa Zsa is so cold to me," he complained. Then he came up with what he considered a bright idea. "I am en route to Santo Domingo. Come with me."

"Rubi, it is impossible. I have seven people who are here with me."

"I will take them all. Come, pack, let's go."

"No, Rubi. I am afraid this is too much. You have been drinking heavily. You have polo ponies in the plane with you and then you would have me and my Hungarian friends and it is late at night and we must leave immediately and you are still fresh from your split-up with Barbara Hutton and it is ridiculous."

So, reluctantly, he left.

Rubi was mad for Zsa Zsa but I told her, "Rubi is not for you. He drinks a lot. At the most you have a white wine *spritzer*. He loves nightclubs. You don't smoke. You hate nightclubs. For a husband he is not good."

"Yes, but for a lover, he is the most exciting," sighed Zsa Zsa.

Then came the great press chase. Reporters on both sides of the Atlantic followed them—will they marry, won't they marry? Zsa Zsa was ruining her career, chasing him all over the world, staying up late, getting no sleep. She was exhausted. Her eyes were redrimmed. She had desperately wanted a career. She had worked for a career. She had gotten a career. And now she was throwing it away. She sneaked into his Paris mansion in a wig. He stayed at a hotel at the airport under a false name. From Hollywood to Vegas to New York to Paris, Deauville, Cannes, they ran. Rubi was a sickness to her.

The truth is my daughters are old-fashioned. They do not play around. They are very honest—they marry every lover. Me, I love love. So even though I didn't approve of their relationship I kept Rubi hidden in my 63rd Street house for three days and nights so they could be together without anybody knowing and I stayed at the hotel which is owned by my friend Evelyn Sharpe.

It was only two months since Rubi was divorced and Zsa Zsa and Rubi captured the excitement of the international press. She had worn an eye patch when he hit her. George Sanders had named Rubi publicly. Barbara Hutton had talked about Zsa Zsa publicly. The street in front of my house was blocked with cameramen and newspapermen day and night and the two lovers were inside.

"Where are they?" the press would ask as I'd run in and out periodically. "Are they inside or where?"

"No comment," was all I could say because Zsa Zsa warned me, *"Nuci,* I know you love to talk but you must not say anything now. It is very difficult with all this excitement and love story going on and I know how much you love both but you must keep your mouth shut."

It was so hard for me. Harder still was figuring out a way to smuggle Rubi out of there. "We both want to leave here," said Zsa Zsa, "but how?"

"Yes," said Rubi peeking out of the curtains at the army of reporters downstairs. "We want to go to Paris separately and meet one another at my house. I will go first in my private plane and Zsa Zsa will . . ."

". . . go by regular plane," I finished.

"But how can I get out?" he fretted. "There is no way."

"I have devised your method of escape," I said. "I will wear an outfit that is a concealing one. I will put on a wraparound mink coat, a big hat with a veil, and high boots and go outside to my shop tomorrow morning in this ensemble. In the afternoon I will return here in this same wardrobe. The press will get used to seeing me in this. Then when it is dark you go out in this identical outfit."

"I should go like a *woman?*" he gasped.

"There is no other way," I reasoned. "You are both worried about scandal. You don't want it and neither does Zsa Zsa so do as I say."

When it came time, I put lipstick on him and put the clothes on him and he ran out to the car. He hid at the airport until his plane was ready and then he escaped. She followed later.

Rubi looked Spanish and dark but immediately I saw him I felt that every girl must be in love with him. Maybe four times he was named correspondent in some divorce action but he was such an elegant gentlemen that you must be in love with him. It is my fault that they never married. I was dead against it although I liked Rubi very much.

There were those heavenly few days we were in Deauville together. I arrived Saturday to go to a party with Aly Kahn, who had been going with Gene Tierney, who became sick from him. Francie and Zsa Zsa were with Rubi and Ellie Rothschild was there and the Maharajah of Jaipur and his beautiful Maharani. Five-year-old Francie introduced her as "A real princess on her own." She introduced Colette as "This is the old lady who wrote *Gigi* and is in a wheelchair, which her husband who is even sixteen years younger than she but adores her pushes for her all the time." Francie, who was educated in all the best schools in Switzerland, such as Sacré Coeur, said the most outrageous things about people right in front of them.

Zsa Zsa had to leave for Paris to do a film.

"Wait here with me for a day or two and then I will drive you to Paris myself," Rubi told me. "Meanwhile I will show you off in Deauville." I could easily understand how any woman could be in love with Rubirosa.

He was a racing-car driver so we drove at 100 kilometers per hour to Paris. I was sure we wouldn't arrive alive. Halfway there he stopped on a dark highway and took off the car lights in front of a pleasant little house situated exactly nowhere that I could figure out. Someone opened the gates and it was a tiny restaurant.

In this little *boîte* with red tablecloths on the round tables there was a bouquet of red roses under my napkin with the note: "To Jolie, the world's most beautiful woman." How could you not be in love with Rubi? It was midnight so he must have called in advance to the man and woman who owned this place in order to have this for me. Iced champagne was on the table and he was so sweet and so gallant, but he died only for Zsa Zsa. "Nobody ever loved Zsa Zsa as I love her, Jolie," he said. "I know what marriage is. I have been married before for many years. Now I want to marry Zsa Zsa. Please help me."

We clinked glasses. "Look, Rubi," I said. "Zsa Zsa has not the time to marry you. She has a career. In the daytime you are an angel but at night you are not such an angel. You drink. You stay out a whole night drunk. Zsa Zsa works in movies and she has to go to nightclubs all night to be with you and it is never enough for you no matter how late she stays. It is not right for Zsa Zsa to marry you."

I swear he was on his knees to marry her, but I told Zsa Zsa no.

"I don't let you do this," I told her. "He is a beautiful creature but unreliable. You cannot marry him."

3 In December of 1949 I was named a correspondent in a divorce action. I couldn't believe it. I thought correspondent meant people who write each other.

Eleven o'clock one evening I was working in the shop and a shortish, fattish man—definitely not my type—knocked on the door and then introduced himself in Hungarian. "My name," he said, "is Baron Stephen Kelen d'Oxylion. Don't you remember, we met at the party last night?"

"So how do you do?" I said to him.

"What are you doing working so late?" he asked, seeing that I was writing a letter.

"Oh, I am so busy," I complained, "because I have a great many foreign manufacturers and I must write in Hungarian, German, French, and English."

"I can help you," he said. "I can take dictation and I can type and I can do many things. I can even lick envelopes."

He told me he was a millionaire from Hungary who had put all his money in a Broadway play and that during the war he was in the Secret Service and that his American wife, from whom he was separated, was a writer. I knew immediately he was a broken-down crookish sort. But I had been working a long day and even though he wasn't my type I was a little interested in what the many things were that he guaranteed me he could do. Meantime I was hungry. He said, "I know a good Chinese place that I will take you to."

It was a cheap place. The whole bill was $5 but he didn't even have that much so I gave him $10 to pay and I let him keep the change.

I hired him for $75 as a sort of secretary. He helped with my plumbers and contractors in Southampton. Also I had my lemon of a Packard convertible but I didn't have a license. D'Oxylion had a license but didn't drive so he accompanied me always to Southampton. Also he took care of my dog. Also he took care of me sometimes.

One late afternoon I came out of my shop and I went to cross the street. As I waited for the traffic on Madison Avenue a thirty-fivish blonde came up to me and said in perfect English, "Mrs. Gabor, $10,000 or bad publicity. It's your choice."

I don't know how but immediately I recognized she must be the wife. "This is blackmail," I said to her.

"Yes it is," she replied grimly.

This was during the biggest business days just before Christmas. In Europe such bad publicity could kill you. When there would be something like this in Europe you would do anything to keep it hidden forever. So I didn't again go to the shop or show myself and I paid $6,000 to the woman and I just stayed home and cried. I thought this was the end of the world.

In turn D'Oxylion gave me in writing that he would stay away. After I threw him out the wife wanted me to take him back because at least when he was with me she was getting $35 a week from the $75 I paid him. After I gave the $6,000 she began to molest me again because she was no longer collecting alimony.

I learned quickly that it was a big difference to be a woman in America. In Europe a husband can throw you out without a cent. Here not. There he is not responsible for nothing. Here it is different. Immediately when D'Oxylion didn't pay his wife alimony, she threw him in jail and I had to get him out. One year this went on.

I liked him. I know he thought he would conquer me and marry me. I had no such intentions but I did keep him around because he could do many things and there were many things he did that I liked the way he did them. Anyway, it ended up bursting into the newspapers. There were big captions quoting her and bold headlines quoting me and there was her picture and there was my picture.

The stories were terrible. She accused him of beating her and of having repeated relations with me. She accused us of being together every weekend in Southampton. She accused him of being seen going up to my New York apartment at 10 P.M. and not leaving until 3 A.M.

She accused us of kissing and embracing in public. Another lie. He was not attractive so we certainly didn't kiss and embrace in public.

The scandal had run its course when Magda, who was furious at this woman, ordered to me, *"Nuci*, you forget all this tonight and you come with me to The Little Club for dinner."

"How can I go, Magduska? I am too ashamed to be seen in public."

She forced me. She literally dragged me. Well, I was a celebrity when I walked in! From the headlines and the publicity I was a terrific somebody. I'd been in the paper so much that everybody was impressed with me and this was the beginning of my fame on my own. I couldn't get over the way this country works!

Romance is very important for my life but as soon as I had a new one I no longer remembered the old one. I never let one lover go until I had another one. A Hungarian friend brought Paul Virag to my shop. I had never met him but I knew about him. For years I had been impressed by his sister in Budapest. She was a demimondaine. She had a lover in those days and she was a famous horsewoman and tennis player. She did all the exotic, exciting, glamorous things.

Paul Virag was beautiful, tall, suave, and he smelled of cologne. I had heard bad things about him; he cheated people but on a very high-class level. I had heard so much about him that he was already under my skin.

He came into my shop, kissed my hand and announced, "I am here, Jolie."

I was deliberately cold to him. "I hear you are married."

He nodded. "It is only a stepping stone, however, it does not really mean anything. We are now separated."

He had married this superwealthy 50-year-old American who owned three houses on the West Side. She was definitely not a beauty. They made a honeymoon voyage for $15,000 which he booked and which I was told really only cost $6,000. He married her strictly for her money.

Paul Virag was charming. He lit women's cigarettes. He played piano. He danced. He sang songs. He had a voice like an opera star. In fact he was asked once to take over a musical role for another Hungarian, Paul Lukas, but didn't want to. He told me, "I have a big business deal in Mexico and I am going to make $200 million so why should I work night after night in a show for a lousy couple of thousand dollars a week when I am set to make $200 million?"

"You are absolutely right," I said. I didn't want he should take this theatrical job. I was afraid with his gorgeous voice and everything I would lose him. We became big, big lovers. Late in the night after hours of passion, he told me about his wife. "To keep me happy and to make me stay with her, my rich wife made me a travel office and to further keep me she even gave me money."

"Then why do you not stay with her?" I asked.

"I don't want her," he replied as he drank my whiskey and lit my cigarette. "I am fifty years old. I want love. I am so dying in love with you that I want nothing more than to stay with you. For you I will officially give up my wife who will give me anything and everything and I will come with you." I was overwhelmed by his willingness to give up everything for me.

I didn't want to stand in the way of his huge $200 million future, so I said to him, "I will give you the money to go to Mexico so that at least when you get there you will have something to live on."

"I hate to have to go and leave you, Jolika," he said. "I am going only to make this money so I can come back and marry you."

I thought he was noble, attractive and talented, and if he would only be successful I thought he would be for me a good catch. I couldn't find a man with all the qualifications I wanted but this one had so much that I thought it is worth that I make an investment in him and then I would have a big rich husband I could adore. I said, "Well, then, in this case, I will give you $5,000 so that you can make this $200 million for me."

"No," he said. "I couldn't take it—I really don't think that I could." But he finally did manage to take $5,000 and it went into his pocket and he was off to Mexico. "I will give you an IOU," he promised.

I received ten-page love letters—typed—from Mexico. All about how much he adores me and he said things like "You are not a woman you are a saint." I thought that the paper would burn the words were so hot. I read the letters in bed and hugged them to sleep.

After this $5,000 was used up he came back to live with me, bringing stories written about himself in Mexico. When he arrived there had been terrific newspaper stories about the American millionaire businessman. There were no stories when he left. In the time he was there nothing happened. Nothing ever happened with Paul. He never made a buck in the two and a half years we were together.

Back again to Mexico with another $5,000 of mine in cash. He made many trips back and forth. And a third time I gave him again $5,000 since I had nobody else and I felt that if he made this big deal he could be very suitable for me.

Because he spoke six languages he was offered a job with Pan American but again, "This is ridiculous," he said, "I am on the verge of making $200 million. How can I be satisfied with $300 a week?" In the meantime mine was the only money he ever saw. Still, I thought my $15,000 was worth it. That is until he beat me up.

That night, I was in the shop until 11 o'clock. He was at home and the phone rang. I forgot that I had an extension which rang in my home as well as my shop. It was a Hungarian girl friend. "Oh, Jolika," she wept, "I am so unhappy with my love affair."

I didn't want to flaunt mine in her face and, anyhow, mine was not so great in those days. My love toward Paul was not so hot anymore, so I said, "Ilona, I'm also tired of Virag's ways and his taking my money and his not working and his lying to me."

"You mean you are really unhappy, too?"

"Yes," I said, wanting to console her. "So don't be so sorry for yourself. Don't think it is only you who is unhappy. I would like to get rid of Paul. I wish he would again go to Mexico and never come back."

"But he is involved in a tremendous business deal, no?"

"Supposedly he is putting up a village of prefabricated houses and I really believed he would come back with big millions because it sounded so good. However, all he does is talk. Nothing ever happens."

I didn't know he was listening. I went home to find him weaving, thanks to a fifth of my liquor in him, and he said, "I heard you say to Ilona that you don't love me anymore."

"Oh, you are such a fool," I said quickly, "I only say this to console her."

His face darkened, "I am bitterly angry, Jolie."

It was winter. He had his hat and his camel's hair coat on. We were standing at the piano. He lunged toward me and I went under the piano. He dragged me out and banged my head against the wall. I shouted for help and nobody heard. I was black and blue and nobody came. When I was a mass of blood he put a compress on my battered head and called the doctor.

The doctor said to Paul, "You smell of liquor."

"I drank a whole bottle of whiskey," mumbled Paul sheepishly.

"I don't know what happened to this lady but she barely escaped a concussion."

"Oh, you must help her, you must fix her," he cried to the doctor. "I didn't know until I saw her like this that I loved her so much."

As for me, I had had it by then. "Get out," I commanded him. But.

"I love you so much," he moaned, stroking me all night. "I want to die."

"I agree with you," I said. "I also want you to die."

When Eva arrived she was horrified. "What did you do to my mother?" she asked him.

"It is just that I love her so much," he said, applying ointment to my wounds.

Then Eva told me, "We must forgive him because his real crime is that he loves you too much."

In any event, I threw him out Friday and Saturday he slept in an empty apartment in my house with a smelly dog with a litter of ten puppies. I locked him out and he could communicate only by letters under my door which one after the other had the same message! "I love you."

Sunday, I had a date to play gin rummy and he plays so good that I had to invite him. The best part about a love affair is the reconciliation. Oh, it is always so beautiful when the man and the woman hate each other and then there is the big drama. This is the best. I found this out even with this Virag. Even after the beating and the everything, the reconciliation—this is the best.

Eva is the only one in our family that didn't get beaten up. I got it from Paul Virag. Zsa Zsa once from Rubi. Magda many times from her fourth husband Tony Gallucci. Only Eva not.

Monday, my face was still swollen. I told Countess Teleky, my friend and employee, that I had an accident in the taxi. When she saw me she said, "Oh, you mean Paul beat you up?"

I was stunned. "Why is it you say that?" I asked.

And she answered, "Because we are Hungarians and we know that our men always beat us up. Hungarian men are like the Irish."

I just shrugged, "Well, it was either Paul or the taxi. I really don't remember."

I learned an important lesson from Paul Virag. I learned from him never never never to surprise a man. After this he went again to Mexico. He was in Mexico nearly a month and he wrote me twenty pages on the typewriter, a big burning love letter, about "I love you, I adore you. I die for you to come. I worship you. I am happy only when I see you. I am miserable still worrying whether or not you love me. If you would come only once I would be in ecstasy. If you would come I would kiss your toes." So, foolish that I am, I came so that he could kiss my toes.

I was dumb, stupid. I actually wanted to show up at his hotel in Mexico City without letting him know that I was coming. I wanted to surprise him and make everything nice. And the one who got the surprise was me. I found he had been cheating me with a Czech lady. Later, much later, he convinced me that he still loves only me. "It is just that I was lonely," he apologized.

"Well, maybe it is that I am naive," I said, "but I will believe you."

So I went to his room and we had a night of passion but it was no good. I had to admit something inside had died. Later, after I went back to my bed, I called him but he was not anymore in his room. He had gone to *her* room.

The next morning he said to me. "I have two days work so I send you to Acapulco and after two days, I come after you."

Never did he come after me. My heart broke. I wanted to kill myself in the ocean. I didn't so much really love him anymore, but I almost died when I found him with another woman.

So, every love affair comes to an end and every lover is bitter when the other goes away.

When love burns out there is nothing left, but if there is nobody else the love stays until you fall in love with somebody else. After Paul Virag, I had not a steady date for a while and then a friend said, "I have a good-looking man for you."

"Is he a man with problems?" I asked. "I don't want to listen to his troubles. I want now in my lifetime only happiness."

Sari, this Hungarian lady, a secretary, but one with great style, assured me, "This man is just perfect for you."

"Good," I said. "Bring him to my summer house this weekend."

Saturday noon, prepared for an overnight stay, came—Sari and my cousin Elsa, a doctor's wife. The doctor came too in another car. From my kitchen window I saw the man who was with him—tall, maybe 54 or 55. He took an enormous suitcase from the car. Then another piece of luggage he carried out. Then again and again.

My two friends began to laugh so that we couldn't stop. "He is packed like he would go to Europe for years," I screamed with laughter. This fool was surrounded by more luggage than a porter. I don't remember what his name was. He was a Lord and he was from the Churchill family somewhere but what his name is I don't remember.

"He was invited to Palm Beach also for a weekend," said Sari, "and he took everything with him, and he stayed four months!"

"Oh, then I have something to look forward to," I said. "Look, how long do you plan to stay here?"

"We have to go tomorrow evening home," said Elsa.

"How about this Lord? Will he go also home with you Sunday?"

They didn't know. I wanted to stay until Monday because I had arranged for that time in my shop.

After lunch, this Lord whipped out an album with Churchill, with his family, and with a photograph of a cemetery stone with his father's name on it. He was showing off but too impressed I wasn't. With a mausoleum at least I would have been a little impressed. So then he threw in how many times he was invited to the Royal Enclosure at the horse races with Queen Elizabeth and with that left to go upstairs. I said to the woman, "Who exactly is he?"

"He lives in a chic East Side hotel," offered Elsa. "He has a small income but a very big life. He's nobility. He isn't quite a nobody or a garbage man. He's a somebody but exactly who I don't know."

Sari, the one who really knew him, said, "His ex-wife is the daughter of a Jewish banker in Berlin and a great beauty. They met when she came to America at the age of twenty and he was a dash of glamor for her. They lived together for twelve years. She became a career girl type who ended up earning $40,000 a year as a big shot with Elizabeth Arden and she left him."

Instantly my friends left on Sunday afternoon, the Lord announced to me, "I would like to marry you." He hadn't been in my house twenty-four hours! He said, "I only know you one day so, of course, you understand I am not in love with you."

I told him, "I didn't even expect it."

"I will take you out when we get back to the city," he said, mixing himself a drink. "I will introduce you to a princess who is my aunt."

He told me everything but that he would support me. However, this I didn't care. I knew that at my age I could not be so stupid as to think a multimillionaire was going to be swept off his feet by me.

Magda was violently against my new conquest. "I heard he is a broken-down man," she said when she called me.

"But, Magduska, this doesn't matter," I told her. "Look, I have friends who are rich widows and they sit around for years wanting to marry only rich men."

"What's wrong with that?" she asked on the phone.

"A rich man will marry a young beauty, not me. I am happy that a poor man who is under sixty and is intelligent and nice and maybe has a few hundred dollars a month income, so that he can pay for the cigarettes and the laundry, comes into my life. It is so stupid for rich old ladies to be looking for support. What they must look for is companionship. And anyway, I was brought up with this thinking. Don't forget my mother also gave her husbands the support. So what is wrong with this?"

Monday as I prepared to leave I said to my houseguest, "Come and we will go back in my car because I close the house."

"No," said the Lord, who was sprawled comfortably on my couch. "I will stay here for the week." With that he went into my refrigerator and helped himself to a tin of caviar.

The following week he visited my house on 63rd Street and promptly went back to the country and called me at my shop on my phone from the house. "Jolie, darling, I am looking for an apartment for us because I hate your 63rd Street house. In those brownstone houses with the view of the court there is not even light in the daytime and in your apartment you can make only suicide."

I again had problems with Magda. Angrily she accosted me, "How can you leave a strange man in your house? Someone will kill you one day."

"Oh, Magduska," I laughed, "you are always anxious and worried about me."

"It is because you are so impulsive. You are the enfant terrible."

"I know that you are the smart one in the family," I said. "It is like you are the mother and I am your daughter because always you are checking after me . . . where are you going . . . with whom . . . when are you coming home . . ."

"Well, do you think it's normal to have a man living endlessly in your house whose name you don't even know and who isn't working because he's spending his time looking for apartments for you to buy?"

"Maybe you will come out this weekend," I said, "so I don't have to be with him alone."

"It is for these stupid things that I feel I must take care of you. You do too many strange things with too many strange people."

The truth was my new houseguest was certainly strange. Two weeks later he had no embarrassment about still staying in my country house. In one week my telephone bill was $50. All day he telephoned me and made hour-long calls to New York real estate agents demanding, "I want a Fifth Avenue penthouse." He had maybe $10 to his name. "I want you to find something next week," he told the agents, "because I wish to move immediately."

Sure enough he found a penthouse on Fifth Avenue but I told him the price was very high.

"High?" he repeated. "Oh well, how much is it you can afford?"

This question I somehow did not think was such a big thrill for me. He was attractive and had good manners so I thought a little bit maybe he would be good for me but I was becoming embarrassed about the whole thing.

On our way to Fifth Avenue, where he was going to show me his find, I asked this Lord of mine if he had worked during the time he was married. "I used to be a wealthy landlord with a hundred acres near London," he told me, "but during the war I forgot to pay the taxes and for this oversight they took away from me my land and now I am suing them for a million pounds."

And on and on and blaaah blaaah he gave me. Whether or not it was true, I didn't think so. I only know it didn't answer my question. I tried again, "Well, what did you then contribute to your marriage?"

"My wife was educated in Switzerland and had a good upbringing but, of course, all she was was a Jewish girl. I made her a Lady. Because of me she developed nobility."

"Then she supported you?" I asked.

"She paid for the privilege of what I gave her," he replied.

At Fifth he showed me a handsome apartment with a wall-to-wall blue rug in the sitting room. The apartment was empty except for the five rugs and five sets of curtains but it was obvious somebody had spent a lot of money. There was a bay window, a terrace, two bedrooms, and a staggering rental. He said to me, "Here I will set my chair. And here I will read the newspaper while I wait for my wife to come home."

This was his mistake. I was to work my head off like a fool while my Lord of a husband was to sit on his throne. This was the picture he presented me with.

That evening, I had visitors, friends from Paris I had gone to school with. He took over totally. He prepared cocktails like he would be the master of the house. I said, "I feel like I am a guest here."

"You are the guest," he answered. "You will be my wife and you will see what a good life I can give you."

In the night hours I waited to see what a good life he could give me. Nothing. Actually I didn't have any feelings toward this man at all. I wasn't angry with him and I wasn't crazy about him. I was neutral.

The next night he made his second big mistake. He invited me to El Morocco. I selected a very chic short velvet dress.

"Oh, no, my dear," he corrected me. "To El Morocco you can come only in long dress."

"It is not so," I retorted angrily. "Women go in short dresses, too. Always."

Icily he said, "The Princess whose guest you are is wearing long."

"This high-class Princess Szeherezade you are talking about is an old French whore who married an Egyptian and became an Egyptian broken-down Princess, which is not so very tremendous," I snapped. "Also, I've seen her house in Southampton and it is a large nothing."

"I do not wish you to speak this way of Her Highness," he said as he smoothed down his dinner jacket.

"Well, maybe for you she is a big thing, but for this big nothing Princess I will not wear a long dress. I've been a hundred times to El Morocco and I know how to dress for there."

It was not one of our better evenings. When we came home he left me at the door and went to his hotel. An hour later, the telephone rang and one of my salesgirls excitedly informed me, "Someone has broken into your shop."

"How come you are there?" I asked.

"The police from the Holmes Protection Service called you, but when there was no answer they got hold of me. It happened earlier this evening."

"But I have been home an hour. Why didn't you call me earlier?"

"Because your Lord walked by and when I told him I was so happy you were now home and I was going to call you immediately, he said to me, 'I forbid you to call Madame. She was dancing with me in El Morocco and she is tired.' "

I was getting very sick of this Lord. The following Saturday I was to go out to the country with Magda but changed my plans. "No, he is out there," I said to her. "I think instead I stay in the city this weekend."

Magda was furious. "Why do you put up with this creep? Throw this crook out."

We had a big quarrel. Magda was so overwrought that she lost her speech. For a few minutes she actually was without the power to speak because of her frustration. From this excitement and tension I saw that she was right and I broke off my "engagement" with the Lord. Years later I bumped into him and he said, "You were not smart, Madame Gabor, that you let me go. I am now well off with Helena Rubinstein."

I used to take friends for the weekend to Southampton. Sunday mornings we'd gather in my bedroom and sip chilled champagne and I remember one of my houseguests, Prince Jarmal Odeskalsky, perched on the edge of my bed typing a love letter for me. He was good at that and I was not. All I then had to do was sign it.

Anyway, the Prince had such a good time that weekend that in gratitude he offered to make love to me. He knocked on my door but I wouldn't open it. "Last night you were so impulsive with your decision not to let me in. Why did you not let me in? If you would only know with what I had been knocking on the door." His suggestion was so romantic. He said, "Jolie, you have given me such a fine weekend that I wished to give you a big night in gratitude for having had me over. This is what I did for my Palm Beach hostess! I always pay off with my manhood."

I thanked him but I didn't really need it. In that time I had somebody. I had a fat millionaire who was my age and who had a villa on 500 acres in New Jersey and a dusty duplex with a butler on the West Side of New York and from his rich corporation a hired limousine and driver and he wanted to marry me. Still I couldn't go through with it because he wasn't interesting for me. I told him, "When I am not even a little bit in love, I don't marry a man."

4 I wanted also an acting career for Magda and besides, she was an expensive employee for me.

I did some calling of agents and friends. I said, "I have a third daughter. She is the biggest talent in the family. Can you not make something with her? She can be an even better actress than Zsa Zsa or Eva." One agent responded, "She doesn't have to go so much to be better than Zsa Zsa or Eva," but this I ignored.

Magda was not happy. She was restless and jealous of the other girls. She didn't know I had pressured everyone and the afternoon the telephone call came from the producer Magda called me excitedly, "*Nucika*, they want me to play Peggy in *The Women* on stage, on the road, for $1,500 a week. But how can I do this?"

"What Zsa Zsa and Eva can do you can do, too," I said.

"But I am different. I don't think I have the temperament to go on stage. I will make a spectacle of myself."

"Tell the producer to come immediately over," I said.

"I am not stagestruck like the others," she continued.

"Tell the producer to come and bring the contract," I said.

This was important for her because she was having a stormy love affair and needed something to take her mind off of Tony Gallucci. Tony was a building contractor with a plumbing factory. He was good-looking, generous, everything. Magda adored him. His only small problem was that he was a drinker. On a Monday a year after they met he said, "This coming Thursday, we will marry." Wednesday night he brought Magda home and said, "Tomorrow is the great day."

Even Coco, Magda's brown poodle, barked with happiness. I thought it was from happiness. Magda thought it was because he had to make. Therefore she said to Tony, "Before you go home for your last night's sleep as a bachelor, take out Coco for a walk."

That was the last we saw of Tony. He got drunk on his walk, ended up at his old girl friend Gerrini's place and got married to her.

When Coco returned to the house the leash was missing. I didn't mind Tony didn't come back but I did mind that he didn't send me back the leash. To Magda, however, this was the end of life. She tried to kill herself, but not

251

too hard. She only took maybe ten pills. I called the doctor who gave her two slaps and forced her to vomit. She had decided to leave everything to our mutual butler, Harry, not to me. I was so mad at her that I also wanted to give her two slaps.

Much later, Magda and her agent, Jeffrey Jones, saw Tony on the street. "Do me a favor, Jeffrey," said Magda, "bring Tony to my apartment for a few minutes. I am no longer angry with him but just for old time's sake, I want to talk with him."

Magda then staged her own little Hungarian drama: she beat Tony with a whip. She cracked a glass of scotch out of his hand with the whip. She didn't really hurt him too badly because he managed to stay alive another twenty years. When she finished she called me. "Now I feel better," she said.

Meanwhile, I introduced her to Count Yailotzie so she could console herself. We four were at El Morocco—Magda with Lotzie and me with some escort—when Magda was wanted on the phone. She left her cape on the chair and I sat with the two men waiting but she never came back. Tony had called and said, "Come," and Magda had taken a taxi.

Tony was against Magda's career. She was doing *This Thing Called Love* in a Coney Island theatre with folding wooden chairs when Tony came and bought a ticket to watch. In the love scene the leading man kisses her. In anger, Tony stood up, pushed back his chair which came clattering down, and rushed backstage to slap Magda across the face.

Tony was a terrific sport. He put down $500 for the actors' closing night to have a hamburger and hotdog party. "If it's not enough," he said to the proprietor, "I will send you another $500." Wherever I went in Southampton with my poor Hungarian friends I was told, "Mr. Gallucci paid already."

The romance went on for eight years.

On Sunday afternoon, April 1, 1956, they were married. They lived in a townhouse in Manhattan plus a castle in Southampton. Tony's regular house in Southampton had seven bedrooms but then he wanted to build dressing rooms and cabanas and the zoning law wouldn't let him so he bought another ten acres for $20,000 an acre and first built dressing rooms for his pool and then put up an actual castle. They used to invite 300 people to their castle parties. This is the way my Magda lived.

Tony's only problem was that he drank. I had a small party of thirty people and Magda wore the most exquisite black lace short dress from Paris. After the party she called me and asked, "How did you like my dress?"

I told her, "You must tell me where you got it. I will not wear it when you do but I have to have a dress like it."

"It is now in pieces," she said. "Tony and I had a fight going up in our elevator."

"But Tony was in such a good mood here. He gave my Hungarian cook and waitress and chambermaid each tips of $100 and he kissed their hands and told them how good the dinner was."

"Yes, but he was drunk."

"Tony is a sweet drunk, though."

"I hate even sweet drunks and I began to nag him about his drinking and in our tiny elevator where there is not even room enough to have an argument he tore off my dress."

The next day he didn't remember the incident. Magda went on hating that he was a drinker and she even beat him up because of it. One time this huge-sized man called me and said, "Help me. Magda is beating me. She slapped my face."

I told him, "So slap her back."

Oh, but this was a very happy marriage. He adored her and she adored him.

Eva was not lucky in her personal life for ten years. She and Tyrone Power had a big big love. He begged my Eva to come to London with him where he was doing a movie. I told her, "Evika, if you live with him he won't marry you." It was all my fault that she didn't go and this was the end of their romance. One night she wept to me, "Everybody says I am so beautiful and who would believe I am like a dog in my house all alone." Oh, they were very much in love and she tore her heart out over Tyrone.

Then for three years her big love was Dennison Slater. I introduced her to Denny and he went every weekend to California to see Eva who was working there. He was crazy for her. She was crazy for him. The weekend he was to bring her home with him to New York, he didn't come. That one weekend he said to her, "I have a little crush on a French singer but this is not a big love. I am sure it will go by." She shed many tears over Denny.

On a visit to Palm Springs Bundy Solt introduced her to a plastic surgeon, Dr. John Williams. They became friends and when she came to New York for a play she said to me, *"Nuci,* this man wants to marry me."

"Do you adore him?" I asked.

"No. I am not madly insanely in love but I don't dislike him either. I am so lonely I think this would be a good idea."

"What does he look like?" I asked.

"Handsome and very nice. What do you think?"

"I don't know him," I said. "so I really cannot give advice."

"But," she pressed, "I must have your opinion."

"A plastic surgeon has a good future. If you help him now, he will repay you generously in the future."

"You know, *Nuci,* a millionaire playboy also is sort of interested in me, but I don't like him at all. I cannot bring myself to marry just for money."

"Of course not," I said. "Without love marriage is too difficult and I didn't tell any of you that you had to marry millionaires."

"No, you didn't," laughed Eva, "you said we had to marry kings."

"Darling, I am like every mother. I want the best for my daughters, but I know more than anybody that money alone will not make you happy."

"John has an office but he makes very little money so far. He practically cannot even afford rent," Eva sighed. *"Nuci,* even if you go to parties and resorts where you can meet men still it is not always so easy to find the right one. I can have many beaux but none is good enough to be the only one. I like John. I think you will too. You must go to Hollywood and spend a few days with him and tell me what you think."

"Okay," I said, "it's worth it to leave my business for a few days to study him."

I went to Hollywood. Dr. John Williams was very nice. He called for me, took me to dinner and a movie and in the movie he held my hand. It was so embarrassing! It was like I would be his girl.

Then, when he told me good-bye he gave me a big kiss. I said to him, "But John, it is not I who is going to marry you."

He said, "You are so sweet that I love you, too."

I told Eva, "But this is a wonderful guy. Just from the handholding alone is enough to tell what a man he is. His hand is so warm and dry. If it was a cold or a sweating hand I would have to tell you don't marry him and in that moment I would be out of the movie and onto a plane for New York."

The wedding was April 8, 1956, in the drawing room of Eva's New York townhouse. It was a quiet ceremony, only thirty persons—almost the same group from Magda's wedding to Tony the week before. That same night they went to my country house for the honeymoon. I put flowers all over and I stocked the bar and put champagne on ice and paid my housekeeper extra to take care of them. I said to them, "I will give you everything. I will give you even my car."

After one week they grudgingly permitted me to come out but only for Saturday afternoon from 6 to 8 P.M. With all I had supplied I could not even stay over. I came with fruits and caviar and *kolbász* and everything which I personally carried and at 8 o'clock I had to turn around and go back. Much later on, when they were living in Hollywood, Eva told me, "John didn't like it that you came out to the house."

A few months later Eva's hello to me on the phone was, "We're getting a divorce."

Out I flew to their $450-a-month rented house which naturally Eva paid for. Eva had rented it from an actress and it was very exotic with many sculptures plus a swimming pool that was practically indoors.

"We had a terrific fight," she told me when I arrived. "Thank God for Marlene Dietrich, she is such a good friend. I called Marlene and she came rushing over and you know how Germans are. With such strength she shouted to him, *'out.'* She threw him out from the house bodily."

"But why? You are only married maybe months."

"With all my shows and things, I am always on the road and he doesn't like it. So I said to him, 'Someone has to pay the rent and since you go to the office but do not earn much it is I who must work for it.' "

"I am sure that you insulted him very much."

"Not any more than he insulted me. After Marlene ordered him out he came back again. But you know for what? For his television set!"

"Are you very unhappy?"

"Yes," she sniffed. "I am going to get it over with quickly. No alimony or anything. We will divide up the wedding presents because he insists that half belongs to him. I don't understand how this can be since all the wedding presents came from *my* friends but he's insisting on taking his half anyway."

This is twenty years ago. Her husband number three has since married many times and now makes maybe $100,000 a year but when my lucky Eva had him he had nothing but a promising future. And they say the Gabors are gold diggers!

The New York *Journal American* newspaper had a centerfold spread in its magazine section about the three girls and me and Zalabondy told me, "The papers speak so much about Jolie Gabor that it is only intelligent to try and make something extra with this big publicity. You must come up with a perfume or a line of cosmetics."

That was a good thought. I had a good thought, too. "One of my uncles was a skin specialist," I told Zala, "and he had a cream which the ladies loved in Budapest. I could package this cream."

Zsa Zsa introduced me to this crookish but Hungarian gentleman, distinguished looking, who lived in the Blackstone Hotel. He was here many years so he was an American type which I needed. At every stage of my life, I had somebody to help me. I think maybe that when you know me you have to love me and they all did.

That he would help me, so I began. I had the most beautiful jars in the world. It took six manufacturers just to make the jar. One made it white, another manufactured the golden top. Still somebody else did the label. So, again, all night and every day I worked. Once I came home from the Bronx factory at three o'clock in the night all alone.

If I had gone my own way I would be today a millionaire. I wanted to stick with only the cream but then people said I had to have with the lipsticks, the powders, the perfumes and this and this.

We had Creme Gabor, "that fountain of beauty in a jar; that unique luscious pink cream containing Hungarian camomile, the beauty guardian which gives you the dewy moist look of youth." The Gabor Foundation Cream was "the secret of lasting beauty now revealed by the Gabors," and the Madame Jolie Gabor Makeup Base, "guaranteed to be used by all the Gabors." The Pearl de Jolie perfume, mounted with pearls and called "a closely guarded secret of Jolie Gabor," "completely continental" sold for $12.50 per ounce. One of the bright notes of this period of my life came when Clark Gable's wife Sylvia wrote me from London, asking me to rush airmail jars of my cream, which she could not do without.

My nephew who was a professor at the University in San Francisco had me get into the wholesale business in great style.

He called I. Magnin and said, "I am the secretary of Madame Gabor" and he laid it on very big. I went with my hat and veil plus my samples and got a Magnin order for $10,000. Then I got into a Fifth Avenue department store and Saks in New York City.

An employee of Elizabeth Arden who later became an employee of mine told me Elizabeth Arden raged in her office that "Jolie knows nothing about cosmetics and she is already in the Fifth Avenue shops."

They didn't have to worry because this never became for me a business. It only costed me money. I didn't ever make a penny. Besides, I became angry with this crookish man. I told him, "I will give my money and my name, you will give your work and I will give you from the business half." At first he worked. Then he said, "The hell with the business. I love you and I want to be with you."

When I refused he became angry and I threw him out. First, however, I demanded a paper from him that he would go out from the business. To get in good with me again he gave me a letter stating he wants nothing more from the business only to stay with me. The next time we fought he sued me for $2 million. This is the one and only thing that made me unhappy for a few days.

Not only couldn't I pay $2 million, but if I was even stuck for $50,000 I would have been *kaput*. There was no way that I could afford this. But, again, it was proved to me how lucky I am. I told his lawyer, "Look here, this man has not a case because I have a signed letter from him." The lawyer admitted his client was a swindler and that he owed here and he owed there and that three women were currently suing him because he took their money away and he ended by suggesting to me, "When you give me $200 I will throw away the case!"

So all I was stuck with was 5,000 of these jars. I couldn't put anything else in my cellar because of all this junk. Zsa Zsa bought them for a dollar apiece and told on the television that she has a marvelous cream, but she regretted very much having paid me $5,000 because she couldn't make nothing with them.

I tried also to go into the wholesale end of the jewelry business. At the Waldorf Astoria there was an exhibition and I hired the most expensive booth. To push the dealers from all over the country I had a party in my shop. I had goulash and *kolbász* and Gypsy music and champagne and I kept urging them, "Have a drink . . . eat something . . . try this. . . ." My personal attention to everyone made of the party a big success. Eventually the police came because my guests were actually outside my shop on the sidewalk dancing in the streets at five o'clock in the morning.

Each guest promised to return with his sales manager and give me a big order. They adored me. I had three proposals—two for sex, one for marriage from a guy I could have loved a little but he was married anyway. My party cost $1,000 and when the gaiety was over not even a single "maybe" order did I have.

The one way in which I could have made money I was too damn stupid to have made it. On a very rainy day, I was crossing Madison Avenue from my shop to my house and an auto came from I don't where and hit me. All I can remember is that I was lying there under the car. Two police officers took me back to my house.

I didn't feel nothing. Only my two knees were blooding and the stockings were *kaput.* My lawyer sent immediately a doctor. "But it is not such a big thing," I said. "It doesn't even hurt me."

My lawyer wagged his finger at me, "Jolie, stay in bed and I make you $50,000. Don't move from the bed for two weeks."

Not even for $100,000 which I badly needed could I lie in bed for two weeks. For two days I stayed in the bed and I became restless. I wanted to work. My shop was like a cocktail party every day. People like Faye Emerson, Maggi McNellis, Betty Furness, and Carol Channing came in just to say hello to me. George, the butler, opened the door with white gloves and served champagne every afternoon. He was tall and black and in love with Harry. My shop was my whole life.

The third day, I couldn't stand it. I dressed myself, made up my face and my hair and an hour after I arrived at the shop a young man came in. Two weeks earlier I had decided that I will not anymore be so stupid with customers who say, "Jolie, how are you?" and I answer, "And who are *you?*" Naturally, I don't recognize them because I don't know them.

I had just made up my mind not be so *ousgalasint*—so without manners —to act to everyone as though I knew them. So this young man says, "How are you, Jolie?"

"I am fine," I smiled.

"But I heard you had a little accident," he said.

"Oh, it's nothing. Nothing happened at all," I answered, waving my hand airily.

Looking at me intently the man said, "But what's with your beautiful legs?"

I thought I knew him from my society life so I said, "Oh, they're as perfect as they were before. It was all nothing."

This nice young guy turned out to be the insurance man. My lawyer nearly died. "Oh, you are so stupid," he hollered at me.

I always had trouble with insurance men. There was a period when I was robbed four times. In one month three times. In the house two holdup men robbed Magda. One was quite gentlemanly, though. His partner grabbed $40 from her purse. Magda pleaded, "Please, this is my weekend money. It's all the cash I have until Monday." The nice one said, "The lady needs it. Don't touch it." The not-so-nice one put it back but took the big diamond ring she had brought out for me from Budapest but never gave over to me. Therefore, I didn't care so much about this particular robbery because to me that ring was lost anyhow.

After that my apartment was robbed of jewelry and my TV and some things but not my ten-year-old mink coat. I was sorry about that. I had gotten it in America to replace the Budapest one that was stolen in the movie theater right after I arrived. A week later, my apartment was again robbed and this time only my lousy mink coat was taken! I thought, "Oh, how God loves me that he would steal the one thing I wanted stolen!"

The fourth time, I had the trouble with the stupid insurance people. I had seemed to have lost my own diamond. It was a good sized stone, maybe four carats.

In order not to upset my insurance I hadn't put in previous claims so this time they paid me quickly in one check. The following week, Bob Schuler, the husband of Patrice Munsel, called, "Jolie, I found your diamond stone."

I had still my hot hands on the check. "You did?" I said, trying to sound thrilled. "Where did you find it?"

"In our fireplace in the drawing room. You must have been leaning up against it when you were here and in cleaning it out today Patrice found it."

"Ohhh," I groaned, "now you find it and I already have the check from the insurance."

"Well," said Bob, "I'll give it to you and whatever you do is your business."

"I have always such trouble with insurance that I think I will show the good will and tell them I found it."

"Okay," said Bob. "That's really the best way."

"Yes, but my heart isn't in it," I said and hung up to phone the insurance people.

Magda was furious. "Why are you so stupid that you call and tell them you found the stone?"

I told her, "Because I don't want that they throw me out from the insurance company."

But you know what? They threw me out from the insurance anyhow so it wasn't worth it to be honest.

Whereas I lost money in lots of ways, I made money in lots of ways.

I bought this adorable, smart French poodle in Southampton. He was a miniature and his breeder wanted $400 and I offered $200. He looked very sad as though he could understand we were bargaining his value. He cocked his head from side to side as we bargained.

This smart dog was plainly insulted. You could tell he knew that the man wanted to sell him. He trotted over to where I was and almost asked aloud with his eyes to "Please don't let there be any haggling over me." Naturally I bought him—for $200.

Unfortunately, this dog was a big tragedy. He made all the time with his behind. I don't know how nicely to explain it but when he did it I only know you have to die. He slept with me and he did it once in the night so bad that I had to go out from the room. Another day I had to stop on the highway because he made in the car.

I didn't know what to do until a very rich widow with a chauffeur came to my shop and she fell for this dog. "Oh," she squealed, "I adore this dog. If you would only give to me this dog. Nothing would be too expensive for this dog."

For me it was very important the money because I was always hanging. I had another payment of some thousand due so I thought selling this animal I no longer wanted would be a help. I told her, "Okay, all right. $450."

Her daughter whispered, "You dope. My mother would give a thousand dollars because she is insane for this French poodle."

The mother gave right away the check for $450. So it didn't look as though I was palming off a lemon, I told her, "Only in this case I am denying myself and giving up my precious beloved dog in that you bring him in every day even if only for a moment."

She was terrified I would reclaim him so she didn't come personally but sent him with the chauffeur. The dog began to cry and to lick me but I had already deposited the check so I was able to stand it. The fourth day the lady came in personally and the dog didn't even look at me. He discovered I had sold him.

An employee, a broken-down princess, was watching this and I said, "The dog doesn't want to come back because he is rich now with a chauffeur."

"But you also have a car plus a villa plus a townhouse," said the *fercrochta* broken-down princess.

"Yes," I agreed, "but nothing is paid. I live in everything but I don't own anything."

When the girls found out I had sold him, Zsa Zsa raged at me, "Oh, *Nuci*, how could you? This dog was a member of your family, close to your heart. Why don't you sell *us?*"

And I answered, "Because nobody asked."

Somewhere along the line I had arrived professionally. Letters from abroad addressed simply "Jolie Gabor, America" reached me. A British Broadcasting Corporation poll listed me as "The number one selfmade businesswoman of America." My designs were being worn by such beauties as Lana Turner and Lauren Bacall. Irene Dunne loved them so much she wore them in her next picture.

My press clippings referred to me as a dynamo of energy. I was always on a revolving circuit. I thought nothing of a last minute quickie trip to Texas overnight or a plane trip to California for a long weekend. Or going Friday for a personal appearance at the Fashion Group in Philadelphia or displaying a special precious jewel collection to the International Fashion Revue at the Chalfonte in Atlantic City Saturday or telling a group of ladies at the Blum-Vogue Store in Chicago on Monday that "Pearls are worn at your ears and around your neck where they can beautify the face so don't cheapen that beauty with cheap pearls."

Everybody was writing about me. A journalist from the London *Daily Mirror* planned a story on me so I invited him home. To fix up the narrow hallway from the main part of my apartment to the bathroom, I had a vanity table lining one side with chic appointments like gold combs and mirrors and jars. It was very impressive.

I told this London journalist for the six-part serial he was doing I wanted $10,000. I'd heard big stars got that. I would have done it for free but I thought I have nothing to lose. He was so impressed with my vanity table that he figured I was really even more than I was. He called London and they authorized him to pay me $6,000. I couldn't believe it!

My shop could have been a daily television serial. There were almost more life and death stories going on than there was jewelry being sold. I had met a lady from Brooklyn who suffered a stroke and was told she'd never walk again. I visited her at the hospital every day. She said I brought her courage. She kissed my hands and said, "I thank God for you. You have given me hope."

Many months later, she hobbled into the shop on crutches and she fell on me. "I promised myself the first time I could walk I would come to see Jolie Gabor." Her eyes began to tear, "But they say I will never really walk again normally."

I told to her, "So what. So you will be on crutches or in a wheelchair, and you will mean something. Before you were nobody and you meant nothing."

The woman started to cry and I gave her a pair of pearl earrings for a present. "Don't cry," I commanded her. "You are now an extra special somebody—now everybody will pay attention to you." Then the pressure of business crowded in on me and I couldn't spend any more time so I said to her, "You must go now. Go, darling, go. I'm very busy and I don't have time for you. But don't anymore be gray. Be happy."

I might have been startling but I was sincere and this she recognized. She left happily and has continued to lead a life under the sun.

Not everyone is grateful when you do a favor for them. My two homosexuals from the Southampton jewelry shop fell into trouble with the 20 percent luxury tax, went bankrupt, and lost all but their little Southampton shop. To befriend them I offered them an apartment, fed them and when they wanted to commit suicide I saved them from it. I saved their business, too. When they were out of cash, I gave them $5,000 worth of merchandise on consignment.

After all this, I saw in their shop months later a little junk bracelet, nothing good.

I said, "Charge it."

They said, "Sorry, we only take cash."

I was so hurt after all I'd done that I just took off the piece of junk and said, "Never mind."

One of them, shifting back and forth from one foot to the other, mumbled, "Well, that's just the way we conduct our business, Jolie."

"Forget it," I said. "Never mind."

Magda wanted to come and hit them but I said, "I don't hold hatreds and I get over things like that and that's why I'm happy."

I don't hold unhappiness inside me and I have the ability to absolutely overcome suffering. This is a greatness I think. My pains are of short duration. I dismiss them quickly.

Another ingrate to me was Jack Paar. I had done his little morning show and when NBC gave him a tryout for the nighttime show he called me. "They are giving me a one-week trial. I want you to come on with me for the whole five nights," Jack said. "You were so good with me before. I feel you'll bring me luck."

"Friday night I cannot. I have an appointment in Southampton and, anyway, you don't pay me."

"Jolie, you must come the whole five nights. I cannot be a hit without you. You're my goodluck piece."

"Who else do you have as a steady?"

"Dody Goodman."

So I came and I was wonderful. I put an earring on his ear and I made great fun for him. The last night I made for him a big present. Zsa Zsa was in town. She and Jean Pierre Aumont had just done the Arthur Murray show and she was at this moment at "21." "How about we call Zsa Zsa at 21," I said while we were on the television, "and ask her to come over quick and be a guest."

"I'd love it," said Jack, "but I can't pay."

"So, anyway, give me a telephone and we will try."

While we were still on camera, I called Zsa Zsa and she said to me, "Who is this Jack Paar? I never heard of him."

"I was on Jack's morning show," I said, "and he is a very nice friend and he is now on late instead of Steve Allen and it would be heaven if you would come because this is his trial. If he is not good then they will throw him off. So do me a favor, Zsa Zsika, come over."

Zsa Zsa came. She was ravishing and exciting and at the commercial break she gave to me a typical Zsa Zsaism. *"Nuci,* you can go now. I will stay for myself."

"No thank you," I replied, "I am the star of this show."

Jack thanked me deeply for what I did for him. The next week he phoned me at home and spoke to me on the air but this way wasn't too successful and for fifteen years he didn't invite me on again. Zsa Zsa and Eva, always, but me never. He never even came to my parties. He never even introduced me the time I sat in his audience.

Only once in all the years did he contact me again and that was for me to get all the Gabors on his show at one time. I said politely, "No, thank you."

One kindness which I did for somebody ended with people thinking what a brilliant public relations trick I had pulled. Columnist Hy Gardner invited me on his television with the mama of Maria Callas. I'd never met Litsa Callas before the taping. When I was brought into the studio, Litsa and I chatted for a few minutes. She was poised, genteel, and refined-looking.

I did not know her story and we just began talking about our children as any two mamas will. I asked her what I thought was a normal question. "When is the last time you spoke to your daughter?"

Tears flooded her face. "We didn't talk for ten years," she said softly. "I don't even know her husband. I wrote to Maria nine years ago and asked her for $100. She answered badly. She told me, 'You're young enough—go to work' and other things I can't tell you."

My eyes widened in horror. "Have you no money at all?"

"I am flat broke," she said. "I have lost everything and for nearly ten years I am bitterly separated from Maria. It is heartbreaking not only to be poor but to have a daughter who won't even speak to you. Still, a mother cannot have hate in her heart."

"All right," I said, "I can't even imagine it or believe it but supposing she doesn't love you. So, okay. But why doesn't she support you?"

"It is hard to state my heartbreak," Mrs. Callas said sadly. "My daughter is temperamental and it is a tragedy because I love Maria more than her sister. Maria is my baby."

The makeup man came in and powdered us and still we sat in our same two chairs and talked. While there was deep despair and frustration, there wasn't bitterness in the soft-voiced Litsa Callas. "Maria offered to finance me if I will return home to Greece. If this means I could never visit America again I would not do it. I was an American citizen when I gave birth to Maria and I lost it because I stayed in Athens too long, not having money to come back. I love America and I could not live anywhere else if I am told I could never see this country again. What has she got to fear? The fact that I write a book? It is a mother's book not a scandal. I wouldn't hurt Maria."

I took her hand in mine. "How can it be so between a mama and daughter?"

"It's strange," whispered Mrs. Callas, her eyes clouding up again.

"Maybe you yourself did something wrong?"

"Never."

"I'm going to bring you and Maria back together. She will come to you."

"Never. Not Maria." She shook her head vigorously.

"We Hungarians never hold a grudge," I said as the director moved our chairs for the best angle. "The Greeks they hold it and hold it. In Hungary we get mad, smash a glass, and then forget it. That's why there are no psychiatrists in Hungary."

"How do you manage to live?" I asked her on the air.

"A poor Greek couple in New Jersey named Zarras gave me one room in which I take in sewing."

This touched me. "I give you a job," I heard myself saying. "You start Monday in my jewelry shop for a salary and commissions."

"I accept," said Mrs. Callas and we sealed it with a hug.

The second day she made her first sale, two gold pins with pearls. "You've brought me much happiness," Mrs. Callas told the customer.

After three years in my shop Litsa Callas sued Maria and won. She is now in Greece.

I do not deny Maria Callas' mother working for Zsa Zsa Gabor's mother created publicity and it helped for the shop and magazines wrote about it and we were invited to the Plaza Hotel for lunch and papers made pictures of us but this was not my original idea. In fact, I was even insulted when Hy Gardner said this was a good, smart idea. "You always did have a great flair for publicity," Hy said to me.

"This is not publicity. This is human being," I said.

BOOK SIX

Mrs.
Edmund de Szigethy

1 I was sure life was over for me in terms of love. I went out with many fellows but I never seemed to find the romantic love.

I almost married a Dr. Louis Bardoly, who owned his own hospital in Roslyn, Long Island. I had a bunion operation and Dr. Bardoly sent an ambulance to steal me out from a big Manhattan hospital to his little hospital because he knew where I was, the girls would also come and so he would make publicity.

Bardoly was good to me. He escorted me to Europe, paid the bills, and even let us have separate rooms. The Duke and Duchess of Windsor were at the Sacher Hotel in Vienna when we were there. I was wearing a black dress with white polka dots and carried a matching umbrella. I was sitting on the terrace sipping a coffee when a newspaperman recognized me and made photos of me and then the papers wrote that there were three celebrities in town: The Duke and Duchess *and* Jolie Gabor. Then I was happy!

Bardoly was short, not good-looking and although he was seven years older than I, he looked older. I kept refusing to marry him because I had a feeling something better would come along. Here I was supposed to be an authority on the gay life and glamor and men and all of that and I was alone.

Having a man for dating purposes was not difficult because men like a woman who is a little bit crazy—especially rich men. They relish a woman who can amuse them. So getting a man to fall for me was easy but I wanted desperately to belong. I wanted desperately to love a husband. I was, maybe, not so very young anymore but the heart has no winter. In her heart a woman is always young.

I had about given up hope of experiencing happiness in marriage and knowing again what romance was when—suddenly—unexpectedly—the good fairy touched me with her magic wand. Life began again for me—about sixty.

In December of 1956 Brigadier General Sidney Wooten, post commander at Camp Kilmer, New Jersey, came to a party at my house for seventy newly arrived Hungarian refugees who had escaped the recent revolution. Kilmer was their point of internment upon arrival in the United States. Among them I noticed this young, slim, handsome, soft-spoken aristocrat who drank only wine. Next day Dr. Bardoly, my escort who was also present, sent me two cases labeled "For your new friend." He telephoned later to say, "I

269

could see you were flirting very much with this freedom fighter so I guess it is Bardoly out of your life and this new man into it."

He was right. Edmund de Szigethy of Transylvania was caught in the revolution and had escaped. We sat in a corner of my apartment that night. He spoke no English. "Like all aristocrats in the old days," said this soft-spoken freedom fighter, "my family were landowners. When our property was seized, I had a friend in the textile business and I found I was able to move his goods for him and so I became a businessman. I learned also to paint textiles and in all these ways I found the means to make a living."

I had a friend whose son had come out of the '56 revolution and the next day I asked him, "Tell me about this Edmund de Szigethy. I never heard of him before yesterday but I am now suddenly very interested."

"Edmund is fine, noble, and courageous," said the son. "I can thank him for my life because when the Nazis were in Budapest Edmund gave over his apartment for Jewish people and I was among them.

"Edmund is a Catholic," he went on, "and since he could go around on the streets he used to shelter us and bring us food. He hid maybe eight people who were in big danger. We who are alive today speak about him like he is a god."

This god of mine was, of course, broke. He came out of Budapest with only two suits—wearing one on top of the other. He made it to Vienna hiding from house to house and eating from hand to mouth. When he finally arrived here he had exactly $27.

His thank you letter after my party was courteous, not overflowery. At the end he wrote his phone number, adding, "If you should want to see me again I'll run happily." I showed immediately this "love letter" to Bimba who said, "This is not a love letter. It is cold. And, anyway, why do you want him so much? He has nothing."

"He has everything," I said. "He has only not money. He is gentlemanly, from a good background. He speaks quietly and you feel it is the truth. Maybe I, myself, am too overpowering and I talk too much but Edmund is everything I ever dreamed about. All my life I have wanted a true aristocrat, a tall, slim, and elegant man, and Edmund is all that."

All of us who had arrived in America earlier helped the new refugees. The Hungarian lady who placed Edmund in Newport, Rhode Island, phoned me and said, "He is housed with a husband and wife and three-month-old baby but the wife is trying to take liberties and he doesn't want trouble and he's terrified to jeopardize his position. I think it would be best to move him. Would you be able to house him?"

"Yes, I would be thrilled," I said truthfully.

He arrived at my house in a white Cadillac. "Where did you get such a car?" I asked.

"A rich Hungarian loaned it to me," he said. "How else would a Hungarian refugee arrive?" he quipped.

When Magda married Gallucci, she gave over her apartment in my house to Harry Karl, who later married Debbie Reynolds. Harry had paid $30,000 for me to decorate his place. I made it not for a businessman but for a French madam with gilt chairs and a round red velvet bed. Harry never lived in it. He just sent his broken-down friends to use it. I'd say to strangers who arrived, "Who are you?" and they'd say, "We're friends of Harry Karl."

When I needed room for Edmund, I called Harry. "Harry, darling," I said, "I would like to use your apartment for a beautiful Hungarian who is broke and so good-looking that you would adore him."

"Okay," Harry chuckled, "but only if you promise to sleep with him in my round red velvet bed."

"Harry, darling, I promise." And I kept my promise. Many times.

Edmund proposed to me after lovemaking. He was stroking my hair and he said, "I love you. I really love you."

"But it is only two weeks," I said. "I cannot believe you would feel this way after only two weeks."

He stroked my hair some more. "You are a very sweet woman."

"And you are a nice guy," I murmured. "Would you like to be my steady?"

We had made love on a thick rug and were lying there on the living room floor just touching one another and kissing. He rolled over away from me and lay on his back alongside me. "I cannot be happy except in marriage. If I love I love, and if we are not married and you get somebody else then you give me heartbreak."

"But you are so much younger than I," I argued. "I wouldn't dare to marry you for this reason."

He kissed me and then he said, "But, *Angyalka*, this doesn't matter. You are entertaining, you are good company. You are younger in spirit than I am."

"I think it is now better if we are just lovers."

"No," he said. "I am a one-woman man. I want to marry you."

The truth is on our first date he had spent $22 of the only money he had, $27, to send me roses and I knew immediately—even then—that I would have to marry such a man. Everybody was against us. People not only told me not to marry him but told him not to marry me. When the young boy whose life Edmund saved heard about the possibility, he ran to Edmund and warned, "You make yourself unhappy when you marry into this family. They will use you up."

And Edmund snorted, "I have nothing. What can they do to me?"

That evening he discussed this. "I cannot understand why the boy would do this to me."

"Only thing I can figure," I shrugged, "is that his mother works for me and she thinks you are sharp and would take over the management of the shop and that you would become right away a boss and she would have to leave. I think for these reasons she and the son are suddenly against you."

My friend Evelyn Sharpe, the hotel owner, was also against. She was a widow for many years and if not for me she would have no romance because I made her to have a lover on a boat once going over to Europe. Anyway she scolded, "How dare you marry a poor man who has nothing and is so much younger than you?"

I told her, "I know this sounds ridiculous but in this short time I knew that here at last was a man I could trust."

"How can you be sure this will last? Are you not afraid?"

"Just because he is a younger man doesn't mean he is necessarily a flirt. An older man can be a worse flirt. Dr. Louis Bardoly is older than I. We were flying to Europe and he flirted outrageously with an 18-year-old girl opposite us. I could have sprung out from the airplane I was so upset. A younger man maybe is *not* a flirt. It depends on a man's makeup not on his age."

"I am flabbergasted at your decision. You only know him two to three weeks."

"Yes, but no matter who will try to tell me no I am very sure about this marriage."

"I am only thinking of your good, Jolie," insisted my friend. "He is much younger . . ."

"Not so much. Maybe ten years. Okay, so twelve."

". . . and it could happen that he will leave you, cheat on you, take your money."

"Those who feel that way never have happiness, Evelyn," I explained.

"Do you deny that he would not marry you if it was not for your villa in the country and your townhouse and your shop?"

"One high-society woman who saw him with me said that he has me under his skin but I know he is not so very insanely in love with me. I also know, though, that I will work hard at making him in love with me. I will be sweet, I will look at him like he is a great man and I am a simple little woman. I am sure he would not be so crazy to marry me if I would be a poor seamstress. I know this therefore I find American rich women ridiculous. Therefore is Barbara Hutton unhappy. Why she cannot make a man love her and why she cannot make a man happy? It is because she buys the man with money and planes like she did Rubi."

"But you have just admitted that all this *can* make a man marry you."

"Yes, but it cannot make him love you. Edmund is such a man who would prefer to work day and night and not marry a woman he couldn't love. Nothing except the woman herself can make a man love her and this I will work at.

I, too, am not so very very in love but I know this man will be good for me."

I didn't tell her I was embarrassed being seen in the halls and that's why I also wanted to get married! Edmund lived directly over me so some nights I went upstairs to him in my pajamas and some nights he came down to me and one of my fairy tenants saw me therefore I thought it would be better to marry him instead of doing this every night.

"What do you think?" I asked Magda, who is like my mother. "Do you think I can marry him?"

"He is a man who carries himself with respect. He has good taste. I am not for a minute afraid that you are doing something bad," said Magda, who was very much for this.

"Everybody says we will probably only have a year together," I said thinking aloud and kind of sounding out her thoughts although I had already made up my mind what I was going to do.

"Does Edmund know how old you are?"

"He knows I am older but not how much. He can figure out approximately but I will never tell him actually. Let it be a fantasy."

"This man is good for you," declared Magda decisively. "He is well-mannered and he's not spoiled or demanding. The question is what will he do for a living?"

"I think he will go with a textile house. He knows where he can get a job for $200 a week."

"No. No good," interjected Magda instantly. "He'll be tired at night and won't be any good to you. You won't be able to take him to parties and he'll have to get up too early to be a good escort. Besides, if he does good then what would he need you for? It is not so terribly clever for a woman to make too many outside opportunities for a man."

"Oh, you are so smart," I marveled.

"Give him $200 a week and put him into your shop where you need the help anyway."

We were dressing to go to City Hall to get our marriage license when Western Union delivered a cable from my sister Dora in Budapest. It was in reply to one I'd sent her requesting any information she could find on Edmund.

Her cable read: "He is a heavy drinker. He beat up his former wife. He is impulsive, throws money away but is smart and can make life even on an iceberg."

This Hungarian proverb, "He can live even on the ice" means that under any circumstances the person will survive.

I showed Edmund her cable.

He made a very short reply, "Maybe they took this out of my divorce papers."

I understood exactly and ran to the telephone. "How quickly," I asked, "can I get a call through to Budapest?"

"It will take about twelve hours," said the operator.

"Well," I said to Edmund, "let us see how famous I am." I called again the telephone company. "I am Jolie Gabor. I have met a beautiful man and I want to marry him but I must first get a call through to my family in Budapest. It is urgent. Can you help?"

In no time my sister was on the other end. "Doruska," I cried, "I want to marry him anyway."

"Oh, Jolika," her voice crackled through the wire. "I am so glad you called because I wanted to get in touch with you again. I was sick that I sent such news to you because since then I have learned that all this dirt about his marriage came from his divorce papers. The information that he is a little sharp should not worry you because all aristocrats had to be crooks a little bit in order to survive. He is all right. He is a decent man. Marry him."

We came to City Hall at 11 o'clock in the morning. Not until 6 P.M. did we go away. They had such fun with me because I could not remember what age I told everybody I was. See, there were photographers surrounding us plus there were complications about my divorce papers, which I didn't have. Each time we had another interruption we would start to fill out another form and each time I would give a different age—whatever came into my head.

I forgot from one hour to the other what I said. Finally the pleasant clerk said, "Mrs. Gabor, please make up your mind. Please decide your age so we can make out the papers." Someday I must call up City Hall to find out how old I am.

The day had developed into the worst downpour in years. The stupid lawyer accompanying us instead of hiring a limousine came for us in a taxi and because of this big rain we couldn't get a taxi back. We saw a lot of people going in one direction downstairs so we followed them. I was wearing an $80 straw hat from Saks with flowers and a veil plus a mink coat and I found myself in the subway.

Our photos were already on the front pages of the late afternoon newspapers. So there we were at rush hour surrounded by people who were reading about us and congratulating us in the subway!

Inside the subway station when we got off there was a flower seller with roses. With the only money he had left, Edmund bought me all the roses. My veil was plastered down on my head from the rain, the glue from the flowers on my hat had loosened and the flowers were hanging down in front of my face and I was carrying a basket of drowned soggy roses and my mink looked like a dead cat and in the pouring rain we had to walk to the house where a dozen newspapermen and photographers waited for us.

The wedding was Sunday afternoon, March 3, 1957, and I was called by society columnists "The Bride of The Year." At 2:45 in Magda and Tony's townhouse. Edmund first came down the staircase and everybody whispered his age as anywhere from forty-four to fifty-two. With his graying temples he looked very distinguished. Magda and Zsa Zsa gave me away. Eva was then in California in the middle of divorcing that Dr. Williams. Best man was General Wooten from Camp Kilmer.

Judge George Postel performed the ceremony, which took maybe 45 seconds and the jammed crowd of about 100—Igor Cassini, who was Cholly Knickerbocker of the New York *Journal American*, Hope Hampton, Betty Furness, Anita Loos, Bobo Rockefeller—broke into applause. I was so happy. I love weddings.

Friends sent thousands of dollars worth of flowers, fruit, champagne and cases of expensive wines and candies and foodbaskets to Magda's house. Edmund said, "Why were we not married in your house so we could have kept all this?" You know, he was right! I realized then how brilliant he was. We ended up without one flower in our house. We had nothing. Magda never sent even one doggy bag of hors d'oeuvres. We dragged back to the empty apartment with not even a bite to eat.

I apologized to Edmund, "The reason I didn't have it here is because it was easier in her house. I didn't have the bother."

"But," he said, "I would have done it." I saw immediately that he is a leader type.

Edmund bought for me an $8 wedding ring. Peter's I threw away because it was cheap. Vilmos' I threw out the window after a fight. Edmund's I would have kept if it was diamonds but it was only a plain gold band so I lost it somehow.

Edmund it turned out not only didn't cost me money but he saved me money and he made me money. I was tired of the shop. I wanted to sell it. It was getting too much for me. It was now a little bit down in its success and I had big debts. The girls' names were doing as much damage as help because thanks to all the high-powered publicity even with the sign of $10 on items in the window, the little people would still say, "I don't dare to come in here."

Edmund took over and threw me out of the business entirely. When he has troubles he takes care that he doesn't come to me. I have not to do anything. I have only to spend the money he earns. Edmund is also a money saver. The last big party I gave was for him eighteen years ago. He stopped all that kind of spending. He is everything that a woman can dream of.

2 I hadn't seen Vilmos in ten years. He had gone back in 1948 after the news that Hungary had become a Republic. The Communists were clever. They had come into a country that was empty. Businesses were dead. Houses were shells. Nothing was making money. So they lied and promised that Hungarian citizens who repatriated themselves would have their confiscated properties returned.

They said: "Go back to your businesses, build up your houses again, rebuild your manufacturing plants." So the people worked like maniacs. They rebuilt what the war and the Nazis had torn down. Then when everything was built up the Commies took it all away. After my sister Janette reestablished The Diamond House it was seized and she was thrown into one room to live along with a princess of the House of Hapsburg. Eventually she and Rozsie made it to Australia.

Vilmos lived in a small cooperative apartment. He married his faithful ugly secretary, Magda, who had been in love with him for twenty years. She didn't get any bargain. She complained to Janette, "When Jolie married Vilmos he was rich, generous, and sexy. Now he is poor, sick, and impotent. It is not a thrill to get your sister's leftover. To take a husband from Jolie is not worth it."

In October '58, after two years of negotiating, I managed to arrange for him a visa to Austria for eight days. All of us were so thrilled that we gave up everything for this family reunion. Zsa Zsa left a film in Rome with Mario Lanza. Eva left playing in a play on Broadway and Magda said not even her husband could keep her from coming. We all brought gifts—a solid gold watch, a cigarette case, a tailor-made suit, a camera.

Vilmos' snow white hair was sparse and he had grown heavy but he was still immaculately dressed. His lot had been helped over the years by each of us sending $100 a month.

We came in like a whirlwind—mink coats, pearls, perfect hairdos, smelling of perfume and wealth, trailing photographers in our wake. It was very moving and we cried all of us. At the end of the eight days he went back behind the Iron Curtain and we returned to our world.

Once a year for four years we did this. The fifth time around I thought,

"I don't go this time." I said to the girls, "Look, children, I don't want to spend a thousand dollars just because the Communists are again letting him out for eight days so you go without me."

Three days after the girls had left for Vienna I was sitting at the hairdresser and the telephone rang. "You must come," said Eva from Austria, "because Papa doesn't speak to us. He just sits and stares at us."

"But, Evika, it is very expensive and I don't want to spend the money right now. Maybe next year."

Then comes Zsa Zsa. "*Nucika*, darling, I swear to you we give you back double the fare. It will cost you nothing and you make four persons happy because if Papa stays like this we are coming right back. He doesn't even speak to us. He asks only, 'Where is Mama . . . ?' "

Two days later I flew out with Edmund. He remained in his room and I went alone to see Vilmos. We had a lovely dinner together and after dessert I told him, "My husband is here with me. He was in the same regiment as you but he wasn't a big shot like you. He was only a little lieutenant."

There was silence a moment then, "Is he a younger man than you?"

"Yes."

"Well," he smiled benevolently, "you are younger than everybody so maybe this is good. I want to see him."

In Hungarian an olderly man calls a young man by a phrase which implies, "Little Brother." This Vilmos did and Edmund was properly respectful. At the end of the evening Vilmos said to him, "You take care of my wife."

I was glad I had gone. It was the last time I saw him.

In 1964 we were in Southampton dressing to go to a party when we got word that Vilmos died suddenly. It was a beautiful death and I want to go the same way. He had been sleeping and when he rose up he said to Magda, "Cook something light because my stomach was not good in the night." She went to the market to buy chicken to make a little soup and when she arrived back at the apartment he was gone.

Come to think of it, I have yet to get that air fare back from the girls!

We had come out to Southampton one Thursday night. Friday morning Magda fell over her black poodle. The dog was always lying before the bedroom and Magda had gone out in the night, tripped over him, and hit her head. The maid put cold compresses on her head for a couple of hours and it looked like she was all right.

Friday all afternoon she was lying in bed and exciting herself about Tony's behavior. *"Nuci,"* she said angrily, "He's drinking. Here I am lying in bed after my fall and he doesn't even come upstairs to ask me how I feel."

"Why are you exciting yourself?" I asked. "You had a nasty fall. You are lying in bed to regain your composure. You have cold compresses on your head and instead of being quiet you are screaming with anger. What is the matter with you?"

She wasn't to be stopped. "He's drinking with the butler and watching the baseball game on TV on the first floor," she snapped.

"But Tony is so good and so generous with you," I said, trying to console her. "Be a little understanding with him and please don't excite yourself. You must stop this or you will have a bitter evening."

Saturday afternoon she brought herself together again and Saturday night she had a big evening as the celebrated guest at the Horse Show Ball. She had been seated atop a wooden horse, photographers snapped her, and she was the belle of the ball. She never was so beautiful. She also never spoke again.

The next morning at my villa I was gazing at her photograph in the paper when Tony called on the telephone. "Come over quick," he said to me in a strained voice. "I don't know what has happened—but it's something terrible. Magda cannot speak. She's like in a coma. Come over right away."

Edmund and I ran over and we saw tragedy has happened. We took her right away to the Southampton Hospital.

Fortunately Zsa Zsa was in town at the Waldorf. "Quickly," I said to Zsa Zsa on the phone, "Get me Dr. Andrew Bernath, the head of the Bellevue Hospital."

"Isn't he a psychiatrist?" she asked.

"Yes. About five years ago also on a Sunday afternoon Magda also lost her speech temporarily. We had had an argument about a broken-down Lord

278

Churchill, who was so broken-down that he wanted to marry me and she overexcited herself. It was this Hungarian Dr. Bernath who helped her then. Tell him I badly need help."

Zsa Zsa arrived in the afternoon with a specialist from Mount Sinai plus this Dr. Bernath. Only for Zsa Zsa would these two doctors drive out on a Sunday afternoon 100 miles to Southampton. Dr. Bernath came out from Magda's room and said, "We are moving her to the city. To Mount Sinai Hospital. This is a stroke."

Zsa Zsa went right away to the telephone. "I'm going to call Eva."

"No," I said, "she is just now arriving in Palm Beach. She is to open tomorrow in a play there. Leave her be. She has enough to think about right now."

Zsa Zsa was determined because she knew that when she did this then everybody would do for her when she needed them. It is something to see how this family keeps together when there is a problem. Zalabondy said, "The Gabors are a great team. They're like a Greek house. When one column falls out everything falls." This is true. The girls are close. Underneath those "dahlingks" are girls who will do anything for one another. They're right there when any of us needs help. Eva turned right around and caught the next plane. Late that same night she was sitting with Zsa Zsa and me in Magda's hospital room at Mount Sinai. *"Nuci,"* she said when she saw me, "You look ninety years old."

We all sat around the bed and stared at Magda. Hours went by and she made no sounds. She looked only. She knew everything that was happening but she didn't speak.

The regulation at the hospital is that you cannot sleep over. When everybody was leaving I hid. I slept under the bed and at five o'clock in the morning I got up and fixed myself because at six o'clock the doctors came in. Oh, this was such a big tragedy for me.

Tony went to his manufactory every day out in Corona, Long Island, but from seven to nine in the morning and in the evening, too, he was in the hospital. He was a little jealous of the way we took charge but he was a good man. He said to the hospital officials, "I want the biggest and the best of everything. Don't think of the cost." When he took her home he made from the bedroom a hospital room. He had two nurses, one for day and another for night, and he slept in the library.

After some months she went to the Rusk Clinic, where they teach you to speak but they told her very cruelly, "You will never speak. Don't even come here anymore. It's a waste of time and money." Magda became bitter and it broke my heart. She kept trying to tell me something but she couldn't. She could manage a word or two but she couldn't connect phrases. She struggled and struggled but—nothing. One evening we spent together at her home with

Tony sitting alone in the library. She cried bitterly. She could get out only three words, "No speech . . . die." I wept that whole night. I couldn't believe such a tragedy could happen to us. "If you die," I said, "then I die, too." We made a pact that night, but as the months rolled into years, she lived and I lived.

Eva's ten years of professional success and personal aloneness had brought her to a five-story Fifth Avenue townhouse overlooking the Metropolitan Museum of Art. Eva had been in such movies as *Gigi, Don't Go Near The Water, My Man Godfrey* and was then appearing in movie theatres in *It Started With A Kiss* with Debbie Reynolds and Glenn Ford.

Nine tenants (mostly divorced ladies) paid her rent. Her own twelve-room duplex was furnished in Louis XV antiques. She was successful and rich but lonely and unhappy. On an evening when her entertainment was going to be looking at the brand new white rugs that had just been laid in her house, old friends came by with Dick Brown. Dick was dark, handsome, and a stockbroker. He had a very nice apartment, many friends, and everybody loved him. One New York girl loved him so much that she committed suicide over him.

Eva and Dick dated for a year. During this period Eva worked a lot in Europe and Richard simply packed up and picked up and went off to Europe, too. In 1959 they were married by a justice of the peace in Las Vegas. Red Buttons gave the bride away and his wife, Helayne, was matron of honor. This wasn't too good an omen because Red had since divorced Helayne and married again. And so it came about that Eva took her fourth husband.

At first everything went as normally as anything could go when the wife is one of the world's beauties, an actress who is devoted to her profession and, of course, a Hungarian. Then came the CBS series, "Green Acres," and they moved to Hollywood into Eva's house naturally. Dick gave up his stockbroker business, which wasn't doing too much anyhow, and as a favor to Eva CBS made him a job as executive producer.

Eva really loved Dick Brown. Even when he wasn't doing anything professionally and she was hysterically busy she would say to me, "I feel so relaxed with him. He is for me like Edmund is for you."

Dick Brown never really liked me. He never got up to greet me when I walked into a room. He just sat there with a long face. He was the one and only son-in-law who didn't respect me. When he saw me at a party he would kiss me but not for real and say sarcastically, "Oh, Mrs. Gabor, don't you know me? I am your son-in-law." When he came to New York he never called. I would meet people who'd say, "Your son-in-law, Dick, is in town, you know." This was so humiliating for me.

Eva was not such a good daughter while she was with him. He turned her against the family. Even when we both had nearby houses in Palm Springs, still she stayed far away. They only came when I had a party. Dick was not cooperative. He was not gracious. Most important was my daughter's happiness so I had to look away.

When Eva wanted a bigger house in California she put up her little one for sale. Edmund and I were in Los Angeles for a few days so she said to me, "You can use it but three real estate people have keys to the house and will be showing it off to prospective buyers."

"Won't that stop the few days we are here?"

"No. But it won't bother you so much."

So, I decided once again, better to go to a motel. Thank heavens we had money enough to go to the Beverly Hills Hotel—as usual.

Eva was terribly busy and supersuccessful. She was president of an interior decorating business and chairman of the board of a wig company. Her Beverly Hills mansion with the priceless paintings and antiques was a showplace. She had a Palm Springs house, Rolls-Royces, four servants, a male secretary, two cats, three Yorkshires and she was chairlady of a cancer crusade and other worthy causes. Besides her series she had starred in more films like *Wake Me When The War Is Over* and such TV shows as the "Tennessee Ernie Ford Special" and "The Pat Paulsen Comedy Hour."

All this time Dick was broke. He tried different things and none of them seemed to succeed. At the time of their marriage, it was not like this. He bought Eva a diamond choker and she gave him a Rolls-Royce. She didn't look at another man for the thirteen years they were married but Dick Brown cheated her with other girls and I'd known it but I didn't say anything to her because I knew she loved him. When Eva found out she went to a psychiatrist. Then she went away to Switzerland to a famous spa. Eva tolerated his brief flings but she was crushed completely when she discovered that Dick had a steady girlfriend for over a year. This she could not forgive.

If Dick wanted to get Eva back when she started to move away from him, I could have done it for him. Even when it came to the end and Eva wanted a divorce, I would have helped him but he never called me. In the last years she didn't love him much anymore and she had become tired of him. Still she stayed. When he wanted to live in London she even went to London after him but he didn't want to come back.

He was so conceited that he believed Eva could not live without him. If he would beg Eva to stay with him she would have. He could have kept her. She didn't leave Dick for any other man. She had nobody at that time. She and Dick were separated before she met anybody else and when this happened Dick wanted to crawl back—but by then it was too late.

5 I think maybe Zsa Zsa was afraid she was going to be the only spinster in the family so she announced her engagement to Hal Hayes. He was a builder, a mild-mannered gentle sort of multimillionaire . . . only he was peculiar.

He had an eccentric mansion built on seven levels right into the mountain over Sunset Strip with a twenty-foot waterfall in the foyer, a live oak tree growing through the living room, a genuine tinkling brook in the floor, and real orchids growing on real coral walls.

But this was not a very deep romance. She knew him maybe a year but the whole big romance was maybe two months. Two months and one week she decided, "I do not really love him madly" and so that engagement was broken. I think it was wise because he had one hundred suits, fifty sport jackets, a dozen tuxedos, and seventy pair of shoes. There would have been no room for Zsa Zsa.

After this she married Herb Hutner but this was not a very big deal either. My best recollection of this period was the one picture we took together when all of us had husbands at one time.

Everybody thinks everybody gives Zsa Zsa. But really nobody buys for her. Nobody buys her jewelry. She buys all alone. When she divorced Hutner she gave back the $36,000 Rolls-Royce car. Zsa Zsa is always involved in scandals. Like the time Rafael Trujillo sent her a $17,000 chinchilla. Well, what would you expect a rich man to send to a beauty like Zsa Zsa—candy?

"I just have a bad reputation," she says, "and it's hard to live up to!"

It is hard to live up to because there aren't enough men around who can feel secure with Zsa Zsa. Women should be soft and feminine and most of all helpless, but it's hard to be helpless and be successful too. Zsa Zsa is one of the most famous, most ravishingly beautiful, most successful women on earth. She is also rich. She has too much, therefore she is not always happy. She's too beautiful, too demanding, too witty, too everything. She can't even keep servants. Men are afraid of her. A little woman who will sit and adore him and admire him and fuss over him is what a man wants. Zsa Zsa is too busy conquering the world to do this. We are all career women. Women like us get nervous just being married.

We were in her Bel Air mansion some years ago and she sighed, "Nuci, it is not easy. A man can always get a woman but a woman cannot always get

283

a man. For me, a man has to be witty, handsome, have *savoir-faire* and at least a little money. I mean, most men cannot have *savoir-faire* without money. This is impossible. Unfortunately this type often has a cold heart. They turn out to be stinkers. What I need is a witty, rich man with *savoir-faire.*"

While she was waiting for this combination along came socially prominent Joshua Cosden. Joshua Cosden was educated at Choate and was tall, lean, handsome and had excellent manners. He was in the oil business. The only problem was that he was the one and only Texan in the oil business who was poor. The wedding was in Zsa Zsa's living room. They were happy for about a year and then they parted as good friends.

Zsa Zsa has a palace. She owns Howard Hughes' old house. She has four bedrooms—and still there's never room for me. Whenever I want to come she complains her cook is off or her butler is sick or she has a paint job going or some drapes aren't up. I always stay at the Beverly Hills Hotel and she comes to visit me there! Anyway, her house is like a petit Versailles. To paint one room cost her $2,400. She has a horse, a German shepherd, a lhasa apso and an angora cat. She pays $250 a month in veterinarians' fees.

She makes big money, she spends big money. She said to me, "I have a friend who told me her husband was stingy. And I said to her, 'Stingy? He pays the food bills, doesn't he?' So God help me, *Nuci,* I would be happy if I could only find that!"

Following *Moulin Rouge* with José Ferrer, Zsa Zsa has starred in more than thirty films in France, England, Spain, Germany, and Italy, always in the native language. She has starred in 300 major television productions including the Bob Hope, Jack Benny, Sinatra, Dean Martin, Red Skelton, and Jerry Lewis Specials. She was twice nominated for "Emmy" awards. She broke all theatre records in Chicago in Noel Coward's *Blithe Spirit.* She's chairman of the board of her own cosmetics firm. The Hollywood Foreign Press voted her Most Glamorous Actress in the world five years in a row. She plays tennis, polo, and she was the Junior Ping-Pong champion of Hungary.

The girls say Zsa Zsa is my favorite. Maybe they feel that way because she looks like me. Zsa Zsa is *ravissante.* She has exquisite breasts that stand up with two points. She is only a little overweight but nobody looks like her. Women her age could *plats,* explode, when they see her because she has not a line on her face; not a flaw anywhere and her hair is like a cloud.

I am a bohemian and a spender. Zsa Zsa not. We were at a casino in Vegas where she was being paid thousands. I quickly lost $500 gambling. Zsa Zsa never risked a cent. "I don't like to lose my money," she said, so the manager gave us $300 to play with. I went right away to the tables. Zsa Zsa pocketed hers. She says to me always, "I know what it means a rainy day." She is always speaking of a rainy day but I don't remember that it ever rained for Zsa Zsa.

Except for her men, with whom she is very generous, Zsa Zsa doesn't spend stupidly. She makes her own living without any man to help her and she has been the victim of robberies, the victim of mash calls and she has suffered through embarrassing headlines. It is no wonder that sometimes she falls down under it all.

It is true that Zsa Zsa had a mixed-up period in her life. In London about five years ago it began with her buying things even she couldn't afford. She bought a house in five minutes and decorated it with the most expensive antiques from the most expensive antique shop in London . . . one single mirror cost her $22,000. Her transportation while she was shopping on Bond Street in the middle of a busy weekday was an Arabian horse. The owner of the store didn't mind. He said, "We were more than happy that Zsa Zsa Gabor was in our place. It was the biggest publicity for us. Besides, she parked the horse outdoors." Ultimately I negotiated a deal to have them take back their antiques with Zsa Zsa paying 10 per cent to repay the loss of the sale.

She was friendly and loving. She gave to one girl her half-a-million-dollar diamond necklace which she was wearing in broad daylight. Of course we got it back immediately. She made all kinds of problems for everyone. She ordered the contents of her Beverly Hills home shipped to her in London. I refused to let this happen and it cost $5,000 to get the furniture that was already taken put back.

Majorca was where Zsa Zsa really misbehaved. She came into a bar in the middle of the afternoon and decided to lie down across three bar stools. She abused people. She told everybody off. She was literally crazy about George, who was in Majorca in the house he shared with Charles Boyer. All she wanted was George and he didn't want her.

In Majorca they arrested her. She slapped a high police officer who was so tall that she had to climb on the plane seat to slap him. They took her down from the plane and the plane was delayed fifteen minutes for this scandal but the passengers were more than happy to be late because they had witnessed such an exciting bit of theatre. They were only unhappy that Zsa Zsa had to remain behind. Someone came from the American Embassy in Madrid to free her. A professor and a board of twelve people were brought in to interview her and by then she was in good humor so they all agreed to let her go. See, she was not really deeply sick; she was only mixed up. It cost her a $3,000 fine for this little slap.

She didn't call me when she was in the trouble. This is a sickness where they don't believe they are sick and they don't want help.

I flew over immediately and arranged for her to enter a private rest house where famous celebrities went to rest from overwork or whatever.

There was nothing I could do that first weekend because they put her to sleep. I couldn't see her so I flew to Pforzheim, Germany. I went to order jewelry because whenever there is tragedy I *do* something. I cannot just sit around and let the tragedy get to me. I handle the tragedy and then try to get out and get around it.

In three days she was all right and she told me in front of the doctor, *"Nuci,* I was mixed-up. They will take care of me a few days more and then you will see I will come out of this whole sickness."

When I arrived they said in the newspaper that "Beautiful Mama Jolie came to spank Zsa Zsa because she has behaved so badly." On TV the emcee asked me, "How is Zsa Zsa? Why is she doing such things?" I said only, "Thank God Zsa Zsa has already been through everything and she feels wonderful. She is in her house in London resting and she apologizes to everyone for her misbehavior."

This was positively all I said and this was very good for Zsa Zsa. In a few days like a miracle Zsa Zsa herself appeared on the same television show. She was perfect and beautiful.

Jolie's #3, Edmund de Szigethy. "The wedding was March 3, 1957, and I was called by society columnists 'The Bride of the Year.'"

Formal wedding portrait: Mr. and Mrs. Edmund de Szigethy.

"The girls have never said outright that they don't think it is proper for a mother to have such blonde hair or low-cut dresses or false eyelashes. They might think it but never have they said it."

"In October, 1958, I managed to arrange for Vilmos a visa to Austria. All of us gave up everything for this family reunion in Vienna: Zsa Zsa left a film in Rome with Mario Lanza, Eva left a play on Broadway, and Magda said not even her husband could keep her from coming."

At another of the five annual reunions in Vienna.

Nightclub columnist Earl Wilson lends an ear.

One of Zsa Zsa's six wedding days.

As a prospective son-in-law, Rubirosa was once
in the running — but he ran off, instead, with
Barbara Hutton.

Ex-secretary and present pearl salon manager
Bimba Beck, at Gabor poolside in Ridgefield,
Connecticut. (Learning Jolie's office filing system, she was told: "Do not be unintelligent—
look under "S" for the names of escorts.")

The one without earrings, Magda plays sheriff;
Mama is a dance-hall hostess; Eva came in
mufti.

Zsa Zsa, Greer Garson, Jolie, Gina Lollabrigida,
Glenn Ford.

"And now a few words from . . ." Hometown radio interview in Palm Springs (Magda in the background; Edmund at Jolie's side).

Zsa Zsa's sixth, Jack Ryan ("a genius inventor,
he made his first million with the Barbie doll")
gets to meet the family.

George Sanders ("The Deep Freeze" to his
mother-in-law) was in and out of the family
twice.

Lunch was, as usual, on Mama.

A trip to Japan — and a Hungarian out-geishas them all.

It's James Mason behind the beard.

The present-day Palm Springs living room.

A one-time president of the United States who called on Jolie for a recipe (Edmund flanks her other side).

"I tried once to re-do Mamie's bangs, but she said the General had liked her the way she was for forty-five years."

A bemused Eddie Albert joins the Jolie line.

With the most famous debutante of all time,
Cobina Wright, on Jolie's left; Nat Dumont,
Eva, and Valerie Dumont.

The pose is loving enough, but Dick Brown
(Eva's fourth) was not a favorite son-in-law
("He never got up to greet me when I came
into a room").

A frequent foursome: Alma and Harry Kessler, who give Edmund and Jolie a magnificent anniversary party every year in Palm Springs.

A group of The Girls (no daughters) surrounds
its favorite girl. On hand: "Princess Blue Eyes"
Barnett, Matilda Barnett, Jolie, Alma Kessler,
and Valerie Dumont.

Dinner-guest time in the New York City apartment.

Violinist de Szigethy woos Jolie's gypsy heart.

With Zsa Zsa's #2, Conrad Hilton. "She got a lawyer from Claudette Colbert and she made a stupid divorce. Not even a permanent suite for life at the Plaza. Wherever Zsa Zsa goes, in a Hilton hotel she must pay herself. Ridiculous."

Lily Pons is in the middle; to her right, another
good friend, Alma Kessler.

Jolie with the limp-watchman of Surrealist
painting, Salvador Dali.

For Jolie, three daughters, seventeen sons-in-law, one grandchild: Zsa Zsa's Francesca.

Jolie Gabor today: "I'm convinced that this memoir will be the end of me: the girls will be unhappy no matter what I say, and Edmund will throw me out when he reads about my lovers."

I truly love Edmund deeply. I would die without my Fairy Prince. Who else would spoil me like this?

Today nobody can live elegantly with two servants. It doesn't exist. Even Bobo Rockefeller with her townhouse and her millions invited me with sixteen people for Thanksgiving dinner and had no servant. She even washed the dishes herself. We only have twice a week a maid. I can't do things like cooking therefore he does it. Before Edmuska goes to work for a full day he will prepare breakfast for me and when I come home from a day of shopping I just ask him, "What's for dinner?" He is a terrific man. I have not to do anything.

I like to go out five nights a week. Edmund is happiest when he is at home. If we are alone we call a favorite restaurant and they bring in dinner to us. Edmund cleans up, too. I always fight for doing the dishes but I always lose. This is good because I don't really want to win. I am organized but not so much as the girls. My citizenship papers, for instance, which are so important to me I couldn't find for ten years. The children are like their father, rigid and disciplined. Their gloves are lined up in their drawers like soldiers. I am not so concerned for neatness and perfection. I care more for life and love and happiness. My own personality is such that if I have love I don't care so much if my gloves are thrown in sideways. With me sideways gloves are also all right. I care only for front ways gloves when I come back from a visit to Zsa Zsa or Eva or Magda.

With Edmund I have love. We didn't have a fight for more than five minutes ever. When I don't speak to him in five minutes he cannot sleep, he cannot eat. Edmund is only happy when he is with me. Thank God he likes to spend time with me because if not I might by now be a cripple. I might even be dead.

We have a summer house in Ridgefield, Connecticut. We are always changing houses. Edmund usually returned to the city Mondays but it came a Monday and he wanted to spend with me another day. "I will make us steak on the charcoal," he said as he busied himself with the preparations. "First I take a swim," I said, running down the five steps to the pool. At that moment I fell. It was a terrific fall.

I screamed and Edmund came running. If not for him I would scream and die and nobody would hear because we were up on a hill and nobody was around. "Edmuska," I screamed when he came to me, "I can not move. My leg is broken." The leg was hanging on one bone and a piece of skin almost at a right angle to the knee. The whole leg was shifted to the side.

He covered me with a big red bathrobe which he had made wet in the pool and then he ran to the telephone to call the nearby Danbury Hospital. Two nice young boys came in an ambulance.

"They are going to tell me I will never walk again," I said to Edmund.

He comforted me as best he could. I saw myself having my leg amputated. I thanked God I had reached the point where I could be sure Edmund would not leave me. I made up my mind I would live with this tragedy in the sunniest way possible. I made up my mind that although I would live the rest of my days in a wheelchair I would still be made up beautifully and I would be wheeled into the best restaurants and parties and life for me would not be over.

I can not be a sufferer. When Bimba was in the hospital for 2½ months for kidney trouble I came daily. Finally I threw a copy of *Vogue* on the bed and said, "Bimbuska, eat your heart out." Bimba started that day to turn upward.

When the doctors got me at the hospital and they took off this red bathrobe my leg had snapped back into position. Nobody could believe this. It was a miracle. They put a cast on me, of course, but I was already at this moment all right. When anybody asks me what was the happiest moment in my life then I must say this was it.

I had only one really bad time during my years with Edmund. I had a stroke. It was a Sunday morning. When I woke up I felt a little funny but nothing hurt me. I went in the bathroom and I felt so strange that I went back to bed. I wanted to read a newspaper but I couldn't see it. It was blurry. The three girls were in New York in one time and they raced over. Edmund was pale as death. Silently my family sat around my bed.

Dr. Vermes, a friend who lived in New Jersey but had spent the night in New York at a party with us came quick. He made me to go up and down. "Go to the piano," he commanded. I went. "Sit down." I sat.

"Play it." I could not. I had forgotten how.

"Speak to me. Tell me how you feel," he commanded.

I tried. I stuttered.

"This is a little stroke," he said to the girls.

They put me to bed and I put on my pink silk bed jacket because when I am sick I put on pretty things. I went to bed in a good spirit because I felt no pain and I looked pretty and I was delighted the three children were together.

In the evening the doctor said, "Jolie, I must place you in the hospital."

I didn't want to go.

"It is only for an examination," he said and had me placed on a stretcher and taken to Mount Sinai.

In moments of crisis the Gabors are not four but one. My daughters, the big stars, sat down on the floor outside my hospital room because there were no chairs. The snobby cold nurse said to Zsa Zsa, "Miss Gabor, you must leave here. You cannot sit on the floor in front of a hospital room in the middle of a busy corridor. I am afraid I cannot permit you to do this."

Zsa Zsa looked up at her from the floor and said, "Only when you call the police will we three leave here. Our mother is in there."

And there the three sat the whole first day. There were many examinations in the spine and the first week was a bitter one. When they brought me home I felt good but little things were wrong. I couldn't speak at all on the telephone. When I could manage to speak a little bit haltingly, the effects of my stroke were that I couldn't remember my English and the German which I had long forgotten suddenly came back. "Forgot English," I cried to Zsa Zsa.

"But you never spoke Shakespearean," she said.

I turned to Eva and Magda for sympathy. "No piano," I said.

"But you are not Rubinstein," Eva said.

And when I spoke even the little bit of German it was a strange voice and it was stuttering. My face was all right. It hadn't gone to the side like Magda's but everybody was terrified I would end up like Magda.

Then Edmund, this angel man who would give his strength into me if he could, said, "I will take my wife to Palm Springs."

"You cannot," the doctor said. "It is too much for her."

"She needs sun and quiet and warmth and she loves it in Palm Springs and there I myself will nurse her back to health," he said. "Everything will be all right."

The day we left was my bitterest day. Magda accompanied me to the airport. A man was assigned to help us and assist us onto the plane. I was standing with Magda and he asked Magda, "Do you have a house in Palm Springs?"

Before I was always quick to give the answers for Magda. This day it was unbelievable pain because Magda couldn't speak and when I tried to answer for her I couldn't speak. The man was gentle and polite. He simply stood there and looked at the two beautiful Gabor women . . . both of us dressed fashionably and neither of us able to speak. I wanted hard to answer for Magda but at this moment I also couldn't say any words. I just stood there my eyes flooding with tears.

When we were on the plane I wanted to tell Edmund but I was excited and in these few weeks when I was excited I couldn't speak even when I stuttered. I cried. It took nearly the whole trip to Los Angeles but I managed finally to communicate to Edmund what had happened.

In Los Angeles airport Eva and Zsa Zsa waited so we could all go on the small plane to Palm Springs. They were so unhappy. "You don't look very well," said Eva. "You have lost weight."

"You wait a few weeks and you will see what I will make of your mother," said Edmund. "Only the heavens I won't bring down."

He sent for the doctors to come. He personally administered my medicine. In a couple of weeks I became the old Jolie Gabor. Jerri Cotten, a friend of mine from the oil business, made a joyous party in my honor. I got up and sang a little "Never On Sunday." I did so well that Edmund began crying. He couldn't believe that this woman who was singing was weeks ago having a stroke.

If not for Edmund I wouldn't be here today. It is unbelievable what this man did. I am lucky to have him. I am lucky for everything. Somewhere up there I have a very special angel watching over me.

In Palm Springs I opened also a shop, and for the short time I had it I developed an excellent clientele. California's then Governor Edmund G. Brown bought from me. One Sunday morning I opened for him especially.

Another frequent visitor was Mamie Eisenhower. One busy day she even helped wait on customers for me. We became so friendly that I gave a luncheon in her honor in my Cahuilla Drive hilltop home. I had tables with candles, centerpieces of red, pink, and orchid carnations, pineapple boats filled with fresh fruits, and I took pictures of the whole party only to have the camera containing the film stolen the next day.

There was a *Jolie Gabor Family Cookbook* published some years ago. When Mamie came over I gave her a copy. "I don't cook," she said to me, "but the General does. He just loves to cook. I'm sure he'll be very appreciative of this book."

Three nights later Ike phoned. "On page 67," he said, "you have a soup but your recipe calls for red wine. I don't have red wine at hand. What do you think, can I use white?"

I didn't know anything about a soup on page 67 or on any other page for that matter, but I said, "Oh, General, of course. In fact it is even better that way!"

I tried redoing Mamie's bangs when we were together at the house.

"But, Jolie," she protested, "the whole nation is imitating me and the General likes me like this. For forty-five years he's liked me like this."

"So therefore he will still like you even if your bangs are a little longer and flatter," I said.

My friends call me the Queen of Palm Springs. Our hillside house with its kidney-shaped swimming pool cut from rock and its spectacular view of the San Jacinto Mountains was always ablaze with Hungarian friends like actor Paul Lukas, international friends like Prince Youka Troubetzkoi and Mrs. Felizia Vanderbilt, and showbusiness friends like composer Frederick Loewe and Lily Pons, my neighbor, who walks down from the top of the hills in the blackness all alone carrying a knife in one hand and a lantern in the other for protection. I also had as a guest Paul Savosdy and Manci. Paul wrote he and his wife would stop in Palm Springs en route to their home in Australia.

When they arrived my heart curled. He still looked good and Manci still looked as she always did. I made myself so beautiful that I was unbelievable. I wore a red satin gown with a matching coat and I had on my arm my young husband.

They had come with their children to stay a few days. I escorted the children into my white and gold kitchen with the passthrough counter that makes a perfect bar for a party. There my servant gave them milk and cookies. I showed Paul and Manci to the frothy, frilly, Continental guest room and they stared with big eyes at the raftered living room with the grand piano and the pictures, photographs, paintings, and portraits of my famous daughters. Paul looked at my house, he looked at handsome Edmund, he looked at mousy Manci, who was so afraid of him that she shivered, then he looked back at me. His eyes really popped.

I took them to a party at Eva's. She was surrounded by the most famous names in the world and her four servants. Zsa Zsa wore a Christian Dior ensemble, a vest embroidered with jewels. Paul couldn't believe his eyes.

I had a profit from this old lover of mine. Even now he still works for Mendel's in Canada so he brought me from his meat company a ham. Then he tried to give me another little profit. He tried to kiss me but I didn't want it.

This man who I had put my whole stupid heart into and who played with me now was jealous of my life and I wanted nothing of his. I told him someday I'd write a book and I'd put him into my book and he was very happy.

Edmund and I were invited to Brazil by President Kubitschek and when we came back Paul had gone. He left me a love note which Edmund didn't show me for one year. It said, "I will die with this love I have for you." I was very happy with the whole experience.

In 1967, Magda became a widow. When Tony died it was a bitter blow. She fell into the habit of smoking forty cigarettes a day and that's between cups of coffee and she is so limited in her happiness that I haven't the heart to make her stop. In every tragedy, no matter how dismal the situation, it is my nature to find something to make light of. With this I cannot.

My heart breaks whenever she calls me. She will try to tell me she's feeling well and contented. She says, "happy." She tells me a couple I know was over last night. She says, "Couple . . . couple . . ." I say, "Who?". . . . She says, "Man, woman . . ." I say, "Think. Try to give me a clue." But she cannot connect words and phrases. She tries and tries and then she says, "Forget it."

Magda's mind, however, is functioning like a computer as it always did. When Tony died there was a bitter fight with his Italian family, who didn't want to give up his millions. Her lawyer advised her, "Stay home. You will only be an interference in the court."

But Magda refused. Magda is strong. She said, "No!" She went to court and fought for her inheritance. She stayed right in the courtroom and steered her lawyer with one-word directions: "Yes . . . no . . . yes . . ."

When her lawyer was ready to accept a settlement Magda's eyes flashed and she said, "Fight . . . fight. . . ."

She was smart. Her lawyer advised, "I suggest you keep your share of your late husband's business." Magda wagged no vigorously. "Sell!"

She was right. His manufactory failed and she had her money. That family would never have given her a rightful share if she hadn't fought every inch for what was hers. She takes care of her money all alone. She has a secretary, Mitzi Meyer. Mitzi is her friend and writes her letters and does her bookkeeping. Magda is very rich. It's all Tony's money and she worked it out by herself.

Magda lives in Palm Springs. Her kitchen is the size of my whole apartment. She overworked the house from top to bottom. Fifteen workers came in every morning at seven o'clock for eight months and she thought when she kissed them they worked better so she kissed every one of them even the black ones. She said, "Good boy . . . work . . . work. . . ."

Magda gave right away gorgeous parties. She made herself a favorite hostess. Her right arm which is useless hangs limply and she does everything with her left—puts on wigs, makeup, even false lashes. With this outlook it was not surprising Magda developed a fiancé, Gar Moore, a former actor who makes delicious strawberry trifle desserts for Magda's parties.

At this time Zsa Zsa and George Sanders, who were divorced in 1954, resumed a little. George was lonely. Zsa Zsa told him, "You don't have to go out to parties if you don't want to but at least move in and be with me. Don't be alone."

Zsa Zsa always loved George. Sixteen years and two husbands later she still loved him. I asked Zsa Zsa, "Why you don't marry him again?"

"I adore George," she said, "but George has dropped out from life. George wants to retire and not go out anymore. It would not be good for us to be married."

George was stingy. When Zsa Zsa wanted to go to a New York restaurant, Chez Vito, George said, "Too expensive."

"Whenever Mother dines there she doesn't get a bill," said Zsa Zsa. In this case George gave his OK. What happened was that he got a bill for $72. He was so furious he didn't speak to Zsa Zsa three days! "It was so unpleasant at this restaurant," Zsa Zsa told me later. For Zsa Zsa it is always unpleasant when she has to pay.

After he'd been staying with Zsa Zsa awhile, George said, "A very rich lady wants to marry me and I am thinking I might go through with it. What do you think?"

Zsa Zsa wanted not to lose him so she suggested, "Look, you are lonely and so is Magda. So why you don't marry Magda?"

Zsa Zsa was not jealous because Magda was not anymore interested in sex. "What do you think about this?" asked Zsa Zsa.

"It's a good idea," he said.

"Magda has money and you can live well with her."

"It seems like it would be a good idea," he repeated.

"It's the best thing that could happen to both of you. You will be comfortable and Magda will be happy. You will be good for one another."

George went to the phone to call me in Palm Springs. "What do you think, Jolie, if I marry Magda?" he asked. "It's Zsa Zsa's idea. She cooked it all up."

"I love the idea. Look, why you don't come up this weekend with Zsa Zsa and we speak it over?"

I right away went to Magda. In her halting way she said, "Unbelievable . . . beautiful." Then she kissed my hands and said, "Nuci . . . sweet. . . ."

George was so eager that he drove up without Zsa Zsa who couldn't get away. I told him frankly, "Magda cannot speak."

"I know but I don't care. I want to marry her right away."

"Take my advice. I suggest you come and stay as my house guest for a month and then decide."

"You have not seen her in fifteen to sixteen years."

"No, but I always loved her."

When we drove up to Magda's house she was waiting at the front door in an elegant hostess gown and she herself is still so beautiful. Also she had invested in a tin of Russian caviar and the vodka George loved. "Let's get married now," said George.

"But it is two o'clock on a Friday afternoon. How can you marry now? You must wait until Monday and then we can all go to Las Vegas," I said.

"I want to get married now," he repeated.

"Now," echoed Magda.

"Wait," I said. "Sleep here tonight, George. Just be happy with the way things are right now. Live with Magda a little. See how things go."

"No," he said, "I am set on this idea."

"Mitzi arrange," Magda said, dialing her secretary.

"But this is impossible," exploded Mitzi on the phone. "George and Magda need a blood test and it's Friday and you can't reach anybody in another two hours."

"Leave the blood test part to me," I said. "Dr. George Kaplan loves me. When I tell him what I need he will do it."

I called Dr. Kaplan. "Are you crazy?" he shouted at me. "I have patients lined up in my office. How can I leave them and go right now? Magda's not a virgin. She can wait three days."

"But you must help me," I begged. "My happiness depends on this. For Magda to marry George Sanders is very important."

He sighed heavily. "Okay, Jolie. In ten minutes you meet me in the hospital."

In the hospital we saw a pair of junk gold-colored hoop earrings for $1.90. "I'll buy that for Magda's wedding ring," said George, "but the thing is I only need one."

"I'm sorry," sniffed the clerk. "We sell earrings in pairs."

"But I only need one," insisted George.

"Okay, I'll take the other one," I said. "We'll split the price." I didn't want 95 cents to stand in the way of my daughter's happiness and by now it was three o'clock and I couldn't afford to waste time. So, George chipped in his half and I raced the five miles to my house to throw on some party dress fast. George had packed completely when he came to the Desert so he put on his red velvet dinner jacket and we took off for Indio, a small town twenty miles away where we had found a judge.

It was 4:30 on December 4th, 1970, and all the employees in Indio's City

Hall were awaiting us. A judge with his elegant wife, who was wearing a ball gown and diamonds, drove up. They were en route to some chic dinner party and had come by City Hall just to marry us.

I never dreamed you could get married so fast in California. We came home about six o'clock and the telephone rang. It was Gar, who was supposedly engaged to Magda and had been escorting her for years. "Jolie, darling, my sweet angel," purred Gar, "tell the redhead I'll be a half hour late."

"Well, but I don't think you can come today because she just got married."

"What?"

"She just got married."

"To whom?"

"George Sanders."

There was nothing on the phone. Nothing. Not a sound. I think he fainted.

My friends Alma and Harry Kessler gave the wedding reception at The Racquet Club. "I am happy that George is back in the family," said Eva with a mischievous smile, "and this time he is married to the nicest sister."

As for me I was ecstatic. I always think it's nice when you get a son-in-law back.

George was generous. He gave Magda a TV set, he repaired her Cadillac for $300 and since he was a tool kit addict he made for Magda a magnificent workroom that costed Magda $8,000. George wanted so desperately to settle into a quiet life. Excitement was too much for him. Once he was so overcome that he insulted me and this was something because George admired me.

This night there was a sit-down dinner in my honor at Lord Fletcher's. Unfortunately I came late. Because I was guest of honor they didn't serve until I arrived. I was seated at the host's right. George was on my right. Unfortunately I brought an escort, Joseph Bolker, who later married Tina Onassis. He wasn't expected so I said, "George, you will have to move down one and everybody will move down one because this gentleman will sit next to me."

Cranky George was forced to move and he was starving and everything was delayed and he had wanted to stay home in the first place so across the table in loud angry tones he called to me, "You fucking Hungarian!"

Nobody laughed or said a word. You could see everybody draw in their breath. They were all tense for the minute. But not me. I took it very easy. I joked, "That's not so bad. Anything that is connected with sex cannot be so bad."

The whole table laughed and it broke the spell. He and Magda left early. When I arrived at Magda's later he was sitting on the terrace and he quickly picked up my two hands and kissed them. "Jolie, you are not angry with me, are you? Please forgive me. It's not such a bad word after all."

I am deeply unhappy that George made his suicide. I liked George Sanders. He was a good guy.

9 Slowly . . . slowly . . . life runs away from me . . . I know I must slow down a little more than before. Now I sometimes take a nap. Now I slowly slowly dress.

Now it takes longer to make myself up. It always takes more and more time and after I make myself beautiful and *soignée* I am very tired. This is something new for me because making myself up was my biggest passion. I enjoy to fix my face and hair. I never used to get tired from this.

I cannot help but see so many changes in myself. In recent years I began *shmeering* leg makeup down my chest and on my hands and up my arms because I developed those ugly brown age spots which come after sixty from oldness.

What bothers me most is my upper arms because I used to wear always sleeveless décolleté. But this is not so any more because it is important to cover what is not good. You can not have arms circled with jewels when the flesh hangs from the upper part like a rooster's neck and there are pleats around the elbows. I keep now the whole arm covered including the elbows. Even I don't go to sleep unless I am wearing long sleeves.

Always I have had to fight weight. Sometimes I go to a spa and I had to starve for two weeks although I don't die to be skinny anymore because it is not good in this age. A few nights ago it was candlelight and I looked well and I had many compliments. I am afraid if I lose weight it will hurt my face.

It is not so tremendously glamorous to put this down in a book, maybe, but I must now take every night a laxative. The only trouble is I forget often. Edmund comes in the bedroom and he says, "Did you take your laxative? Did you put the drops in your eyes?" I say, "I put in the oil but the laxative again I forget." So he brings it with the spoon and stands there until I swallow. It really is very romantic that a man will care for you so much.

I try to help myself yet more by making some exercise every day. I put cha cha music on the phonograph and I jump jump jump and do what my sweet friend Gayelord Hauser tells is the best with the stomach in and out all to the music.

When you get old you must take very much care of your facial muscles. I make all kinds of funny faces. The best is to put out your tongue as far as

298

you can. About ten years ago I had two frown lines between my eyes. I said to a plastic surgeon, "These are little but deep and I would like not to have them. Can you take them away?"

"Of course," he assured me. "This will cost you $800 plus two days in the hospital."

I was thinking which doctor to use when a friend, Sonja Loew, said to me, "Jolie, I am going to a doctor about my nose. Why don't you come along?"

"Okay. Who is this doctor?"

"He is a great man. His name is Dr. Rish."

While I was there I said to him, "I would like to have these lines between my eyes done away with."

Without asking a word he came to me with a needle and I panicked.

"Please . . . please . . . don't do this. . . . I am just now ready to go to a cocktail party. Please, don't do anything now."

"They won't even notice it," he said and quick put in two injections.

I ran to the mirror and I shouted, "But you have made it straight immediately. I can't believe it. It is not even red and the lines are all gone. What did you do?"

"Nothing," he said calmly, putting away his instruments. "What I gave you was silicone."

When I went out I asked the secretary, "How much are you charging for this?"

She said, "That will be $25."

I couldn't believe it. I quickly paid out the money and I never had any trouble with my forehead from then on.

Four years ago I again had my face lifted. In five days I made an unveiling party for fifty-two women. This I did with two young doctors in Palm Springs working together. Rona Barrett, a gossip Hollywood columnist, said, "Jolie Gabor is not satisfied with her beauty so she made herself a Christmas present with a brand-new face." The picture she put of me on television was so beautiful that if I knew I looked that good I wouldn't have made the face again.

I can't look forty-five anymore. I tell flatterers, "Look, I am happy when I look now not a day over sixty." The face lift does not hold so perfectly as you get older but still it is always a plus. Now I have only a little loose skin under the chin, on the throat and neck, which I will tuck up someday.

I always want to look the best. In our early days Bimba saw me in the shop after midnight, making up my face. "Where do you go at this hour?" she asked.

"I go home," I answered. "Where do you think I'm going?"

"But you only live a block away. What's with all the makeup?"

I turned around and explained to her, "Bimbuska, dear, learn from me something. I can go out from this door, turn the corner and by accident meet the one man I will love for the rest of my life or, worse, I can meet the one woman who hates me the most so I must be my most glamorous always."

Edmund has to help me dress a little, but he never sees me putting makeup on and he never sees me getting into a girdle which is very unelegant for a man to see.

There are women who go around not combed and in the nude. This is ugly. When my hair is not good I don't come out of the bedroom without I wear a turban. My husband never sees me looking badly. I wouldn't step from my room unless I put a line on my eyes then dark glasses, just a little lipstick and perfume. I always am in bed before Edmund because I like when he comes in that the room is dark. In the dark I look beautiful.

I take bubble baths, wash with any kind of soap and wipe cologne over every inch of my body including my bust. And that's it. I don't put oil in the tub. I have not the patience to cream. It's just that when the skin is good it's good. The only oil I use is to clean off my makeup. Sometimes I use a little water and soap on the face. I go to bed with the tiniest bit of moisturizer.

In the morning when my husband is gone I put on a thick night cream for while I am in the steaming tub and wipe it off with kleenex. No astringent even though I have the most expensive kind from Zsa Zsa. It's too much trouble and I'm too lazy. Nothing makes any difference anyhow.

My makeup is inexpensive. I use Cover Girl Foundation liquid base with a wet sponge then I *shmeer* cream rouge then loose powder. I don't redo my makeup during the day and if I'm going out later I let it go for the whole night. I don't even repowder because my face does not perspire. I adore Woolworth's for makeup. What I spend much for is the good smell. I use mouthwash, body powder, eau de cologne, deodorant, everything that smells good.

Being a celebrity costs much money because salesladies always bring out the most expensive. In a strange shop when the lady recognizes me looking at a sale rack and she says, "Oh, Mrs. Gabor, we have much better things only they are not on sale," I don't mind to say back to her, "But I want what's *here.*"

When I became a little rich I became not exactly stingy but more careful. Another reason I don't overbuy is that before I used to send to Budapest my clothes but now they are choosy. They say, "This is not good . . . that is not good. . . ." First they were happy with everything. Now they are not even grateful, let alone enchanted. Edmund won't let me send there anymore.

Edmund . . . Edmund . . . for me everything is Edmund. Because of Edmund even I look better. Edmund orders me, "Don't stay so long looking at the television" so instead of seven hours sleep I now get ten hours. Edmund insists, "Take a nap" so I take. One reason to write this book is to tell women they don't have to be afraid anymore of birthdays after seventy. The heart has no wrinkles.

Women are always after him but he doesn't care about them. I would love him even more if he would flirt. Once I almost thought he was making a little pitchy potchy with a neighbor and my arm began to ache with excitement. If he would flirt I would be tortured with pain but then I would be *in* love with him.

Women are stupid when they throw out their man for having a little sex with another woman. I would instead conquer him. Anyhow, I also don't cheat on Edmund. Maybe the reason is nobody asks me anymore.

Women are never really impotent. I don't understand women who tell me from change of life they have no more interest in sex. I don't even know what that is. In Budapest when I was in my thirties I had to have a minor operation. The doctor told me many courtesans have this operation so they don't have children. I have been free already many years of the mess of menstruation so I never knew the change of life. Some of my friends had nervous breakdowns from it as they grew older. Me, nothing.

For me almost everything improved as life went on. My daughters and me—we are like good wine. Look at the pictures of us fifteen, twenty years ago. We look better now. The Gabors improve with age.

September 21, 1973, Eva married her fifth husband in a double-ring ceremony and the organist played, "More Than The Greatest Love" and it was beautiful. Zsa Zsa caught her bouquet even though she aimed it at Tina Sinatra.

Frank Jameson is from Beverly Hills and he's not so tremendously rich but he's among the industry barons of the world. He is tall and very good-looking.

Under his influence Eva is so sweet to me so even if he wasn't such a bigshot I would adore him. Now she says to me, "Next time you come to Hollywood, *Nuci*, I give a big party in your honor." Always she forgets but at least I am happy that she bothers even to promise to me. So at last I know Eva is happy personally and emotionally. Financially I know she is also all right. With Zsa Zsa also it is the same. She is very smart. She knows what she is doing all the time. Zsa Zsa was a little nervous last year and she cried to me once she married this last husband, "My house costs me just in taxes $14,000 and when I don't have this big income I don't know what I will do."

But this was before she met and married Jack Ryan, her sixth husband, the biggest catch in the whole world. He's good-looking and she adores him. He is a genius inventor and the one man she respects. He made his first million from the Barbie Doll, which he put together. This man is out of the world. He has a castle with a waterfall, nineteen bathrooms and eight kitchens but also fifteen inventors are always living there most of the time. Therefore they are living together in Zsa Zsa's house because it has more glamor and less people. They made the wedding in January in Las Vegas in two minutes and Zsa Zsa told me, "I didn't dream to own such a man. I am the happiest woman in the whole world."

Zsa Zsa and I would die for each other but we can't live together.

Before I opened my house in Palm Springs last winter Zsa Zsa announced, "I will come out the same day you arrive and I will stay with you in Palm Springs a while."

"No, Zsa Zsika," I said on the phone from New York. "You must let me get settled first a few days."

"But I want to come immediately," she insisted. "I will help you open the house."

"No, darling, this is not so. You will make for me a busy *kop,* a busy head.

302

You know you won't help me fix up the house. When you come you make for me a big guest." I didn't add that I knew she'd just sit and complain about Eva, which wasn't too helpful in terms of opening the house.

Zsa Zsa was offended that I told her no, but Edmund said to me, "They never have time for you but they always expect you to make time for them." He doesn't find any of the three of them are so out of the world. Last Easter they didn't send me a flower, they didn't call me and Edmund sees this and he says a little sarcastically, "What good children they are!"

They are each the same. I admired a tiny gold evening bag at Eva's. "That's what I want for Christmas," I said. "But that's $250," said Eva, "without tax." When she saw my face fall she added, "But if that's what you want you can have it."

Only once was I smart with my daughters. One Christmas, when they were all working and had rich husbands, I asked them to chip in for a mink coat for me. I explained to them that if I had taken the $3,600 they each once promised me a year they would have given me $100,000 apiece. Instead, all I wanted from them was a mink coat. This, the darlings, they did give me.

Sometimes they send me things that have been sent them that they don't want. Everybody thinks my rich high-class famous daughters support me. I send three Christmas presents and they send one and even then they sometimes think it over.

They can be hard and selfish. When we were arranging for Eva's wedding in Claremont, California, I called Zsa Zsa and said, "I will fly out for overnight and stay with you."

"Why don't you go to a hotel?" she asked me.

"Why? You have two houses with many bedrooms and many beds. I only need one."

"Even so," she said, "there is no room. Anyway, there is no place for you in my limousine."

"I will come to you," I said to Magda on the long-distance phone call I paid for, "because Palm Springs is even nearer the chapel than Beverly Hills."

"*Nuci*, I am redoing my house and it's not yet ready. And anyway, my butler is off. Better you should stay in a hotel."

It's the old saying that one mother can find a place in one room for ten children but ten children cannot find a place in ten rooms for one mother.

Anyway, I went to the Beverly Hills Hotel and I went to the reception and everyone was happy to see me. And I was happy to see them.

When I was in Palm Springs two winters ago before Zsa Zsa married Jack Ryan, she called me from Beverly Hills. "Please, *Nuci*, I want you to come to me in my brand new house which belonged to Howard Hughes and stay a few days."

"Look, Zsa Zsa," I told her. "When you come to me you always have a good time but whenever I go to you always there is trouble."

Edmund listening in on the conversation whispered to me, "Don't go . . . don't go. . . ."

"It is better I don't go," I said to Zsa Zsa. "You will not have time for me. You will have with your secretary and your servants and your dogs and your telephone and your friends and someone from Bangkok will call and while I sit there alone someone will offer you some movie role or something and you will be busy with arrangements."

"Don't be so spoiled," she scolded me. "I will take off time for you specially. I will put everything aside and I will make in your honor a special one-day *Nuci* day."

"Why did you not request Zsa Zsa sends for you a limousine if she wants you so badly?" Edmund asked.

"Because she did not suggest it. Look, I will go with the public limousine, which only costs $12.50 a person."

"This is not so elegant. It's more like a small bus because it takes twelve people and it takes so much longer because you have to first pick up everybody and then before you come to Hollywood you must drop them all off."

"Eddika, please," I said. "I will go. I have made up my mind."

My friend Matilda Barnet found out about this so she put for me her Rolls-Royce with a chauffeur.

After all this Zsa Zsa telephoned the day before I was to come. "Can we postpone it to next Tuesday?"

Meanwhile Eva, who is jealous, took it poorly that Zsa Zsa wanted to make a *Nuci* Day so she said, *"Nuci,* you must come to me, too, not just Zsa Zsa alone."

Here my two big film star daughters with their chauffeurs and their Rolls-Royces were fighting over me and again I had to hire this mini bus. I did not even sit in the front seat with the driver alone because there was another girl sitting there. When Edmund took me out with the suitcase and my little overnight case he nudged me, "This you need, right?"

I went first to Eva's house and Zsa Zsa had promised she comes for me 4:30 the latest. So, she came instead at seven. While I was waiting, Eva ordered her Japanese couple to prepare an elegant dinner for the three of us. This I didn't mind. Also, Eva gave me a Louis Vuitton handbag. "You must swear," she said, "that you don't give this to Zsa Zsa."

"I don't swear but I also don't give to Zsa Zsa," I said accepting the bag which she knew I didn't like but which I knew was expensive.

I had arrived with two suitcases. The small one was for me the most important. It had the laxative, the vitamins, the nightcream, the eyelashes, everything that I need. I had pushed it all in and jammed it down because

I needed absolutely everything in it. Immediately Zsa Zsa and I arrived to her house tragedy struck, "Oh, my God, Zsa Zsa," I said in panic. "I find I have left my little bag at Eva's."

"Forget it. It is now 9:30 and I have had a long day," she snapped.

"For me this is impossible. I must have my little bag," I repeated.

Zsa Zsa became nervous, "I will give you everything. We make the best vitamins and the best everything in my cosmetics manufacturing company."

"Oh, God, I cannot be dependent on that," I thought. This means that for everything I will have to ask her and she will not have time to give. "That case is for me a miracle case. I must have it," I said in a frantic tone. "Zsa Zsa, if it costs me $100 I don't mind but I must get this little white bag back immediately."

Impatiently she flung over her shoulder as she disappeared into her room. "Call Eva."

I called and Eva said, "Yes, I know. I saw it but there is no way I can send it now. Everybody is in bed. My chauffeur already retired hours ago."

My *Nuci* Day was only in the starting hours and I was so nervous not to have a fight with Zsa Zsa about anything yet the tragedy was already unfolding. The problem was finally solved when I had the idea to send a taxi driver for the bag.

Zsa Zsa's house has walls with mouldings like in Versailles and she pushes a button in the living room and up comes the swimming pool and proudly she showed off everything to me and said, "Here is your room and look at your own private bathroom." It was ornate and impressive—pink marble—only the lousy jacuzzi in my bathtub wasn't connected, but what it did lying there was make it so there was no place to bathe. I tried the shower but it didn't have a hot water faucet. The faucet was gold but it was laid aside neatly for the someday day when the plumber would arrive. So, in this pink marble bathroom, I had no way to use the jacuzzi and no way to use the tub and no way to use the shower.

I like also a glass for brushing my teeth but there were no glasses. Also there was a giant statue of soap weighing maybe five pounds but you cannot take this in your hands. I tried to wet my hand and rub it but no soapsuds would come that way so quietly I sneaked into Zsa Zsa's bathroom and stole out a piece of soap.

I said to myself, "Jolie, don't open your mouth." Also there was no light so like a horse I carried in this heavy lamp from the bedroom to do my makeup.

When she saw that lamp she snapped, "How can you do this? This is a very expensive lamp."

"I don't want to eat the lamp and I don't want to steal it. I only want to see," I replied.

She dragged it back herself and brought another one so tall that it made light on the ceiling. Anyway, she saw the look on my face and she saw it was something bad and she was angry. There were no words but just a feeling. We both knew things had gone wrong.

The next morning on the beginning of my *Nuci* Day Zsa Zsa already left for work at seven o'clock. She has a Spanish couple but they speak not a word English, so there I am in this huge house with nobody to talk to.

She came back about ten o'clock and the telephone rang. "I am here with my new wife," a newly arrived cousin from Australia told her. "I married an English model and I am dying to introduce you to her."

Usually Zsa Zsa would say, "Oh, I am so busy. Call me another time." This time she invited them right over. "Come up," she said.

"It is your sister Janette's son," she said to me when she put down the phone.

I felt disappointed. This was not good. I was leaving at two. Meanwhile she had these two for lunch.

"Either you have been gone from the house or you are busy," I said. "I wanted to spend a few hours alone with my famous daughter but we will have not even five minutes alone. Janette's son Tibi and his family are coming to Palm Springs next week so I didn't need them for the few little hours I could be with you."

Zsa Zsa became very busy bustling around organizing a big salad and lunch. With nobody to talk to me I sat down to read. After fifteen minutes I looked up. "Oh, it is so cold here, may I have a shawl?"

And she answered over her shoulder, "Don't speak to me. I am so busy."

"Can you not ask to the maid?" I said shivering a little.

"Don't ask her," she warned. "She doesn't understand a word." But never did she say, "I will give you." And so I sat there cold because I wanted to be unselfish and not bother her. There was never a fight between us—only a feeling.

My friend had sent her Rolls-Royce to take me back to Palm Springs and when I stepped into it I said to Zsa Zsa, "Your house is gorgeous and I wish much luck to you" and I kissed her. In the evening when I got home I called her. Coldly she said to me only, "Oh, how nice that you arrived safely."

"I want to tell you again how nice the house is," I began, "and to say that . . ."

"I cannot speak with you now," she interrupted, "because I am still busy."

Her tone hurt me very much and I cried. "Edmund," I said, "I do not know what is the matter with Zsa Zsa." I get very upset when my daughters hurt me. These damn daughters of mine can sometimes give so much heartache. All three girls and myself we are very sensitive and it happens we hurt each other and then begins the drama—the big Hungarian tragedy.

Zsa Zsa didn't call me for ten days. The eleventh day came this five-page letter. We all write letters when we are hurt because we don't want that we hang up on each other.

She wrote, "Maybe you forget that I came home from London when you wanted me at your big party last month even though I would have liked to have stayed over another two days . . . but with you my sacrifices never count . . ."

The next paragraph she said, "I was so happy that you were coming to my new house but you could speak only of yourself. You never talked about me at all. You discussed only your parties and your friends." (This I don't remember.) "And you will please remember that I gave you a beautiful $500 St. Angelo dress and you threw it back to me like it was nothing." This about the dress I don't remember either except maybe faintly. I am sure she bought it for herself and she don't like it so after she has worn it once she gives it to me.

Zsa Zsa now has trouble with her daughter, too. If Zsa Zsa wouldn't care it would be better but she does. Zsa Zsa would die for a smile from Francie but always she whips her mother with words. She says to Zsa Zsa, "Mother, it's about time you grew up."

I have nothing with Francie—not since she was five years old. Always I send her a lovely present for Christmas and her birthday and she sends me a nice letter.

Zsa Zsa worries because Francesca doesn't want to get married. She worries maybe Francesca will have a baby before marriage. We are modern but this we don't like. I know at least that Francesca doesn't live like I did where I didn't kiss a boy or even see one until I was married. I'm sure Francesca will never suffer from my feelings because she has had so far an interesting life.

This overly bright child rejects everything we were all taught to believe in. She doesn't care about money or jewels or glamor or marriage. When we were fourteen, we were already plotting to get a husband. Now she's a good over twenty and doesn't care. Meanwhile she is in love with life. Francesca is very independent and very hard to handle. I was a good mother but I have heard from Zsa Zsa frequently that I am not a good grandmother. For this I am sorry but I can not help it.

Today Magda has a very successful man in her life, the artist John Morris. Let's hope they have a good relationship. Also, she has a great house on a hill overlooking Palm Springs. Although Morris is her one man right now, he is often busy painting. When he is, she goes with Prince Umberto Poliolo, among others. I am overjoyed that Magda once again is living the good life.

In this crazy family everything changes so fast that by the time you get to this page all could be a different story. I only know that right now Eva is divinely happy with her handsome new husband and her only complaint is Zsa Zsa, who is also ecstatically happy with her handsome new husband and whose only complaint is Eva. For life to be calm and normal with my daughters doesn't exist. In some ways Magda is the happiest of the three. Anyhow the richest. She has suddenly developed a new zest for life again. For years she didn't want. She closed the bedroom door when the last husband, Tibor Heltai, wanted to come in. She shuddered. I don't know whether it was the thought of sex or the thought of Tibor but I only know that she shuddered.

CLOSING

And so slowly . . . slowly . . . my time runs away. I hope only that I will be alive when this book comes out. Bob Hope said, "Jolie has made three daughters, carbon copies of her guts, her looks, and her female-ness but none of them matches her inexhaustible energy." That is true. I have for years been the sun around which my daughters revolved and from which they absorbed strength. But slowly, slowly my strength runs away.

"*Nuci,*" Eva said to me, "you are the youngest of us all." I have a love of living. I will relax only when I die. Inside I am happier than I was at twenty. It's just that I know I am nearing the end and there is still so much I want to do. I have just made my first TV commercial and there is still so much more I want to do.

My life is living proof that it is never too late. If I am sitting here at my age writing a book then you can know it is never too late to do what you want. Fifty times I started this book, each time with someone different. Once it was a man who brought his troubles to me. He was in love with a doctor's wife and she made suicide but she didn't die and this became my problem. Another time with a lady who sued me. Another time with I don't even remember who else. Anita Loos wanted to do my life story. Zalabondy told me, "Jolika, you will wind up in American history." So far this hasn't happened but I have certainly wound up in many front pages beginning with my trip to Paris when Art Buchwald put me on the cover of the *International Herald Tribune*.

In Chicago last year I did not feel so well and Edmund made an alarm to everybody and two handsome young firemen about twenty-five rushed in with their equipment and gave for me artificial respiration. My breath came back just knowing their hands were on me. While they clamped the mask over my face they asked, "You are really Jolie Gabor?"

I nodded, "Yes."

"You mean," the muscular one said to me, "you are the mother of Zsa Zsa and Eva?" I bobbed my head up and down. He was so excited at meeting me that he took the mask off my face to see me better. Thank God my breathing had already returned or they would have been so impressed with me they would have killed me.

Edmund tries hard to preserve everything for me including my strength and my money. Before Edmund I never had anything in the bank. He made me to stop having elaborate parties and spending foolishly. He also made me to stop working in my shop.

"But I love to work," I said when he brought up the subject.

"But, *Angyalka*, I must make you not to work. Always people want to talk to you and meet you and ask you questions about the girls and take your pictures and get your autograph and it is too much."

"I know how to relax, though, Eddika," I reasoned.

"Yes," he sighed, "but you work as hard at relaxing as you do at working. You have canasta parties and people over for bridge and you are on the telephone and you go to cocktail parties and you invite for backgammon and you go to Connecticut for the weekend. It is too much."

I stared at him. "You know, years ago if someone told me that I would stop working ever in my shop I wouldn't believe it."

"*Angyalka*, people wear you out. You are a celebrity and the days you go in there are many people before the window and they look in and they come in but they don't always buy. What they do always do, though, is ask you, 'How is Zsa Zsa . . . where is Eva . . . what is Magda doing.' "

"Yes, and I answer, 'Buy the newspaper and you will learn because that's the way I have to find out myself.' "

"People want to know everything about you. They want to talk to this beautiful woman with all the strength from whom such famous beauties have come. As soon as they walk in they want to meet you."

"Maybe we will lose some business if I do not come to the shop."

"It is enough that you will continue to design the jewelry, giving the world the benefit of your excellent taste."

So I know I have accomplished something in this world and now I write a book. Also at this stage of my life I make lectures. The Robert Keedick Bureau asked me, "Can you make a lecture?"

"How can I know when I have never been to one?"

I was a little nervous but when Mr. Keedick guaranteed a fee with all expenses paid I became less nervous. Imagine to be paid money just for talking! I said to Mr. Keedick, "From age twelve I was determined to be an actress. Always I put on my Magda and Zsa Zsa and Eva what I could not achieve and I hurt so much for it. Now here I am. Here I will finally have a stage, lights, microphone, an audience. It's like being an actress."

I did not tell him I was so excited that I would almost have done this for no money. Well, *almost.*

"Don't do this, *Nuci,*" Zsa Zsa said. "It will tire you. All the traveling and speaking and preparing and maybe they will not understand your English."

"Sweetheart," I said, "if they can understand yours they can understand mine. I have been on many TV talk shows—Merv Griffin, Mike Douglas— and always they tell I am a wonderful guest."

"But, *Nuci,*" she said. "You shouldn't do lecturing. I will tell Edmund not to let you do this. It will tire you out."

"No, Zsa Zsika, darling," I said. "It will stimulate me. Also I will be very good. I have never failed at anything and I will not fail at making a lecture." I think maybe she was a little bit jealous.

I worked at it. I had a secretary take down my stories and I memorized and my theme was "Never Too Late" and I went to many cities in Michigan and I had pink lights and an audience of 2,500 and a podium and the newspaper said I was a sensation.

Most exciting for me was that one newspaper printed big headlines of me and down in a small story on the bottom of the page was something about Archduke Otto. When I was a young girl I went to his father's coronation in Halasz Bastya. The Archduke Otto was then a boy of five wearing a crown with emeralds and I stood on the outside near the gates peeking through watching him and his father, King Karoly, riding a big white horse to the church. Otto stood with his mother, Queen Zita, and he wore an ermine cape with tails. Oh, I was so impressed. Now I am on the front page and Archduke Otto, who is also coming to the town, has a little story. I was so happy.

The women all wanted to know beauty hints. I told them the best beauty parlor in the world is to be contented. Much of a woman's beauty is inside. When you're angry you actually look ugly. I have had disappointments and frustrations but I have never permitted myself to be bitter. I can't stand it to hold a grudge. I never refuse to forgive somebody.

There is this Mimi Bass, who took large amounts of my jewelry in the days I couldn't afford it and never ever paid for it. Last Thanksgiving at Bobo Rockefeller's I again saw this Mimi Bass. Bobo was afraid we would kill each other with knives but Edmund signaled to me. I didn't say a word but she said to me, "Oh, Jolie, you must come to the Grenouille for lunch with me."

I said, "Okay, I come." Naturally she never called me. She also told how she still adores my jewelry and how she has it securely locked away in the vault. But I never said, "Why don't you take it out of the vault and give it back to me?" Instead I was very nice and smiling and I even accepted her invitation to lunch which I so far didn't get. But I have forgiven her.

Besides being forgiving another thing a woman must be is herself. I cannot stand hypocrites who pretend to be sweet little girls next door while all the while they are trying to steal your husband. A woman must be honest. I cannot tell a lie. Maybe only a little bit of a white lie but that doesn't count.

One little white lie that doesn't count is the matter of my age.

I cannot bear to be associated with sickness or old age. The manager of my shop, Bimba, claims that "The best way to describe Jolie is to tell you it's August. It's hot. Jolie invites me to go with her into the car. I have a dreadful cold. I'm sneezing and I'm coughing and she turns around and wags her finger in front of me and says, 'Bimbuska, stop coughing. It's so oldish.' If you have a cold in August and you see 1,000 people they will make 1,000 different remarks but nobody else but Jolie Gabor will ever think to comment, 'Stop coughing it's oldish.' "

I gave my age years back but I discovered it is not smart. Some people look more than they are and others less and even when you tell the truth people add some because they automatically figure you are lying—which, mostly, you are. Anita Loos who wrote *Gentlemen Prefer Blondes*, always told her age. Now everyone remembers exactly how high up in the eighties she is. This is not good. I saw her on TV lately and she looked like a woman of fifty.

I used to always tell my age until I was sixty. It was then at a party that Perle Mesta told me, "Oh, Jolie, you are so beautiful."

I replied, "Oh, I am so old."

And she said, "How old are you?" Stupidly I told her like I told everyone. "I am sixty," I said. For years she always remembered. Maybe she thought I was five years younger. I could use now those five years. Even though I am a miracle for my age I don't want to tell any more. I make every living creature younger.

I admit that I am still romantic. Before my husband comes home I freshen up so I am perfect before he arrives. And always I spray on more perfume. A woman must smell good even if she looks not so good. And whenever a man is ready for romance a woman must be ready.

Romance and love depend on the woman. A woman is born for love. A man is almost always tired. When he sees an attractive woman with a delicious aroma he will want to be with her.

I am now in the twilight of my life. As I look back on my memories I have no regrets. Maybe even my unhappiness was valuable. I learned from this. I appreciated what I had. I don't even regret my twenty-two years with

Vilmos. If I would have been only a little nice to him he would have brought the stars down for me, but from this union with a man I didn't love came three exquisite children. For this I am grateful.

Eva says always I love Zsa Zsa the most and she hates it. Once Eva and Zsa Zsa were at Eva of New York, the hairdresser, at a time I was angry with Zsa Zsa and wasn't speaking to her. I don't even remember what it was. I only know I didn't like Zsa Zsa that day. So I went into Eva's booth and Eva insisted we make up. "Don't be that way," she insisted. "Go into the other booth and speak to Zsa Zsa. Go ahead." I pulled out my mirror, fixed my hair, put on lipstick, and went into Zsa Zsa's booth.

Moments later one of the hairdressers came after me. "Eva is crying," she whispered, motioning me outside.

"Why? What is it?" I asked.

"You don't know what troubles you caused," lamented the girl wringing her hands. "Eva is so angry that you went to Zsa Zsa."

I looked at her in shock. "What are you talking about? Eva told me to go into Zsa Zsa."

I immediately went back next door to Eva and it was true. She was blue with anger. She shouted at me, "You fix your hair like you go to your lover. For me you just walk in however you are but you touch up your makeup and fluff up your hair and everything before you go in to Zsa Zsa!"

Actually the four of us are trying to outdo and out-impress the others. Often we come home in flaming tempers because one has stolen the show. We can be so competitive and we all argue at the top of our voices. But it means nothing. Let an outsider say one word against the family and we will unite to tear the stranger to pieces. We may be crazy but we are the Gabors.

I am satisfied with my daughters. I love them dearly and they love me. They give me sometimes pain but they give me great happiness. It has happened a couple of times that their secretaries will call to say they are going to be on TV at such and such a time. And I get so excited at what I have created, at my children the stars, that I say, "Aren't they marvelous to call us like this?"

And my Edmuska will say, "Oh, yes, they're just wonderful. They're so good to us. Look, we can turn on the television and we can see them for free and we have not to pay for this privilege!"

I have done a good job with them. I taught them well. I have been accused of pushing them to marry millionaires. To this I answer, "Every mother wants for her daughter a Prince Charming. When a mother has beautiful, blonde, angel-face daughters she doesn't say to them, 'Look, darlings, when you grow up you will marry truck drivers.' " After this statement had been printed I was afraid I'd be hollered at by truck drivers but I was on Madison Avenue in the Fifties, riding in my convertible, and one big man in his underwear shirt hollered down at me from the cab of his truck, "Hey, Jolie, you're damn right not to want a truck driver!"

I am different from my daughters. No matter how much aggressiveness and competitiveness and desire to succeed and be gorgeous and famous that they may have, I still have more. People have said the reason they are anything is because of my push. People have said the riches of the whole family is in the mama. I don't know if this is true. I only know that I would like to be what the three of them are.

Mostly what has pushed me forward is my hunger. I have a hunger for living. Even today I am afraid to stop. I am afraid to go to bed, afraid to miss something, anything—a program, a party, a person.

Perhaps I am not normal. I only know I hunger for everything the world can give. I have to this day many people around me from whom you can hear something or learn something or profit in some way.

Even at this age I have yet to eat my fill. I hunger more with each passing day because I don't know how much longer I have left to satisfy myself. Now, before I leave for Palm Springs I walk around the apartment. I touch my paintings. I run my hands over the furniture. Maybe I won't come back. I invite my friends for a good-bye party. I touch their faces. I make them come closer. Maybe I won't see them again.

My family, my sisters, and I, we have always been healthy. However, I was in Palm Springs in the spring of '74. Eight o'clock in the morning the phone woke me up. The voice of my secretary Bimba in New York said, "I have bad news for you." I knew right away. I'm psychic. I said, "It's Janette." My sweet sister, Janette, was gone. It was starting. The first of us the eldest of us, was gone. It starts. Now it starts. Less than a year later, in December, my youngest sister, Rozsie, who also lived in Australia, was gone from leukemia. We were always healthy and strong and now at this age it starts.

Years back Edmund sold our 63rd Street house and we bought a magnificent apartment. But it is too magnificent. I want to move so I can feel more life. This beautiful cooperative apartment overlooks the East River. I love to watch the boats go by but this large apartment with its huge picture windows is too pretty. It keeps me at home enjoying it and I don't always make enough effort to get out. This is not good for me. I want to move to the Plaza in the heart of the shopping and business district so I can force myself to experience life.

When I am in the bathtub sometimes I say, "Please, God, not now. I don't have on my makeup . . . not now." I want my friends to bring in the best makeup man when my time comes so I will be gorgeous when everybody says good-bye to me. But I am not ready yet. I want so much to be alive for all the excitement of this book. Please God, not yet.

Even at this stage of life there are so many things I would like to do. I would like to fly to the moon. I would like to climb Mount Everest. I would like to go on a safari. So many things I'd like. Maybe I'll still do them.

I wanted very much for this book. I wanted other ladies of all ages to know they, too, can find their dreams. I wanted them to know that they, too, can find love and happiness even when they are seventyish. I wanted them to know there are no wrinkles on the heart. I wanted them to know it is never too late.